Instructional Strategies for Middle and High School

"This book breaks the mold of traditional secondary methods texts. Readers will feel empowered as they connect and apply content through the 'guidelines' and 'step-by-step procedures' sections in each chapter. The succinct chapter reviews, graphic organizers, and bullets make this text reader-friendly. The balance of these great attributes makes it a practical and long-awaited resource."

—**Sherese A. Mitchell**, Hostos Community College

"I am pleased to see this text retains its strong focus on lesson design in its second edition. *Instructional Strategies for Middle and High School* serves as an excellent bridge from what my students initially learn in previous courses to what they must master in terms of curriculum design in my secondary methods course."

—**Joseph M. Shosh**, Moravian College

"Quite often, texts such as these suffer in their 'readability' for college students who are grasping (for the first time) some of the nomenclature and terminology of the field. This text provides the necessary information in a manner that is usable for a student beginning his or her professional coursework."

—**Doug Feldman**, Northern Kentucky University

Instructional Strategies for Middle and High School is an accessible, practical, and engaging methods textbook that introduces pre-service teachers to various instructional strategies and helps them to decide how and when to use these methods in the classroom. Classrooms are comprised of diverse learners, and aspiring teachers will face complex decisions about the assessment of student learning and classroom management. Veteran teacher educators Bruce E. Larson and Timothy A. Keiper offer practical suggestions for ways to integrate effective classroom management and valid assessment techniques with *each* instructional strategy. *Instructional Strategies for Middle and High School* equips pre-service teachers with the methodological tools to promote understanding, conceptual awareness, and learning for every child in the classroom.

Features and updates to this new edition include:

- Clear, step-by-step descriptions of seven instructional techniques that pre-service teachers can realistically implement within the classroom setting;
- "Teaching with Technology" and "Teaching English Language Learners" features now included in every chapter;
- Fresh interior design to better highlight pedagogical elements and key features, all to better engage students;
- Fully revamped and comprehensive companion website with both student and instructor materials that stress real-world application of strategies, classroom assessment, and management.

Bruce E. Larson is a Professor of Secondary Education and Social Studies at Woodring College of Education, Western Washington University, Bellingham, WA, USA.

Timothy A. Keiper is an Associate Professor of Secondary Education and Social Studies at Woodring College of Education, Western Washington University, Bellingham, WA, USA.

Instructional Strategies for Middle and High School

Second Edition

Bruce E. Larson
Timothy A. Keiper

Routledge
Taylor & Francis Group

NEW YORK AND LONDON

First published 2013
by Routledge
711 Third Avenue, New York, NY 10017

Simultaneously published in the UK
by Routledge
2 Park Square, Milton Park, Abingdon, Oxon OX14 4RN

Routledge is an imprint of the Taylor & Francis Group, an informa business

Library of Congress Cataloging in Publication Data
Larson, Bruce E.
  Instructional Strategies for Middle and High School/Bruce E. Larson and
  Timothy A. Keiper—2nd ed.
  p. cm.
  1. Teaching—Handbooks, manuals, etc.   2. Lesson planning—
  Handbooks, manuals, etc.   3. Educational tests and measurements—
  Handbooks, manuals, etc.   4. Classroom management—Handbooks,
  manuals, etc.   I. Keiper, Timothy A.   II. Title.
  LB1025.3.L367 2012
  373.1102—dc23
  2012013189

ISBN 13: 978-0-415-89814-0 (hbk)
ISBN 13: 978-0-415-89813-3 (pbk)
ISBN 13: 978-0-203-09652-9 (ebk)

Typeset in Sabon and Helvetica Neue
by Florence Production Ltd, Stoodleigh, Devon

Acquisitions Editor: Catherine Bernard
Textbook Development Manager: Rebecca Pearce
Editorial Assistant: Allison Bush
Production Editor: Sarah Hudson
Marketing Manager: Lori Kelly
Text Design: Susan R. Leaper, Florence Production Ltd
Copy-editor: Florence Production Ltd
Proofreader: Georgi Bellingham
Cover Design: Jayne Varney
Companion Website Designer: Marie Mansfield

Printed and bound in the United States of America by Sheridan Books, Inc. (a Sheridan Group Company).

Contents

PART 2

Instructional Strategies 123

Figures

Tables

Boxes

Acknowledgments

This book is written with the help of many. We continue to learn a great deal from the aspiring teachers we have as our students and from the many classroom teachers we are privileged to work with on a frequent basis. Their insights and suggestions are invaluable. On the companion website, the following teachers appear in videos with their students: Kirsten Jensen, Bruce Mansfield, Scott Smartt, Doris Sjoquist, and Megan Vigre. We appreciate them for opening their doors so we can learn from them. Kirsten Jensen also helped coordinate the videos, and Alaura Ogle visited the classrooms and made the recordings. We also acknowledge the helpful critique of the anonymous reviewers. We believe this book is improved because of their comments and questions. We had a great editorial team at Routledge; Rebecca Pearce and Catherine Bernard provided timely direction and encouragement. In addition, they completed behind-the-scenes tasks that we will never fully appreciate but have made the book better and more accessible. Finally, we wish to acknowledge the foundational support we receive from our families. They encourage us daily.

Introduction

In short, this book is written to help teachers be successful. We define successful teachers as those who help all students learn important facts, concepts, skills, and attitudes, and enjoy the process along the way. We believe teaching is a wonderful and exciting profession, and we hope the pages of *Instructional Strategies for Middle and High School* serve to excite and empower the next generation of classroom teachers. The second edition of this text is designed to be the primary text for secondary education teaching methods courses in which curriculum development, instructional strategies, classroom management, and student assessment are examined. This book prepares pre-service teachers effectively by using seven powerful instructional strategies and clear guidelines for writing unit plans and lesson plans. Since effective classroom management and valid assessment techniques are important parts of student learning, we illustrate practical ways to manage the learning environment—including a special focus on making your lesson plans meaningful for English language learners (ELLs) and incorporating technology into your classroom—and assess student learning for each instructional strategy.

WHY THIS BOOK?

As we wrote this book, we were mindful of our students: pre-service middle school and high school teachers who are enrolled in instructional methods courses. We call these students aspiring teachers, because they aspire to become effective teachers who help their students learn. We frequently notice, however, that aspiring teachers struggle with selecting instructional strategies, and often the strategies they select do not line up with the curriculum. For example, a teacher will decide to lecture because it is efficient, not because it is deemed to the best strategy for helping students learn a set of key concepts; or, a teacher will use a simulation or group project to "add some variety" to the day, not because these approaches will promote student learning more effectively than others. Similarly, decisions about the assessment of student learning, making the lesson work for all the students in a classroom, classroom management, use of digital technology, and many other common areas of the classroom are difficult for aspiring teachers to make because each decision is modified based on the content being learned and the instructional activities planned for the class session. Aspiring teachers need guidance as they make decisions, and this is why we decided to write *Instructional Strategies for Middle and High School.*

LINKING INSTRUCTION, ASSESSMENT, AND MANAGEMENT

In this book, we explore the assessing students and managing of classrooms with a different approach than other textbooks. We introduce assessment of student learning and ideas for managing the classroom in Chapter 1, and then build on that introduction in each of the succeeding chapters, thus contextualizing the roles of classroom management and assessment within the framework of specific instructional strategies. Along with teaching, newly qualified teachers often report that they struggle with valid and authentic assessments of their students' learning. This book provides a concise overview of assessment and offers many concrete examples of assessments to use with *each* of the instructional strategies. For example, valid assessments of what students learned from a role-play activity will be different from assessments following a classroom discussion. Appropriate assessments are integrated into each of the chapters for the instructional strategies, with contextualized examples to provide tangible ideas for the reader. We provide examples of unit plans, lesson plans, and rubrics that we gathered from the many teachers who provided input to the content of this book. Another common worry for aspiring teachers is how to manage a classroom with thirty students and how to discipline students who are disruptive. We have observed that many student teachers will not try student-centered activities for fear of "losing control" of their students. This book addresses concerns such as these by providing specific classroom management ideas for each of the instructional strategies. *Instructional Strategies for Middle and High School* acknowledges that it is impossible to use a strategy effectively without considering unique management concerns and assessments for each strategy.

Over the course of the text, we explore seven instructional strategies. Our decision for including these strategies was informed by conversations with many middle school teachers, high school teachers, and principals. All agree that the seven strategies included in this text are those most commonly used by teachers, are effective for helping students learn, and are necessary for all teachers to understand. By listing step-by-step procedures for using these instructional strategies, this text gives aspiring teachers a deep understanding of each strategy and the tools to determine how best to use each with a classroom of adolescents. Students are then given the opportunity to observe these strategies in an actual classroom by watching the accompanying videos on the companion website. We recorded videos of teachers using the strategies in their own classrooms so that pre-service teachers have the opportunity to see the strategies "in action" before practicing it themselves.

All of the ideas presented in this book are theory-based, and our practical suggestions are built on extensive examinations of current and long-standing research. In our writing of this text, we made great efforts to focus on the day-to-day teaching and learning that need to occur in classrooms because we want to provide future teachers with the tools to proactively manage their classrooms and ensure that all students are able to learn. The following ideas directed our development of the content:

- Effective teaching promotes student learning of the course content; teachers matter!
- Students bring diverse abilities, interests, and needs to the classroom that the teacher must accommodate.
- Teachers need skill with a large and diverse set of instructional strategies to help their students learn.
- The content students will learn will help determine the instructional strategies selected by the teacher.
- Each instructional strategy has unique assessments, and teachers must closely match the assessment to the strategy if they are to accurately and validly know what their students have learned.
- Aspiring teachers need tools for developing effective classroom management skills and student discipline strategies. Teachers often forget that each instructional strategy presents unique classroom management considerations, so part of a teacher education program needs to apply management theories to each instructional strategy.
- Teaching requires constant decision making. As such, decisions about class activities, student discipline, classroom management, and student assessment will be better if the teacher engages in a thoughtful decision-making process.
- Teachers need to account for the needs of a diverse group of students and are likely to encounter ELLs. It is imperative that teachers are mindful of ELLs when they are planning and implementing their lessons.
- More and more classrooms are technology-enabled, so it is important that future teachers know when and how to make effective and appropriate use of technology in the classroom.

STRUCTURE OF THE BOOK

Instructional Strategies for Middle and High School is divided into two Parts. Part 1 is titled "Teaching on a Solid Foundation," and Part 2 is titled "Instructional Strategies."

Teaching on a Solid Foundation

The four chapters of Part 1 explore theories and research about learning and adolescent development and provide the foundation for the content of the book. Teaching extends beyond pure methods and strategies to include areas such as tone of voice, subtexts of curriculum, classroom environments, and classroom management. Part 1 describes contextual factors that all teachers need to consider when planning, teaching, assessing learning, and reflecting on their teaching. These factors include:

- motivating students to learn;
- diverse characteristics and needs of students;
- differentiated instruction, with a focus on ELLs;
- the use of digital technology;
- guiding principles for classroom management and discipline;

- national, state, and local standards and the Common Core State Standards;
- determining classroom curriculum;
- domains of learning;
- assessing student learning.

In addition, Part 1 presents reasons for course goals and objectives, the components of a lesson and unit plan, and ideas for appropriate sequencing of content.

Seven Instructional Strategies

The seven chapters in Part 2 provide ideas for teaching effectively and will help a teacher to provide instruction that is engaging, varied, and most appropriate for the content being learned. In each chapter, we provide guidance about the process of selecting classroom activities that are appropriate and are based on current ideas from educational researchers and theorists. Each chapter is devoted to a specific type of instructional strategy to allow an in-depth examination and provides step-by-step procedures for implementing the strategy in the classroom. To accomplish this, we very purposefully explore the following areas for each strategy:

- an overview of the strategy;
- a description of what research has found about the strategy;
- step-by-step procedures for planning and implementing the strategy;
- a realistic exploration of the logistical concerns related to each strategy, including benefits and obstacles when using the strategy;
- classroom management and student motivation unique to the strategy;
- appropriate assessment techniques to use with the strategy;
- ideas for integrating technology to enhance student learning;
- specific suggestions for making lessons more meaningful for ELLs;
- guidelines for deciding if a strategy is appropriate for the content of a lesson;
- opportunities for you to consider how to use the strategy with content you will teach;
- a corresponding online video demonstrating the strategy "in action".

We start with instructional strategies that are teacher-centered, and move to strategies that are increasingly student-centered. These chapters integrate and contextualize the management, assessment, and learning theories developed in Part 1 of the book by examining many examples from a wide range of middle school and high school classrooms.

PUTTING IT ALL TOGETHER

It is our hope that all teachers will establish classrooms that have a positive impact on all their students' learning. Consider this example: if students need to learn the history and context around the development and writing of the U.S. Constitution, why might a teacher use a simulation, as opposed to a class discussion, classroom lecture, or an inquiry-based research project? Might these other strategies be more effective? How will I determine that students learned? These questions are not easy to answer and are a continual part of the teaching process. The strategies that a teacher selects for engaging students requires a complex series of decisions that include the learning preferences of the students, the content being learned, the setting of the classroom, assessment procedures, and the teacher's comfort level with a particular approach to leading the class. When a teacher selects an instructional strategy without considering the content or student, all sorts of problems abound. This text provides clear guidelines for helping aspiring teachers to engage in a thoughtful and effective decision-making process.

Classrooms are comprised of diverse learners, so we want future teachers to consider how each strategy might allow for differentiated learning, ideas for appropriately integrating digital and computer technology into the lessons, and how to make the lessons meaningful for ELLs. In addition, each chapter has at least one section titled "Making It Work in Your Content Area." In these sections, the reader is asked to determine how to apply the ideas presented in the chapter to a specific subject area. This helps contextualize the chapter within the notion of a content area and is a helpful tool for encouraging student teachers to explore what is taught in middle school and high school, and note the differences to and similarities with how subjects are taught at the university level.

Video

New to this edition, our companion website contains video examples of instructional strategies across a variety of settings, grade levels, and content areas. When used in concert with the text, readers will learn the theoretical underpinnings for each strategy, understand the step-by-step procedures for planning and using the strategy, and then be able to have a "virtual" classroom experience by watching the related video. Typically pre-service teachers learn several instructional strategies during their teaching methods courses and will hopefully observe these strategies in a middle school or high school classroom. However, these observations have no "quality control" on the teacher's effective use of a strategy, or even whether a variety of instructional strategies were modeled, while the student sat in the classroom. In addition, pre-service teachers' reflections on their observations are done independently, simply because they cannot all attend the same middle/high school classrooms together. A streaming video with examples of the instructional strategies allows pre-service teachers to observe the strategy and debrief as a group about the effectiveness and utility of what they observed. We have placed this icon

throughout the text to alert the reader when online videos will enhance what is described in the text. These icons are in the second part of the book, where the seven instructional strategies are examined. Videos will not replace being in an actual classroom but could be used in conjunction with experiences in a classroom practicum. Videos are available on the companion website for this text: www.routledge.com/cw/larson.

Companion Website

In addition to the videos, the companion website for this text (at www.routledge.com/cw/larson) contains resources for students and instructors. For the student, the site includes:

- samples and templates of useful documents (i.e., lesson plans, graphic organizers, rubrics, etc.);
- links to useful websites;
- access to online journals.

For instructors, we have included resources such as:

- suggested activities;
- PowerPoint lecture slides;
- examples of well-written objectives/learning outcomes tied to strategies/models;
- compatibility of content for use with online course management systems, such as Moodle or Blackboard.

We have placed this icon

throughout the text to alert the readers when the companion website offers material or information that will enrich the book.

NEW IN THE SECOND EDITION

We are excited about revisions, updates, and completely new features in this second edition. For this edition, we have added learning objectives for each chapter. This provides readers with a summary of the chapter. We also use these objectives as an outline for the chapter review.

We have added a feature called "Reality Check," which provides directions for integrating field-based experiences into the chapters. Ideally, the readers will have access to middle school or high school classrooms as they read the text. These check points provide concise tasks for contextualizing the ideas in the book. If students are not in a classroom setting, then they can easily return to these highlighted reality checks when they have access to a middle school or high school classroom. We have also updated and expanded a section in each of the seven instructional strategies chapters that is labeled "Enhancing Your Lesson with Technology." We provide websites, links, and many other ideas for appropriately integrating recent technologies into the classroom for the purpose of enhancing student learning.

A very important addition to each of the instructional strategy chapters (Chapters 5–11) is the feature "Making Your Lesson More Meaningful for ELLs." Chapter 1 has an extensive overview of ELLs and effective strategies for promoting learning among this important and growing group of students. The "Making Your Lesson More Meaningful for ELLs" feature builds on Chapter 1 and provides ideas for engaging ELLs that are specific to each instructional strategy. We base our ideas on current research and theories about these learners, as well as suggestions from our network of middle school and high school teachers. The number of students who do not speak English as their primary language is increasing, and teachers must be able to help all students learn. In addition, many students who do speak English as their first language do not understand the language of the classroom; this is often referred to as "academic language." This feature will prepare you to help all students learn.

We begin each instructional strategy chapter with an opening vignette to help describe how it might be used in the classroom. In addition, we have ordered the chapters from "most" teacher-centered to "most" student-centered. Therefore, the first instructional strategy chapter, Chapter 5, Lecture, is about a teacher-centered approach. Chapter 11, Student-Directed Investigations, describes a student-centered approach. To help you think about these ideas, each chapter has a chart to illustrate where the instructional strategy falls within a student-centered and instructor-centered continuum.

We wish you well as you embark on your journey to develop your own ideas about helping your future students learn!

BL/TK

PART 1

Teaching on a Solid Foundation

CHAPTER 1

The Classroom Learning Community

CHAPTER OBJECTIVES

In this chapter, you will learn about:

- adolescent development and its implications on learning and teaching;

- general theories and ideas about learning;

- motivating students;

- diverse characteristics and needs of adolescents;

- the role of appropriate technology for helping students learn;

- importance of classroom management.

When you think about your future as a teacher, it is encouraging to realize that you will help students to understand the wide range of topics, **concepts**, **facts**, skills, and **content** in your subject area. You will help your future students in middle school and high school to examine themes and ideas and to develop skills that will, in turn, help them make better sense of the world around them. The content is ready to be learned, and you will be able to engage with your future students as they learn. This probably seems exciting and daunting at the same time. Exciting because you either have, or are developing, a solid **knowledge** and appreciation of the content in your subject, but daunting because you have not had much experience teaching and helping students to learn and understand.

The purpose of this first chapter is for you, the future teacher of adolescents, to consider many issues that surround student learning. By understanding how adolescents develop and how they perceive the world, you will be able to more effectively help them learn academic content, critical thinking skills, and interactive social skills. You will be able to create classroom communities with your students that foster their learning. In this book, we will return to many of the ideas introduced in this first chapter that pertain to learning, teaching, and classroom management. Our intention is for this chapter to provide a foundation for thinking about your future students that will allow you to develop an increasingly complex understanding of how to effectively promote your students' learning. As a future teacher, you will face many challenging tasks. Knowing your students is one important issue, **classroom management** is another, and understanding the perspectives and backgrounds of your students and community and knowing the content of the courses you will teach each provide opportunities and challenges. In addition, your students are wrestling with their roles in the world and are trying to understand their growing and developing bodies as they leave childhood and become young adults. All of this contributes to making teaching an exciting profession.

ADOLESCENT DEVELOPMENT AND INSTRUCTION IN THE SECONDARY SCHOOL

When you walk down the halls of any middle school, you will be amazed at the vast physical differences of the students. Some sixth grade boys and girls look as though they are still in elementary school, and some eighth grade boys and girls appear to be like high school students. Even students who are the same age develop very differently. All adolescents' bodies are going through dramatic physical changes, but they are not necessarily experiencing them at the same time. Nonetheless, all middle school and high school students are growing, developing, and changing at a very rapid pace.

The exciting news about this is that opportunities abound when teaching adolescents because of their newly developing cognitive skills, social interactions, and awareness of the world around them. One fruitful approach for thinking about middle school and high school students is to consider three areas of human development:

- biological and physical
- psychological and cognitive
- sociological and cultural.

Biological development considers the influence of the body's physical changes on the adolescent. This applies to learning and teaching because physical changes impact adolescent body size and shape, nutritional needs, mood swings, and the many other changes that are occurring in the body. In many cases, your future students will be observers of their own body, wondering how the changes will affect them. Girls and boys develop at different rates within their same sex, but they are also developing very differently between the two sexes. In sixth grade, girls are often the tallest in the class, and this slowly changes as boys experience growth spurts around the ninth or tenth grade. Puberty, and all of the hormonal influences occurring at that time, occurs for all students eventually. Mood swings are a huge aspect of hormonal secretion. Not only do moods change, they are also magnified to extremes (e.g., high highs and low lows). The fact that students develop at different rates means that you will have students who are much more physically mature than others. The challenge is to realize that physical development is not linked to social maturity, emotional stability, or cognitive ability. For example, a 15-year-old student may look like an adult, but still have the maturity level of a child. Physical changes will affect girls differently than boys (a topic we will explore later in this chapter), and physical changes will affect the social, emotional, and academic worlds of the adolescent. These physical changes will influence the instructional strategies you choose, the ways you manage the learning environment, your relationships with students, and many other elements of teaching.

Psychological and cognitive development considers how the mind impacts the adolescent. As children grow physically, they also increase their cognitive abilities. Thinking skills improve as they develop, and adolescents begin to have cognitive abilities that were only emerging in fourth and fifth grade. For example, your students in middle and high school will become increasingly able to think about possibilities, hypotheses, and abstract concepts. Adolescents gain the exciting ability of introspection: analyzing and evaluating themselves and others. Specific theories about how adolescents develop cognitively are examined in the next section. The important idea to think about is that your future students have very capable cognitive and thinking abilities. You will help your students enhance these abilities by providing opportunities to practice using them. At times, this presents a paradox for adolescents and teachers alike. Beamon (2001) suggests several of these following contradictions that may be resolved simply with practice in your classroom:

- Adolescents may be technologically "savvy," yet lack skills to organize, evaluate, and synthesize data.
- Adolescents may be used to fast access of information, yet lack motivation to see a task to completion.
- Adolescents may be socially active, yet lack the skills for purposeful social interactions.
- Adolescents may be independent-minded, yet vulnerable to peer and societal lures.
- Adolescents may be intellectually capable, yet unpracticed in higher cognitive thinking.

Your classroom becomes an ideal place for developing and refining these cognitive abilities.

Sociological and cultural development receive a tremendous amount of attention when thinking about teaching adolescents because they are closely linked to physical, psychological, and cognitive development. As adolescents struggle with their own identity, they experience a series of identity crises (Erikson, 1959; 1968). These crises are closely tied to one's self-concept—literally our ideas/thoughts about who we are. As we make decisions about our identity, we question how we love, with whom we have intimacy, whether we have autonomy and initiative, and the effectiveness of our work ethic. Our culture, ethnicity, economic level, social status, athletic ability, academic prowess, and self-esteem are a few of the many aspects that are part of our identity. They each have a role in shaping our sociological development.

In *All Grown Up and No Place to Go: Teenagers in Crisis*, David Elkind (1998) suggests that the cognitive and physical development of adolescents puts them sociologically in a time of extreme egocentrism. Children demonstrate this "crisis" as they deal with an "**imaginary audience**" and a "**personal fable.**" These two phenomena are initiated in early adolescence, and while we learn to manage them, they may never leave us completely. Imaginary audience "accounts for the teenager's extreme self-consciousness. Teenagers feel that they are always on stage and that everyone around them is as aware of, and concerned about their appearance and behavior as they are themselves" (Elkind, 1998, p. 40). The idea of a personal fable stems from their thinking that they are "special, different from other people . . . [it gives them] courage to participate in many necessary but frightening activities" (pp. 43–44). In addition to creating a sense of invulnerability ("I won't be in a car accident"), the personal fable helps convince the adolescent that no one has ever loved so deeply, been so excited, or experienced such emotions as they have. As Elkind summarizes, bringing the fable "in line with reality is part of maturing . . . only in finding out how much we are like other people, paradoxically, can we really discover our true specialty and uniqueness" (p. 45). The impact of sociological and cultural influences on adolescents, and implications for teachers, will be expanded upon in the following pages of this book.

LEARNING

Our adult memories of adolescence can be detailed and specific. However, an adult thinking about his or her adolescence is very different from thinking like we did when we were actually adolescents. Adult memories of overcoming an obstacle, confronting a peer, interacting with a teacher, or studying for an examination are influenced by the fact that we know how the situation ends. Adolescents are in the process of living out these scenarios without this perspective; therefore, they may look at them differently than adults. When teachers consider how to best help students learn in school, their memories of school should serve as a guide but not the driving force behind decisions. Certainly teachers have all been apprenticed by the teachers who taught them. In fact, teachers tend to teach in the manner they were taught (Lortie, 1975). So our memories are useful, just not as reliable as we may think.

It is important for you to think about learning, since that is what teachers help students do in school. Many different theories attempt to understand how people learn. One definition of learning that we find helpful for teachers is provided by Jeanne Ormrod (2012). She suggests that learning is a "long term change in mental representations or associations due to experience" (p. 18). Teachers, then, work with their students to help bring about this change. For example, some suggest that memorizing is not "learning" because it is usually not permanent; it takes rehearsal, and memorized information usually fades over time. Others suggest that memorization is one form of learning because the process has brought about change. More importantly for you, however, is the realization that your opinion about this will impact the type of instructional strategies you select. If a sixth-grade science teacher wants her students to learn about the habitats of grizzly bears, she will choose classroom activities that are based on her belief about learning.

Consider for a moment whether students typically memorize particular facts or concepts in your content area. If they do, think of specific examples. Students in geometry often memorize theorems; in geography, students often memorize countries on a map; in English, students often memorize poetry. What do you think about memorizing? Does it help students learn? Do they remember what they memorize?

Behaviorism is a long-established approach for thinking about learning. According to behaviorists, learning occurs when the overt behavior changes. Over 100 years ago, the famous behaviorist experiment by Ivan Pavlov involved a person ringing a bell and feeding a dog. After repeating the stimulus of ringing and feeding, the person rang the bell only. The dog had learned to associate the bell with food and began to lick its lips in anticipation of food. This idea that behavior (salivating) could be influenced by a particular stimulus (the bell) ushered in behaviorism. Skinner (1953) believed that an organism's interactions with the world (or the environment) conditions behaviors. In other words, people are continually coming into contact with stimuli. At times, these stimuli encourage us (e.g., praise when doing a good job), and at times, they discourage us (e.g., punishment when doing something inappropriate). Skinner suggested that these stimuli shape who we are and what we learn.

The idea that behavior indicates learning is unsatisfying for cognitive approaches to learning. Cognitive approaches attempt to address what is happening inside our brains when we are learning. Piaget (1970), Vygotsky (1978), and other cognitive psychologists investigated how our brains function, and not just our behaviors. For example, Piaget believed that the brain becomes increasingly able to learn complex and abstract information as we grow. Adolescence begins in the final years of Piaget's "Concrete Operations Stage." During this stage children organize their thoughts logically and sequentially. Piaget suggests that near age twelve children engage in "formal operations," where their thought becomes more abstract. They are able to generate abstract propositions, multiple hypotheses, and possible outcomes. Thinking becomes less tied to concrete reality. Vygotsky theorized about a **"zone of proximal development"** that exists between our current level of understanding something and the next level. To arrive at this next level, we need help. Tutoring, modeling, and guiding provide examples of how to expand on our current levels of understanding. Current thinking about ideas tied to Vygotsky's initial theory have led to terms such as "scaffolding," **"constructivism,"** and "hands-on learning." These imply that learning occurs when some additional source provides a support network to promote learning (e.g., in the same way that a scaffold provides support for a building).

The main **goal** of learning is to promote student achievement. In *How People Learn: Brain, Mind, Experience, and School*, Bransford et al. (2000) suggest that three findings consistently emerge from "research on learners learning and teachers teaching" (p. 14) to promote student achievement. Below we list these three, and follow each with a brief explanation:

Students come to the classroom with preconceptions about how the world works. If their initial understanding is not engaged, they may fail to grasp the new concepts and information that are taught, or they may learn them for purpose of a test but revert to their preconceptions outside the classroom.

(p. 14)

Students come to classes with a wide range of experiences and **prior knowledge.** If this knowledge is accurate, then teachers have the opportunity to tap into a wealth of background insights and understanding that comes from these students (imagine how a unit on Japanese culture could be enhanced if one of your students had lived in Japan). Conversely, misconceptions need to be "unlearned" and taught, so students can relearn proper information (a common misperception of middle school and high school science students is the nature of the moon's orbit around the earth and the earth's orbit around the sun).

> To develop competence in an area of inquiry, students must: (a) have a deep foundation of factual knowledge, (b) understand facts and ideas in the context of a conceptual framework, and (c) organize knowledge in ways that facilitate retrieval and application.
>
> (p. 16)

Researchers have examined the performances and learning of experts and novices in several subject areas. An expert understanding of key concepts facilitates understanding of new knowledge. This allows experts to identify patterns, and note similarities or differences in a manner that novices cannot. Therefore, teachers should be able to teach key concepts and/or facts in depth. These "defining concepts" are important if students are to learn additional ideas and information, and they are important for helping students learn content on their own.

> A metacognitive approach to instruction can help students learn to take control of their own learning by defining learning goals and monitoring their progress in achieving them.
>
> (p. 18)

Metacognition, or "thinking about one's thinking," frequently takes the form of an internal conversation. Adolescents can be taught effective internal dialogues that will promote learning. For example, predicting outcomes, explaining an idea to oneself to improve understanding, noting when you do not understand, referring to background knowledge, and using strategies for studying are all elements of learning to be metacognitive. These are not used by all students and should be taught by the teacher through modeling and other explicit ways of bringing out the hidden/internal voice for the students to observe (p. 21).

LEARNING STYLE PREFERENCES

Litzinger and Osif describe learning styles as "the different ways in which children and adults think and learn" (1992, p. 73). Often teachers engage students in a wide range of learning activities to provide a variety of learning opportunities. Given our earlier definition of learning, the concept of learning preference does not imply that students will learn the material differently. It means that students may prefer one type of instruction over another. For example, some students may prefer to work on inquiry or research tasks, others may prefer to listen to a **lecture**, and still others may prefer to see examples as they hear new information. If you believe that all students have different learning preferences, then you will quickly realize that you have preferred styles, too. The challenge is to teach with varied styles and not teach using the style you prefer the most. The second part of this book provides detailed ideas for seven different instructional strategies that will assist you in determining how to appropriately use a variety of instructional techniques with your students. Each strategy meets specific purposes, and determining when to bring in different strategies is an exciting part of **planning** and of teaching.

MULTIPLE INTELLIGENCES

The theory of **multiple intelligences** was developed at Harvard University by Howard Gardner (1983). His multiple intelligence theory (MIT) suggested that long-standing ideas about intelligence such as the intelligence quotient, or IQ, were limited. Gardner says that our society tends to value linguistic skills (speaking, reading, and writing) and logical-mathematical skills (number sense and reasoning). People who are "well-spoken," logical, and "calculated" are highly esteemed. This value might overlook students who have intellectual capabilities in nonlanguage or mathematics areas. Actors, designers, musicians, dancers, counselors, encouragers, and naturalists may not be as highly valued by our society because their capabilities are different. Gardner's MIT (1983, 1999) suggests that there are eight different intelligences, and that these account for a broader conception of what we think about human potential.[1] In a recent keynote address to members of the American Educational Research Association, Gardner stated that he was concerned about educators confusing multiple intelligences with learning styles (2003). Where learning styles are preferences that a learner has in how they are taught, intelligences are learning aptitudes, or ways of thinking about the world around us. The eight intelligences proposed are:

1. *Linguistic and verbal intelligence*: This involves abilities with spoken and written language, the ability to learn languages, and the capacity to use language to accomplish certain goals. Writers, poets, lawyers, and speakers are among those who usually have a high linguistic intelligence.
2. *Logical-mathematical intelligence*: This consists of the capacity to think logically, carry out mathematical operations, and investigate issues with a systematic and scientific approach. This intelligence includes the ability to detect patterns, reason deductively, and think logically.
3. *Musical intelligence*: This involves skill in the performance, composition, and appreciation of musical patterns. It encompasses the capacity to recognize and compose musical pitches, tones, and rhythms.
4. *Bodily kinesthetic intelligence*: This gives rise to the potential of using one's whole body or parts of the body to solve problems. It is the ability to coordinate bodily movements. Gardner sees mental and physical activity as related, since the brain tells the body what to do.

5. *Spatial intelligence*: This involves the potential to recognize and use the patterns of wide space and more confined areas. The world around you makes sense because of patterns and organizations that others without this intelligence may overlook.
6. *Interpersonal intelligence*: This is the capacity to understand the intentions, motivations, and desires of other people. With this intelligence, a person works effectively with others. Educators, salespeople, religious and political leaders, and counselors utilize this intelligence.
7. *Intrapersonal intelligence*: This entails the capacity to understand one's own feelings and emotions. With this intelligence, a person has a useful understanding of himself or herself and is able to use this information to regulate his or her life.
8. *Naturalist intelligence*: This involves abilities for sensing patterns in and making connections to elements in nature. People with a naturalist intelligence may have a strong affinity to the outside world or to animals and may show unusual interest in subjects like biology, zoology, botany, geology, meteorology, paleontology, or astronomy.

Gardner does not suggest that teachers teach to all eight intelligences. However, he does suggest that teachers will have students who look at the world and understand it in terms of any one or more intelligence. The principal implication of this is that teachers should provide a variety of activities that focus on different intelligences. Consider how this might impact you in the classroom. If you were teaching eighth graders in a world geography class, you might have your students read about a particular region in the world (linguistic), look at a map of that area (spatial), and examine demographic inform-ation about that region (logical-mathematical). They could then record their impressions of that region in a journal (intrapersonal) and discuss them in groups of four (inter-personal). What Gardner's theory provides is a challenge for the teacher to help students learn content by thinking about it in ways that benefit the students' strengths.

MAKING IT WORK IN YOUR CONTENT AREA

Cognitive development during adolescence is dramatic. Thinking skills improve and develop, and adolescents begin to have cognitive abilities that were only emerging in fourth and fifth grade. Adolescents gain the exciting ability of introspection, or the abilities to analyze and evaluate others and themselves. Think of at least one way that you can make use of these cognitive abilities when teaching your content area. For example, how might a language arts teacher use students' introspection, **analysis**, or **evaluation** abilities? How might a chemistry teacher build on these newly forming abilities?

If you are able to attend a middle school or high school classroom in your content area, watch the students and try to focus on their cognitive thinking. What are some instances where they think abstractly? How do they move beyond merely "knowing" and actually demonstrate deeper "understanding" of the information?

MOTIVATING STUDENTS TO LEARN

Motivation might best be thought of as a force, or energizer, that helps us accomplish a task. We are motivated by many things, and when we lack motivation, we usually accomplish very little. Theories and research about motivation are expansive, so our purpose of this section is to focus on the most salient aspects so that you can consider how to best motivate your students. Students will arrive in your classroom with different motivations. Some will have little interest or motivation to attend class, while others will have a high interest in learning your subject. On more than one occasion, we have taught high school students who received money from their parents for the grades earned at school (e.g., $50 for an A, $40 for a B, etc.). At the same time, many students will be motivated to simply complete an assignment because they want it to be their best work. As we begin thinking about motivation, it would be interesting for you to consider what motivates you to do various tasks. These are often called motivating factors. What factors motivate you in your life? A few might be: personal satisfaction, a sense of accomplishment, financial rewards, increased status among peers, or pleasing a teacher or supervisor. Motivating factors leads us to consider two different forms of motivation: **extrinsic motivation** and **intrinsic motivation.**

Extrinsic motivation is when we are motivated to do something by outside, or external, factors that we believe will provide desirable outcomes such as praise, a reward, or even avoidance of negative consequences (Pintrich and Schunk, 2002). Extrinsic motivation is a means to an end; we are motivated to do something because the end result will be better. Teachers extrinsically motivate their students in a variety of ways, such as points for assignments, letter grades, praise for good behavior, after-school detention for misbehavior, free time if students all read silently for 30 minutes, or allowing students to revise their assignment for a higher score.

Intrinsic motivation refers to motivation to engage in an activity because of the satisfaction derived from the activity itself. Students who are intrinsically motivated view the learning process as valuable and genuinely want to understand the content. Teachers can encourage intrinsic motivation, though it is more challenging. Researchers suggest that the following types of activities tend to intrinsically motivate learners: challenging tasks that question existing understanding and create a sense of curiosity, tasks where the learner has some control over their own understanding, and tasks that evoke some aspect of our emotions (Lepper and Hoddell, 1989; Ryan and Deci, 2000).

Extrinsic and intrinsic motivations can both be used effectively in the classroom. Although it is important to realize that only motivating your students with extrinsic factors may promote learning for the sake of a reward (or for the sake of avoiding punishment), extrinsic motivation is appropriate to use. For example, most people gain some motivation to go to work for the extrinsic reward of a paycheck. However, teachers need to consider how they might also provide opportunities to promote intrinsic motivation—where students want to learn because they genuinely enjoy the process. Researchers in this area are quick to remind us that motivation is neither intrinsic nor extrinsic exclusively (Pintrich and Schunk, 2002). For example, a student might study so she can receive a good grade and be eligible to play on the basketball team (extrinsic) and at the same time study because the course content is genuinely interesting to him or her (intrinsic).

While it is important to think about intrinsic and extrinsic factors, as a teacher it is equally important to consider what Jere Brophy calls "Motivation to Learn" (2004). Brophy described this as the "students' tendency to find academic activities meaningful and worthwhile and to try and get the intended learning benefits from them" (p. 162). Students who are motivated to learn may not have intrinsic motivation for all tasks, but they see the purpose and value of school. As a result, they are motivated to attend class, think about content, complete assignments, and engage in the activities because they believe that learning will be worthwhile. When you help your students understand how the content and activities are useful and beneficial, you promote their motivation to learn. This might be accomplished by modeling to your students your interest in the content and sharing how you motivate yourself to learn. Creating a classroom environment that exudes your enthusiasm for learning your subject, as well as your interest, care, and concern for your students' learning, will help develop your students' motivation to learn.

"FLOW" EXPERIENCES AND MOTIVATION

An interesting approach for thinking about motivating students comes from a theory of intrinsic motivation called **"flow"** (Csikszentmihalyi, 1990; 1997). When someone is highly motivated from within, he or she is in a flow experience. This stems from a general belief that our abilities match the challenge of a task so well that we can simply enjoy the experience. During a flow experience, we are unaware of time because we are so involved and concentrated on a task that we are only aware of the present. In addition, we have confidence in knowing what needs to be done and how to accomplish it. This engagement creates a sense of calm and reward of its own. Most of the people who theorize about "flow" suggest that we can learn how to create a flow experience. Figure 1.1 below operates on two axes: one is the perceived challenge of a task and the other is a person's perception of their skill or ability to accomplish the task.

Consider how this figure might help you understand motivation and, more importantly, help you provide appropriate motivating factors for your students. When we perceive that a task presents a low challenge, we will respond with either apathy or boredom, depending on our perception of our skill or ability. If we see ourselves as highly capable, an unchallenging task will bore us. If we see ourselves as having low ability, it will lead us to not care. Contrastingly, a task that is perceived as highly challenging will promote anxiety (if we do not perceive our abilities or skills as being capable of completing the task), or it will promote a "flow" experience if we perceive a match between our ability and the challenge (Csikszentmihalyi, 1990; 1997).

This can be directly applied to the middle school or high school classrooms in several ways. Low challenging tasks rarely serve to motivate students. According to Figure 1.1, students will feel varying degrees of apathy and boredom. Therefore, you need to consider how to challenge students. If the task is so challenging that the students believe it is above their ability level, then they may be so distressed that they cannot complete the task. Students also need help in their perceptions. Tasks may appear too difficult when only focusing on the final product. However, when the task is broken

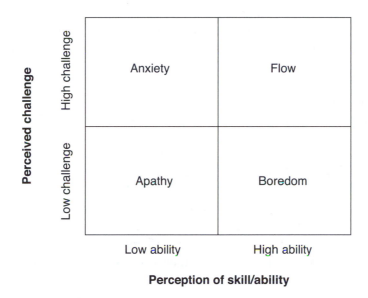

FIGURE 1.1: Intrinsic Motivation and "Flow"

into smaller, sequential activities, it becomes more manageable. Likewise, students may perceive themselves as lacking sufficient skill for a task, at first. Often with proper modeling or scaffolding, the student learns that he or she does have the skill after all. Consider the following examples, and possible ideas for moving students closer to a flow experience:

• Boredom: A student who is an advanced reader may show little interest in reading an assigned book that is far below her reading level. She appears bored because the challenge is far below her ability. If the reading task is made more challenging, boredom will be less of a problem.

• Anxiety: A shy student may decide to skip class on the day he is scheduled to make a 10-minute presentation to the class, because the stress of standing in front and talking is too great. If the student is coached on how to present, given opportunities to practice, or even allowed to present privately on a videotape, he may perceive his ability to more align with the task.

• Apathy: A student in an art class may simply give up if he cannot accomplish the first drawing assignment of the year. He thinks that he will never be able to do well in the class, because he had such difficulty with the easiest task. If the teacher expresses her own challenges with drawing, and some of the strategies she has come up with, she provides a model of how to work through problems. If the student is provided with opportunities to practice on specific areas, and master those areas, he may see his skills improving.

- Flow: A low-achieving student who loves to work on the computer is able to provide technical support to her classmates as they develop their personal websites. Classmates' challenges become her opportunities to see how well she can solve problems, and it makes her happy when others people begin to rely on her to help with the assignment.

You will not be able to motivate all of your students for every task, but if you think of their motivation in these terms it will help you focus your effort to help them.

SELF-EFFICACY AND LOCUS OF CONTROL

Self-efficacy is our self-expectation or belief about what we can accomplish as a result of our efforts. This in turn influences our willingness to attempt tasks, and what our expectations are (Dacey et al., 2004, p. 174). Albert Bandura has researched efficacy extensively, and his ideas can be directly applied to the expectations you might have for your future students:

> Self-efficacy beliefs determine how people feel, think, motivate themselves and behave . . . A strong sense of efficacy enhances human accomplishment and personal well-being in many ways. People with high assurance in their capabilities approach difficult tasks as challenges to be mastered rather than as threats to be avoided . . . In contrast, people who doubt their capabilities shy away from difficult tasks which they view as personal threats. They have low aspirations and weak commitment to the goals they choose to pursue. When faced with difficult tasks, they dwell on their personal deficiencies, on the obstacles they will encounter, and all kinds of adverse outcomes rather than concentrate on how to perform successfully.
>
> (Bandura, 1994, p. 71)

Self-efficacy is developed by a wide range of factors, including family, peers, cognitive ability, and previous experiences. As a teacher you can work to increase a sense of self-efficacy by modeling successful strategies for students, providing opportunities for success, and helping your students develop strategies for overcoming obstacles. Similar to self-efficacy is the idea of "locus of control." This is a concept that examines how much control people believe they have over events in their life. If you attribute your success or failure to forces beyond your control (e.g., you believe you were "just lucky," or "not sure why you failed"), you express an external locus (location) of control. If you attribute your behavior to forces you can control (e.g., you "studied hard for the test," or "won because of practicing"), you have an internal locus of control. As a teacher, opportunities to help your students develop internal attributions will be beneficial, since control over their achievements and behavior will be from themselves and not from unpredictable outside forces. We will explore locus of control more in the strategy section of the text, because each instructional strategy has unique opportunities (and challenges) for you to consider.

MAKING IT WORK IN YOUR CONTENT AREA

Partner with someone who will teach in the same content area as you. Generate examples of how students might behave in your classroom for each of the four student behaviors proposed on Csikszentmihalyi's flow diagram. For example, how might a student be apathetic in a geometry class, and how would he or she behave? How might students be anxious? Bored? In flow? For the three behaviors other than flow (apathy, anxiety, and boredom), come up with at least one approach where you could modify either the student's perception of his/her skill, or the perception of the difficulty level of the task.

DIVERSE CHARACTERISTICS AND NEEDS OF MIDDLE SCHOOL AND HIGH SCHOOL STUDENTS

The learners in your classrooms will be very diverse. When considering some of the ways in which students might be different from one another, the following provides an adequate but incomplete list: students will have different cultures, ethnicities, primary languages, economic backgrounds, religions, family structures, physical abilities, and learning abilities. These differences are not exclusive, either. For example, some students who are **English language learners** (**ELLs**) are also gifted, and some will have physical disabilities. In this section, we will examine several aspects of diversity in your future students so that we can establish some key ideas. Before we move on, pause and consider what a wise teacher will remember: we *don't* teach social studies or science or English— we teach people.

Prior to addressing the specifics of diversity, we would like to introduce you to an important concept related to the diverse needs of students in your classroom: *differentiated instruction*.

Your students will learn best when you are informed about their interests, ability and readiness levels, learning preferences, and other areas of their lives that allow you to maximize their specific learning potential (Tomlinson, 1999). As with any examination of adolescents, a caveat needs to be in place about exploring student diversity: **generalizations** about any group are not intended to create stereotypes. Since there are not universally applicable generalizations about teaching adolescents, it will be up to you to get to know your students as individuals. Diversity is a characteristic of your future students that should be enjoyed and considered for the range of ideas, viewpoints, and experiences that it will provide. Differentiated instruction is a learning methodology based upon the premise that instructional approaches should vary depending upon the diverse students in the classroom. The practice of differentiating instruction requires flexibility on the part of the teacher to adjust lesson planning to the students rather than requiring students to adjust to the **curriculum**.

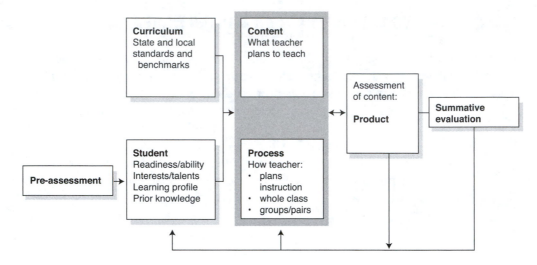

FIGURE 1.2: The Learning Cycle in Differentiated Instruction

According to Hall et al. (2003), differentiating instruction is to

recognize students' varying background knowledge, readiness, language, preferences in learning and interests; and to react responsively. Differentiated Instruction
is a process to teaching and learning for students of differing abilities in the same
class. The intent of differentiating instruction is to maximize each student's growth
and individual success by meeting each student where he or she is and assisting in
the learning process.

In Figure 1.2, these authors help us visualize the learning cycle used in differentiated
instruction.

Note the three primary elements of curriculum that can be differentiated are
content, process, and product (Tomlinson, 2001). However, these start with understanding the student. You will find as you continue learning about this topic that
student-centered instructional strategies, such as **student-directed investigation** or
cooperative learning, are highly conducive to the principles of differentiated instruction. As a result, we will revisit these ideas when the instructional strategies are
examined in Part 2 of this book.

MAKING IT WORK IN YOUR CLASSROOM

To learn more about practical suggestions for your content area
classroom, consult the Tomlinson (1999) article "Mapping a Route
Toward Differentiated Instruction" that can be googled and retrieved
online (we also have a link to it on the book's companion website).

Turn to a lesson you have written for one of the courses you are likely to teach during your first year (e.g., a commonly taught course for new English teachers would be Freshman English as opposed to A.P. Literature). Explain how you think this lesson might address differentiation in terms of

- interest
- readiness
- learner profile.

Is the lesson you selected conducive to adjusting for all three of the above? Two, one, or maybe none? If you were to adjust this lesson, what information would help you plan more effectively?

ETHNIC AND CULTURAL DIVERSITY

A common term closely tied to diversity is **multicultural education**. James Banks defines multicultural education as follows:

> Multicultural education is a field of study and . . . discipline whose major aim is to create equal educational opportunities for students from diverse racial, ethnic, social-class, and cultural groups. One of its important goals is to help all students to acquire the knowledge, attitudes, and skills needed to function effectively in a pluralistic democratic society and to interact, negotiate, and communicate with peoples from diverse groups in order to create a civic and moral community that works for the common good . . . *consequently, we may define multicultural education as a field of study designed to increase educational equity for all students that incorporates, for this purpose, content, concepts, principles, theories, and paradigms from history, the social and behavioral sciences, and particularly from ethnic studies and women studies.*
> (Banks and Banks, 1995, pp. xi–xii)

One implication of this definition is that multicultural education moves students' stories and experiences into the school curriculum. Instead of feeling as though they are not a part of the school and curriculum (a term often referred to as being "marginalized"), students from ethnic minority groups see their culture, history and perspectives incorporated into the standard curriculum. In addition, students in the "dominant culture," or the culture of the social or political group that holds the most power in a school and community need to learn about and embrace stories, cultures, and experiences that are not the same as their own. Gloria Ladson-Billings has called teaching with students' culture and background in mind "culturally relevant teaching" (1995). An excellent place to read a summary of culturally relevant teaching is from the Education Alliance at Brown University (www.alliance.brown.edu). For example, the Education Alliance suggests seven principles for meeting the needs of ethnically and culturally diverse learners. Our summary of these principles are represented in the following chart[2]:

PRINCIPLES FOR MEETING THE NEEDS OF ETHNICALLY AND CULTURALLY DIVERSE LEARNERS

1: Positive Perspectives on Parents and Families

Parent involvement should not be limited to participation in school functions. Oftentimes, religious and cultural differences preclude active participation in school activities. However, parental involvement also includes how parents communicate high expectations, pride, and interest in their child's academic life (Nieto, 1996). Teachers should try to understand the parents of their students, because that will often provide insight into the student at school. This requires communication with parents through such avenues as phone calls/e-mails, school visits by the parent, home visits by the teacher, and even informal conversations at community events. In addition, teachers can help inform parents of the various social and academic services offered by the school and by organizations associated with the school. If you have not had experience with the culture of a parent, you should learn about their cultural activities and beliefs. This will provide a level of knowledge that will help you begin to communicate with parents.

2: Communication of High Expectations

All of your students should hear that you expect them to attain high standards in their school work. This message must be delivered by teachers, counselors, coaches, administrators, and other school personnel. Teachers should understand students' behavior in light of the norms of the communities in which they live, which is why the first point above describes the importance of talking with parents.

3: Learning within the Context of Culture

Schools have a dominate language. Typically, this is the standard American English that is common in middle and upper socioeconomic groups. Your students who do not live in a home and culture that is close to that of the schools may be inhibited from learning because of "language barriers." Other barriers also exist, including preferences for learning. Some cultures emphasize speaking, while others value silence. Some cultural groups put value on cooperation and others do not, preferring individual work. By gaining knowledge of the language and culture of your students, you will be able to create lessons that promote learning because they will use contexts with which your students are familiar.

4: Student-Centered Instruction

During student-centered instruction, learning is a cooperative joint venture. Students are engaged in learning the content more so than when the teacher is the center of attention. This may entail everything from brainstorming topics to study, to student-led discussion groups, to cooperative learning projects, to service learning activities in the local community. These types of activities provide opportunities for students to develop their own ideas, and receive feedback on these ideas. Students from diverse backgrounds are able to bring their ideas and cultural perspectives to the classroom and to work on projects that are culturally and socially relevant to them.

5: Culturally Mediated Instruction

Culturally mediated instruction and learning occur in an environment that encourages multiple viewpoints and allows for inclusion of knowledge that is relevant to the students and to their diverse cultures and backgrounds. Your goal should be to create an environment that encourages and embraces culture by using management and learning strategies familiar to students' culture, provides students with opportunities to share their cultural knowledge, and even questions and challenges students' beliefs and actions. Students should learn that there are often multiple ways to interpret a statement, event, or action. By being allowed to learn in different ways or to share viewpoints and perspectives in a given situation based on their own cultural and social experiences, students become active participants in their learning (Nieto, 1996).

6: Reshaping the Curriculum

The curriculum should use resources other than textbooks for study. For example, students could research a topic within their community, interview members of their community, or provide information on alternative viewpoints or beliefs of a topic. Students' strengths in one subject area will support new learning in another. If your students use their personal experiences to develop new skills and knowledge, a more meaningful connection between school and real-life situations is established (Padron et al., 2002).

7: Teacher as Facilitator

Teachers should develop a learning environment that is relevant to and reflective of their students' social, cultural, and linguistic experiences. You will act as guides, mediators, consultants, instructors, and advocates for your students, helping to effectively connect their cultural- and community-based knowledge to the classroom learning experiences. Teachers should use the students' home cultural experiences as a foundation upon which to develop knowledge and skills. Teachers can do this by encouraging students to share artifacts from home that reflect their culture, write about traditions shared by their families, or research different aspects of their culture. Teachers should also work to accommodate learning preferences of their students that are linked to cultural background and take into account varying levels of English language proficiency. This might also occur by using a community speaker, or inviting parents who can demonstrate alternative ways of approaching a subject or a problem to class (Ladson-Billings, 1995; Padron et al., 2002).

TEACHING ENGLISH TO STUDENTS OF OTHER LANGUAGES

You might relate to the following **reflection** from a recent student teacher:

> My university supervisor came to my World History class one day to observe. After class he was encouraging me to consider ways I could include all the students and not only the ones that volunteered to speak-up. He asked if I noticed the three students sitting in the back corner that didn't say a word the entire class. I did notice them. They speak Ukrainian and I had no idea what to do.

The demographics of the United States, including the number of those who speak languages other than English, are changing rapidly. Teaching students who are learning English as their second or third language is not new, but it has become increasingly common. In addition to immigration from the traditional European regions, a new and profound wave of immigration from Asia, Africa, and Latin America occurs today. As seen in Table 1.1, the percentage of those self-identifying as foreign-born has approached the 1900 highs and the total number of recently immigrated is double that of any time in the history of the nation.

As immigration nears record numbers, it follows that the number of our students with limited English proficiency is growing rapidly. Statistics that reflect school population change have been used to support what has been referred to as the *demographic imperative*. It is imperative for us to prepare ourselves to teach all of our students.

Obviously, not every new teacher will choose to become a certified expert in teaching English as a second language; however, there are several ways to prepare. An important start is learning about the four basic elements for engaging students who are not proficient in English. First, it is important to be able to understand some basic terms used so that when you are placed in your internship or begin your first teaching position, you can ask informed questions. The terminology can be tricky, if not head spinning at times. A person could walk into the teacher's lounge and hear talk of **ESLs**, **TESOLs**, **ELLs**, **ESOLs**, **bilinguals**, emergent bilinguals, and **LEPs**. The glossary of terms that follows will prepare you with some key words and phrases.

TABLE 1.1: Immigration and Your Students

Year	Number of foreign born	Foreign born in U.S. population (%)
1850	2,244,602	9.7
1880	6,679,943	13.3
1900	10,341,276	13.6
1930	14,204,149	11.6
1950	10,347,395	6.9
1980	14,079,906	6.2
2007	38,059,694	12.6

Note: For more information on the topic of immigration and the social studies see the special issue on immigration and citizenship education in the November 2009 issue of *Social Studies and the Young Learner* (A journal of the National Council of the Social Studies).

Source: www.census.gov.

A BRIEF GLOSSARY FOR TEACHING STUDENTS WITH ENGLISH AS A SECOND LANGUAGE

Academic Language: The language used to describe complex ideas, higher-order thinking processes, and abstract concepts, especially within a specific discipline. This term is used for native speakers of English as well as ELLs. See CALP.

Bilingual: An ability to speak two languages.

Bilingual Education: An approach to instruction that includes the continued development of the student's native language, the learning of a second language, and the use of both languages to teach academic content.

Biliteracy: An ability to read and write in two languages. See Freire (1978) for information about the implications of **biliteracy** or literacy on issues of social justice.

BICS: Basic interpersonal communicative skills. This might be thought of as conversational language. A distinction between BICS and CALP was introduced by Cummins (1979). See CALP.

CALP: Cognitive academic language proficiency. Immigrant children typically take 2 years to acquire a conversational fluency (BICS) in a new language. It may take the same child at least 5 years to reach an academic proficiency (CALP) in the new language.

ELL: English language learners or students who are not proficient in English.

ESL: English as a second language. A program or system of instruction designed to teach English to those who speak other languages. This system typically will use academic content and is usually thought of as a component of **bilingual education**.

ESOL: English to speakers of other languages. Some prefer this to ESL because it recognizes that English could be the third or fourth language of the student and that this should be acknowledged. For example, a student from Mexico may speak Mixteco (a Native language) as their first language and Spanish as their second language.

Immersion: Technically, this is a bilingual immersion program developed in Canada where 90% of the early elementary-aged student's day is in the minority language (the non-mainstream language). Many times, however, this term is used in schools to refer to placing a student in a mainstream classroom (not necessarily as part of a well thought-out program).

LEP: Limited English proficient. This is usually used as an adjective to describe students as in: 'the LEP student'. Some prefer not to use this term for the same reason that some prefer not to use the word "disability"—it focuses on what a student *cannot* do instead of what they *can* do.

TESOL: Teaching English to speakers of other languages or the professional organization Teachers of English to Speakers of Other Languages.

Second, it is important to know that you are not alone. There usually will be a teacher in your school that specializes in teaching ESL. Her program could look like one of the many possible varieties of teaching English but most likely will reflect current trends of teaching ESL. This means that students of all levels of English proficiency come to her class to either learn the academic subject (ESL content class) or have class time to support them with their assignments from mainstream monolingual English classes; support may be in English or in their first language, depending upon obvious variables. Of course, some students will attend introductory-level English classes as well. This is important to keep in mind, but—without question—conscientious teachers will not shift all of the responsibility for the learning of an ELL onto the ESL teacher.

A third element to consider is the way people acquire new languages. Having a basic understanding of language acquisition theory will help as you try to design or modify lessons. While taking a course on second language acquisition theory would undoubtedly benefit any teacher, here we will focus on two of the components that influence language acquisition in a school context (Cummins, 1979; Thomas and Collier, 1997). Students learning English will tend to begin by learning social language. They learn what they use in everyday conversations. Immigrant children typically take 2 years to acquire a conversational fluency (BICS) in a new language. Students take much longer to negotiate their way into the more formal academic language. It may take the same child at least 5 years to reach an academic proficiency (CALP) in the new language. The catch is this: an unknowing teacher may assume that because he hears a student speak English during class that the student is equally proficient in academic language, the language of teaching and learning. This will most likely not be the case. In addition, because textbooks are written in academic language the student's actual proficiency could easily be overestimated and not be provided with adequate assistance for understanding what they read for class.

The teaching of academic language isn't something unique to those with limited proficiency, however. Some of our students will certainly have advantages if they come from homes that speak dominant dialects with access to computers, books, conversations, and other mainstream English language resources. By contrast, other students may have recently immigrated and come from homes with non-mainstream English language resources, no computers, few educational resources, or come from homes where dominant English is not common in their homes. While this group clearly has unique needs, both groups are academic language learners.

All of our students need to be taught academic language, and many of the techniques used to assist with teaching academic language are beneficial for both groups (Zwiers, 2008).

Another consideration for teachers is that some students may not have a literacy base at all. In other words, they may not read or write in their first language. This obviously would have an impact on their ability to read or write English even if they are verbally performing well.

The final element for you to consider is inclusive methods of teaching. TESOL specialists tell us that many of the techniques used to support ELLs are also helpful for every student. You will see in Part 2 of this book that techniques of teaching are unique to the instructional strategy chosen by the teacher. Techniques for implementation,

assessment, and classroom management used during a **discussion** will be different from those in a lecture. When working in mainstream social studies classes with varying English ability levels, a teacher will choose common instructional strategies but purposefully modify or add techniques that aid language development. For example, in a world history class you may have decided to have a discussion about the similarities and differences between South African apartheid and Jim Crow laws in the U.S. South. Providing discussion time in class between native and ELLs is an outstanding aid to language and content learning. Student peers can often speak in a way that is more comprehensible to the ELL and a good mix of small group and large group discussion helps the ELL to feel more comfortable participating. In this apartheid discussion, the teachers then might begin by spending time building background before jumping into the discussion, they might be sure to use plenty of visuals to help students understand concepts, and finally, they might choose to ask small groups of students to review and discuss background materials they provide prior to starting a large group discussion. As with most every aspect to teaching, there is no one-size-fits-all approach to teaching ELLs.

In Part 2 of this book you will find ESL strategies and ideas that could be beneficial for each of the instructional strategies we discuss. In addition, you can easily find lists of ideas on the internet that will be helpful as you consider a variety of approaches based upon your instructional strategy choice. A good place to continue your learning can be found at Dave's ESL Café (www.eslcafe.com), a link to which is provided on this book's companion website.

MAKING IT WORK IN YOUR CLASSROOM

Imagine you are planning a lesson on a specific topic in your discipline; for example, you might choose Wilbur Wilberforce and his attempts to end the slave trade in Britain. You have determined that this lesson will rely on lecture and discussion. Next to each of the ideas below used by TESOL instructors to help support ELLs, either leave blank or write down the name of one of these two instructional strategies that you think might be a good match.

- Activate prior schemata by making connections to students' background knowledge, or providing contextual information to help provide that background.
- Handout a paragraph with blank words for students to fill in.
- Provide a graphic organizer.
- Stop speaking every 10 minutes and ask a question.
- Explain your lesson objective.
- Use exit slips.
- Be aware of your speech patterns.

- Let them know straight out what you want them to do or produce at the end of the day.
- Break the class into pairs before a large group debriefing.
- Show common language patterns on a poster in the room: for example, "I see what you mean, but I think . . ."
- Place students in mixed ability groups.
- Provide participation roles like timekeeper or note taker.
- Ask for written notes on a poster in a different color for each student.

EXCEPTIONALITIES

In your future classrooms, you will teach students with unique needs, talents, and interests. One challenge you will face will be to differentiate the curriculum so every child has opportunities to learn in an environment that is safe and least restrictive. What this means is that you need to consider how you might make your daily instruction individualized for each of your students. You can manage this task for many of your students, but you will also have students who will need special services—or special education. These students are frequently referred to as "exceptional students," and teachers have a legal, and we believe ethical, obligation to provide lessons to them that will promote maximum learning. Culatta and Tompkins (1999) developed this list of exceptionalities that your future students may have: mental retardation; learning disabilities; behavioral or emotional disorders; communication disorders; physical and/or health impairments; hearing and or vision impairments; severe or multiple disabilities; and giftedness.

Exceptional students may receive special services from an instructional assistant who attends classes with them or receive special services from courses and programs that pull a student out of the general education classroom. When possible, exceptional students are kept in the general education classroom. This is known as the "inclusive model," because the general education classroom is a place that includes all students. It is easy to understand that many educators disagree about how to educate children with exceptionalities. Proponents of a fully inclusive model speak of the benefits that all students have when learning in a room with diverse learners. Students of all capabilities work together to help one another learn. The challenge for teachers is to provide opportunities for learning that allow the wide range of students to learn. Opponents of inclusion suggest that placing students in programs separate from the general education classroom allows for more individualized instruction and learning. They argue that the burden on the classroom teacher will be too great if all students are placed together. The challenge for these "pull-out" programs is to ensure that academic expectations remain high. In addition, boys are identified as needing special services more than girls, as are students of color, and students from homes that are economically disadvantaged. Whether these students should be taught separately, included in the general classroom, or taught with some combination of these two is a raging debate in schools. In any case, you will need to consider how you will help students who have exceptionalities learn in your classroom.

One of the most powerful tools that you will have as a teacher in an inclusive classroom will be your exceptional students' **individualized educational program**—or their IEP. When a public school child needs special services, an IEP must be designed. These are developed by the special education teachers/specialists in your school, with the help of parents, other teachers, school personnel, and at times, the student. An IEP give details about the educational supports and services that will help the child with a disability to receive appropriate instruction. An IEP may specify instructional strategies, strategies for managing behavior, motivational techniques, and other insights about how to best help the student learn. Test scores, physician reports, and other psychological, cognitive, and/or medical reports might also be included. By contacting your special education expert(s) in the school, you will have powerful strategies for meeting the needs of your exceptional students. New regulations emphasize that the IEP team must consider a student's strengths as well as areas of weakness, when formulating an educational plan. An IEP is required by federal law whenever a student has a recognized disability. In 1997, the Individuals with Disabilities Education Act (or IDEA) was passed into law, and this act specified disabilities and strengthened the expectations of learning for all students. Each state, or in some cases, each county or each school, designs their own IEP's for their students with disabilities. Some students do not have disabilities that require special education services. They might not receive an IEP, but they could receive a "504 Plan." A **504 Plan** is a program of instructional services to assist students with special needs who are in a regular education setting. A student who has a physical or emotional disability, or who has an impairment that restricts one or more major life activities (e.g., caring for one's self, performing manual tasks, walking, seeing, hearing, speaking, breathing, working, and learning), or who is recovering from a chemical dependency should receive a 504 Plan.

The instructional strategies that we will examine in the second part of this book can be adapted to meet the individual needs of the students. They allow for all students to learn, whether they are considered a general education student, a student with learning disabilities, or a gifted student. Specifics for differentiating the instructional strategies to help your students learn most effectively are described for each strategy.

GENDER CONSIDERATIONS

In their book *Choosing Democracy: A Practical Guide to Multicultural Education*, Campbell and Steinbrueck (1996) write that teachers often communicate different expectations of males than they do of females. Teachers often give male students more attention and provide them with more opportunities to share during class activities. Others have observed teachers and concluded that teachers tend to praise boys for the intellectual contributions to class, and praise girls for their proper behavior in class (Sadker and Sadker, 1982; McCormick, 1994; Sadker and Sadker, 1994). As a result, teachers may reinforce societal norms about gender-biased behaviors that actually limit girls' academic performance and enhance boys' achievements. During the last decade, a series of programs have encouraged girls' participation in mathematics and science classes, and increases in girls' performances in these areas are starting to be realized. Now concern is beginning to rise about the low number of boys who attend colleges, with some estimates suggesting that in the near future two females will graduate from college for every male. Suffice to say, gender differences exist, and you need to reflect on your interactions with students to ensure that gender bias is not affecting your students' opportunities to learn.

For years, reports have concluded that in early adolescence girls' IQ scores drop and their math and sciences scores fall behind their male counterparts (Pipher, 1994). This could be partly due to changes from leaving elementary school and entering middle school, changes brought about by puberty, and/or increased awareness of peer and societal influences on their behavior. More recently, however, gaps between girls and boys are narrowing. Achievement in mathematics and science are not as wide as they were even a decade ago. The emphasis on closing the gender gap seems to be having a positive effect, especially on girls. Boys are changing as well, and at times feel pressured to repress emotions and feelings; some find that using aggressive behavior helps them to fit in with societal expectations (Sadker and Sadker, 1994; Thorne, 1994; Sadker and Zittleman, 2012). Boys engage in more at-risk behaviors (gang membership, drug use, physical risks, etc.) than girls in middle schools and high schools. Boys tend to receive lower grades, and make up the majority of students referred for special education services (Gurian and Stevens, 2004). For example, 71% of students identified as "learning disabled" and 80% of those identified as emotionally disturbed were boys (Sadker and Sadker, 1994).

For these reasons, and more, it will be important for you to consider the role gender plays in your content area. Many high school students perceive poetry as being "feminine" even though famous poets throughout history have been men. Mathematics is often misperceived as being masculine even though women have made significant contributions to that discipline. Women's roles are often omitted from historical accounts; men's conquests dominate the conventional "stories." Check your curriculum to identify if you are missing important opportunities for clarifying misrepresentations of women and men, or if you are underrepresenting the roles of women or men in the content your students are studying. When teaching, reflect on the nature of your interactions with students. If you teach in accord with the sample that McCormick examined in 1994, you will likely give boys five times more attention than girls. Work to provide gender equity in your classroom.

POVERTY IN SCHOOLS

According the United States Bureau of the Census, 37 million Americans are living in poverty. Of these, 13 million are under 18 years old.[3] The social economic status of your students will likely impact their learning and the educational resources available to you. The National Commission on Teaching and America's Future issued a report that supports over 20 years of research on poverty and schooling. This commission states:

[C]hildren at risk, who come from families with poorer economic backgrounds, are not being given an opportunity to learn that is equal to that offered to children from the most privileged families. The obvious cause of this inequality lies in the finding that the most disadvantaged children attend schools that do not have basic facilities and conditions conducive to providing them with a quality education.

(NCTAF, 2004, p. 7)

Paul Gorski (2005) follows up on this report with the following summary:

[S]chools with large percentages of low-income students are more likely than schools with large percentages of wealthy students to have an abundance of teachers unlicensed in the subjects they teach, serious teacher turnover problems, teacher vacancies and large numbers of substitute teachers, limited access to computers and the Internet, inadequate facilities (such as science labs), dirty or inoperative student bathrooms, evidence of vermin such as cockroaches and rats, and insufficient classroom materials.

(p. 3)

Many implications can be derived from these accounts. It is important to recognize the impact of poverty on schooling—both in terms of educational opportunities for your students, and the support systems available to your students outside of school. You will want to consider whether your assignments and activities unfairly allow students with more resources to have an advantage over poor students. Teachers used to be discouraged from finding out the socioeconomic status of their students out of concern that it might bias them against students. Today, the thinking is that teachers must be aware of the student differences so that they can help each child uniquely. When you know students are living in poverty, then you check if you are assuming that all students come to school from the same background. Poverty is systemic, and it is difficult for schools and teachers to devise a list of strategies for overcoming poverty. We developed the following list of topics related to poverty and wealth that we hope you will think about when you are planning your classroom activities. This is not an inclusive list, but a beginning point for considering economic diversity in your classroom:

- Some students work for pleasure, some work to help pay bills, and some will not work at all.
- The value of education varies dramatically in the homes of your students.
- Opportunities to travel, to have access to materials and resources, and to use the internet outside of school are correlated with higher economic status.
- Parent/guardian availability to help with students' school work is widely varied.
- Some students have nutritious breakfasts and lunches, while others will eat little or eat poorly.
- Crime rates and other safety issues could impact students' opportunities to complete school work.

MAKING IT WORK IN YOUR CONTENT AREA

Think of three specific strategies that you might use in your future classroom that will raise the status of your students who are typically "marginalized" due to ethnicity, exceptionality, or gender. Consider the following examples to get you started thinking about this: if you are a woman who plans to teach mathematics, then you could tell girls how you overcame any stereotypes about girls and mathematics. If you plan to teach American literature, you might select a story by Alice Walker because African-American women are often underrepresented. If you plan to run a mock congress in your civics course, you might consider having students who are not in leadership roles at your school hold offices of class president or ambassador during the simulation.

CONTEXTS OF TEACHING IN A CHANGING AND TECHNOLOGICAL SOCIETY

You will find that in educational circles technology is defined in many different ways. Some, such as the Association for Educational Communications and Technology (AECT, 1994), define educational technology very broadly so that it would include procedures and resources for learning. This could include the process one uses while including a tool for learning as a type of "technology." Others would define it almost exclusively as the use of resources as tools for learning. "Tools" could include many resources from common pencils to sophisticated systems for interactive communication (e.g., laptops or cell phones). For the purposes of this text, we will be using the term technology to specifically refer to modern electronic resources found in classrooms that can be used for teaching and learning. Most often we will be referring to digitally oriented resources used by and found on computers.

The technology available has changed dramatically over the last 5 years. This is obvious to many of us, but to others, especially those in your classes, that have grown up with the changes, it might have gone unnoticed. The frantic pace of technological change is an unremarkable way of life to many middle and high school students of today. These students have spent their entire lives learning new software, playing video games, updating their operating systems, and looking forward to the latest versions with the latest audio and graphics. Some have described these students as native speakers of the digital environment or "digital natives." That, interestingly, would make those not born into the digital world "digital immigrants"; those trying to hang on to the myriad technological changes, those who tire of learning new software again, those who speak with digital "accents," those who may be like you, your building administrators, or fellow teachers, and those who according to some, think differently (Prensky, 2001; Owston, 1997).

As long as we are considering this metaphor it is important to note that some have purposefully decided to stay in the "old country" and not (or tried not to) immigrate at all. These note how technology does not always have a positive impact on our society and, in fact, takes more than it gives (Postman, 1995; Oppenheimer, 1997). We believe that just as it is important to consider ways to include ESL students while planning lessons, it is also important to consider ways to include the digital language of our students as well as take into account our own fluency in that language. Some teachers are naturally apprehensive about using the new language (a computer), while others do not realize that they are speaking with a "heavy accent" and that their students are the native speakers (highly skilled with computers). In addition, it is important to remember that asking your students to use technology implies that students may need access to computers and other electronic devices. Much has been written about the "digital divide," or the socioeconomic gap between communities and people who have access to computer technology and those who do not. For example, if you assign students to access the internet as part of a homework assignment, you are assuming that all students can do this outside of school. If some do, and some do not, then you are placing students who do not have access at a disadvantage. This is not equitable. Care needs to be taken when implementing student activities tied to technology.

Through the years as we have discussed using technology with teachers and aspiring teachers there has been a common agreement: most teachers do not want to be "technologists." Teachers are less interested in learning about the gadgets than learning how they can be used in a lesson. One of the most important things a person can learn about using technology for teaching and learning is that the focus in the classroom should not be on the technology but on how it can be used to promote student learning. Digital immigrants can be a skeptical group because most of us have seen the well-meaning use of technology that adds little value to a lesson or, worse, becomes a distraction. Adding technology has become the easy part of teaching—not necessarily the best part. The question we ask ourselves should not be "How can I infuse technology into this lesson?" but rather, "Can value be added to the lesson by using technology, and if it can then how?"

We have also seen technology used in well thought-out, valuable ways. Some have argued that technology helps increase student motivation. Of course, any teacher would be interested in something that is motivating. Unfortunately, motivation due to the use of a new gadget is somewhat shallow and often expensive. However, motivation due to increased control of your own learning is empowering and technology can help accomplish this. This would take a rethinking of the way we teach, not simply adding more technology to our classes. Technology can also be used to promote, establish, and support dynamic instructional strategies that are designed to meet **learning objectives**. In fact, in a review of cases studies, the CEO Forum (2001) concluded that technology has the greatest impact when it is integrated into the curriculum for the purpose of achieving clear, measurable educational objectives. In the chapters describing instructional strategies that follow, we show how technology could play an important role when using specific instructional strategies to help students learn.

MAKING IT WORK IN YOUR CONTENT AREA

Thinking critically about the use of technology in classrooms

Go to the technology-infused lesson plan database created by in-service teachers in Mississippi at CREATE: www.create.cett.msstate. edu/create/classroom/lessons.asp.

We link to CREATE from our companion website.

Choose a lesson to review from the areas of language arts, science, math, and social studies. What technology is to be used? Do you think the technology will help students learn the content more effectively? If so, why? If not, why did the teacher use technology and what could the teacher have done differently? What caveats would you give any teacher who is interested in trying the lesson?

GUIDING PRINCIPLES FOR CLASSROOM MANAGEMENT AND DISCIPLINE

After many interviews with teachers (both pre-service and in-service), we have concluded that classroom management and student **discipline** are closely linked to the instructional strategy you are using. Each instructional strategy has its own management requirements and logistics considerations; the seven chapters on instructional strategies specify how best to manage the classroom while using a particular strategy, and how you might effectively discipline students during each strategy. Therefore, the chapters in Part 2 build on the management and discipline principles that we will examine in this section of Chapter 1. We intend for this section to provide some general terminology and overviews of key components for managing an effective learning environment.

One of the greatest worries in the minds of many student teachers has to do with management and discipline problems. Pre-service teachers often wonder if they will be able to maintain order, earn student respect, oversee group activities, or effectively handle all of the logistical and organizational tasks of the classroom. Specific questions arise from working with teachers as well, such as "Am I really not supposed to smile until December?" or "What should I do if a student says 'no' when I ask him to do something?" These are real concerns. Many worries fade when you meet your students, but new concerns often arise. Effective teachers can manage the classroom and discipline students so that optimal learning can occur. In addition, teaching will be much more enjoyable for you when the classroom is a community of learners in which you and your students are comfortable.

DIFFERENCES BETWEEN MANAGEMENT AND DISCIPLINE

When preparing to help students learn, you will use a series of instructional strategies. While these strategies will help you determine appropriate ways to assess your students' learning, they will also provide guidance as you identify the activities students will engage in, select materials and resources that you and the students need, and consider the logistics of having the day's events work together to promote student learning. The best planned lessons can be unsuccessful, however, if you do not think through how you will manage the learning environment, and if you are unable to effectively discipline students who are behaving inappropriately.

We differentiate between classroom management and discipline as follows: *Classroom management* is a proactive approach to helping students learn, and *discipline* is a reaction to student misbehavior. Classroom management addresses all of the aspects of the classroom that will promote student learning. You are overseeing all that happens in your classroom. Many educators refer to the classroom as a "community of learners," where you and your students are committed to making the classroom environment a safe place where knowledge, skills, and dispositions are developed over the school year. As the adult leading that community, you need to ensure that students are supported, cared for, challenged, and meeting the learning outcomes for your course. Classroom management involves overseeing the classroom so this happens. *Discipline* specifically refers to how you can effectively control students' behaviors so as to maintain the sense of community in your classroom. Part of discipline enables students to self-monitor their behaviors (so they literally become self-disciplined), but part of discipline involves the specific action that teachers take when a student disobeys a rule or an expectation. While teachers need to discipline students, we suggest that many potential problems can be avoided simply by having a well-managed classroom.

Consider the following real dilemma that a teacher might face: Students are seated in groups of four around the room. One group of students needs the teacher to help them understand the assignment. A second group of students, on the opposite side of the classroom, is being disruptive and not working on the assignment. The teacher knows that her proximity has a significant impact on disruptive behavior; that is, when she is in close proximity to the disruptive group, they quiet down and work. However, this keeps her away from the group of students needing her help. What could the teacher do to manage this situation? How could she address this proactively? What discipline issues are at work? As you consider answers to these questions, you are engaging in the type of thinking that teachers do when considering the management of their classroom and learning environment.

RELATIONAL TEACHING

Many conflicts and problems can be avoided if teachers try to build appropriate relationships with their students. The term we use for this is ***relational teaching***. As the name implies, relational teaching places high value on the relationship the teacher has with the whole class as well as with each student. Rather than thinking of your students as a group of adolescents that come to your classroom, you think of them individually, with each possessing their own unique experiences, struggles, strengths, and weaknesses. During the school year, you look for opportunities to build teacher/ student relationships with each member of your class. This takes time and effort, but it is surprising how quickly you can get to know your students. Benefits from a relational teaching approach include: knowing how to assign students to groups because you know each students' strengths and weaknesses; understanding pressures and influences on a student that may affect their behavior in class; developing a sense of mutual respect for one another; reducing "acting out" or misbehavior by students because they do not want to harm the relationship you have developed; and, increasing interest in the development and learning of your students as you become more invested in their lives.

A wonderful example of relational teaching is seen in the work of Wolpow et al. in their free online handbook *The Heart of Teaching and Learning: compassion, resiliency, and academic success* (2011). The handbook informs us of the enormous difficulties faced by youth exposed to traumatic events, such as abuse, neglect, homelessness, and domestic violence. Students who have experienced traumatic conditions often have difficulties, with learning, forming relationships, and behaving appropriately in school. The handbook provides guidance and background information about trauma and learning, self-care, classroom strategies, including vignettes and case studies, and building supportive partnerships.

Relational teaching also has to do with developing what is often called "**withitness**" (Kounin, 1977). When teachers are "withit" they are described as being keenly aware of all that is happening in the classroom. Sometimes it seems as though a "withit" teacher has eyes in the back of her head, or has an extraordinary sense of hearing and can hear comments whispered on the far side of the room, or is able to preempt a potential problem before it starts. A significant part of being so tuned in to your students that you are "withit" requires developing a positive rapport with them.

With a partner, consider how you might develop positive relationships with students. What are some ideas for getting to know the interests of your students? As you talk about these ideas, check if you understand the idea of "withitness." Have you observed teachers or coaches who are withit? What did they do? On our companion website, we provide an overview of ten "truths" about effective schools developed by Doda et al. (1987).

APPROACHES TO CLASSROOM MANAGEMENT

Every teacher develops his or her own approach for managing a classroom. Successful teachers will often claim that they "do not have management or discipline problems." However, when you watch them teach, they are continually monitoring and interacting with students to ensure everyone is acting pro-socially and adhering to the classroom expectations. If a student begins to fall asleep, the successful teacher casually walks by and taps him on the shoulder. If two students are passing notes, the teacher does not draw attention to the behavior but simply continues talking while standing next to the two students. His proximity makes them put the note away. If a challenging assignment is beginning on Monday, the successful teacher anticipates students' questions and is able to address most of them when the assignment is described. In this way, students feel as though their ideas and worries are considered. In each of these situations, the teacher managed the learning environment with an approach that worked. In this section, we will describe seven effective and long-standing approaches to classroom management. What you end up using will undoubtedly be a hybrid of these, but an initial examination of these seven will allow you to start thinking about effective management approaches.

Behaviorism

Skinner (1953) did not describe an approach to classroom management, but the principles of behaviorism that he established provide some general ideas. The most useful principle for management is *behavior modification*. Behavior modification operates on positive and negative behaviors. True to the stimulus–response of behaviorism, a teacher notices a student behaving properly and acknowledges, praises, or in some way reinforces that behavior. The reinforced student, along with his classmates who witnessed the reinforcement, will likely repeat this behavior and perceive it as a beneficial behavior. Students who are misbehaving are not acknowledged, and in an effort to earn praise they would also behave appropriately. Students receive external rewards for behaving appropriately. These often take the form of tokens or other tangible items. For example, a teacher might put a pencil in a mug whenever all of the students are sitting down before the bell rings to start the period. When the mug is full (about fifteen pencils), the class receives a "free day" to learn about a topic of their choice, or even to have a pizza party. Rules are established and rewards are provided for following them. Earlier in this chapter, we described intrinsic and extrinsic motivations. Behaviorism relies largely on extrinsic sources of motivation.

Canter's Assertive Discipline Model

This model (Canter, 1976; Canter and Canter, 1992) provides a set of clear-cut expectations for the classroom. Students can expect teachers to provide a safe learning environment, and teachers can expect students to pay attention and not disrupt the class. The teacher establishes clear expectations, justifies why these expectations are needed, and lists the consequences for misbehavior (not meeting expectations). Once established, the teacher expects adherence to the classroom rules. Students have the choice to behave in accord with the rules, or to misbehave. Misbehavior is considered to be a poor choice and the teacher must be assertive and follow through with the stated consequences. This will teach students to behave responsibly in the classroom. When helping students remember the expected behavior, the teacher should state the expectations to the student ("Chris, remember to bring your book to class"), or to praise a student in front of the class for behaving properly ("Chris remembered to raise his hand. Nice job!"). If a student perpetually misbehaves, then the teacher "moves in" close to the student, establishes eye contact, restates the expectations, and indicates the next consequences of continuing to misbehave.

Dreikurs/Albert Model

Dreikurs (Dreikurs and Cassel, 1972) suggests that the classroom needs to be democratic, but his ideas became more applicable after Albert (1989) refocused them specifically to classroom management. This has implications for how the rules are decided and the instructional strategies that are employed. Students impose limitations on themselves for the purpose of directing behavior so it promotes learning. The teacher and students cooperate to determine classroom procedures, rules, and even the discipline for misbehavior. Democratic teaching is very different from "autocratic teaching" (where the teacher is always in charge of the classroom policies and disciplining students, and where students have no need to develop self-discipline), and it is different from "permissive teaching" (where the teacher does not help enforce the classroom policies and students do not learn about responsibility, accountability, and self-discipline). The democratic teacher engages students in the process, and fosters a sense of self-discipline among the students. Students have goals that they strive to attain, one of which is a sense of belonging to the classroom community. If a student does not follow the class-developed rules, then authentic consequences result. Dreikurs suggests that misbehavior is the result of a student seeking one of four wrong goals: (1) getting attention; (2) seeking power; (3) getting revenge; or (4) withdrawing and not participating. As the teacher manages the classroom he or she looks for students who are pursuing these wrong goals and then redirects them by enforcing the natural consequences of breaking rules.

Ginott's Model

This model is built around the key term of congruent communication, or communication that is about situations rather than student character or personality. In other words, instead of telling students that they are being rude by interrupting during a classroom discussion, the teacher might say: "This is a whole class discussion. We need to allow everyone a chance to express their ideas." Students' behavior, thus, is managed by addressing the situations that students are in and inviting students to cooperate. In the teacher's comment above, the first sentence addresses the situation (a class discussion), and the second sentence asks for cooperation (letting everyone speak). By not attacking students' character or personality, the student may be more willing to discuss his or her feelings about a situation in the classroom. This open line of communication, along with the teacher modeling appropriate behavior, enables the teacher to change the attitudes and beliefs of students, not merely their behavior. This takes time, and depends on repeated opportunities to communicate with students. Ginott also felt strongly about the powerful role that teachers play in students' lives. In his book titled *Teacher and Child* (1971), he wrote:

> I am the decisive element in the classroom. It is my personal approach that creates the climate . . . As a teacher I possess tremendous power to make a child's life miserable or joyous. I can be a tool of torture or an instrument of inspiration . . . in all situations it is my response that decides whether a crisis will be escalated or de-escalated, and a child humanized or de-humanized.
>
> (p. 13)

As a result, Ginott suggests that communication without attacking the students' character will lead to a well-managed classroom.

Glasser's Model

According to this model (Glasser, 1992), the teacher expects all students to produce quality work. Teachers must lead students in learning activities that students and teachers agree are worthwhile and useful. This model suggests that students want their basic needs met: survival, belonging, power, fun, and freedom. Survival is not always tied to the school (though it can be if the student feels unsafe), but the other four needs can be met at school. When these basic needs are not met, students are frustrated. When they are met, students are satisfied. If students needs are not being met, the frustration leads to apathy, and the learning is seen as irrelevant. Teachers must manage the classroom to create an environment that has some fun, allows students a certain amount of power, has some degree of freedom, and helps students feel part of the classroom learning community. This can be partly accomplished when the teacher has high expectations for quality work and provides opportunities to learn course content in depth. Students then need encouragement to determine their own paths for attaining this level of quality. The teachers' role is to encourage quality work by challenging students to solve problems, building relationships with students, and continually being available to help. This can be done individually or during class meetings where expectations for quality work are further refined.

Jones' Model

This model (Jones, 1987) differs from the others in its emphasis on nonverbal communication. The teacher's "body language, facial expressions, gestures, eye contact, and physical proximity" (Charles, 1996, p. 128) each send important messages to the students and help manage the learning environment. The messages from teachers to students about their behavior can be very powerfully sent without saying anything. Some teachers allude to this when they proclaim that when they simply give their students "the look" everyone knows it is time to behave. The importance of proximity is also highlighted by Jones. By simply standing near students who are misbehaving in some fashion, a teacher is able to quickly end the behavior without drawing a lot of attention to the situation. This model also suggests that teachers provide incentives for students that are genuine and will motivate all students in the class. Incentives such as extra credit will motivate select students, while an ice cream party will likely motivate most students. Tied to this is Jones' suggestion to follow "Grandma's Rule": First eat your vegetables, and then you can have your dessert. Translated to the classroom, teachers should remember that students should behave properly before receiving any rewards for their behavior. Teachers must not reward students based on students' promises to behave well.

Aside from nonverbal communication, Jones suggests that teachers should not spend too much time with any one student. Part of managing the classroom is to move around to all students. By spending too much time or attention with one student, the other students in the class are not monitored—for behavior or for understanding. Also, students need opportunities to work through academic problems without building dependency on the teacher to answer every question. Jones suggests that teachers should provide efficient help to students, and limit interaction to 20 seconds intervals. He suggests three steps: (1) acknowledge what the student has done correctly; (2) suggest what needs to be done next; and (3) leave the student to work on the details.

Kounin's Model

Jacob Kounin's (1977) ideas about classroom management centers on the teacher's behavior that engages students in the lessons. He suggested that misbehavior rarely occurred when students were actively learning. Kounin's principal concepts are succinctly described by Charles (1996, pp. 45–46):

- The **Ripple Effect**: is a phenomenon where the teacher's words or actions are directed at one student, but spread out and affect behavior of other students. Similarly, if misbehavior is ignored by the teacher, the ripple effect could spread a belief that the teacher will not enforce certain rules.
- Withitness: This term refers to teachers knowing what is going on in the classroom at all times. Students do not think they can "get away" with anything if their teacher is "withit."
- **Momentum** and Smoothness: Lessons need to keep moving by not spending too much time on details ("overdwelling"), having smooth transitions from one lesson to another, and varying class activities to keep students engaged.
- **Student Accountability**: This phrase refers to teacher's efforts to keep students alert and involved in the lessons. This may involve calling on students to answer questions, or other requests that require students to be attentive.
- **Overlapping**: This is Kounin's term for multitasking; the ability to attend to two or three tasks at the same time. For example, the teacher is able to write on the board while answering a question, and redirecting a group of students working on a group project.
- **Satiation**: This means that students are done thinking about a topic, and that the teacher needs to change his/her approach. Satiation can be brought about by boredom, repetition, or frustration.
- **Valence and Challenge Arousal**: This is Kounin's term for how teachers might make activities more enjoyable/challenging. Variety of activities, teacher enthusiasm, and multi-media are ways to keep students aroused (and not satiated).

MANAGING THE LEARNING ENVIRONMENT

As we mentioned before, exuding a sense of being "withit" and using your proximity to students for making your presence known will help a classroom environment. Establishing classroom rules and routines will also help you manage the learning environment. Rules might be established by students, the teacher, or in concert together, but they need to be consistently adhered to by everyone in class. It is more effective to state your expectation in terms of what should be done, rather than what you do not want. For example, the rule "Do not be late to class," is not as effective "Be ready to start class when the bell rings." Or, the rule "Do not interrupt" is more clearly stated as "Let classmates finish their thought before you talk." In the discussions that we have done with teachers, it appears that fewer, more general rules and expectations are more effective than many specific rules. "Respect other's opinions" is vague, but it may be a better rule then ten specific rules about respect. If you are going to ensure that all students follow the rules, then you do not want to provide so many rules that it gets in the way of your planning and instruction. In many ways, the teacher who is effectively managing the classroom is like a good baseball umpire. Everyone knows he is there and is not afraid to enforce a rule, but he does not allow the rules to overshadow the game, or in the case of the teacher, the rules do not overshadow the activities of the day. Similarly, the placement of tables, chairs, and students can help the management of the classroom. The classroom set up needs to vary depending on the instructional strategies you use. For example, you might have students in neat rows during a lecture, but they need to be sitting in circles during a group project. More specific rules are examined later for each instructional strategy.

Effective teachers also establish classroom routines. Routines help address questions such as when to turn in the homework, when to raise hands, what is expected when the bell rings at the start or end of the period, what is the procedure if someone needs to leave class, where will class announcements be posted, or what materials are needed for class (e.g., textbook, binder, pencil). By establishing clear routines, students are able to focus more on the learning and less on the logistics.

MAKING IT WORK IN YOUR CONTENT AREA

To put some of these theories into practice, we want you to complete three tasks:

First, consider how "daily life" in your classroom might operate. Explain what you will do regarding the following elements of classroom management:

- What routines will you use (e.g., beginning/ending class, homework collection/return, bathroom passes, etc.)?
- What will your policy be about late work?
- How will you determine seating assignments? Desk arrangements?

Second, create an introductory assignment or student interest survey that you might use to get to know more about your students. Be creative in what you ask of students; try to find out information that will assist your management of the classroom; it will give you insight into their lives that will help you be a more effective teacher of your content area.

Third, generate a one-page handout that you might give to your students that articulates your classroom guidelines and/or expectations. These can be developed by taking "bits and pieces" from the management theories presented above. Keep in mind the following:

- Strive for a suitable level of generality.
- State your guidelines positively (say what you expect them to do) and clearly.
- Specify your expectations about students' behavior, respect for property, respect for people, academic achievement, safety, and other elements you think are important.
- List positive and negative consequences of adhering or not adhering to your guidelines.

CHAPTER REVIEW

- Adolescent development and its implications on learning and teaching:

  - Adolescents' bodies are changing rapidly.
  - Cognitive development advances: thinking skills develop and improve.
  - Social development advances: adolescents learn how to interact with the world around them.

- General theories and ideas about learning:

  - Learning defined: "relatively permanent change, due to experience, either in behavior or in mental representations or associations" (Ormrod, 2006, p. 184).
  - There are many theories about learning (e.g., Gardner, Piaget, Vygotsky, etc.).

- Motivating students:

  - Motivation: A force, or energizer, that helps us accomplish as task.
  - Intrinsic motivation differs from extrinsic motivation.
  - Self efficacy.

- Diverse characteristics and needs of adolescents:

  - Classrooms will have students with different cultures, ethnicities, primary languages, economic backgrounds, religions, family structures, physical abilities, and learning abilities.

- – "Exceptional students": those who have disabilities, impairments, giftedness, or disorders.
  - – Number of ESL students has increased dramatically.

- • The role of appropriate technology for helping students learn:

  - – Focus on how technology can promote student learning.
  - – Be mindful of finding ways to include ESL students.

- • Importance of classroom management:

  - – Proactive approach to help students learn.
  - – Discipline is a reaction to student misbehavior.

NOTES

1 Gardner admits there may be more than eight, and is currently considering additional forms of intelligence such as an existential or spiritual intelligence (Gardner, 1999).
2 Please visit this website for more details about culturally relevant teaching: www.alliance. brown.edu/tdl/tl-strategies/crt-principles.shtml (retrieved June 2012).
3 Census Bureau data about poverty can be retrieved at www.census.gov/hhes/www/poverty/ poverty04/pov04hi.htm (retrieved May 2012).

CHAPTER 2

Constructing Classroom Curriculum

CHAPTER OBJECTIVES

In this chapter, you will learn about:

- five parts to the school curriculum;

- four ways to construct your classroom curriculum;

- what students should learn;

- hierarchy of curriculum influence.

As you work to become an effective teacher, you will gather ideas for teaching and consider ways to implement those ideas. Perhaps you have heard about or seen a teaching strategy that you would love to try, and want to learn the best way to plan for using it. This is an issue related to the curriculum. Before helping you do that, however, we first need to address one of the questions asked most often by prospective teachers: How do I know what I should teach?

DEFINING THE CURRICULUM

When teachers think about what they will teach, they are thinking about the curriculum. The term "curriculum" is used in many different ways and has many different definitions. Consider the following examples: a teacher's daily plan that provides detailed information about how he will help students to read and understand the works of the Harlem Renaissance and Langston Hughes is a form of curriculum; a biology textbook is a type of curriculum; when a teacher tells her class to not raise their hands before speaking, she is making a decision related to the curriculum; if half of your afternoon class is excused to attend the cross country meet, that is part of the curriculum as well. Keep in mind that in this text when we use the term curriculum we will be using it to help answer questions related to "*What* do I teach?" and "*How* do I teach it?" Or even more appropriately, "*What do I want students to learn?*" and "*How can they learn it most effectively?*" Our use of the term curriculum includes the expected learning outcomes of the classroom, the content students will learn, and the **lesson plans** that provide a detailed description for each class period.

There is much more to the school curriculum than deciding what should be included in the courses. Before we get to the practical aspects of constructing classroom curriculum, it is important to offer some background on the idea of curriculum for you to consider so that you can have added insight when you start making decisions for your students. We find it helpful to think of the curriculum as having five parts, though some suggest there may be more (Eisner, 1985; Cuban, 1996). While these may have different labels and subheadings, the five basic parts to the school curriculum are: the **formal curriculum**, the **delivered curriculum**, the **learned curriculum**, the **hidden curriculum**, and the **null curriculum**. The basic premise behind this partitioning of the curriculum is that to plan curriculum you need to be aware that your students will not always learn what you intended. Sometimes they will, and other times they will learn more and learn less than you planned. Consideration of this will help with planning for your class. A review of each part follows.

THE FORMAL CURRICULUM

The formal curriculum consists of all that educators purposefully intend to teach students. This is also referred to by some as the intended, planned, explicit, or official curriculum. This is the part of the curriculum that most think of first and includes syllabi, **unit plans**, lesson plans, national and state standards, or textbooks. The word curriculum is derived from the Latin word meaning "the course of the chariot race." In the academy-award-winning movie *Ben Hur*, Charlton Heston has his famous chariot race around the "curriculum." This visual can be used as a helpful metaphor in that while there is a course to be followed, there is also ample room to swerve the chariot in any way and to make timely decisions to avoid pitfalls or gain advantage to successfully cross the finish line.

The formal curriculum takes many forms. It might be a document that a school district distributes to parents describing the content of a seventh-grade earth science course. It might be a calendar used by an English teacher that identifies what his or her students will learn during each week of the course. From the name you can infer that the formal curriculum has been authorized, or formalized, as being the acceptable curriculum. If a school board decides to ban a particular book, then the board is contemplating changes to the formal curriculum. Decisions at this level often results in debates and deliberations, because the changes will become official policy for a school. This curriculum is usually developed without students and sometimes, as you will later see, even without teachers. It is also heavily influenced by theorists and a variety of stakeholders.

THE DELIVERED CURRICULUM

The delivered curriculum is also known as the taught curriculum, and can be thought of as the instructional processes or methods used to communicate the formal curriculum. This would include course organization, instructional strategies, and the **sequence** of learning activities designed for a lesson. In the chariot race metaphor, the swerving of the chariot would be part of the delivered curriculum. There is an "acting out" of the official course of the race. A quality teacher does not always follow the formalized written plan, but may decide to change the course and follow up on a "teachable moment," or for deeper reflection. These may be spur-of-the-moment decisions. Of course, a teacher will need to balance spontaneity with purpose. For example, during a planned lecture about gravity, a student may ask how satellites orbit the earth. The teacher did not have anything about orbits in his planned lecture, and must make a quick decision about leaving his plan to consider this student's question. For the sake of example, say that he spends the rest of the class period talking about this question with the students, and is able to explain gravity from a different perspective that actually enhances his students' understanding. The delivered curriculum may have actually been better than the formal curriculum. However, if the student in the above example proceeds to ask whether the international space station should always have an American astronaut "on board," the lecture and discussion will swerve way off the subject, and the delivered curriculum will no longer support the intent of the formal curriculum. The question is certainly interesting, but it does not fit in with the overarching curricular plan for the day. The delivered curriculum is heavily influenced by learning theories that we explored in Chapter 1. These theories help determine the activities used during class. The teacher and the students also influence the curriculum that is delivered or taught.

THE LEARNED CURRICULUM

The learned curriculum is a representation of all that a student learns in school. Some refer to this as the "realized" curriculum and it comes into play when assessing the students and the curriculum itself. We cannot assume that the "planned curriculum" or the "delivered curriculum" will be the same as the learned curriculum. This is one reason that most educators refer to what they intend for their students to learn, and not what they intend to teach. The difference is subtle, but important. If you focus on what you will teach, you may be less aware of your students' understanding. If you think in terms of what your students will learn, then you will be focused on how closely your formal planned curriculum aligns with student learning. The learned curriculum has been of major concern to educators in recent years as the accountability movement has given rise to standardized tests that are used to measure student learning. Test scores are not the only way observers judge the educational system and student performances. A good example of this is the Sputnik era in the 1950s. Americans viewed their educational system as lacking because the Soviets were the first in the world to send a manned spacecraft into outer space. This was a perception about the learned curriculum that had far-reaching effects on the educational system for many years. At the classroom level, teachers also play a role with this curriculum as they seek ways to assess their students. They use this information to evaluate both their students' learning as well as their own teaching.

THE HIDDEN CURRICULUM

The hidden curriculum can be thought of as part of the delivered and the learned curriculum but is worth mentioning separately. The hidden curriculum consists of learning that is not part of the formal curriculum. It is "hidden" because teachers and other curriculum writers are often not aware of what students may be actually learning. For example, attitudes, values, or beliefs are learned through observation or participation in the normal routine of the school day. This is the curriculum that people "pick up" through immersion into school culture. Philip Jackson has been credited as one of the first to make educators aware of the hidden curriculum in his book *Life in Classrooms* (1968). However, John Dewey also mentioned that in addition to course content, students learn values, socialization cues, and other important content simply by being in school together (1938). Dewey thought this "untaught" content might even be learned more than the planned curriculum. Given its hidden status, however, you will want to think about how you can reveal some of the hidden curriculum in your future classroom. Often the hidden curriculum is criticized as a tool for maintaining the status quo in the classroom and in society. Theorists such as Michael Apple (1986) suggest that the hidden curriculum is a misnomer and that it purposefully enables some students (typically those in the dominant culture) and "disables" others (typically those students who are marginalized by socioeconomic status, ethnicity, and ability). Thus, the hidden curriculum is not perceived by all as learning "by accident," but is thought of as a way to perpetuate the current social and power structure of a school. The hidden curriculum might be a teacher calling on boys more frequently than girls in a mathematics class to answer difficult questions (thereby students "learn" that boys may be better skilled at problem solving than girls), or a school canceling classes during the state basketball playoffs, so students can all attend the games (thereby students may "learn" that athletics have equal footing and importance to academics at the school). Both of these examples portray the hidden curriculum as a negative influence. This portion of the curriculum can be a positive learning element such as when a student learns that hard work pays off or that there are rewards for determination. However, this curriculum is most often referred to when pointing out such learning that reinforces misperceptions such as studying hard to get good grades is "acting white" or girls are not scientifically inclined. Negative elements range from oppressing students (based on gender, ethnicity, ability, etc.), to "sending the wrong message" that one aspect of school is more important than it should be. Cornbleth (1991) suggests the following examples of the hidden curriculum in schools:

- grading policies and systems;
- separating schools into subject areas;
- elevating textbooks as the most accurate and important sources of information;

- arrangement of the daily school schedule;
- distribution of materials and resources;
- school rituals and traditions.

Consider Cornbleth's examples above and identify examples for each of the categories listed. If you think about it, you will probably be able to come up with several things you have learned along the way through "courses" in the hidden curriculum.

NULL CURRICULUM

The null curriculum is simply the content that students do not learn. Consider Eisner's (1992) detailed comment on the null curriculum:

> There is something of a paradox involved in writing about a curriculum that does not exist. Yet, if we are concerned with the consequences of school programs and the role of curriculum in shaping those consequences, then it seems to me that we are well advised to consider not only the explicit and implicit curricula of schools but also what schools do not teach. It is my thesis that what schools do not teach may be as important as what they do teach. I argue this position because ignorance is not simply a neutral void; it has important effects on the kinds of options one is able to consider, the alternatives that one can examine, and the perspectives from which one can view a situation or problem.
>
> (p. 97)

This component of the curriculum may send implicit messages to students about the importance of some information over others. As a teacher, you cannot teach everything. We often share with future history teachers the obvious point that three-and-one-half decades of history occurs during a 35-year teaching career. Yet, the days in a school year will be the same, and teachers need to determine what to include and what to leave out of those 35 years of history. It is a difficult task to consider what you leave out, when most of your energy is spent trying to determine what you want the students to learn. However, it is important to reflect on the range of possible topics that you *could* teach, to insure that you are planning for students to learn the most important content, skills, and abilities.

MAKING IT WORK IN YOUR CONTENT AREA

We will revisit these components of the curriculum later in this chapter. It is interesting to ask teachers how much control they have in developing their course curriculum. Talk with teachers in your content area, and ask them who develops the following parts of their course curriculum:

1. the units for their course;
2. the textbooks and/or other supplemental texts they use in class;
3. the videos they show in class;
4. the software they can install on their computers;
5. the tests/examinations students take;
6. the daily lesson plans.

Do teachers feel a good deal of autonomy, or do they feel constrained by outside sources? Compare your findings with others.

WHAT SHOULD STUDENTS LEARN?

We originally thought that this section should be labeled "What Should You Teach?" However, now that we have reviewed the five parts of the curriculum, focusing on what students should learn seems much more appropriate. Decisions about both curriculum and curriculum plans reflect philosophical assumptions about the way adolescents learn and what they should know. You read in the previous chapter that the way we believe students learn affects the way we plan instruction. A "constructivist" lesson plan will look much different from a lesson plan designed by a "behaviorist." A constructivist approach is based on the idea that learners construct, or build, meaning and understanding as they learn. It usually implies hands-on activities where students spend a good amount of time processing the information so they understand it in depth. A behaviorist approach will tend to focus more on the final product and place less emphasis on the process that was followed to attain the information. Decisions about what we teach will be influenced by what we believe is important based upon our view of the purpose of education.

Our educational philosophy also influences how we teach. For example, the ideas of E. D. Hirsch (1987) and James Banks (2003) provide two different approaches to making curricular decisions. Cultural literacy is an idea advocated by Hirsch to respond to concerns that American youth are not learning a shared knowledge. According to proponents of this view, the lack of common knowledge adversely affects our ability to communicate with one another, and it weakens the commonalities that hold the country together. Hirsch's "Core Knowledge Curriculum" attempts to address this concern by detailing a sequential approach to acquiring the knowledge that is essential for becoming a fully functioning citizen. Critics might contend that the knowledge necessary to be culturally literate is determined by the dominate group. They would ask: "literate of whose culture?" Another curricular perspective is multicultural education, advocated by Banks (2003). Banks responds to the concern that there has been little respect in the school curricula for the contributions made by the many diverse cultures that make up our country. Banks advocates creating curriculum that moves classrooms beyond merely mentioning the names or celebrating holidays of ethnically diverse heroes and heroines. Proponents of this view intend to transform the curriculum into one that represents a wide variety of perspectives and encourages students to become socially active. Critics of this perspective might contend that this approach contributes to the balkanization of America by focusing the attention of the students on our differences rather than commonalities. Both views, as well as many others, continue to emerge as educators think about the implications of each. We have several links to different approaches to making curricular decisions on the companion website for this book.

You should be aware that making these decisions can be highly charged politically. In general, while new teachers are attentive to the curriculum (what students do need to learn) they are most concerned with the curriculum plan (how students will learn most effectively). This is interesting because at the same time the public eye is focused on the content and skills being learned, and most controversy surrounds this issue. For example, you will make critical decisions about what you intend for your students to learn. As we mentioned in the previous section, selecting one topic causes others to be omitted because of the limited amount of time in the school year (this "limit" enforces the hidden curriculum that schools must promote efficient learning). This decision may prove to be highly controversial, such as teaching evolution and not intelligent design, ignoring a certain perspective in history such as the impact of Chinese migration, or choosing one novel over another.

School curriculum should be purposeful and have an aim. Figure 2.1 may help explain the links between three elements: School, Education, and Life.

The "Life" box represents all the time and experiences that people have. A significant part of our life is when we learn, or are educated. This is represented in the "Education" box. We learn information, skills, and attitudes in both formal and informal settings. One formal educational setting is school. The "School" box stands for the time and place in which people receive their formal education. Of course,

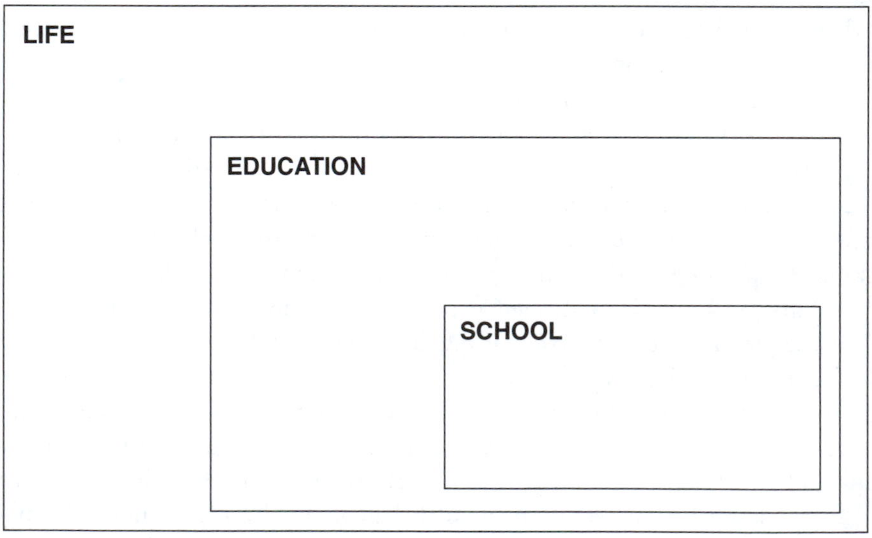

FIGURE 2.1: Linking Life, Education, and School

learning occurs both inside and outside of school. Our focus in this illustration is the link between "School" and "Life." Here, school is separated from life because it provides a time in the day when students focus on learning. Some of the things students learn at school have little or no connection to life but are part of their education. For example, students learn strategies for taking tests. A curriculum problem arises when school and life are separated. Most curriculum theorists argue that school should enable a student to live a good fulfilling life. The curriculum questions that follow this are simply "What kind of content, skills, attitudes, and thought processes enable a person to live a good fulfilling life?" and "How can your course curriculum improve your students' lives?" Schubert (1986) contends that this should be the question behind all curriculum decisions. If you take some time to discuss these questions with your classmates, you will soon realize that finding satisfactory answers proves difficult; it's contextual, and perspectives vary widely. Try splitting up the class by discipline and try to answer these questions or start with: *What does it mean to improve a student's life? How will teaching about (blank) help improve a student's life? Does teaching (blank) improve the lives of all my students or just some?*

Understanding assumptions and purposes behind curriculum theory is not merely an academic exercise. Decisions based upon these theories have deep significance, because they will impact your future students!

EXPANDING YOUR THINKING ABOUT CURRICULUM

Many different approaches to curriculum development exist that we have not touched upon here. All curriculum development has an aim or intention that is focused on student learning. If you are interested in exploring a range of curricular perspectives, consider the following curricular theorists and/or philosophers:

- Michael Apple (1986)
- Catherine Cornbleth (2002)
- Larry Cuban (1996)
- John Dewey (1916)
- Elliot Eisner (1985; 1992)
- Paulo Frerie (1970)
- Genva Gay (1988)
- Diane Ravitch (1985)
- Theodore Sizer (1984).

We list a well-known article, book chapter, or book for each theorist in the references section of this book, and on the companion website for this text, or for a quick review of each, you could merely search the internet for their work.

Have you considered why it is important for students to learn about your content area? The disciplinary knowledge of your content area provides background and insight needed to participate with others in our society. Without this knowledge we are unable to make informed and reasoned decisions for the public good.

When we think about civic competence, it is useful to start thinking about what makes an effective citizen in America. One group defines an effective citizen as "one who has the knowledge, skills, and attitudes required to assume the office of citizen in our democratic republic" (NCSS, 2006).[1] We do not often think about citizenship as a political office that we all hold. This is a useful idea, however, because by doing so you start to think about the duties and responsibilities needed to be a citizen (in the same manner that a mayor or senator would need to be aware of the duties and responsibilities of those offices). John Dewey, one of the leading thinkers in American education, suggested the value of schools as a location for learning the skills, social dispositions, and perspectives needed to engage with other citizens about public issues. In Dewey's estimation, schools, and as a result your future classroom, could become laboratories of democracy, where you and your students engage in activities aimed at developing civic competence in a democratic society in much the same way that science lab activities are aimed at developing scientific competence.[2] This is not just a task pushed off to the social studies or civics teachers. It is an opportunity for all teachers to see their course as part of a big plan to help students participate in society and democratic life.

Paul Carr (2008) states that "thin" and "thick" democracy are helpful metaphors when thinking about civic competence and participation. Democracy could be characterized in terms of representative democracy (where the focus of your participation is voting for appropriate representatives) versus participatory democracy (where the focus of your participation is critical engaging in promoting social justice). In a representative democracy a citizen does not engage in the political system, and has little invested in engaging with others about the betterment of society. This is what Carr calls "thin" democracy, because engagement is very basic. In a participatory democracy, the citizen is engaged in and challenges the current state of affairs to work at improving the status quo—a much "thicker" type of democratic action. James Banks (2003) suggests that classrooms have the capacity to enable students to become active and transformative citizens, or citizens who take action beyond voting and begin to support, maintain, and challenge laws, conventions, and political structures (p. 136)—thick democratic work. To this end, Banks proposes a typology of citizens that differentiates the level of participation in society, and it is helpful to look at these types of citizens when thinking about civic engagement and your future students:

Legal Citizen: A citizen who has rights and obligations on the nation-state but does not participate in the political system.

Minimal Citizen: A citizen who votes in local and national elections on conventional candidates and conventional issues.

Active Citizen: A citizen who takes action beyond voting to actualize existing laws and conventions. The actions of active citizens are designed to support and maintain—but not challenge—existing social and political structures.

Transformative Citizen: A citizen who takes action to actualize values and moral principles beyond those of conventional authority. An interest in taking action to promote social justice even when their actions violate, challenge, or dismantle existing laws, conventions, or structures.

(Banks, 2008, pp. 136, 137)

The legal and minimal citizen practice thin democracy, and the active and transformative citizen engage in a thicker form of democracy. Engagement as an active or transformative citizen will lend itself to promoting the common good in the broader community.

A HIERARCHY OF CURRICULUM INFLUENCE

Standards and guidelines for the curriculum exist at the national, state, and local levels. These standards will impact the curriculum that your students learn. The following chart shows the different levels, or the hierarchy, of the curriculum. National standards are the broadest and, in some respects, furthest removed from the classroom. However, they impact other aspects of the curriculum or, for example, may even be identical to state standards. Lesson plans are the most specific, lean heavily on these other standards and plans, and are developed with your students' names and faces in mind. "Stakeholders" are groups who exercise some influence on the classroom curriculum. Given the level of the curriculum, and the content you are teaching, stakeholders hold different amounts of influence.

Think about the levels of curriculum each stakeholder will most likely influence, and why they are considered stakeholders in the curriculum. For example, what level

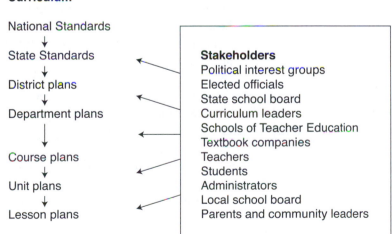

FIGURE 2.2: Curriculum and Stake Holders

(Adapted from Garcia et al., 2001).

will parents influence? How about elected officials? Also, consider what each stakeholder might contribute to the curriculum, and potential problems that could arise from their involvement.

NATIONAL STANDARDS

In 1983, the United States Department of Education's National Commission on Excellence in Education published the report *A Nation at Risk* (National Commission on Excellence in Education, 1983). As the title states, the report proclaimed that our nation is at risk because of problems in education. This report was heralded by some as pinpointing the key problem with public education: students were not learning. Others criticized the report as unfairly blaming schools for societal problems. Many other publications followed that both refuted and praised the report (Boyer, 1983; Sizer, 1984; US DOE, 1991; Reed and Bergman, 1992) and were instrumental in sparking the national movement toward content area standards. Professional organizations from each discipline have since published what they consider to be the essential elements that every student should learn. These documents became the national standards for the content areas. Each organization brought together teachers, university professors, and other experts in their discipline to identify the most important content and skills. These national standards will impact your future teaching, because they influence the standards that the states created. State standards influence the local school district standards for your content area, and ultimately your classroom curriculum. At the time we are writing this book, forty-four states have agreed to use **Common Core State Standards**. This initiative intends to have the United States aligned with common expectations for student learning. We describe this in more detail later in this chapter.

Before going further, we want you to think about this series of events since 1983. Some believe that the "standards movement" provides an excellent guide for states, districts, and teachers to develop the formal curriculum. Some worry that these standards take away from the professional judgment of teachers in determining what their students need to know. As you probably know, the standards movement has led to an "assessment movement" where most states have developed standardized competency tests for many content areas. These tests assess how well students learn the content identified in the standards; these assessments are praised for holding schools accountable, and criticized for reducing teaching to "test preparation."

- What do you know about the standards movement? What effect has it had on your middle school or high school experiences?
- How does a set of national and state standards impact your content areas positively?
- What negative impact might it have?

The list of educational professional organizations below will guide you to websites where you will find the national standards for each content area. When you visit these sites, search for the "standards" documents. Most of the standards documents are available for free, though some, such as the National Art Education Association, charge a nominal fee. You can also join these organizations. Members receive information about research and teaching in the content area. Usually membership dues include a subscription to a journal or magazine that provides ideas for helping students learn content and skills in that subject area. We encourage you to "play around" in these websites and locate the standards as well as to identify how the national organization affiliated with your content area might help you as you prepare to teach. The standards for your content area are an excellent starting point for focusing your lesson plans. They are a planning resource. Near the end of this chapter we describe how an experienced teacher develops curriculum. This teacher suggests that the first step is to read the standards. If you visit the site for the following organizations, you can search within the site for their standards documents.

Professional Organizations with National Standards[3]

- Art (National Art Education Association; www.arteducators.org)
- English (National Council of Teachers of English; www.ncte.org)
- Foreign Language (American Council on the Teaching of Foreign Languages; www.actfl.org)
- Mathematics (National Council of Teachers of Mathematics; www.nctm.org)
- Music (National Association for Music Education; www.menc.org)
- Physical Education (American Alliance for Health, Physical Education, Recreation, and Dance; www.aahperd.org)
- Science (National Science Teachers Association; www.nsta.org)
- Social Studies (National Council for the Social Studies; www.ncss.org)
- History (National Center for History in the Schools; www.sscnet.ucla.edu/nchs)
- Geography (National Council for Geographic Education; www.ncge.org)
- Economics (National Council on Economic Education; www.ncee.org)
- Civics (National Standards for Civics and Government; www.civiced.org)

Links to each of the above standards are also provided at the companion website for this book.

STATE STANDARDS AND THE COMMON CORE STATE STANDARDS

These national organizations may direct the content taught in your future classroom, but they have no legal authority to determine curriculum. In the same way, the classroom teacher has no legal authority to decide what is taught. This legal authority has been granted to the state. Traditionally, this authority has been passed along to the local level—to the district, school, department, and on to the classroom teacher. Along with the national standards movement an emphasis on assessment and accountability has come from the federal government. The rationale being that for federal funds to be expended evidence of students' progress must be shown.

As we mentioned earlier, most of the fifty states crafted their own standards so as to specify what students are expected to learn. The creation of the standards varied from state to state, but typically they were completed through committees of representatives from the various stakeholders. Some states use these standards as guidelines for schools but most states have accompanied them with a high-stakes testing component.

At the companion website for this book, we provide a chart with links to each of the states' standards. At these state sites, you can download information about content skills in your endorsement area, the name of each state's academic standards, and the consequences of the assessment (e.g., whether the assessment is "high stakes"). We include the myriad abbreviations and initials that each state uses to help you become familiar with the jargon each state has adopted relative to their standards and assessments. When we state that a test has "No Child Left Behind (NCLB) consequences," we refer to the fact that the state's test is used to demonstrate partial fulfillment of the federal government's NCLB requirements. Each school and district must demonstrate that they are making "adequate yearly progress" (AYP) toward meeting their learning goals. The state tests are the source of data most states use to show this progress. You can read more about this legislation at the United States Department of Education site: www.ed.gov/nclb.

In addition, the Education World website has an excellent links page to all of the state standards. We find this useful for understanding the learning expectations of each state, and for comparing state standards to national standards. We encourage you to access this site at www.education-world.com/standards/state/index.shtml or from the link we provide at our companion website.

The Common Core State Standards is an initiative that intends to provide a consistent, clear understanding of what students are expected to learn across the country. It is a state-developed plan to have a common set of agreed-upon standards across the United States. The Common Core State Standards Initiative states:

> The standards are informed by the highest, most effective models from states across the country and countries around the world, and provide teachers and parents with a common understanding of what students are expected to learn. Consistent standards will provide appropriate benchmarks for all students, regardless of where they live.

These standards define the knowledge and skills students should have within their K-12 education careers so that they will graduate from high school able to succeed in entry-level, credit-bearing academic college courses and in workforce training programs. The standards:

- are aligned with college and work expectations;
- are clear, understandable and consistent;
- include rigorous content and **application** of knowledge through high-order skills;
- build upon strengths and lessons of current state standards;

- are informed by other top performing countries, so that all students are prepared to succeed in our global economy and society; and
- are evidence-based.

(www.corestandards.org)

Currently, Common Core State Standards have been developed for two content areas:

- English/language arts (addressing areas such as reading, writing, speaking/listening, language, media technology);
- mathematics.

Additional endorsement areas are likely to be developed in the coming years. With forty-four states adapting these two standards areas, the projection is that these states, and most likely many of the remaining six states, will replace their current state learning standards with the Common Core Standards as they are developed. We encourage you to visit the Common Core State Standards Initiative website to get a more robust understanding of this project.

You can see then, how state influence on the local classroom curriculum has increased dramatically in recent years. However, there still is a great deal of local control and influence over the curriculum:

District plans: Each school district has at least one administrator who is in charge of the curriculum. These coordinators are usually former classroom teachers who are sympathetic to the balancing act a teacher must perform between the various influences on the curriculum. Their role is to help ensure that state initiatives are being implemented by working with department chairs. A curriculum coordinator oversees how the state standards are being addressed in a department. Curriculum coordinators also ensure that the departments' course offerings are aligned and presented in a logical order for students. For example, school districts will often articulate the grade levels at which students will learn American history. Traditionally, eighth grade is when students learn about European contact with the Americas up through the United States reconstruction after the Civil War. In eleventh grade, American history picks up in the mid-1880s and continues to current day. By identifying the content (in this case, the chronology of American history), districts help insure that the content students learn, and the order in which students learn it, is the same across the district.

Departmental Plans: At most schools, department chairs work with district administrators, department chairs at other schools, and classroom teachers to outline content and skills for both individual courses and all departmental course offerings. District plans are used by the departments to help facilitate this. In the case of our American history example, the social studies departments at the middle schools and high schools work to insure that the teachers organize their course curriculum around the district plan. Teachers are then in a position to design their course, the units in their course, and their daily lessons to fit with this plan. This type of organization allows for the district to better utilize resources when purchasing textbooks and materials for the classroom. Therefore, daily lessons, units, course outlines, and department or district outlines all are curriculum plans.

Many departments prefer to entrust the classroom teacher with these decisions. Even with the influences that affect the curriculum, most teachers have considerable freedom to develop plans for the classroom because they are supported and trusted at the local level. The curriculum will be a fluid document pushed and pulled by those with keen interests. As with any truly democratic pursuit, parents, students, and the local community have the right to be involved with decisions related to the classroom and their involvement should be embraced. However, in the final analysis, the teacher is almost always the final gatekeeper of the curriculum and instruction that occurs in his or her classroom. Stephen Thornton (2005) has expanded on the idea that teachers are the curricular gatekeepers who have the final say about how local, state, and federal standards are learned by students. If we expand this metaphor, it means that you will determine what your students will learn. This is a sobering, yet exciting aspect of teaching. Sobering in that the expectation for student learning is great and exciting because it should make you feel as though you can make professional decisions about the needs and interests of your students. We know many excellent teachers who express the following sentiment: "Good teachers will meet content standards without too much extra effort. The assessment test will merely confirm what we do." We also have many of our beginning teachers report that state standards provide excellent direction about the content and skills to teach. Many teachers, however, worry whether the assessment tests will accurately determine what their students have learned. Teachers as gatekeepers cannot escape the fact that their teaching is being assessed when their students are tested. In Chapter 4, we will discuss classroom-level lesson plans in detail.

PRACTICAL SUGGESTIONS FOR DETERMINING CLASSROOM CURRICULUM

Sometimes a new teacher simply needs a practical way to get started. With all the talk of educational philosophy, curriculum theory, and influences, it can be somewhat overwhelming. We would like to suggest four practical ways to begin the process.

- asking the important questions;
- seeking advice from experienced teachers;
- beginning to write course goals and year-long **scope** and **sequence**;
- determining the role of available materials.

ASKING THE IMPORTANT QUESTIONS

The most well-known curriculum writing prompts are commonly referred to as the Tyler rationale (Tyler, 1949). Oftentimes, you will see these prompts used to help with school-wide curriculum decisions; however, they are helpful at the classroom level as well. The Tyler rationale is organized around four important questions that we will modify for the classroom level:

1. What educational purposes should the class seek to attain? Tyler suggests that these purposes should be determined by considering studies of the student as a learner, the practices of society, and recommendations from subject-matter experts. These purposes should then be translated into the stated course goals.

2. What educational experiences can be provided that are likely to attain these purposes? Tyler suggests that once goals have been formulated the teacher should begin collecting ideas, activities, and materials that can be used to meet the goals. This collection can show alignment with the goals.

3. How can these educational experiences be effectively organized? Tyler recommends that each class would have organizing elements from which to build around. This might be related to a value (respect) in a history class or certain skills in a math course. Considering these elements is useful in building lessons, or in integrating several topics or content areas.

4. How can we determine whether these purposes are attained? Assessing student learning and evaluating if they have attained the desired aims is a key component of Tyler's rationale. Assessment techniques should go hand in hand with the stated goals of the course.

We find it interesting that this approach is still dominant in schools today—over 50 years later. It provides a rational and systematic approach for developing curriculum. It is this sequential, four-step process that has made it so popular and provides a starting point for curriculum development (Ornstein and Hunkins, 2004). Tyler's approach is certainly flawed. It is built on behaviorism (which assumes that the taught curriculum will be close to the learned curriculum), and it may oversimplify curriculum development as being a series of small performances. Nonetheless, it is a proven and long-standing approach for developing course curriculum.

SEEKING ADVICE FROM EXPERIENCED TEACHERS

Another suggested step in making decisions about your classroom curriculum is to seek the advice of experienced teachers. Some schools assign first year teachers with a mentor, but even if you have no one at your school to lean upon, you will find that there are many teachers who will be able to offer you insight from their experience. Obviously, every teacher experience will vary to some degree. However, it may be helpful for you to read about one high school social studies teacher's process for deciding what to teach in her government course. Jen Reidel's district did not have an outline for her course, and her department had only generally agreed-upon classroom-based assessment—one suggested by the state. She had the opportunity to create her own curriculum, and describes this process as follows:

> I typically use both state standards (grade level expectations) and the national strands in determining the essential concepts, terms, and ideas to be taught. Often I will also consult education organizations (Center for Civic Education, Foundation

for Teaching Economics, Street Law) for their view on what they believe is most essential to teach in that specific discipline. Once I have determined what the essential concepts/terms are to be taught I start investigating what sources of curriculum exist to help me amass materials to teach the course (textbooks, simulations, Internet resources, videos, primary documents, etc.). I shy away from running a textbook driven classroom which tends to discourage students' passion regarding the subject. I try to use the textbook as the starting point—not ending point for the teaching of specific concepts and for the kids that need information in black and white to best comprehend it. I do use pocket constitutions though to teach students about the guarantees and structure of the Constitution and I'll use other textbook material as a supplement.

Consequently, I have created all my own materials to teach about our governmental system, structure, and current issues related to it. This does give me the ability to modify my curriculum as the times change and when a current event is in the news that effectively illustrates what I am teaching. The downside to creating all my own materials is that often I as the teacher become the sole source for knowledge (versus a textbook). This fact alone can cause a teacher to become incredibly worn down creating their own curriculum on a daily basis. I have drawn my materials from the Internet, from conferences I have attended, from materials purchased from civic education organizations, and from materials that I have purchased/located on my own.

For a new or a pre-service teacher, I would definitely encourage them to seek some sort of guidance from their district's plan. If the district does not offer one, they can't go wrong consulting the state and national standards for their discipline to narrow down what should be taught. They also might look at both the state and national standards in terms of any potential building or district goals (i.e. increasing reading, writing, math skills, or emphasizing diversity). Once the essential concepts that must be taught have been identified, I think then the teacher can choose to teach what they are passionate about concerning the subject. Students more times than not will become most interested in a subject that they see their teacher excited about. My government class is proof of this. I love the subject . . . and yes I am geeky about it—particularly the court system. So as a result, I have a huge amount of knowledge to draw from when teaching the students. That translates to the ability to give in depth responses to a student's question as well as the fact that I can develop much more meaningful assignments and assessments when I am excited and knowledgeable about my subject.

Jen's approach is helpful. She suggests that the district curriculum plan, state standards, and national standards will provide you with a starting point for knowing what to teach. Her message is that these standards are not to be feared, but used as a tool for determining critical skills and concepts. When this is determined, the teacher is "freed up" to decide how to best promote student learning. She is the gatekeeper (Thornton, 2005), but she leans on others to help her determine what will be let in to her classroom.

WRITING GOALS

A third step is to write goals and consider a year-long scope and sequence (this is described in more detail in Chapter 4). As Tyler suggested, the creation of written goals is a natural outcome of determining the purposes of the course. Goals, not to be confused with objectives or targets, are broad general statements that allow a teacher to focus. For example, the physicist Stephen Hawking once wrote: "My goal is simple. It is complete understanding of the universe." Now that is a broad goal! Goals are usually written for the entire course as well as for segmented sections of the course called units of instruction. Course goals will be made more explicit by the unit goals and unit objectives or targets. It might be helpful to think of it like creating an outline for an essay. It would look like the following:

1. Course Goal
   a. Unit goal
      i. Objective or Target

The idea is to help you focus on your overarching aim while not becoming overly burdened by prescriptive paperwork. Unit objectives or targets will be discussed in detail in the next chapter.

Goals should be written so that they convey broad expectations. For example:

- Students will expand their leisure-time activities.
- Students will become familiar with the music developed during the Romantic period.
- Students will appreciate the role of civil rights activists.

State and national standards are filled with broad expectations that could be helpful in determining goals. In fact, sometimes these expectations are thought of as less than helpful when someone is looking for more specific learning targets rather than a broad goal. When writing a goal keep in mind two things. First, that it is something that you want the students to accomplish over an extended period of time, and second, that it is something that you hope your students will learn. Because of this it is helpful to consider for a moment which verbs might be used. Some of the verbs we have found to help broaden goals include:

Apply	Demonstrate	Grasp	Recognize
Appreciate	Expand	Imagine	Think
Believe	Enjoy	Know	Understand
Comprehend	Familiar	Like	Value

If it is not provided by the district or department, writing the year-long plan naturally follows the development of course goals. Usually a teacher will sketch out the year into units of instruction to begin getting an idea of the amount of time they can spend on certain topics. These topics become the foundation for writing unit plans.

DETERMINING THE ROLE OF AVAILABLE MATERIALS

Determining the role of materials that are available is often decided at the same time that plans are being made for the year. For example, math or science courses will often have a textbook that the district has chosen as the formal curriculum guide. The internet is filled with materials that could be used in the classroom. You will find lesson plans, primary source documents, pictures, audio, and much more. As you sift through this material, you will be getting ideas that will help your curriculum planning. One of the many websites you might visit is the "Federal Resources for Educational Excellence (FREE)" sponsored by the United States Department of Education. This site (www.ed.gov/free) organizes hundreds of free lesson plans into content area categories. If you visit the site map, you can locate your content area, click on the link and view or download many lessons for your future courses. It is stated on this site that: "More than 30 Federal agencies formed a working group in 1997 to make hundreds of federally supported teaching and learning resources easier to find. The result of that work is the FREE web site." This is not the only website with lesson and content information, but it might serve as a useful starting point for thinking about lesson planning. We will examine lesson plans in Chapter 4 and in Part 2 of this book.

MAKING IT WORK IN YOUR CONTENT AREA

Consider for a moment some of the predominant metaphors of schooling. This is important as you develop the curriculum because if the "student is the worker" (Sizer, 1984), then what is the role of the teacher? How would this affect the curriculum? Kliebard (1987) came up with three predominant metaphors of schooling for curriculum literature. In other words, these are three ways to think about education in order to develop curriculum in an educational setting.

1. Production—industrial model
    Teacher = overseer of production
    Student = raw material
    Curriculum = skilled worker who shapes and forms the raw material into a product. A rough diamond becomes expensive jewelry. The teacher is able to help the students to meet a predetermined goal. In this model, the students are passive, and viewed more as a commodity that brings little to the educational setting except potential. The teacher is the primary determinant for what a student will learn.

2. Growth model
   Teacher = insightful gardener who nurtures, feeds, prunes, and nourishes the plants.
   Student = the potential-filled plant that relies on the gardener if it is to survive.
   Curriculum = the gardner cares for plants and helps them reach their potential. Unlike the first metaphor, students in the growth model will develop and learn without the teacher, but they will not reach their full potential unless the teacher interacts and assists the process. The teacher knows what is best, and the students depend on the teacher's insights.

3. Journey model
   Teacher = the tour guide
   Student = traveler
   Curriculum = student and teacher are touring the knowledge, information, skills, and learning experiences. Student is a traveler who focuses on many different things depending on their interest, and much of what should be seen is pointed out by the teacher/guide.

Your metaphor of teaching will likely be better than these. Consider your metaphor for schooling. Choose a metaphor that seems to fit your perspective of how you envision your class. Share your ideas with a group or the class. After you have written some of your first curricular materials come back to this idea. How does what you have planned reflect your stated metaphor? Do you suppose students would use a metaphor for schooling? What might students suggest?

CHAPTER REVIEW

- Five parts to the school curriculum:

  - formal
  - delivered
  - learned
  - hidden
  - null.

- Four ways to construct your classroom curriculum:

  - prompts found in the Tyler rationale;
  - seek the advice of an experienced teacher;
  - writing course goals and a year-long outline;
  - determine the role of available materials.

- What students should learn:

  - content (knowledge and skills) required in your subject area;
  - ideas for improving life;
  - knowledge, skills, and dispositions needed to be a citizen in a democracy.

- Hierarchy of curriculum influence:

  - National standards are developed by national organizations related to your content. For example, organizations for teaching mathematics (NCTM), English (NCTE), science (NSTA), and social studies (NCSS) have developed national standards.
  - State standards, and Common Core State Standards are developed by each state, and usually build on the national standards. The Common Core standards are the result of an initiative to have all state standards align.
  - District and department standards build on national and state standards, and provide additional levels of specificity in regard to the knowledge and skills that students are expected to learn in a given district or school.

NOTES

1. National Council for the Social Studies (2006). Creating effective citizens. Retrieved June 2012, from www.socialstudies.org/positions/effectivecitizens/.
2. Dewey, J. (1938/1965). *Experience and education*. New York: Collier Books.
3. Even though this list provides the national standards for each content area, it raises several questions for social studies teachers. If you plan to teach history, geography, economics, or civics you can contact professional organizations in your content area, and you can contact the National Council for the Social Studies (NCSS). The NCSS has ten standards that attempt to integrate all of the social sciences. We suggest starting with these standards, then visiting the content specific organization (e.g., history, economics) and identifying the additional content that they suggest should be learned.

CHAPTER 3

Preparing Learning Targets and Assessing Student Learning

CHAPTER OBJECTIVES

In this chapter, you will learn about:

- long- and short-term learning targets;

- different domains of learning;

- assessing student learning, and the specific importance of formative assessment.

Learning targets and assessments provide specific details for meeting the goals of a lesson or unit. When you write targets, you provide a focus for the lesson and unit, and you determine how you will assess students' learning. But that is only part of the purpose. Your students must know how they will be assessed in your classroom before a lesson or unit even begins. Current thinking about student learning suggests that teachers and students must know how they will be assessed before a lesson or unit even begins. This idea is often referred to as **"backward design,"** because you design lessons with the end goal in mind. Wiggins and McTighe (2000) describe backward design as follows: "One starts with the end—the desired results—and then derives the curriculum from the evidence of learning called for by the standard (learning target) and the teaching needed to equip students to perform" (p. 8). Thus, targets and assessment are closely connected, and that is why we will examine them together in this chapter. We will revisit this in Chapter 4 as well, when we look at long-range planning. At that point, these planning components will be understood even more robustly.

PURPOSE OF LEARNING TARGETS

Before teaching a lesson, you will want to write learning targets. Learning targets help teachers answer three basic questions related to teaching and student learning:

• What content do students need to learn?
• How will student learning be assessed?
• What activities will students engage in to promote learning?

A concise examination of these three areas helps to clarify the content and purpose of learning targets.[1]

What Content Do Students Need to Learn?

Textbooks, state curriculum guides, and district/school curriculum plans provide direction about what to teach, but teachers are left with the freedom to decide how to best teach the content in the classroom each day. Consider the following example: If you are going to be teaching a high school biology course, you will likely have a biology textbook, and local/state standards to consider when thinking about the course's content. In addition, as we mentioned in Chapter 2, the National Science Teachers' Association has developed national standards for biology (www.nsta.org). Before the class session starts, you need to consider these content recommendations, and then determine the most effective way to help your students learn. If, for example, these documents lead you to decide that students need to know about symbiosis, you will need to consider how to help your students learn this effectively. Learning targets help you narrow down the content so that you can promote student learning. The number of targets you have for each day is determined by the complexity of the content your students are learning.

How Will Student Learning Be Assessed?

The second component of a target helps you determine whether students have learned the content during the activity. It is this area that serves as an assessment of student learning and helps you find out whether your students have met the target. By placing the assessment in the target, you are ensuring that it coincides with the content to be learned and the activities planned for the class session. Assessments need to be observable, but they do not always need to be graded or quantified into points. Learning is assessed using a variety of approaches. For example, you might have a student present her results of an internet search activity, take a quiz, or write a book report. As the teacher, you determine how well students need to perform on the assessment in order for you to feel confident that they have learned. A score of 100% on a review vocabulary quiz might be your minimum because the students have used the words before. A book report that identifies the theme of a chapter might be what the students produce to show that they learned about a particular piece of literature. Therefore, the assessment in a target has two components: (1) a plan for how students will show their learning and (2) the degree or the "performance expectations" that students need to meet for you to know that they have learned (e.g., 10 out of 10, support all claims with a primary source, or expectations provided in a **rubric**).

What Activities Will Students Engage in to Promote Learning?

Once the content and assessments have been determined you will need to select learning activities for your students. These activities may last 15 minutes (e.g., a brief introduction to the day's topic, or a review of previous content), or they may last several days (e.g., a research project using online resources). Sequentially, the activities derive from the content you want students to learn, and the activities prepare students to demonstrate their understanding when they are assessed. An old adage among teachers is to change the activity every 20 minutes so that the students stay engaged. Although changing an activity every 20 minutes is not required, it is important that you observe students to be sure that they are engaged during any activity. Generally speaking, when students learn more difficult content and engage in more cognitively demanding tasks, the activity requires more time. For example, a twenty-word vocabulary quiz generally requires less time than a research activity. Often you may find that an activity lasts longer or shorter than you planned. By reflecting on this, you will become more skilled at determining how long an activity will last so that all of your students can learn. Targets specify activities that will help your students learn the particular content.

LONG- AND SHORT-TERM TARGETS

Goals provide the general direction for a course. Simply said, they are what you hope your students will learn and accomplish over time. Targets specify how and when you can help students meet those goals. A social studies teacher might have the following goal: *Students will appreciate the personal sacrifices of civil rights leaders.* This does not specify how the students will learn about the sacrifices, how they will develop an appreciation for the sacrifices, or how to determine if the students meet this goal. These specifics come from the targets. Targets can be long term or short term. *Long-term targets* will be accomplished after a longer unit, semester, or even an entire course. Targets that are met during an activity or after a few class sessions are *short-term targets*. These labels are not critical, except to help you understand that long- and short-term targets provide a sequential approach to meeting your goals. Figure 3.1 below shows the relationship and level of specificity regarding goals and targets:

Consider again the goal stated earlier:

Students will appreciate the personal sacrifices of civil rights leaders.

Long-term targets could be:

- After learning United States history from 1950 to 1980, students will be able to list two sacrifices that a leader made for the cause of civil rights.

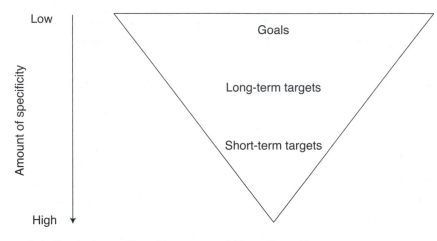

FIGURE 3.1: Goals, Long-Term Targets, and Short-Term Targets

- Students will show how they have benefited from the sacrifices of civil rights leaders by stating at least one area where their life is better now than it would have been in 1960.

Short-term targets could be:

- In a three-page biography, students will identify three sacrifices that Rosa Parks made during her involvement in civil rights movements.
- During a class discussion, students will be able to describe the hardships suffered by Martin Luther King Jr. and his family as a result of his involvement in civil rights protests during the 1960s.

Long- and short-term targets will reoccur if students need repeated assistance to learn a skill or to understand a concept. For example, adolescents have difficulty criticizing ideas and not people during discussions about controversial issues. A target for developing this skill could be: *During all classroom discussions, students will respect classmates' human dignity by critiquing ideas and not the person bringing forth the ideas.* This target is certainly attainable as a short-term target, but it is a skill that students will need to continually practice. Therefore, you could have this target reoccur whenever you plan to have classroom discussions.

In the above example, you can see how clearly a target might tie to an instructional strategy, in this case discussion. In later chapters dealing with specific strategies, we show how certain instructional strategies might be chosen to help students reach specific targets.

MAKING IT WORK IN YOUR CONTENT AREA

Think of a goal that would be appropriate for your content area. In Chapter 2, we described the utility of national and state standards, and you may want to refer to those again to help you determine an appropriate goal for a course you will teach. Devise at least one long-term and one short-term target for this goal. Refer to the examples above on civil rights as a guide for the level of specificity for these two types of targets. Be sure that the targets have an assessment component so that you can be sure to help your students meet the target during the lesson and/or unit.

DOMAINS OF LEARNING

Bloom (1956) and Krathwohl et al. (1964) have suggested that educators should categorize learning targets to help focus instruction on specific areas, or *domains*, of learning. This type of focus helps teachers to select course content and activities that will promote more specified learning. Since the mid-1960s, three domains are considered by teachers, when writing learning targets:

- cognitive domain
- affective domain
- psychomotor domain.

These three areas provide hierarchies for learning. They move from less complex (and typically easier to attain by your students) to very complex (and thus more difficult to attain at first). As a teacher, you will write less-complex targets, but you should continually consider how you might progress to a higher level on each of these domain hierarchies. Bloom et al. (1964) worked together to suggest the three domains of targets (cognitive, affective, and psychomotor). While they developed in-depth taxonomies for the cognitive and affective domains, they did not develop much for the psychomotor domain. Fortunately, others have thought about types of student learning that fit in this third domain, and several taxonomies exist for the psychomotor domain. Consider the following descriptions for each of these three domains.

Cognitive Domain

The *cognitive domain* addresses the thinking skills and academic content to be learned in the classroom. Of the three domains, this is the one that is most common, most easily assessed, and the focus of most educational reforms. When you hear about "getting back to basics," "academic learning," or "concepts and skills," it is usually referring to the cognitive domain. Cognitive targets are synonymous with research done by Benjamin

Bloom in 1956. His six-level taxonomy classified the types of questions that teachers pose to their students, and the type of thinking that is required when answering these questions. Today, Bloom's theories are used for more than categorizing questions. His taxonomy helps evaluate the cognitive tasks in which students engage. Commonly used terms such as "higher level thinking," or "higher-order thinking skills (HOTS)" have their roots in **Bloom's Taxonomy**. The base level of the taxonomy is called "knowledge," and the pinnacle of the taxonomy is the level called "evaluation." As students move in the taxonomy from knowledge to evaluation, the types of questions, activities, and cognitive tasks they engage in are more difficult and require different understandings of course content. The following outline provides a sample question and brief description for each of the six levels of Bloom's Taxonomy (Bloom, 1956; Biehler, 1971)[2]:

1. KNOWLEDGE
   Can Students recall information?
   The issue is recall of information. At this level, it is important that students remember what they have read, were told, or saw.

2. COMPREHENSION
   Can students explain ideas?
   The target at this level is to ensure that students can explain ideas.

3. APPLICATION
   Can students use ideas?
   Targets developed at the application level have as their purpose something of practical use.

4. ANALYSIS
   Can students see relationships?
   Targets written at the analysis level are designed to enable students to see relationships, make comparisons and contrasts, and look for patterns.

5. SYNTHESIS
   Can students combine ideas?
   Synthesis represents a pulling together or combining of elements.

6. EVALUATION
   Can students make judgments?
   Targets for the evaluation level include those that encourage students to take their own points of view or to express their ideas on issues.

During the 1990s a group of cognitive psychologists revised Bloom's Taxonomy, and its use has also become widespread. You probably will come across both versions and, since this is a foundational taxonomy in the field of education, should be familiar with both. Briefly, the later version is as follows:

1. *Remembering*: Can the student recall or remember the information? This level is crucial because students who do not possess basic knowledge cannot carry out

meaningful analyses of language issues or exercise any disciplined creativity. This is the "starting point."

2. *Understanding*: Can the student explain ideas or concepts? It is one thing, for example, to be able to identify different regions of the world (remembering) and another to be able to explain (understand) their various influence in international relations.

3. *Applying*: Can the student use the information in a new way? The issue at this level is whether students can use skills, concepts, and information in new situations. For example, in history, one needs to know how to remember events in time sequence to understand concepts and to apply these ideas appropriately in an essay or story.

4. *Analyzing*: Can the student distinguish between the different parts? Analyzing, as the term implies, is an attempt to break down whole entities into their component parts. For example, in the study of advertising and other persuasive techniques, students will identify appeals made to status, power, group affiliation, and gender.

5. *Evaluating*: Can the student justify a stand or decision? At the evaluation level, divergent thinking is encouraged and differences of opinion are to be expected. Students make judgments and determine "best options" based on their evaluations of all information and factors. A class debate or papers including students' individual opinions or judgments are examples of evaluating.

6. *Creating*: Can the student create a new product or point of view? As a creating-level target, you might ask students to develop and record the various arguments for and against a controversial issue. Otherwise, having taught your students the mechanics of letter writing, you could ask them to create/write a letter using the fundamentals they have learned.

Figure 3.2 provides a brief comparison of the original and updated stages of Bloom's work.

A site from Iowa State University, www.celt.iastate.edu/teaching/RevisedBlooms1. html, offers an excellent visual of the revised Bloom's Taxonomy and examples of

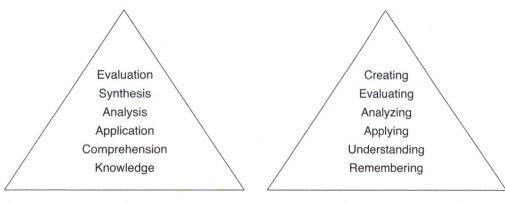

Original version	Revised version
Evaluation	Creating
Synthesis	Evaluating
Analysis	Analyzing
Application	Applying
Comprehension	Understanding
Knowledge	Remembering

FIGURE 3.2: Updating Bloom's Taxonomy

targets/objectives for each level. These targets include the action that students will carry out to facilitate their achievement of particular content/information.[3]

Affective Domain

The *affective domain* refers to learning that is tied to feelings or emotions. Learning in this domain does not require students to develop particular feelings or emotions, but it helps the students to use their emotions and feelings to learn. Where Bloom is usually associated with the cognitive domain, David Krathwohl is most often associated with the affective domain (Krathwohl et al., 1964). Krathwohl suggests that attitudes, beliefs, and value systems should be identified so that children can learn about them and with them in a cohesive manner. Below is a summary of the affective domain, and examples of activities students may do in a classroom[4]:

1. RECEIVING
   Targets written at the receiving level are aimed at helping the students become aware of or sensitive to the existence of certain ideas, materials, or phenomena. Students engage in such actions as looking, asking, accepting, listening, and noticing.

2. RESPONDING
   Responding involves some degree of interaction or involvement with the ideas, materials, or phenomena being learned in class. The interactions promote greater awareness and appreciation than simply "being aware" or receiving the content. Examples include complying, discussing, and supporting.

3. VALUING
   At this level, the students show a commitment to certain ideas, materials, or phenomena. In short, they are able to find value in them. For example, they may participate freely, share, volunteer, and withhold judgment and support.

4. ORGANIZING
   Targets written at the organizing level encourage the students to defend their values and to consider how consistent they hold these values when confronted with new ideas, materials, or phenomena. Examples of student activities include theorizing, **questioning**, comparing/contrasting, and examining.

5. CHARACTERIZING BY VALUE
   For this target, the students act consistently with the values they have already organized. They are now able to "put into practice" their values. For example, students will adhere to a belief, influence others, verify a feeling, defend a belief, and solve problems.

Psychomotor Domain

The *psychomotor domain* helps students learn the coordinated use of the body's muscular system. Physical education is most often associated with this domain, but any time you want the students to learn how to use their body you tap into this domain.

For example, a French teacher could have a psychomotor target that students will be able to shape their mouth and tongue in a way that allows for clear enunciation of a word. An English teacher may focus on the psychomotor domain when using drama in the classroom, or when helping students understand the messages given by "body language." One approach for developing appropriate psychomotor targets was developed in 1970 by R. H. Dave, and is applicable even today. Dave's list is also a hierarchy, ranging from how a learner might begin to develop a psychomotor skill and ability up to attaining proficiency in the skill and ability. These levels are listed below with examples:

1. IMITATION

   Targets for the imitation level are repeating the movements from someone else. Students observe and pattern their behavior after someone who usually has more proficiency than they do. In this way, students can see a model of the behavior or movements. During imitation, students' performance may be of low quality. Examples of the imitation level might be enunciating a Spanish word with the teacher, copying a work of art, or imitating the teacher as he or she kicks a soccer ball.

2. MANIPULATION

   At this level, the students are able to perform certain actions more autonomously after receiving instructions and being given opportunities to practice. For example, practicing finger positions on a violin, or working to develop skill at shooting a basketball.

3. PRECISION

   Targets at the precision level are simply focused on improved skill at manipulations. Students begin to refine their movements and become more exact. The number of errors decrease noticeably, and performance quality shows significant improvement. Examples of this level include practice on more difficult skills, or working and reworking movement so that it approaches being "error free."

4. ARTICULATION

   Targets at this level involve coordinating a series of actions and movement so that they are synchronized and efficient. Movement and body position approaches that of an expert, and practice sessions emphasize "minor adjustments" rather than significant changes. Examples of this level include developing a tumbling routine for a performance, playing in a recital, or competing against other skilled players during a game.

5. NATURALIZATION

   At this final level, a "high-level performance" is natural. While movement can still be refined and improved upon, body position, actions, and skills become automatic. Students do not need to think about their movement, and they can attend to other stimuli while performing. Examples of this level might be driving a car, playing basketball at a highly competitive level, or performing a dramatic interpretation in front of a live audience.[5]

MAKING IT WORK IN YOUR CONTENT AREA

Consider a favorite topic of yours in your content area; something that you look forward to helping students learn. What would be a cognitive target for a lesson on that topic? Some content benefits from the affective domain, and others do not. If your topic would benefit from an affective domain, write one that would explore this area. How about the psychomotor domain? If you expect students to learn kinesthetics, or body movement skills, add a target for this domain. Refer to the categories for each of the three domains, and try to write targets that are as high on the hierarchy as possible.

CONTENT, SKILLS, AND SOCIAL INTERACTIONS: A DIFFERENT APPROACH FOR THINKING ABOUT LEARNING TARGETS

Another way to think about these three domains is in terms of *content, skills,* and *social interactions* (CSS). By thinking of student learning in terms of these three domains, you must consider the academic content your students will need and use, the skills that are required for them to perform effectively, and the social skills required for interaction with classmates.

While schools often adhere to the domains of learning advanced by Bloom and his colleagues, the **CSS approach** for thinking about what the students will learn in your classroom will enhance your learning targets. This approach does not overturn the domains just reviewed, but simply attempts to make student learning more specific. In class, your future students will learn academic course content, develop intellectual thinking skills, and be asked to develop the ability to work with others in groups. It is therefore helpful to think of the classroom as a place where students attain content, skill, and social targets. When you want to be sure that the students learn the facts, concepts, ideas, or other content-based information, you must plan with a *content target*. When your students need to learn processes or thinking skills, such as supporting an opinion with facts, searching the internet, or developing a hypothesis, you must plan with a *skill target*. If your students need to develop specific skills that have to do with interacting with classmates, cooperating with one another or supporting each others' learning, then you must develop *social targets*.

Consider the following activity to demonstrate how targets in these three areas might help your planning, and allow you to back-up into the lesson activities and assessments after you have identified the objctives: *Identify a current event that is slightly controversial.* Here are a few ideas to get you thinking: a current case of banning books; a recent Supreme Court ruling; a foreign policy decision; or a news item about immigration. Next, consider this question, "If a civically minded adult were to develop an informed opinion about this issue, what content and skills would he need to have?" Also, "What social abilities would be needed to interact with others in a civil discussion?"

Often it is helpful to think of this in terms of a four-column chart delineating *issue/event* and *CSS interactions*. By completing this chart for several different issues/events, you will find that the attitudes and skills remain fairly consistent, but the information changes depending on the issue. For example, if you decided to complete a chart for global warming, it might look like this:

Issue/event	Content	Skills	Social interactions
Global Warming (GW)	Causes Effects Current U.S. Policies Case Studies Opposing Viewpoints	Critiquing Ideas Discussing Controversy Researching a Topic Supporting Opinions Listening to Others	Openness to Opposing Ideas Interest in the Topic Desire to Identify Truth Respect for Other Opinions Belief that Sharing Ideas Is Helpful

If this is what an adult needs when developing an informed decision, then what should you do with your students in your classroom to prepare them for adulthood? More than likely, the contents of the "content" column will change as you teach your course. The skills and interactions, however, can be addressed throughout a course. You may be able to write more specific and appropriate targets by thinking of the cognitive and affective domains in terms of content, skills, and interactions.

While the traditional domains (cognitive, affective, and psychomotor) of Bloom and his colleagues are commonplace and useful in the public school, the CSS approach allows for diagnostic target writing: you determine the learning needs of your students, then write out daily learning targets for specific CSS interactions.

FOUR ELEMENTS OF A TARGET: THE ABCD OF TARGET WRITING

Targets, when written correctly, will help you design a lesson. They serve as a tool to help you think through what students will learn, and what types of activities will help them learn best. A target is written as a concise statement, and writing them takes some skill and practice. Armstrong and Savage (1994) proposed that one approach for writing a target is to think in terms of the letters "ABCD." Each of these letters represents a part of the target. Consider the following modified approach for using this technique:

AB—Audience and Behavior (Who will be learning, and what activities will they engage in?)

In this first step, you specify the students' performance, and what they will produce with their actions. This is the first verb of the target. For example, "Students will list reasons"; "Students will write a 300-word essay"; "Students will be able to graph the amount of rainfall during March."

C—Condition (When will students be doing the above activities?)

In this second step, you describe the conditions under which students will produce/perform. The condition might be on a test, after given a ruler and calculator, using class notes, etc. Thought of in another way, though your students will be with you during the entire class session, you will not necessarily assess their learning at all times. By including the condition in your target, you are better prepared to determine when your students will demonstrate that they learned the desired content.

D—Degree (How well do you want students to perform?)

This final step simply states the criteria for the students. While this may be based on predetermined criteria (e.g., your school expects all ninth graders to be able to write out all ten of the Bill of Rights), you will often need to determine your own criteria for student learning. When the students meet your criteria at this level or degree, then you could have the confidence that the students have learned the content. Examples of criteria might be "9 out of 10 times," "whenever asked to do so," "with no spelling errors," or "according to guidelines provided on the rubric."

These elements do not need to appear in the order presented above, but any learning target should have all four of the elements. Consider the following examples:

- Students will demonstrate their understanding (**A, B**) of the parts of a microscope by completing a worksheet (**C**) with 100% accuracy (**D**).
- After a classroom discussion about the reasons for and against the Electoral College (**C**), students will write a one-paragraph opinion statement (**AB**), and support their ideas with at least two reasons (**D**).
- On four out of five story problems (**D**), students will be able to correctly identify the pertinent information (**AB**), and write it down in a mathematical equation (**C**).

THE ROLE OF TARGETS IN DAILY LESSON PLANS

Targets help you focus on the critical content or processes that you will teach during an activity, day, unit, or academic year, therefore they need to be thought about each day. Targets also help you identify the learning you expect of your students and the specifics for how you will determine if they have learned the content adequately. Learning targets help your students, too. Telling them your expectations for their learning, and identifying how the day's activities will help them learn, prepares your students for the expectations of your lesson. The previous section explained why targets use a concise formulaic language. When telling students these targets, you should adjust the wording so that the targets are easily understood. For example, in the previous section you read this target: *After a classroom discussion about the reasons for and against the Electoral College, students will write a one-paragraph opinion statement, and support their ideas with at least two reasons.* Although you could write this on the board for your students, it will be clearer for your students if you write, *Discussion on opposing views of the Electoral College: one-paragraph opinion article using at least two reasons*. You could then tell the students, "We will have a discussion on the opposing points of view about the Electoral College. Following the discussion, you will have the chance to write a paragraph where you state your opinion about the usefulness of the Electoral College, and support your opinion with at least two reasons."

The point is that targets should be explained and be accessible for your students (Slavin, 1999). Students should know *what* they will learn, *why* they will learn it, and *how* they will be assessed. This will help them master the content, especially if they know how they will be assessed. Telling students ahead of time how they will demonstrate what they have learned helps them concentrate on what they learn during the activities. Rather than causing angst or worry in the students, this approach can relieve pressure to perform because the assessment technique is no longer a mystery. Again, in the previous section you read this target: *On four out of five word problems, students will be able to correctly identify the pertinent information, and write it down in a mathematical equation*. Students know from this target that they will be expected to identify the pertinent information from a word problem. By being aware of this, they will be prepared to focus their learning on this skill. This not only helps you focus your instruction, but it helps the students focus their attention and learning.

As you teach, you will want to consider the relevancy of your course content to your students' lives outside of school. Not everything needs to be readily applicable to the world outside school. Sometimes students need to learn facts and concepts simply to help their thinking skills and for helping to understand more complex content. However, your students will appreciate opportunities to understand how information learned in your class might help them outside the classroom.

MAKING IT WORK IN YOUR CONTENT AREA

Identify a state or national standard in your content that you have not worked with before, and compose three targets according to the following criteria:

- Write one target for learning the course content (e.g., a key concept, fact, or perspective).
- Write one target for a skill that students will need in your class (e.g., skill in researching a topic, skill in discussing issue with others).
- Write either an affective target or a social target (e.g., appreciation for the subject, respect for other opinions).
- Make sure each target has the "ABCD" elements.

You could ask a middle/high school teacher to critique your targets, and to tell you when during the school year this content is conventionally learned.

INTRODUCTION TO ASSESSMENT

Assessment is a key component of teaching. By assessing student learning, you can determine how effectively you taught, whether you need to re-teach a particular area, and how engaged the students were in their learning. Assessment is not merely assigning grades. Assessment is a plan that allows you and your students to monitor their progress toward meeting specified goals and targets. Assessments certainly provide information that can be graded, but more importantly assessment provides a systematic approach for guiding student learning. In this section of the book you will be introduced to the basic elements of assessment. The aspiring teachers we work with find it useful to think of assessments as opportunities to gather "student-based evidence," or evidence of student learning. Did students understand the key learning target for an activity? What evidence can I collect, observe, identify, gather, that will help the teacher answer this question? Thought of this way, assessments are merely ways to collect evidence of learning, and evidence of student confusion. Teachers then can use this information to extend the learning for some students, and review what needs to be learned for other students. Assessments and the evidence they provide are critical components to effectively helping all students to learn.

Wiggins and McTighe's Idea of Understanding by Design

We have found the work of Grant Wiggins and Jay McTighe to be helpful when thinking about assessment, learning, and planning. Understanding by design is an approach that highlights the important role of assessment when planning learning activities; the teacher and students promote student understanding by intentionally designing what happens in the classroom. The following points describe the key elements of understanding by design, and reveal the importance of assessment (Authentic Education, 2011)[6]:

- A primary goal of education should be the development and deepening of students' understanding.
- Students reveal their understanding most effectively when they are provided with complex, authentic opportunities to explain, interpret, apply, shift perspective, empathize, and self-assess. When applied to complex tasks, these "six facets" provide a conceptual lens through which teachers can better assess student understanding.
- *Effective curriculum development reflects a three-stage design process called "backward design" that delays the planning of classroom activities until goals have been clarified and assessments designed.* This process helps to avoid the twin problems of "textbook coverage" and "activity-oriented" teaching, in which no clear priorities and purposes are apparent.
- *Student and school performance gains are achieved through regular reviews of results (achievement data and student work) followed by targeted adjustments to curriculum and instruction.*

- *Teachers become most effective when they seek feedback from students and their peers and use that feedback to adjust approaches to design and teaching.*
- Teachers, schools, and districts benefit by "working smarter" through the collaborative design, sharing, and peer review of units of study.

As with our introduction to classroom management in Chapter 1, specific assessment ideas are addressed later in the book for each of the instructional strategies. Each strategy requires specific assessment approaches. By contextualizing the assessment principles for each of the strategies, you will be in a strong position to appropriately determine your students' progress and learning.

Validity, Reliability, and Usability

Students commonly complain that they studied information that was not on the test. They also wonder why examinations sometimes include "trick" questions—questions where the obvious answer is not the correct one. These complaints are challenges of **validity**. *Validity* means that the assessment is an accurate and appropriate measurement of student learning. An implication of this is that assessments have to be tied to the instructional strategies. If you are lecturing to your students and ask them to prepare for a test the next day by studying their notes, then the assessment needs to be closely tied to the content in the notes. If they engage in a debate about the information, or write an essay about a topic loosely related to the notes, the validity of the assessment is questioned.

Targets help to ensure that an assessment is valid. An infamous phrase in education is "teaching to the test." It is often used as a way to express frustration that some outside authority is determining the content of the tests, and teachers are in the unfavorable position of merely teaching students the content of the impending tests. Testing is certainly a significant part of the education scene these days, and many stories are available about how teachers have needed to abandon their conventional curriculum to prepare students to know the content upon which they will be tested. However, as a teacher, you will have many opportunities to develop assessments for your students. When you develop the assessments/tests based on what you want your students to learn, "teaching to the test" becomes a tool to help students learn. The ABCD approach to developing targets is one example of how you might teach to the test or assessment. By being very aware of the condition and degree to which you will assess student learning, you help to ensure that the assessments are valid. If an assessment is not valid, it should not be used.

Along with validity, assessments need to have a high degree of *reliability*. Reliability refers to the degree of confidence that an assessment tool will produce the same results over time. Theoretically, if a student were to take a test several times, his or her scores would be very similar on a reliable test. SAT tests are designed to be highly reliable so colleges have confidence that all students taking the SAT have been assessed on similar information. Reliability is a concern when teachers grade an essay. If the teacher does not have a rating scale (also known as a rubric or a series of components he or she is looking for in the essay), then grading will be less reliable. This is sometimes referred to as "subjective" grading. If you have 75 essays to grade, how assured are you that you will grade the 75th essay the same way as the first? The more assured you are the greater the reliability.

Usability is simply how difficult an assessment tool is to administer. One of the reasons that the traditional true–false test or multiple-choice test is popular among teachers is because of its ease of use and grading. Imagine that a teacher has three classes of thirty students (ninety total students). If students can complete a true–false test in 15 minutes, and the teacher can grade each test in 1 minute, the teacher uses only 15 minutes of class time and needs 90 minutes of grading time. However, if the students each make 5 minutes presentations, and the teacher needs 5 minutes to compose a written evaluation for each presentation, the teacher uses 450 minutes of class time and uses 450 minutes of grading time. The true–false test is a more usable assessment than the presentations. Chances are, however, that the presentations will provide a more valid assessment of student learning than the true–false test.

All three of these components need to be considered when determining how to assess your students. Assessments must be valid, first and foremost. They must also provide information about your students' learning that is reliable. Finally, assessments need to be usable.

To make the assessment of student learning more valid and reliable, educators are utilizing different techniques for determining how well students have learned. The quiz or test is not the only tool that you have for determining learning, and it is often not the most valid assessment tool. Tests or quizzes emphasize competition among students when they are norm referenced (scores are ordered based on students' performance. The opposite of this is criterion referenced. We discuss this under the section "Three More Important Assessment Terms," later in this chapter). They can easily overemphasize lower-level thinking if the students are merely asked to recall information and/or create a particular product. Instead of using an examination, the trend is to look at the whole picture of students' performance in class and during all assignments, and to assess students' understanding of the process they engaged in to create product. For example, the National Council of Teachers of Mathematics recommends that teachers should have their students verbalize the process they went through when solving a problem, and not simply assess the final answer. If the process is correct, the final product will be, too.

Students are engaging in more self-assessments, where they are taught about the tools needed to examine and evaluate their own performances. Earlier you read that telling students your learning targets will help them learn. Similarly, students need to be aware of the assessments ahead of time, so they can master the relevant content. Assessment is seen not as an end in itself but as a critically important feedback loop for instruction. The traditional test at the end of a unit may not be as valid of an assessment as a presentation 3 days earlier. If the presentation reveals that a student's understanding is incorrect, then the teacher is in a position to help the student relearn the content. Assessment is now seen as a tool for learning and not just for grading. Glen Hammond (2004) has done considerable work on this subject. Table 3.1 summarizes some of his findings on recent trends in classroom assessment.

We will discuss ideas from this chart later in the chapter, but an important principle from this chart is that assessments are used to look closely at students' formation of knowledge, skills, concepts, etc. in your classroom. This type of measurement, known

TABLE 3.1: Recent Assessment Trends

From	Toward
Written examinations	Coursework
Teacher-led assessment	Student-led assessment
Implicit criteria	Explicit criteria
Competition with classmates	Cooperation with classmates
Product assessment	Process assessment
Content (facts/concepts only)	Competencies (facts and skills)
Assessment for grading	Assessment for learning

as "**formative assessment**," is useful for the student, because he or she can use the assessments to see what still needs to be learned, and for the teacher, because he or she can use the assessments to direct future learning experiences.

Authentic Assessment and Performance Assessment

What is it that a historian does? What skills does a novelist need to write a manuscript? How does a chemist identify the molecular make-up of an unidentified clear fluid? **Authentic assessments** resemble tasks that might occur outside of the school as well as in the classroom (Wiggins, 1993; Hiebert et al., 1994). For example, authentic assessments ask students to read real texts such as primary source documents, to write for authentic purposes about meaningful topics such as a newspaper editorial page, or to conduct an experiment and draw conclusions in the school science laboratory. Both the material and the assessment tasks look as natural as possible. In addition, authentic assessment values the thinking behind the work, or the process, as much as the finished product (Wiggins, 1998). **Performance assessment** is a term that is often synonymous with authentic assessment. Performance assessments require students to demonstrate what they have learned and emphasize problem solving, thinking, and reasoning (MSEB, 1993). Even the United States Congress determined that performance assessments are valid measures of student learning, and composed the following definition for educators:

> Performance assessment . . . require[s] students to construct responses, rather than select from a set of answers, . . . are criterion-referenced . . . [and] in general, they focus on the process of problem solving rather than just on the end result.
>
> (Congress of the United States, 1992)

Authentic or performance assessments are usually longer and more complex than traditional pen and paper tests. Grant Wiggins suggests the following about authentic assessment:

> Do we want to evaluate student problem-posing and problem-solving in mathematics? Experimental research in science? Speaking, listening, and facilitating a discussion? Doing document-based historical inquiry? Thoroughly revising a piece

of imaginative writing until it "works" for the reader? Then let our assessment be built out of such exemplary intellectual challenges ... Comparisons with traditional standardized tests will help to clarify what "authenticity" means when considering assessment design and use:

- Authentic assessments require students to be effective performers with acquired knowledge. Traditional tests tend to reveal only whether the student can recognize, recall, or "plug in" what was learned out of context.
- Authentic assessments present the student with the full array of tasks that mirror the priorities and challenges found in the best instructional activities: conducting research; writing, revising and discussing papers; providing an engaging oral analysis of a recent political event; collaborating with others on a debate, etc. Conventional tests are usually limited to paper-and-pencil, one-answer questions.
- Authentic assessments attend to whether the student can craft polished, thorough and justifiable answers, performances or products. Conventional tests typically only ask the student to select or write correct responses—irrespective of reasons.
- Authentic tasks involve "ill-structured" challenges and roles that help students rehearse for the complex ambiguities of the "game" of adult and professional life. Traditional tests are more like drills, assessing static and too-often arbitrarily discrete or simplistic elements of those activities.

(Wiggins, 1990, p. 1)

Wiggins's use of the term **"ill-structured"** allows for the students to determine the structure and organization of their approach. The notion of a "clearly defined" but "ill-structured" task might help you think through authentic assessments in your content area. For example, student teaching for pre-service teachers is a powerful authentic assessment that is both clearly defined and ill-structured: Student teachers are asked to promote student learning on par with the cooperating teacher (a clearly defined task), but the planning, organizing, implementing, managing, and assessing of myriad classroom elements is left to the student teacher (an ill-structured task). We mentioned "backward design" earlier, but if we revisit it again here you can more clearly see how it impacts learning (Wiggins and McTighe, 2000). Consider how a conductor assesses the performances of the musicians in an orchestra. Or, consider how a coach assesses the performance of the players on a basketball team. Both might be based on the performance during the very **authentic tasks** of playing a musical score and competing during a game, and the performances are clearly understood before the very first practice session. This assessment is much more valid than a paper and pencil test (imagine how strange it would seem to not have a concert, but to have orchestra members complete a true–false test about the musical composition). When each of the instructional strategies is described in Part 2 of the book, appropriate authentic assessments are contextualized and examined in depth. Each instructional strategy lends itself to particular assessments and a thorough examination of valid, reliable, and usable assessments are addressed in the respective chapters. However, some examples of authentic, performance assessments are:

- writing to real audiences such as a newspaper or magazine;
- short investigations about a local community issue;
- translating text into a foreign language;
- developing a museum display;
- engaging in a service-learning activity;
- portfolios of work showing progress over time and examples of self-selected "best" work;
- self-assessment by students of their performance.

Table 3.2 compares five different assessment techniques. By looking over the chart, you can see that deciding how to assess your students' needs to be a thoughtful process that is as important as any other part of the curriculum.

TABLE 3.2: Comparing Five Assessments

Assessment method	Advantages of the method	Disadvantages of the method
Traditional pen-and-paper test (e.g., multiple choice, true–false, etc.)	Students are familiar with format High in reliability and usability	Often not a valid test of real-world actions Time-consuming to develop
Essays	Highly valid in that it allows students to demonstrate understanding of a concept, opinions, and attitudes Possibility for student to express an unique understanding is greater	Reliability—less control, therefore harder to quantify Usability—time-consuming to write questions and grade responses
Interviews and oral examinations	More relaxed and personal feeling may enhance validity Confusion can be clarified and jargon defined	May not want to be critical face-to-face Hard to transcribe and quantify
Performance assessment (e.g., presentation, recital, game, etc.)	Student demonstrates skill Close to real-world Rubric (rating scales) help focus student performance	Reliability—can be difficult to grade Usability—time-consuming because it depends on direct observation
Product assessment (e.g., homework, research paper, photo portfolio, etc.)	Useful to determine accomplishments Able to provide a standard to measure	Validity—does not show the process, but emphasizes the end result Reliability—can be difficult to grade

MAKING IT WORK IN YOUR CONTENT AREA

What is the equivalent of a concert or a game in your content area? In other words, how might the students in your content area engage in assessment tasks that are authentic measurements of what they have learned, and tasks that they might engage in outside of school? Refer to the list of examples in the previous section to get you started, and brainstorm at least three different activities that are authentic and/or performance assessments.

Rubrics

Like any evaluation process, authentic assessments must provide fair and reliable measurements of student learning. A rubric is a tool that lists the criteria for student performance and describes levels of quality for each of the criteria. For example, the rubric in Table 3.3 might be used to assess students' presentations. It clearly lists the criteria and levels of quality in three categories: demonstrated knowledge; use of visuals; and presentation skills/mechanics. Students receive a score from zero to three in each category:

It is difficult to rely on premade rubrics, because you may want to emphasize particular areas to your students. In the above example, the students know that they will be assessed on the three items in the left column (demonstrated knowledge, use of visuals, and mechanics). Nothing is mentioned about other areas such as "demonstration of skill," or "use of vocabulary," or any of a number of additional criteria, because the teacher using this rubric wants to focus student learning on these four areas. You will also notice that "knowledge" only accounts for 3 of the 12 points (or 33%). This may be too low for some teachers, but for the developer of this rubric, and the assignment for which it will be used, this was determined to be appropriate.

Rubrics help students and teachers define "quality." They increase reliability and reduce subjective or biased grading. Rubrics also help teachers to clearly explain to the students why they received a particular score. If students receive a rubric at the beginning of a project, they can accept more responsibility for their learning, because they know the expectations of the assessment from the start. If a student needs extra assistance with one area of the rubric, then you will be able to focus on the criteria listed on the rubric for that area. In addition, when you create a rubric at the beginning of a unit, you can plan your lessons in ways that allow your students to meet the criteria stated in the rubric. As we mentioned earlier, this is a form of backward design. We first suggest identifying the categories that you will assess students on by thinking through your expectations. Once the categories are established, you should consider the criteria for two extremes of student work for each category: excellent and unsatisfactory performances. What evidence do you want to see that reveals student learning? The remaining criteria can then be modified for the number of levels you are willing to let students attain. The example above has four levels, so we had to identify different

TABLE 3.3: Presentation Rubric

Categories	Criteria for student presentation				Points
	3	2	1	0	
Demonstrated knowledge	Shows complete understanding of the content he or she researched and answers questions accurately.	Shows substantial understanding of the content he or she researched and answers some questions accurately.	Shows limited understanding of the content he or she researched and has difficulty with questions.	Shows a lack of understanding of the content he or she researched and is unable to answer questions.	/3
Use of visuals	Clear diagram, PowerPoint slide or poster, highlighting main ideas.	Clear diagram, PowerPoint slide or poster, but missing some main ideas.	Inappropriate or unclear diagram, PowerPoint slide or poster.	No visuals.	/3
Mechanics	Presentation is well-rehearsed, fits in the time allocation, and easy to understand.	Presentation is practiced, and/or is close to the time allocation.	Presentation needs more rehearsal, and/or is not close to the time allocation. Difficult to understand main points.	Lack of preparation is apparent. Main points are unclear.	/3
				Total	**/9**

Teacher comments:

criteria for each. With more levels, you will be able to differentiate the quality of student work more, but it will be a more difficult task to create unique criteria for each level. RubiStar (www.rubistar4teachers.org) is one of many internet sites that are designed to help teachers design, develop, and use rubrics. We encourage you to visit this site, because it will help you to think about the categories and criteria you could have for an assignment. The down side of the rubric software is that they are usually very generic, and do not provide specific expectations for each criteria level. Ideally you will have criteria and even examples of work for each of the levels of the rubric. You want the expectations to be clearly understood by students. This is not always possible with ready-made rubrics. We suggest using generic rubrics as a starting point, then adding your own details specific to your expectations of an assignment. We provide more examples of rubrics designed specifically for an instructional strategy in Part 2 of the book, and at the companion website for the book.

DIAGNOSTIC, FORMATIVE, AND SUMMATIVE ASSESSMENT

Diagnostic Assessment

Although some authors describe **diagnostic assessment** as a component of formative assessment, most consider it a distinct form of measurement (Kellough and Kellough, 1999; McMillan, 2004). Just as a medical doctor looks at a patient and comes up with a diagnosis for treatment, diagnostic assessments usually occur prior to instruction and attempt to determine students' strengths, weaknesses, knowledge, and skills. Identifying these helps the teachers differentiate the curriculum to meet each student's unique needs. For example, a history teacher might give a pretest on the first day of class to see how much information students remember about the Civil War. Depending on the results, the teacher is able to determine the course content that needs to be learned. At one high school, the mathematics department gives a series of diagnostic measurements to all entering freshmen. Teachers then use the scores to place students into the appropriate mathematics course. The teachers also use the scores to help monitor the progress of each student during their first year of high school.

Formative Assessment

Formative assessment occurs continually during each school day so that the teacher is able to monitor student learning. Formative assessment provides information on how students are "forming" their understanding. An excellent definition of this type of assessment is from Black and Wiliam (2009):

> Practice in a classroom is formative to the extent that evidence about student achievement is elicited, interpreted, and used by teachers, learners, or their peers, to make decisions about the next steps in instruction that are likely to be better, or better founded, than the decisions they would have taken in the absence of the evidence that was elicited.
>
> (p. 9)

The National Council for the Teaching of Mathematics (NCTM) developed *Principles and Standards for School Mathematics* in 2000, and while it is designed for mathematics, their principles around formative assessment transcend content and are applicable to all subjects:

> Assessment should be more than merely a test at the end of instruction to see how students perform under special conditions; rather, it should be an integral part of instruction that informs and guides teachers as they make instructional decisions. Assessment should not merely be done *to* students; rather, it should also be done *for* students, to guide and enhance their learning.
>
> (The Assessment Principle, ¶ 1, emphasis in the original)

Formative assessment provides information to the teacher about how to appropriately "form" targets for future lessons and promote student learning. For example, if several students misunderstand photosynthesis, formative assessments will identify this learning problem and allow the teacher to take strides toward remediation. Formative assessments often are not graded, and allow the teachers and students to develop a deeper understanding of the curriculum. They provide information for adapting teaching and learning to meet student needs (Boston, 2002). Sometimes formative assessment is labeled "**progress monitoring.**" When teachers monitor students' progress, and are able to identify where students are having trouble, they can make necessary instructional adjustments, such as re-teaching, trying alternative instructional approaches, or offering more opportunities for practice. These activities can lead to improved student success (Black and Wiliam, 1998a). Teachers can formatively assess students' understanding in the following ways (Black and Wiliam, 1998a, b; Boston, 2002):

- Have students write their understanding of vocabulary or concepts before and after instruction.
- Ask students to summarize the main ideas they've taken away from a lecture, discussion, or assigned reading.
- Have students complete a few problems or questions at the end of instruction and check answers.
- Interview students individually or in groups about their thinking as they solve problems.
- Assign brief, in-class writing assignments (e.g., "Why is this person or event representative of this time period in history?").

We believe that most of the assessments you will use in class will be some form of formative assessment, and that such assessments provide opportunities to meet your students at their current level of understanding. With diagnostic and formative assessments working together, you will be better able to differentiate your instruction so that all of your students can learn. In Part 2 of this book, we provide extensive examples of assessments that are specific for each instructional strategy. Most of the assessments are formative.

Summative Assessment

Summative assessment is the attempt to summarize student learning at some point in time. This is the assessment that students, parents, and the public tend to value most because it is so closely tied to grades. Where diagnostic and formative assessments provide direction for future instruction, summative assessments typically do not. Consider this analogy for understanding the difference between formative and summative assessment: When the cook tastes the soup, it is formative assessment; When the customer tastes the soup, it is summative assessment (Stevens et al., 1996). Summative assessment occurs at or near the end of a unit, chapter, term, or course. The purpose is to evaluate or grade student learning. The Scholastic Aptitude Test, the Miller Analogies Test, and most standardized exams are also examples of summative assessments. Most statewide assessments are summative (including testing to address such federal initiatives as the "No Child Left Behind" Act). They are not designed to provide the immediate, contextualized feedback useful for helping teachers and students during the learning process. High-quality summative information can, of course, shape how teachers organize their courses or what schools offer their students. However, it is not often useful for helping teachers work to improve the learning of individual students.

THREE ADDITIONAL IMPORTANT ASSESSMENT TERMS

When thinking and reading about assessments, three other terms will often be used: norm-referenced assessment, criterion-referenced assessment, and self-referenced assessment.

Norm-referencing allows for people to be ranked, or put in an order based on their scores. It is competitive. For example, in a class of twenty-five students, a teacher might use norm-referencing to assign grades to students by determining that the top 20% receive "A"s, the next "B"s, etc. Such a scale looks like:

A   The five students with the highest grades
B   The next five students
C   The next five students
D   The next five students
F   The five students with the lowest grades

While this is a traditional grading scale, these figures are arbitrary. If the results of any assessment allow you to rank students from high score to low score, then the test is norm-referenced. Many standardized tests are norm-referenced, as is an IQ test. This approach is not used very often by teachers. Rather than having students compete against each other for a grade, teachers would rather have them focus on meeting specific criteria.

Criterion-referencing is the term used for assessment against fixed criteria. Potentially everyone can pass a criterion-referenced assessment—or everyone can fail. While norm-referencing also has criteria (e.g., the criteria for an "A" grade is to have the top five-point totals in the class), criteria-referenced assessments determine whether a student has adequately met a minimum level or standard. Criteria are usually determined in advance to ensure that they are valid and appropriate. For example, a driver's license test is often criteria-referenced. It does not matter how well you do, as long as you do not make a prespecified number of errors. A pass or fail grade might serve as another example. If you earn a specific number of points (e.g., 70% of the total), you pass the course. It does not matter how many points you earn, as long as you meet the criterion. The concern with this assessment is that it identifies only a minimum level of achievement. This is often justified by the advantage of not basing the success on comparing scores with others.

Many teachers determine the criteria needed for different grades. For example, a percentage of the total points is needed for an "A" grade. A grade scale that uses multiple criteria could look like this:

A   90–100% of the possible points
B   80–89% of the possible points
C   70–79% of the possible points
D   60–69% of the possible points
F   59% or less of the possible points

Self-referencing is an assessment by the students against themselves, or more particularly against previous best performances. Students are able to determine their performance by referencing their performance to their previous performances. A keyboard class may use this to help the students assess their improvement. A baseline score indicating number of words per minutes is taken at the start of the course, and this is compared with measurements taken throughout the year. Grading with this is problematic because students who have prior knowledge or skill will not be able to improve as much as someone who enters with no prior skill. Self-referencing is most relevant to helping students meet individual goals.

MAKING IT WORK IN YOUR CONTENT AREA

Return to the targets you wrote earlier in the chapter. For each target, develop appropriate diagnostic, formative, and/or summative assessment activities that will help students meet your target. For example, if you are teaching a world geography class or an earth science class, you might have the target: *Students will be able to distinguish between "renewable" and "nonrenewable" resources.* You could diagnostically assess students' understanding by handing out a list of resources in each of these two categories on the first day of class and have each student sort the list. This information will help you know the content knowledge students have prior to the unit. You could formatively assess students during the unit by having them write down the resources on a particular continent, and then asking them to identify the renewable resources, and explain why they are not likely to run out. This will allow you to assess how accurately students are acquiring knowledge. A summative assessment could be a PowerPoint presentation through which the student provides slides and descriptions of each of the two types of resources, and details about where supplies of several resources are located throughout the world. This serves as a cohesive plan for helping meet the target.

Using this as an example, develop assessments for your targets, and what the purpose of each assessment might be.

CHAPTER REVIEW

- Long- and short-term learning targets:

  - Targets specify how and when you can help students meet those goals.
  - Long-term targets will be accomplished after a longer unit, semester, or even an entire course.
  - Short-term targets are met during an activity or after a few class sessions.
  - The ABCD approach helps keep targets focused:

    - **AB**—**a**udience and **b**ehavior
    - **C**—**c**ondition
    - **D**—**d**egree.

- Different domains of learning:

  - cognitive domain
  - affective domain
  - psychomotor domain
  - content, skill, and social interactions (CSS) provides another useful approach for considering domains of learning and student learning.

- Assessing student learning and the specific importance of formative assessment.

  - Assessments must be:

    - valid
    - reliable
    - usable.

  - Authentic assessments resemble tasks that might occur outside of the school as well as in the classroom; performance assessment is synonymous with authentic assessment.
  - Assessments should be developed at the beginning of a unit so that you can "design backward" by developing lessons that prepare students to meet the assessment expectations.
  - Rubrics help students and teachers define "quality."

– Assessments occur at different points in the learning process:

- Diagnostic assessment are used near the start.
- Formative assessment occurs continually during each school day to monitor student learning.
- Summative assessment provides a summary of what students have learned.

TABLE 3.4: Verbs to Help Identify Student Behaviors at Each Level of Bloom's Cognitive Taxonomy

Knowledge	Compre-hension	Application	Analysis	Synthesis	Evaluation
Cite	Arrange	Adapt	Analyze	Arrange	Appraise
Choose	Associate	Apply	Appraise	Assemble	Approve
Define	Clarify	Catalog	Audit	Build	Assess
Label	Classify	Chart	Break	Combine	Choose
List	Convert	Compute	Calculate	Compile	Conclude
Locate	Describe	Consolidate	Categorize	Compose	Confirm
Match	Diagram	Demonstrate	Certify	Conceive	Criticize
Name	Draw	Develop	Compare	Construct	Critique
Recall	Discuss	Employ	Contrast	Create	Diagnose
Recognize	Estimate	Extend	Correlate	Design	Evaluate
Record	Explain	Extrapolate	Criticize	Devise	Judge
Repeat	Express	Generalize	Deduce	Discover	Justify
Select	Identify	Illustrate	Defend	Draft	Prioritize
State	Locate	Infer	Detect	Formulate	Prove
Write	Outline	Interpolate	Diagram	Generate	Rank
	Paraphrase	Interpret	Differentiate	Integrate	Rate
	Report	Manipulate	Discriminate	Make	Recommend
	Restate	Modify	Distinguish	Manage	Research
	Review	Order	Examine	Organize	Resolve
	Sort	Predict	Infer	Plan	Revise
	Summarize	Prepare	Inspect	Predict	Rule on
	Transfer	Produce	Investigate	Prepare	Select
	Translate	Relate	Question	Propose	Support
		Sketch	Reason	Reorder	Validate
		Submit	Separate	Reorganize	
		Tabulate	Solve	Set up	
		Transcribe	Survey	Structure	
		Use	Test	Synthesize	
		Utilize	Uncover		
			Verify		

Adapted from work by Kathy V. Waller, PhD, CLS (NCA), National Accrediting Agency for Clinical Laboratory Sciences (NAACLS) Board of Directors: www.naacls.org/docs/announcement/writing-targets.pdf (accessed November 2004).

TABLE 3.5: Verbs to Help Identify Student Behaviors at Each Level of Krathwohl's Affective Taxonomy

Receiving	Responding	Valuing	Organization	Characterizing by value
Accept	Agree	Adopt	Anticipate	Act
Acknowledge	Allow	Aid	Collaborate	Administer
Attend (to)	Answer	Care (for)	Confer	Advance
Follow	Ask	Complete	Consider	Advocate
Listen	Assist	Compliment	Consult	Aid
Meet	Attempt	Contribute	Coordinate	Challenge
Observe	Choose	Delay	Design	Change
Receive	Communicate	Encourage	Direct	Commit
	Conform	Enforce	Establish	Counsel
	Cooperate	Foster	Facilitate	Criticize
	Demonstrate	Guide	Follow through	Debate
	Describe	Initiate	Investigate	Defend
	Discuss	Interact	Judge	Disagree
	Display	Join	Lead	Dispute
	Exhibit	Justify	Manage	Empathize
	Follow	Maintain	Modify	Enhance
	Give	Monitor	Organize	Excuse
	Help	Praise	Oversee	Forgive
	Identify	Preserve	Plan	Influence
	Locate	Propose	Qualify	Motivate
	Notify	Query	Recommend	Negotiate
	Obey	React	Revise	Object
	Offer	Respect	Simplify	Persevere
	Participate	Seek	Specify	Persist
	Practice	Share	Submit	Praise
	Present	Study	Synthesize	Promote
	Read	Subscribe	Test	Question
	Relay	Suggest	Vary	Reject
	Reply	Support	Weigh	Resolve
	Report	Thank		Seek
	Respond	Uphold		Serve
	Select			Solve
	Try			Tolerate

Adapted from work by Kathy V. Waller, PhD, CLS(NCA), National Accrediting Agency for Clinical Laboratory Sciences (NAACLS) Board of Directors: www.naacls.org/docs/announcement/writing-targets.pdf (accessed November 2004).

NOTES

1 Our use of the term "learning targets" is widely used, but not the only one educators will use. Synonymous terms that you might hear are "instructional objectives," "student learning objectives," or "learning outcomes."

2 See Table 3.4 on p. 87 for a list of activities/verbs that can be used when writing cognitive targets at each of the six levels.

3 The Iowa State website is included at the book's companion website.

4 See Table 3.5 on p. 88 for a list of activities/verbs that can be used when writing affective targets at each of the five levels.

5 Some of these ideas are adapted from work done by Donald Clark, www.nwlink.com/~donclark/hrd/bloom.html (accessed March 2012).

6 These bullet points are from the website "Authentic Education," a company to which Grant Wiggins is president. We added emphasis to these points. The website for this overview is located at: www.authenticeducation.org/ubd/ubd.lasso (accessed February 2012).

CHAPTER 4

Long- and Short-Range Planning

Planning helps teachers organize what they will teach during the school year, the semester, the unit, and the daily lesson. Planning also helps teachers organize and structure the school day so that student learning is maximized. We believe that many classroom management and discipline problems can be avoided if the teacher is organized and well planned. If you have a clear idea of what you intend for the students to learn, not only during that day's lesson but also for the coming weeks, then you will be in a good position to address student concerns about the content, and have a better understanding of your expectations for student learning.

YEAR-LONG SCOPE AND SEQUENCE

According to the National Center for Education Statistics,[1] American schools are open an average of 180 days a year. These days are divided by districts and schools into smaller segments such as two 90-day semesters, three 60-day trimesters, or four 45-day quarters. "Scope" and "sequence" are two terms that many educators use to refer to the breadth of content and skills students should learn (the scope), and the order in which students will learn this content (the sequence) during these 180 days. Year-long planning is simply the scope and sequence for a course during the school year. Each state usually determines the scope and sequence for courses in each of the grades from kindergarten through twelfth grade. Consider these two examples of the scope and sequence for two courses:

Virginia's scope and sequence for Algebra I[2]:

- using algebraic topics
- linear equations and inequalities
- systems of equations
- relations and functions: linear
- relations and functions: quadratic.

Washington's scope and sequence for United States history (high school)[3]:

- industrialization and the emergence of the U.S. as a world power (1877–1919)
- reform, prosperity, and depression (1918–1938)
- World War II, Cold War, international relations (1939–present)
- post-World War II domestic, political, social and economic issues (1945–present).

Many states and districts have developed or are developing expectations for the content that should be taught at each grade level to ensure that as students move through the grades they learn content in a predetermined sequence. They are available online, and are usually based on the national standards for each content area, and in the coming years will be based on the Common Core State Standards. A familiar example of scope and sequence is offered by mathematics courses. Students enroll in Geometry, and then proceed to Algebra 1 and 2, Algebra 3 and 4, Trigonometry, and Calculus. Not all students complete these levels, but the scope of each course and the sequence in which each course is taught is clearly specified. Most content areas have a scope and sequence for the year and a scope and sequence across grade levels. This is a great help for beginning teachers because it provides insight into what content students should have learned prior to your class; it suggests the content that students need to learn in your course, and it identifies the content that students will need to know for the years after your course.

School districts and individual schools also develop a year-long scope and sequence for each grade level. These are tied to the state expectations, but may include additional content that districts or schools believe are important. In our work with schools, we have found that some districts provide teachers with incredible freedom to develop their own scope and sequence, while other districts require teachers to adhere to a specific program. For example, a common set of topics and concepts for a middle school earth science course is as follows:

- geologic time
- plate tectonics
- plate tectonics
- earthquakes

- volcanoes
- mountains
- rocks
- fossils.

You might teach in a district where you are expected to teach just these topics, and to teach them in this order. If that is the case, your year-long scope and sequence is predetermined. You still have opportunities to determine how to promote student learning as you select instructional strategies, but the overall content of the course must meet these expectations. Just as likely, however, you might teach in a district that allows you to add to these topics, and does not specify the order (sequence) in which students should learn them. In this latter situation, you will need to determine the instructional strategies and the overall topics for the school year.

As the planning moves closer to the daily lesson, the level of specificity increases. As we found with the Virginia and Washington examples, the year-long scope and sequence is often not very specific. It usually does not specify the number of days to be spent on a topic, subtopics students should learn, assessment tools, or learning targets. They simply provide an overarching idea of the content students should learn during the school year, and the order in which topics and concepts should be learned.

Textbooks present content in an order that attempts to match the year-long scope and sequence of a course. For example, world history textbooks usually present content in the chronological order that most teachers use when teaching that subject. Students, then, are able to read through the textbook as they learn the course content. Mathematics and science textbooks are similar. Language arts and literature textbooks are not as easily organized, and teachers do not necessarily teach the course in the order of the chapters. Physical education and music often do not use textbooks at all. Often, textbooks provide superficial coverage of too much information. We suggest that you determine how the textbook might supplement your planning and curriculum, and not depend on the textbook to determine the scope and sequence of your course. As you learned in Chapter 2, textbook publishers are one of the many powerful influences on a teacher making curricular decisions. Teachers gather information from these stakeholders, but in most cases you will have considerable freedom to pull the course scope and sequence together by using your professional judgment while collaborating with others in your district.

Scope and sequence usually are used in reference to long-range planning; any time a teacher plans he or she should think about the scope and sequence of the content. However, scope and sequence also are important when planning a series of lessons that will comprise a unit plan, and even when planning for a single day's activities. The scope of the content and the sequential ordering of events need to be thoughtfully considered when planning. Teachers develop lesson plans for each day they teach. Lesson plans are placed in a sequence, or order, that the teacher thinks will help the students understand the content. Often a series of lesson plans are placed together to form a unit plan. Unit plans are ordered, or sequenced, together to form a course plan, and the courses are sequenced to form a year-long plan. We will explore this more as we examine unit planning and lesson planning.

MAKING IT WORK IN YOUR CONTENT AREA

Look at the national standards available in your content area (see Chapter 2 for an initial list), and standards that your state may have for teaching your subject or course. For quick access to the standards of all states, visit this website, which has links for each state:

www.education-world.com/standards/state/index.shtml (retrieved May 2012).

Using the state and national standards, write down the year-long scope and sequence for your course. Talk with a teacher who teaches this course, and compare what you came up with to what the teacher has developed for the 180-day school year. Consider discussing: What is the difference between what you wrote and the teacher's plan? What is similar? How do the two plans reflect the state standards or national standards? How did the two of you go about the process of making your selections?

FOUR COMMONPLACES IN SCHOOL

Awareness of the standards, goals, and suggested scope and sequence for your course is the first step in planning. As we mentioned earlier in this chapter, these will be available to you at the national, state, district, school, and even department levels. The scope and sequence plans provide topics for more focused unit plans, which in turn provide direction for the specific lesson plans. Before we start to describe these unit and lesson plans, however, it is important to consider all that is involved when planning. Joseph Schwab (1973) developed the idea that all classrooms have four elements in common. They all have a teacher, students, a subject matter that is to be learned, and a milieu or environment in which teaching and learning take place. If any one of these four commonplaces is hindered, then learning is thwarted. Any planning or thinking about curriculum—of what should be taught and learned—must consider how these four aspects of every classroom interact.

These four commonplaces should not be thought of as a hierarchy. Though it is tempting in an age of testing and accountability to think of "content" as the most important aspect of the classroom, Schwab's ideas remind us that all four commonplaces must work together if learning is to occur. As illustrated in Figure 4.1, below, if any of the four sides is removed, the entire structure collapses. Consider the following examples that show how the teacher, students, content, and milieu codependence affect teaching and learning:

- If your students already understand the key concepts you want them to learn, then the content will impact what you have planned for the day. Similarly, if the content

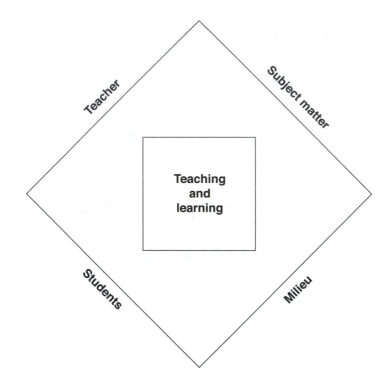

FIGURE 4.1: Schwab's Four Commonplaces

is too difficult for students to understand (e.g., the reading level of a text is too high, the premise of your main point is not accepted by the students, or students do not have adequate prior knowledge), then the learning will be impacted by the "content commonplace."

- If the students are not prepared, or not engaged, or distracted they will not be ready to think about the content you planned for them to learn. This might happen if they did not complete a reading assignment, or if your class meets immediately following a pep assembly, or even if a noisy lawn mower is cutting grass outside your classroom. In each of these instances, the students will affect you (the teacher), the content, and the milieu.

- If you are discussing a controversial subject in your classroom, students may perceive the milieu as unsafe, and feel uncomfortable sharing their ideas. In turn, this will affect the depth that a topic can be examined, and your selection of an instructional strategy.

- If students are making presentations to the class, and the desks are positioned in groups of four (so that the students are facing each other and not the front of the room), the physical set up of the room may distract students from listening to the presentations. This will affect the students' opportunity to learn from the presentations, to present to classmates who are listening, and you might even get frustrated that students are talking too much.

When we work with student teachers, often we will encourage them to reflect on a lesson after they have taught. The four commonplaces provide focus for that reflection. By asking questions, such as "How prepared was I (the teacher) for the lesson?" "Were the students engaged in the learning process?" "Was the content age or ability appropriate?" and "Did the classroom environment promote learning?", teachers are able to critique the class session. For example, consider a case in which students were distracted by the PE class playing soccer outside the classroom (affecting the student) and the student teacher became annoyed and frustrated (affecting the teacher) putting a damper on the positive tone that had been established (affecting the milieu) which caused the **role-play** that was occurring to fizzle (affecting the subject matter learned). While reflecting on the lesson, a student teacher might mistakenly think that students don't learn much during role-play and become wary of trying the strategy with another class. Realizing the interdependence of the commonplaces will help a teacher more clearly reflect upon the events of the classroom. This reflective approach could lead to the conclusion that to simply shut the shades quietly without responding emotionally could positively affect the other commonplaces.

Our point for thinking about Schwab's work is simply to remind you that part of planning is taking into consideration all the aspects of the student (maturity, diversity, ability, motivation, etc.), the content (standards, goals, targets, etc.), the milieu (perception of safety, community of learners, perceived threats to students, etc.), and the teacher (knowledge of the content, knowledge of the students, skill at managing the classroom, choice of instructional strategies, etc.). These four commonplaces direct your planning, and determine how effective the instruction has been in promoting student learning.

MAKING IT WORK IN YOUR CONTENT AREA

Decide on a concept that you might teach in your content area. Imagine that you will be able to spend about 45 minutes on this concept with your students. After you have come up with the concept, consider each of the following situations that could occur in your classroom, and consider the commonplaces that are most affected (remember that if one commonplace is affected, all four will be).

Situation #1: Twenty of the thirty students in your class are in the gifted program at your school. What "area" is affected? How does it impact your classroom and all students' learning?

Situation #2: A fire drill occurs for the first 10 minutes of class. By the time you have students back in class, you have 10 minutes left. What "area" is affected? How does it impact your classroom and student learning?

Brainstorm other situations where different commonplaces might interact to impact student learning.

DIFFERENTIATION AND PLANNING

Schwab's work reminds us of the importance of considering the individual student when we begin the planning process. Tomlinson (2004) suggests three aspects of differentiation that will help us focus on planning appropriately for our diverse classrooms. Student *interest* can be addressed by allowing students to pursue questions tied together by the topic and learning targets. For example, students could create questions they would like to purse on the topic of ancient Rome, such as "How did the Roman arch successfully improve architecture?" "What were the lives of gladiators like?" "What medical treatments were available for illnesses?" Second, student *readiness* can be differentiated by allowing for writing and research tasks that reflect criteria for success agreed upon by student and teacher. For example, an agreed-upon writing project and rubric are supported by a wide range of print and media resources, a variety of support from peers, teacher, or access to experts. Third, *learner-profile* differentiation is reflected by the variety of ways a student prefers to learn or present their learning. For example, the student might be given an option to express their findings through journal writing, an oral presentation, or through a video they have created. Keeping these three aspects of differentiation in mind while planning for learning will help create an environment that assists all students.

THE UNIT PLAN

The unit plan is the compilation of lesson plans during a specific amount of time, for example, 2 weeks, and provides specific focus on course content. By placing daily lessons in a unit, the content that the students learn is connected. Students are able to recognize relationships among each daily lesson, because of a conceptual or thematic link that the unit plan provides. A few examples help explain this:

- A geography teacher is able to examine five common geographic themes (location, place, human–environment interactions, movement, and region) during a unit studying China. Since the unit is on China, students know that the different geographic concepts will all be applied to the content about that country.
- A biology teacher connects 2 weeks of lesson activities that include dissecting a frog, watching a video, reading from the textbook, and completing laboratory tests on blood-sugar levels and blood pressure, when teaching a unit on the circulatory system.
- A Spanish teacher presents a series of lessons about beliefs, foods, religion, and traditions during a unit on Mexican culture.

By segmenting the school year into units, you are able to think clearly about needed resources for upcoming units, prerequisite knowledge for each unit, and key concepts and skills that a unit presents. The 180 days of school could be divided into 18 10-day units. We do not mean to imply that units must be about 2 weeks long. Often they are 3 or 4 weeks long, or they can be merely 1 week. Rather than thinking of a unit as a specific number of days, think of a unit as helping the students learn a specific portion of content and/or develop particular skills.

When thinking about long-term planning, the work of Grant Wiggins and Jay McTighe provide the metaphor of "backward design," which we described in Chapter 3. We provide links to ideas around their work on the companion website to this book. In addition, their work with curriculum development reminds us all that students do not learn and understand automatically as a result of teaching. Student learning is the result of designing effective lessons to match student understanding. Wiggins and McTighe rightfully remind us that understanding is the result of appropriately designing learning opportunities.

Students reveal their understanding most effectively when they are provided with complex tasks that allow for authentic opportunities to

- explain
- interpret
- apply
- shift perspective
- empathize, and
- self-assess.

When applied to complex tasks, these "six facets" provide a conceptual lens through which teachers can better assess student understanding and determine what to plan next to ensure student success.[4]

Essential Questions

Without a unit, daily lessons lack focus. Lessons should be developed because they will help students learn the specific knowledge or skills identified for the unit. As you can see, units are an effective tool for designing lessons that meet your objectives, goals, and curriculum standards. They allow teachers to map out the activities and strategies that will help ensure that students learn specified course content. Erickson (2002) suggests that unit plans should be developed around "**essential questions.**" Essential questions are about the big ideas or fundamental concepts that we want students to think about and learn during the span of a unit. By posing questions, students and the teachers are able to focus their attention on content that will help answer the questions. Wiggins and McTighe (2005) indicate that essential questions provide a focus for the unit and have several important characteristics. Essential questions:

- don't have one obvious answer;

  - e.g., *Why is winter colder than summer?*

- raise other important question often across disciplines;

  - e.g., *What can be done to reduce CO_2 emissions?*

- address philosophical or conceptual foundations of a discipline;

    - e.g., *In nature, do only the strong survive?*

- recur naturally and are important enough to show up periodically;

    - e.g., *What evidence of patterns of change is illustrated within . . . (the rock cycle, seasons, adaptation)?*

- are framed to provoke student interest;

    - e.g., *Why or how do we see color?*

We provide a unit with essential questions as an example of how to organize curriculum at the end of this chapter.

Components of a Unit Plan

While unit plans can have many components, the following eight are frequently used by teachers when planning:

1. overview and rationale
2. goals and essential questions
3. targets
4. outline of content (the scope of the content in the unit)
5. calendar (the sequence that students will learn the content)
6. daily lesson plans
7. assessments and evaluations
8. materials and resources.

The following description of these components will clarify their purpose in the unit plan.

1. *Overview and Rationale*
   The rationale for the unit provides a general overview and justification for teaching a unit on the topic you are selecting. The overview and rationale allows you to consider your reasons for developing the unit, and to determine how the content will build on your students' prior knowledge and skills. The overview also prepares you to consider available materials and resources, and how the unit fits into the overall scope and sequence for the school year. An overview and rationale often include:

   - A title for the unit.
   - The course in which this will be taught (e.g., world history, algebra, Spanish II).
   - The grade level (e.g., ninth grade).
   - A full introduction to the unit that addresses the question, "What is it you will be teaching, and more critically, what is it that students will be learning?" Be specific about the content of the unit and the activities that the students will be engaged in to learn the content.

- A description of how the unit fits into the existing curriculum. For example, what topic would precede the unit? Which will follow it? Why? What existing skills and abilities should students possess before studying this unit? What skills, abilities, and knowledge will the students gain from this unit?
- Your rationale statement considers the idea that of all the possible topics you *could* have selected, what *did* you select for this unit and *why*? The rationale also prepares you to answer colleagues, parents, students, and others who are wondering why this content is important for the students to learn. You might also consider how students will be able to use the content and skills learned in the unit outside of school.

2. *Goals and Essential Questions*

   Goals (described earlier in Chapter 2) are often clearly connected to a skill or content standard at the state or national level. As mentioned in Chapter 2, these standards are being replaced or modified in many states by a set of Common Core Standards that will be shared across state lines. Many teachers will list the number of the associated standard on the lesson plan, but at minimum it should be listed in the unit plan. Unit goals should include both academic content goals and skill goals. Often essential questions come from these goals. These are broad questions that will help the development of the unit. A unit typically has two to four essential questions.

3. *Targets*

   These are concise, formulaic learning outcomes that you want students to achieve during the study of your unit. Before teachers compose these targets, they often pre-assess their students to see what content and skills students already have (or what deficits exist). These pre-assessments could be during an informal question and answer session or discussion, or from a more formal pretest, survey, or series of interviews. Teachers also use their knowledge and previous experiences of what students typically know when they come to class. Concise, well-articulated and focused targets are critical for a well-organized unit, because they focus the unit, and will assist your daily and long-range planning. Many unit targets are not met until partway through or at the end of a unit. Therefore, they are broad and not tied to specific daily lessons. Targets should be written for academic content and information that you want the students to learn, skills that you want the students to gain, and social interactions that you want the students to experience. Follow the criteria for well-written targets that you utilized in Chapter 3, and include the following:

   - What content will students be learning, and what activities will promote student learning?[5]
   - How well should students be able to perform to demonstrate that they have learned?
   - Try to list the unit targets under each learning goal you have established. This will establish a link between the goals and targets.

4. *Outline of Content (the Scope of the Content in the Unit)*

   This provides a concise overview of the content in your unit. It answers the question "What academic content will students learn from this unit?" The content outline is not a list of activities or instructional strategies. Those will be determined after you determine the content that needs to be learned by your students. You should not feel that you are creating this outline on your own. National and state standards provide guidance, as do some scope and sequence guides and teacher resource guides. Unit content outlines do not list everything that students will learn. Rather, they provide key concepts, categories, and topical areas in the unit. For example, part of a content outline for a unit on American democracy might include the following:

   I.   Branches of Government

        A. Executive Branch

            1. President

                a. Terms
                b. Requirements

            2. Powers

                a. Chief Executive
                b. Chief of Staff
                c. Commander in Chief

            3. Checks and Balances

                a. Veto
                b. Nomination

        B. Legislative Branch
        C. Judicial Branch

   II. Elections

5. *Calendar (the Sequence that Students Will Learn the Content)*

   The unit calendar gives an overview of the sequence of lessons. It provides the teacher with a "unit-at-a-glance" in regard to content, instructional strategies, and classroom activities. This aids in developing daily targets and lesson plans. Each day of the unit calendar identifies the topic to be taught, possible instructional activities, and assessments of student learning. The calendar becomes a device for considering the order in which the content will be taught or learned. It also helps you think about how much time you need to spend on each topic. By putting the unit targets into the calendar, you will be able to ensure that your targets are fully addressed during the unit. Similarly, by listing the instructional strategies you might use, you can check that you are using a variety of activities, both within and across days. Notice that a calendar is *not* a lesson plan. Student interns new to a classroom sometimes misunderstand the cooperating teacher's depth of knowledge and experience and think they too can teach from lesson notes. Often this turns into lack of focused "winging it" and unhappy cooperating teachers.

   The unit calendar could look like the following example for a high school Art 1 class (Table 4.1) (we also include one in the unit example at the end of this chapter).

TABLE 4.1: Unit Title: X-Ray Animals by Kate Obukowicz

Day 1	Day 2	Day 3	Day 4	Day 5
Topic: Intro to unit	Topic: Native American Lore	Topic: Norval Morriseau	Topic: Art Criticism	Topic: Skit Day
Obj: 1.1 and 1.2	Obj: 2.1	Obj: 3.2	Obj: 2.2	Obj: 2.2
Event: Morrisseau Hook, discussion of the qualities of Morrisseau's paintings, review color theory and patterns, introduce X-ray painting assignment and go over rubric	Event: Listen to Native American lore, go to computer lab, internet worksheet	Event: Read articles on Norval Morriseau and work on art criticism worksheet	Event: Art criticism group time to plan out 3–5 min. animal skit	Event: Skits at the beginning of class, sketch three possible animal symbols compositions, assign journal write using a web for brainstorming on student's positive qualities and the connections to the animals that represent these qualities
Assessment: Formative observation of listening	Assessment: Formative observation of working independently on the computer and exit slip	DUE: Internet worksheet Assessment: Evaluation summative rubric for internet worksheet	Assessment: Formative observation of participation in groups	Assessment: Summative rubric for art criticism worksheet

Day 6	Day 7	Day 8	Day 9	Day 10
Topic: Color Theory	Topic: Work Day	Topic: Work Day	Topic: Work Day	Topic: Written Critiques
Obj: 1.1 and 2.1	Obj: 1.1 and1.2	Obj: 2.2	Obj: 2.2	Obj: 1.1 and 1.2
Event: Color theory and pattern worksheet given out and sketch animal symbol on paper bag	Event: Work on artwork and color theory and pattern worksheet	Event: Work on artwork	Event: Work on artwork	Event: Work on artwork, introduce written critique form
DUE: Journal write using a web for brainstorming on student's positive qualities and the connections to the animals that represent these qualities	Assessment: Formative observation of participation	DUE: Color and pattern worksheet and animal sketches ready for artwork Assign journal write on why they chose the animal they did	DUE: Journal writing on why they chose the animal they did	Assessment: Formative observation of participation
Assessment: Formative exit slip of journal write		Assessment: Formative exit slip of three sketches and summative rubric for color and pattern worksheet	Assessment: Formative exit slip of journal write	

continued overleaf . . .

TABLE 4.1: Unit Title: X-Ray Animals by Kate Obukowicz . . . *continued*

Day 11	Day 12	Day 13	Day 14	Day 15
Topic: Peer Critiques	Topic: Work Day	Topic: Work Day	Topic: Work Day	Topic: Sharing of Work
Obj: 3.1	Obj: 1.1 and 1.2	Obj: 1.1 and 1.2	Obj: 1.1 and 1.2	Obj: 2.2
Event: Work in progress, in-class written critiques on peer's artwork, introduce artist statement assignment	Event: Work on sketches and artwork	Event: Work on artwork	Event: Work on artwork	Event: Share the finished artwork and written artist statement with the class
DUE: In-class written critiques	Assessment: Formative observation of participation	DUE: Artist statement worksheet	Assessment: Formative observation of participation	DUE: Artwork and artist statement
Assessment: Formative observation of participation and summative rubric of written critiques		Assessment: Formative observation of participation		Assessment: Summative rubric for final explanation and rubric for the use of elements of art

6. *Daily Lesson Plans*

   Lesson plans provide the structure and instructional strategies for each day. While the lesson plan is used each day, practically speaking, the daily lesson plan itself might cover several days depending on the lesson. For example, a teacher might have one lesson plan that takes 3 days as students are researching in the library. Functionally, the lesson plans are expansions of the unit calendar, providing much more detail about each of the activities, content, assessment, and other particulars needed. The lesson plan is a document that takes many forms. They range from fully scripted comments by the teacher to a brief outline for the day. The lessons in a unit need to show in detail how each of the unit goals, essential questions, and targets are met.

7. *Assessments and Evaluations*

   What could you do to determine that your students learned what you planned for them? Unit plans should address the range of diagnostic, formative, and summative assessments you will use during the unit. Assessment principles were described in Chapter 3, and assessment will be considered throughout Part 2 of this book when each instructional strategy is examined. For purposes of planning a unit, assessments should be taken directly from the unit goals and targets. Assessments should also be sketched onto the unit calendar to match them with the content that the students are learning. When we work with pre-service teachers, we have them describe each assessment tool they will use, and explain why that tool is a valid way to determine whether their students have learned. Assessment is a recursive process, where the teacher and students are continually examining what they are learning and using this insight to help determine future instruction and learning. Assessments are not merely the "final unit test." Rather they occur throughout the unit, and planning for them ahead of time is crucial.[6]

8. *Materials and Resources*

    This includes both the sources used in writing your unit and the sources you will need as you write lesson plans, develop assessments, and generally prepare to help your students learn the unit content. Some resources will provide materials that only you will access, and some will be materials that your students will need. Examples of materials and resources include:

    - resources list/references:

        - print resources (books, texts, articles);
        - media resources (films, videos, recordings, computer software, internet);
        - community organizations, field trip ideas, businesses, guest speakers, or other potential resources;

    - materials list for each day of the unit (e.g., 15 Bunsen burners; 50 ml hydrochloric acid; 30 tennis balls; 30 copies of *The Crucible* handout, etc.);
    - graphic materials such as transparencies/overheads, charts, graphs, diagrams, photos, etc. (many of these will be developed with each lesson plan).

If you have not written a unit plan before, these eight components may seem daunting. Unit plans do require a significant amount of time and energy, but if they are written thoughtfully then the individual lessons are taught in a well-sequenced order that promotes student learning. It is important to develop the skills necessary to write a thoughtful unit. Pre-service teachers who have this ability are more likely to be successful during student teaching than those who do not (Harwood et al., 2001).

Although the calendar is important for the reasons we listed above, it is often the most revised section of a student teacher's unit plan. When you actually teach a lesson, you may find that it takes more or less time than you planned on the calendar. It is not uncommon for the calendar to be 2 days off after you finish teaching the first week of a unit! For example, compare the calendar below, presented as Table 4.2, with Table 4.1.

In addition, schools are using block schedules. Block schedules extend the class session. Conventionally, students meet in class for about 1 hour 5 days a week. In a block schedule, students may meet in class for 2 hours every other day for 90 minutes every day, or for some other combination of hours and days. By the end of the school year, any given course will have met for 180 hours, but you will not necessarily have met every day. Block schedules are varied and provide excellent opportunities to reduce the number of students you teach, integrate the curriculum, and meet for longer sessions and explore topics more in depth. For these reasons, we suggest that the lesson plans are outlined in the calendar (so you know the order the content will be learned, and so you can prepare materials and resources in advance), but the actual lesson plans are finalized about a week in advance.

TABLE 4.2 Unit Title: X-Ray Animals by Kate Obukowicz (Calendar Modified during Teaching)

Day 1	Day 2	Day 3	Day 4	Day 5
Topic: Intro to Unit	Topic: Native American Lore	Topic: Norval Morriseau	Topic: Art Criticism	Topic: Skit Day
Obj: 1.1 and 1.2	Obj: 2.1	Obj: 3.2	Obj: 2.2	Obj: 2.2
Event: Morrisseau Hook discussion of the qualities of Morrisseau's paintings, review color theory and patterns, introduce X-ray painting assignment and go over rubric	Event: Listen to Native American lore, go to computer lab, internet worksheet	Event: Read articles on Norval Morriseau and work on art criticism worksheet	Event: Art criticism group time to plan out 3–5 min. animal skit	Event: Skits at the beginning of class, sketch three possible animal symbols compositions, assign journal write using a web for brainstorming on student's positive qualities and the connections to the animals that represent these qualities
Assessment: Formative observation of listening	Assessment: Formative observation of working independently on the computer and exit slip	DUE: Internet worksheet	Assessment: Formative observation of participation in groups	Assessment: Summative rubric for art criticism worksheet
		Assessment: Evaluation summative rubric for internet worksheet	*Track meet—half of class gone; reformed groups and let those present begin planning*	*Half of skits presented—those missing yesterday formed groups— skits took longer than expected so finished one quarter of class*

Day 6	Day 7	Day 8	Day 9	Day 10
Topic: Color Theory	Topic: Work Day	Topic: Work Day	Topic: Work Day	Topic: Written Critiques
Obj: 1.1 and 2.1	Obj: 1.1 and 1.2	Obj: 2.2	Obj: 2.2	Obj: 1.1 and 1.2
Event: Color theory and pattern worksheet given out and sketch animal symbol on paper bag	Event: Work on artwork and color theory and pattern worksheet	Event: Work on artwork	Event: Work on artwork	Event: Work on artwork, introduce written critique form
	Assessment: Formative observation of participation	DUE: Color and pattern worksheet and animal sketches ready for artwork	DUE: Journal write on why they chose the animal they did	Assessment: Formative observation of participation
		Assign journal write on why they	Assessment: Formative exit slip of journal write	

continued . . .

TABLE 4.2 Unit Title: X-Ray Animals by Kate Obukowicz (Calendar Modified during Teaching)
        . . . *continued*

Day 6	Day 7	Day 8	Day 9	Day 10
DUE: Journal write using a web for brainstorming on student's positive qualities and the connections to the animals that represent these qualities Assessment: Formative exit slip of journal write *Finished skits— skits took longer than expected so did not begin color theory*	*Bumped this work day back one day and began color theory*	chose the animal they did Assessment: Formative exit slip of three sketches and summative rubric for color and pattern worksheet		

Day 11	Day 12	Day 13	Day 14	Day 15
Topic: Peer Critiques Obj: 3.1 Event: Work in progress, in-class written critiques on peer's artwork, introduce artist statement assignment DUE: In-class written critiques Assessment: Formative observation of participation and summative rubric of written critiques	Topic: Work Day Obj: 1.1 and 1.2 Event: Work on sketches and artwork Assessment: Formative observation of participation	Topic: Work Day Obj: 1.1 and 1.2 Event: Work on artwork DUE: Artist statement worksheet Assessment: Formative observation of participation	Topic: Work Day Obj: 1.1 and 1.2 Event: Work on artwork Assessment: Formative observation of participation	Topic: Sharing of Work Obj: 2.2 Event: Share with the class finished artwork and written artist statement DUE: Artwork and artist statement Assessment: Summative rubric for final explanation and rubric for the use of elements of art ***Finished unit on Day 16***

We include a portion of a unit plan on short stories that could be taught in a high school literature course. You can read how each component is applied to this particular content area.

Box 4.1 Unit Plan Example

READING AND WRITING SHORT STORIES

Tenth Grade English

Partial Overview and Rationale

This tenth grade short story unit is designed to examine this genre from two angles: Reading and writing. Students will read and listen to classical and contemporary short stories, and then they will explore together the literary elements of plot, character, and dialog. The purpose of these explorations is to discover how different authors used these elements, and for students to consider how they might use them in their own short stories. The second half of the unit will allow students the opportunity to compose their own short story.

In the process of reading and writing short stories, students will gain skills in the state standards of reading, writing, and communication. In addition, the unit is designed to help students enhance their appreciation and **comprehension** of literature, and their skill at writing in a particular genre. These are also fitting with state standards and recommendations by the National Council of Teachers of English. Editing will help students refine their understanding of writing styles and conventions.

Ideally, this unit will be taught toward the end of the school year, so students can apply their understanding of literary elements. This will allow an engaging opportunity for students to use the skills and abilities they have learned during the year. That said, this unit could fit anytime into the school year, as it is a new exploration into the short story genre, and it does not necessarily build on previous units "setting the stage" for the content explored. The unit is planned to use 15 1-hour class periods.

Possible Goals and Essential Questions

Goals

1. Students will explore the short story genre by reading, thinking critically, and discussing various authors' use of language, style, purpose, and perspective. (State St. L.A. 3)
2. Students will be able to recognize and understand the following literary elements of the short story: plot, character, dialog, and theme. (State St. L.A. 6)
3. Students will compose their own original short story and receive and provide feedbacks on their writing style and skill. (State St. L.A. 2)

Questions

1. How does an author's style and perspective affect the plot of a short story?
2. What are effective strategies for developing the characters in a short story?
3. What does an author do with critique and feedback about his or her writing?

Sample Targets

1. Upon completion of this unit, students will be able to identify the central conflict in a short story, describe the conflict in a journal entry, and support their thoughts with one example from the short story (this ties to Goal #1 and Question #2). Content target.
2. Upon completion of this unit, students will be able to identify all the elements of a short story on a written quiz (this ties to Goal #2). Content target.
3. Upon completion of this unit, students will be able to demonstrate their understanding of the writing process by composing their own short story that fully develops the characters in the story through the use of characterization and dialog (ties to Goal #3 and Question #2). Skill target.

Partial Outline of Content (the Scope of the Content in the Unit)

1. Introduction: Why do we read and write literature?

    a. explore cultural values
    b. cause an emotional response from the reader
    c. expose us to the world in new way.

2. Short Stories

    a. *Riki-Tiki-Tavi* by Rudyard Kipling
    b. *Hills Like White Elephants* by Ernest Hemingway
    c. *The Father* by Raymond Carver
    d. *Everyday Use* by Alice Walker
    e. etc.

3. Parts of plot

    a. exposition
    b. complication
    c. climax
    d. resolution
    e. plot of *Riki-Tiki-Tavi (RTT)*
    f. plot of the other short stories etc.

4. Writing short stories

    a. Review of the writing process

        i. prewriting
        ii. writing
        iii. revising
        iv. editing or peer editing
        v. publishing.

  b. Review of literary elements

      i.   plot
      ii.   theme
      iii. character
      iv.   dialog
      v.   etc.

Selected Days from Calendar

Day 1	Day 2	Day 6
Introduction	Lecture: Intro "Plot"	Concept Formation: "Theme"
What is a short story?	Exposition	Read *Everyday Use*
Begin reading Kipling's *RTT*	Complication	Groups: Discuss possible themes in *Everyday Use*
Homework: Finish Kipling	Journal: Elements of plot in *RTT*	Homework: Select and read a short story from the anthology by tomorrow
Day 9	**Day11**	**Day 15**
Review "plot," "dialog," "theme," and "character" for test on Day 10	Mini review: writing process	Student story sharing day!
Share with a partner the main characters in the story that the students are composing	Brainstorm session: Appropriate forms of feedback when peer editing	Peer and self-evaluation worksheet completed in class.
Finalize "setting" of their short story	Writer's workshop: Feedback on students' short story (at whatever stage of the writing process the students are in)	(Meets Target #2)
	Tell expectations and remind of deadlines for short story assignment (due Day 14)	

Daily Lesson Plans

These are described in the lesson plan section of this chapter, and expanded on extensively in Part 2 of the book.

Assessments and Evaluations

- Students will be awarded participation points for their journal responses, which include the examples of characters from their short story.
- Students will be formatively assessed on their understanding of plot, dialog, theme, and character on a test.
- Student's short story will be evaluated for having the elements of a short story. A rubric will delineate these elements.
- Students will provide brief evaluations of peers' short stories, focusing on the stories' plot, character development, and dialog.
- Students will write a self-evaluation of their own short story, focusing on their story's plot, character development, and dialog.

Materials and Resources

Graphic/overheads

- Hemingway background information
- Kipling background information
- character overhead
- theme overhead.

Print resources:

Atwell, N. (1998). *In the middle: New understandings about reading writing and learning*. Portsmouth, NH: Boynton/Cook.

Twenty great American short stories: www.americanliterature.com/SS/SSINDX.HTML

Classic short stories: Bibliography and on-line full text: www.classicshorts.com/bib.html

Materials list:

Day One: Thirty copies of *Riki-Tiki-Tavi*
            Thirty copies of Intro to short stories handout
etc.

Interdisciplinary Unit Plans

Interdisciplinary unit plans integrate topics from more than one course around a common theme or idea. These are being used more and more in middle schools and high schools, because they allow the students to identify connections across several content areas. Teachers develop interdisciplinary units to provide learners with opportunities to think about course content in relation to other courses (or disciplines). The above eight components are the same for an interdisciplinary unit. The unit is more complex because it takes into account more information and also because it needs to describe how the content areas will be integrated. The most common approach for developing interdisciplinary unit plans is to focus the plan around a common theme. Interdisciplinary units are built around a theme that multiple content areas could address. For example, "conflict" might be addressed in a world history course (studying causes of a war), in an English course (studying the use of conflict in plot development), in a mathematics course (learning to graph data related to population growth and conflict with natural resources), and in a biology course (examining the conflict of people and natural resources). These topics would be taught anyway, but the teachers agree to teach them at the same time to help students make connections across disciplines. Some schools promote "team teaching" where students share the same teachers during the course of a day. These teams often represent the core subject areas of mathematics, science, language arts/English, and social studies. This allows the teachers to know what was learned in the other classes related to the theme. Other subject areas (e.g., music, physical education, foreign language) are often electives for students. While they can join the thematic approach, it is more difficult to have the structure in place that ensures interdisciplinary units. We have placed several examples of interdisciplinary units on the companion website for this book.

MAKING IT WORK IN YOUR CONTENT AREA

Think about how you could develop each of the components of a unit plan for a course you hope to teach at a middle school or high school. Think of a topic that would require at least 2 weeks of curriculum, and has connections to state and national standards. Consider how you would answer these questions: What would you write for a unit introduction and rationale? What goals and essential questions would students meet or answer? What information or content targets would students meet? What skills will they develop? What social interactions will students form? What would a content outline for the unit include? How could you assess student learning during the unit? Some teachers teach interdisciplinary units, for example, language arts and social studies teachers' content might be combined for a "core" class at the middle school level. Discuss the above prompts with a student from another content area.

THE LESSON PLAN

A lesson plan is most commonly thought of as the daily plan. Though a lesson may span more than a day (e.g., a mock trial could take 3 days from start to finish), the plan specifies the "look and feel" of a day in your classroom. In this section, we will provide you with the components of a lesson plan, but we will return to lesson planning with each of the instructional strategies described in Part 2 of the book.

Components of a Lesson Plan

Many formats for lesson plans are available, and you will develop your own preference for a lesson plan as you prepare to teach. The following nine parts of a lesson are commonplace in the schools, and will provide structure to your class sessions:

1. lesson targets
2. language targets
3. assessments
4. initiation or start of lesson
5. teacher activities
6. student activities
7. closure
8. materials and resources
9. reflections.

Each is briefly described below.

1. *Lesson targets*

   These are the specific learning targets (some call these objectives) that you have for the lesson or day. They should meet the criteria described in Chapter 3, so we will not go into much detail about targets here. Consider including information, skill, and social interaction targets. Students should be able to accomplish these objectives by the end of the lesson. We suggest two to four targets for each day. You should plan to tell students the daily targets, because they need to know what they will be learning. Some teachers write the targets on the board so everyone can see them.

2. *Language targets*

   As we discussed in Chapter 1, all students need to be focused on improvement of academic language, not only the ELL students. These are specific targets related to the academic language focus you have for the lesson. These daily targets can be directed by the teacher or created democratically with the class. What language do *they* think they should be accountable for at the end of the day? This language can be added to a board or butcher paper at the front of the room each day to help create a unit language list. In each chapter of Part 2, we offer specific examples and ideas for addressing language targets for ELLs, and these can be easily modified to use for all students as they develop academic language.

3. *Assessments*

   These are closely tied to the targets. The assessments may be diagnostic, formative, or summative, depending on when the lesson will be taught in the unit. Formative and summative assessments occur near the end of a lesson, but planning a lesson with a "backward design" (Wiggins and McTighe, 2005) means that you think of the assessment before you plan the lesson's activities. This will ensure that the activities are authentic tasks that prepare students to demonstrate their learning on the assessments. Refer to the descriptions of assessment in Chapter 3.

4. *Initiation or start of the lesson*
   Another phrase for this is "**anticipatory set,**" or the manner by which you will help the students anticipate what will be happening for the day (some refer to this metaphorically as the "hook" by which you catch the students' attention). This could be a question, a poster, music, or even a short activity. The initiation of the lesson is important to consider because it helps the students focus on the lesson. The initiation should have some connection to the content of the lesson. For example, a biology lesson on the skeletal system might start with a skeleton in front of the class, or a video clip about splinting broken bones, or simply the number "206" written on the board (the number of bones in the human body). Another way to think about the initiation is this: Students will be coming to your classroom with many things in their minds. What can you do at the start of your lesson to gain their attention and help them start thinking about your course?

5. *Teacher activities*
   These are the activities you will do during the course of the lesson. By specifying your activities during the lesson, you can think about how you will present information, where you will stand, or the order in which you provide information to your students. These will be described in detail, when the logistics for each instructional strategy are outlined in Part 2 of this book. When planning what you will do to lead the class, consider student diversity, IEPs, student motivation, and classroom management. Many beginning teachers choose to write a script for difficult portions of their lessons. If they are concerned about placing students in groups, or about their lecture notes, scripts help them think through what they might say. We find that teachers rarely read these scripts, but the process of writing the script helps them think through the ideas and content. Scripts can easily be placed in the "teacher activities" section of the lesson. This section of your lesson plan is also a good place to estimate the amount of time each activity will take. At the end of the lesson, your estimation can be compared to the actual time needed. For example, how long will it take for the initiation? How long for a quiz? How long for introducing a concept?

6. *Student activities*
   The emphasis of any teaching activity is whether the students have learned. By specifying the student activities, you can plan for direct connections between the activities you are engaged in and the activities of your students. It allows you to be clear about your expectations for student behavior that will help maximize learning. For example, if the teacher activity is to present information in a PowerPoint presentation, then what should students be doing (taking notes? listening?). If you are facilitating a **simulation,** then what are the students to do during the simulation? Your estimation of minutes for student activities should also be included. Taken together, the minutes for teacher activities and the minutes for student activities must equal the amount of time allocated for your class session.

7. *Closure*
   Just as the initiation started the lesson, closure brings an end to the day. When planning the closure, consider how the lesson should be concluded, how the

content and skills stated in the learning targets can be reviewed to be sure students have learned them, or even a comment that will set the stage for the next class session. Sometimes, teachers close a lesson with a short quiz or other assessment activity. **Exit cards** can be used to determine what students learned. Students write down one or two main ideas that they learned during class, or they respond to a question from the teacher. As they leave the class they must turn in their work (it serves as a card that allows them to exit the classroom). If a lesson has good closure, the students feel confident about the teacher's management of the classroom. The clock should not signal the end of class, the end of the closing activity should. Some lessons need to continue into the next day. If that is the case, then the closure activity should help students see how the day's activities will be revisited the next day.

8. *Materials and resources*
    This list provides a quick overview of the materials needed for the day. You are safe to assume that your classroom will have paper, pencils, chalkboard/whiteboard, and an overhead. Materials and resources are those out of the norm items. This could include handout for your students, student copies of a novel, or other materials that you will use during the lesson. In addition, materials and resources include lecture notes, primary source artifacts, a DVD, or anything that you will need to successfully conduct the lesson. The material and resources will be specific to each lesson and should be similar to the list you created for the unit plan.

9. *Reflections*
    It is important to reflect on a lesson after you have taught it. In Chapter 2, we described differences among the "planned," "taught," "hidden", "null," and "learned" curricula. By including a space at the end of a lesson plan to reflect on your assessments and targets, you can determine what your students learned. If you planned something different than what they learned (e.g., if the content was too difficult and your students did not meet a learning target), then you can modify the lesson plan for the next day. Your reflections can also be directed by the four commonplaces. Consider the role of the teacher, the students, the content, and the milieu on student learning. It is important to reflect and comment on the lesson plan as well so that you can improve your lesson the next time you teach from it. This could be the next period, or it could be a year later when you teach from a unit plan again. Every time you teach a lesson it should improve because of the reflections. We will explore reflections more in the last section of this chapter.

The following lesson plan template (Box 4.2) is a sample that teachers might use. You can identify each of the components in the plan. In addition, this template includes a title, and names the unit from which the lesson comes.

Box 4.2   Sample Lesson Plan Template

TOPIC FOR THE LESSON: Date:

Grade Level/Course:

Unit:

Lesson Targets (information, skill, and social interaction targets):

1.

2.

3.

Language Targets:

Activities:

Initiation/Opening		Time
Teacher's Activities	Students' Activities	Time
Closure		Time

Assessment Tools:

Pre-Planning:

Materials/Resources:

☐ Camcorder   ☐ VCR/DVD   ☐ Worksheets   ☐ Computer Lab   ☐ Handouts

☐ Notes   ☐ Other (list items needed):

Instructional Strategies to be Used:

☐ Discovery Learning ☐ Cooperative Learning ☐ Simulations ☐ Debate

☐ Discussion ☐ Concept Formation ☐ Questioning ☐ Lecture ☐ Inquiry

☐ Other

Multiple Intelligences:

☐ Verbal/Linguistic ☐ Musical/Rhythmic ☐ Interpersonal

☐ Logical/Mathematical ☐ Intrapersonal ☐ Body/Kinesthetic

☐ Naturalist ☐ Visual/Spatial

Reflections/Notes:

_____

_____

The following lesson plan (Box 4.3) shows how the template might be "filled in" by a teacher prior to class:

Box 4.3 **Lesson Plan Example**

TOPIC FOR THE LESSON: *Probability–Unit Introduction*   Date: *Day 1*

Grade Level/Course: *Grades 10–12/Trigonometry*

Unit: *Probability*

Lesson Targets:

1. *In groups of four, students will show their understanding of events and sample space by listing all combinations of numbers that are possible when rolling two dice.*
2. *Students will demonstrate their understanding of "sample space" and "events" by successfully completing a discovery learning activity.*

Language Target: *Students will be able to appropriately use academic language vocabulary during class, such as: probability, integer, concept, and exhaustive as observed by the teacher.*

Activities:

Initiation/Opening *Start the class by shuffling a deck of cards.*	Time
Start talking about different cards, and in the middle "accidentally" scatter the cards onto the floor. Ask students how likely it would be if you closed your eyes and picked out the ten of hearts. Tell students that their answer requires thinking in terms of "probablility."	4 min

Teacher's Activities	Students Activities	Time
Have a student privately select a card from a complete deck, and have the class vote on the color of the card (red or black). Repeat with another student, but ask the class to vote on the suit of the card.	*Participate with answers and comments.*	
	Write notes in math notebook:	
	Sample Space *is an exhaustive list of all the possible outcomes of an experiment. Any subset of the Sample Space is an* Event.	5 min
Ask why color was easier than suit?		10 min
Lecture on EVENTS and SAMPLE SPACE as they relate to probability	*Groups of three. Each group has two dice. Write down all of the possible outcomes when someone roles one die, and when someone roles two dice. Share result with the class.*	10 min
Introduce group project and help students begin.		
Write on board the equation for counting elements in a list:		
n–m+1 (integers between n and m inclusive). Explore examples.	*Write equation in math notebook. Provide examples for the class to consider together.*	5 min
Small group discovery learning activity: List of questions about probability that use the equation. Groups will try to come up with answers quickly and accurately, and will apply the equation. Ask students to share how they came up with the solution for each question.	*Students work in groups, answer questions, and share with the class how they came up with the correct answers.*	10 min

Closure *Review the key concepts by asking questions to the students. Demonstrate the key ideas by using coins (heads and tails). Assign homework that reinforces the introduction to probability.*	Time
	6 min

Assessment Tools:

1. *Successful accomplishment of projects in group activities*
2. *Homework (to be assessed on Day 2)*

Pre-Planning:

Materials/Resources:

☐ Camcorder   ☐ VCR/DVD   ☑ Worksheets   ☐ Computer Lab   ☐ Handouts

☐ Notes   ☑ Other (list items needed):   *deck of cards*
list of questions for group project
homework assignment
two coins
ten pairs of dice

Instructional Strategies to be Used:

☑ Discovery Learning   ☐ Cooperative Learning   ☐ Simulations   ☐ Debate

☐ Discussion   ☐ Concept Formation   ☑ Questioning   ☑ Lecture   ☐ Inquiry

☐ Other

Multiple Intelligences:

☑ Verbal/Linguistic   ☐ Musical/Rhythmic   ☑ Interpersonal

☑ Logical/Mathematical   ☐ Intrapersonal   ☐ Body/Kinesthetic

☐ Naturalist   ☑ Visual/Spatial

Reflections/Notes:

_____

_____

_____

_____

_____

_____

_____

_____

_____

Pre-service teachers often notice that some veteran teachers do not have a lesson plan with them when they teach. It seems as though the in-service teacher simply guides the students without referring to the written document that is required of most student teachers. When you observe teachers, you may find this same thing. However, we encourage you to consider that the teachers you observe may not *have* a written lesson plan, but they do *use* a lesson plan. Their plans may not be written, but they have thought through the components of a lesson plan. If asked, these teachers could usually produce a written plan. The Interstate New Teacher Assessment and Support Consortium (INTASC)[7] and the ETS Praxis II and III[8] assessments require that beginning teachers thoughtfully consider and document lesson planning. Lesson plans provide documentation of what students should have learned in your classroom, and they document how your class is helping students learn content that is tied to district, state, and national content standards. During your student teaching and when you are observed as an in-service teacher you will be expected to write lesson plans. By having a written document, you will be able to ensure that you deliver all you planned, that you pace your lesson to maximize class time, that your lesson efficiently moves through the learning activities, and that you are able to assess student learning and determine when your targets have been met.

THE IMPORTANCE OF REFLECTION WHEN PLANNING

Under the section on lesson planning, we wrote that reflection is an important part of the plan. When teachers talk about reflecting, they often refer to what happened after a lesson has been taught. For that reason, we included the "reflection" component at the end of the lesson plan. Reflection is a progressive process where you consider what happened, good and bad, so your future actions are improved. In this section, we suggest that reflection and planning should take place during the lesson, after the students have left the classroom, and when planning future lessons. Killion and Todnem (1991) describe these three types of reflection as "**reflection-in-action**," "**reflection-on-action**," and "**refection-for-action**" (p. 15).

Reflection-in-action: This is the process of monitoring students' work and progress during the class meeting. This involves noting whether time spent on an activity needs to be extended or shortened based on your students' understanding and engagement. The lesson plan is what you take into the classroom, but reflection-in-action is a continual process of determining whether the plan optimizes student learning. The opposite of this type of reflection is being oblivious to the various phenomena occurring in the classroom. Consider how a history teacher might reflect in action: If you are teaching about an historical event and a student brings up a current event that is related and similar, you need to make a quick decision. Is the time needed to talk about the current event an appropriate step to take? You might quickly assess if you have enough time in class, and if the current event will make the historical event more relevant and understandable. You might gauge student interest to determine if they are interested in the current event. Finally, you might decide to spend the rest of class time exploring the current event, and revisit the historical event tomorrow. All of these thoughts are reflections while you are teaching. They impact the lesson at the moment, and will modify and adjust what your students are learning.

Reflection-on-action: This is defined by Killion and Todnem as "reflection on practice and on one's actions after the practice is completed" (1991, p. 15). This is the most well-known reflection. You ask yourself what went well? What needs improvement before the next period starts? What need to be changed before teaching this lesson again? This reflection is a powerful way to benefit from your successes and failures. For example, if you allocated 15 minutes to read a four-page article, and your students needed 30 minutes to read it, then you can plan for longer reading times in the future. As we mentioned earlier, using **Schwab's four commonplaces** (1973) is a helpful heuristic tool for reflecting on your practice. These questions could guide you to consider each of these commonplaces:

- How did the teacher impact student learning in today's lesson?
- How did the student(s) impact learning in today's lesson?
- Was the content learned? If not, was the content appropriate? Inappropriate? Too difficult? Too simple?
- How did the classroom environment help or hinder student learning in today's lesson?

Reflection-for-action: The third type of reflection that is important for teachers is reflection-for-action. Reflection-for-action is assumed in the previous two types of reflections, but singling it out helps teachers focus on how to make future teaching promote student learning. We assume that when you reflect while teaching, you will also determine what actions to take during class so that learning is enhanced. When you reflect at the end of a class, the intent is to improve the lesson. Reflection for action simply puts a label to this type of thinking. You reflect with an eye toward improving future actions. Teachers reflect on what they did, what their students learned, and gain insights from these reflections that will inform future actions. Figure 4.2 outlines this process.

Often reflections simply identify problems that occurred. Reflection, for example, might help you realize that shy students are not talking during discussions, or that laboratory supplies are being mishandled, or that the students lack note-taking strategies. The point of reflection, however, is to create meaning from your observations

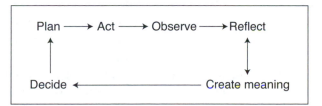

FIGURE 4.2 Planning for Improving Future Lessons
(Adapted from Killion and Todnem, 1997, p. 15).

and reflections, and develop strategies for your future teaching. Shy students may need more opportunities to share in small groups, rules and expectations for handling equipment may need to be restated, and students may need modeling from you about taking notes.

Many schools have adopted a "peer coach" model, where teachers observe one another and help reflect on a lesson. Another term for this is a "critical friend" model. The observations are not an evaluation of the teacher, but an opportunity to identify outcomes of your teaching and strategies to improve your teaching—and to ultimately improve your students' learning. It is an effective approach for pinpointing areas of your teaching. For example, Mr. Green and Ms. Lamb, two social studies teachers, have decided to adopt the **peer coaching model**. Ms. Lamb observes a world geography lesson in which students listen to Mr. Green's lecture on sweat shops in Third World countries. The students are then asked to create posters that display examples of sweat shops in various countries around the world.

Ms. Lamb has reflective prompts for Mr. Green that include:

- What did you do that effectively impacted student learning?
- How did the students positively or negatively impact learning in this lesson?
- Were your targets met in the lesson? How do you know? Did you ask too much from them? Too little?
- Was the environment of the classroom conducive to learning today? What could you have done about it?

Mr. Green and Ms. Lamb discuss the prompts on a teacher work day. Mr. Green indicates that the students seem to "go along" with the lesson but are not overly enthused. He is looking for a way to generate more enthusiasm and also to help students "do something more" with the information. From this discussion Mr. Green decides that a change in instructional strategy will improve the lesson. Next time he will try an inquiry approach (see Chapter 11) in which the students in teams are asked to create webquests (internet inquiry lessons) on child labor. He decides they could create their own specific questions to pursue such as "should you buy tennis shoes made by sweatshop labor?" After completing the webquest, students will have a classroom discussion to help them create a list of possible socially responsible actions related to what they have learned. At the end of their meeting, Mr. Green and Ms. Lamb agree upon a time to observe a U.S. history class of Ms. Green's the following week.

For more information on webquests and web inquiry projects, visit the book's companion website.

Action Research: **Action research** is another form of reflection that teachers use. Action research is often defined as a structured approach to examine and learn from your experience. For teachers, action research is a purposeful way to identify a phenomenon in your classroom, determine an approach for gaining insight into this phenomenon, and determine if the approach was effective. When a teacher engages in action research he or she intends to improve his or her practice. Teachers may do so to evaluate their use of particular instructional strategies, or to find a solution to a problem they are facing. It is usually carried out by the teacher, and not outside "researchers," and the results or findings of the research are usually limited to the classroom or school in which the teacher works. For example, if a group of students have difficulty comprehending a textbook, then a teacher may devise a strategy for improving comprehension, and develop an assessment tool for measuring the effectiveness of the strategy. This strategy should be based on research findings from other studies, but the teacher often will modify it to fit the needs of particular students in his or her classroom. After using the comprehension improvement strategy, the teacher then uses the assessment tool to determine the effectiveness of the strategy. In this manner, teachers are engaging in a type of research that relies on their reflections about a problem, and systematically analyzes strategies for solving the problem. This gives teachers greater confidence that their planning is going to have a positive impact on student learning. There is much more to action research than we include here; however, this introduction may be helpful as you consider the importance of reflective teaching.

CHAPTER REVIEW

- Four common classroom elements to consider while planning:

  - students
  - milieu
  - teacher
  - content.

- Writing Unit Plans that contain eight frequently used components:

  - overview and rationale
  - goals and essential questions
  - targets
  - outline of content (the scope of the content in the unit)
  - calendar (the sequence that students will learn the content)
  - daily lesson plans
  - assessments and evaluations.

- Lesson Planning:

  - lesson targets
  - language target
  - assessments
  - initiation or start of lesson
  - teacher activities
  - student activities
  - closure

- – materials and resources
- – reflections.

- Reflection to improve student learning:

  - – reflection in action
  - – reflection on action
  - – reflection for action
  - – action research is a term that describes various approaches to identify a phenomenon in your classroom, determine an approach for gaining insight into this phenomenon, and determining if the approach was effective.

NOTES

1 To access this data and other statistics related to education, visit the Center's website at http://nces.ed.gov/surveys (retrieved February 2012).
2 Virginia Department of Education (2002). *Algebra I standards of learning sample scope and sequence*. Richmond, VA.
3 Washington State Office of the Superintendent of Public Instruction (2003). *Social studies frameworks: Grades 9–12*. Olympia, WA.
4 This is from the Authentic Education website that provides information about professional development taken from Wiggins and McTighe's work. www.authenticeducation.org/ubd/ubd.lasso (retrieved May 2012).
5 As you read about each instructional strategy in Part 2, you will be much more knowledgeable about how selecting appropriate and effective activities will help you meet these objectives.
6 We encourage teachers to not have a test or examination on the last day of the unit. The traditional unit test is often used by teachers as the closing activity of the unit. Too often students will "cram for the test," and then move on to the next unit. If you want your students to take a test, we suggest having them take it a few days before the end of the unit. End the unit with a simulation, presentation, or some other activity that will allow students to think about the unit content at a high level. Their studying for the test not only will help them for that task but also will help them as they access the information during a more authentic activity at the end of the unit.
7 The INTASC Standards can be found at www.ccsso.org/projects/Interstate_New_Teacher_Assessment_and_Support_Consortium/.
8 The Praxis II exam is reviewed at www.ets.org/praxis (retrieved May 2012).

PART 2

Instructional Strategies

Lecture/Interactive Presentation

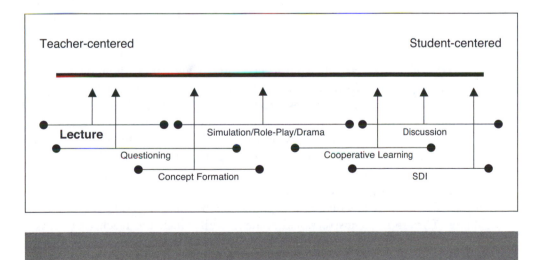

"I didn't think I was going to get out of that fireball alive . . . and after the crash landing off the coast . . . I thought I was going to drown because I can barely swim. When I saw the raft pop up I went for it . . . I sat in the raft for hours, just trying to remember our survival training . . . and all I could think of was my wife and how I wanted her to know that I would be okay . . . I just sat there, sweating, and praying . . . but then the Viet Cong patrol boat spotted us . . ." Marvin's voice trailed off to a whisper as he spoke to the wide-eyed class.

Mrs. Murphy knew she wanted to do something unique with her U.S. history unit on the Vietnam War, but she couldn't take a lot of time. She loved teaching about the impact of the Vietnam War on society but she had to be realistic with her time constraints. It was already getting late in the semester and so she decided to invite a guest speaker, Marvin Roth, to tell his story and hopefully, energize her class for a series of two to three lectures that could move the class quickly and efficiently through the unit. She hoped that maybe these lectures could even turn into question and answer sessions after students were introduced to this topic in this unique and interesting way. Some friends had referred her to Marvin and she had discussed his story with him about a month ago. He seemed like he had the engaging personality that the class would respond to and his story of being a prisoner of war (POW) in Vietnam was fascinating. Mrs. Murphy knew her class might need some help speaking up to ask Marvin questions so she encouraged them to come to class with one or two questions on a paper and to write down questions while he was speaking. She also had a collection of images that she posted around the room to help set the tone. So far, her plan seemed to be working.

OVERVIEW

We have all experienced lectures where the teacher was a gifted speaker and the students were enthralled by the stories, anecdotes, and details being delivered. Most of us have watched a teacher use pictures, artifacts, video, and/or other visual aids to highlight key points and help us understand the topic. Most of us have also been a student in a class where a guest speaker comes and tells about first-hand or real-life experiences. However, just as likely, we have all had teachers who talk and talk without much regard for their students. Lectures from those teachers and guest speakers become something to endure because they contain an excessive amount of facts, do not engage the students' minds or require much thinking, or are simply boring. We suggest that lecturing to students is overused, because it is easy for the teacher to control students and the content being presented. However, lecturing, be it from the teacher or a guest speaker, has the potential to be a powerful strategy that you need to consider using as part of your repertoire of instructional strategies.

Let us define a few terms that will help describe instructional strategies that fit in this chapter. *Lecture* is an instructional strategy with which the teacher presents a specified set of information to students. These presentations take a variety of forms that will be examined in this chapter. For lecture to be most effective, it should provide opportunities for interactions among students and with the teacher. That is why the title of this chapter includes *"interactive presentations."* Another category of teacher-centered and teacher-directed instructional strategies is often called **direct instruction**. The teacher directs students purposely to ensure that specific content or skills are learned. This is not the focus of this chapter, but we will describe its usefulness in the classroom later in this chapter.

DESCRIPTION OF LECTURE AND RESEARCH FINDINGS

Lectures and Presentations

We believe that lecturing offers several advantages and reasons for use in the class-room (Barbetta and Scaruppa, 1995; Heward, 2005). Lecturing allows the teacher to present a specific amount of information quickly and efficiently. It can be used with large or small groups and can be used in every content area. When lecturing, the teacher has a tremendous amount of control over how much emphasis will be placed on certain concepts, facts, and course content. Lecturing enables you to present important content that your students may not be able to learn on their own (e.g., a scientific theory that may be too complex for your students could be presented at the appropriate level of understanding during a lecture). During a lecture, you control the content and information, and use the class time to focus students' attention on topics that are particularly important or difficult to learn. Lectures allow you to highlight the key points that students may overlook or not understand during independent reading, working on the internet, or participating in project-based activities. In addition to the efficiency that lectures allow, if you are passionate and enthusiastic about the topic of the lecture then this excitement for the content is often passed on to the students. We have witnessed a teacher excite students about the Supreme Court through simple 35-minute lecture. She talked about the personal lives of the justices, the role of the Court in deciding issues that impact our daily lives, and how the Court serves as a check and balance to the President and Congress. More importantly, however, was her excitement about the topic. She was animated and enthusiastic, brought in personal stories about her interest in the Supreme Court, and generally exuded a passion about the topic. The students' excitement stemmed partly from the content of the lecture, and partly from the emotional, or affective, impact of the teacher's enthusiasm. Lecture is not always thought of as a strategy for exciting students about content, but we contend that it has tremendous potential for this.

As we mentioned earlier, students are often passive observers during lectures, because most lectures do not require students to participate beyond listening, note-taking, and asking periodic questions. This role is one that many students will enjoy, because it is non-threatening and easy. One of the most consistent and important educational research findings is that students who make frequent, relevant responses during a lesson learn more than students who are observers (Fisher and Berliner, 1985; Brophy and Good, 1986). This applies to any teacher-centered activity, and especially to lecture, because students are often not deeply engaged during them. Donald Bligh

(2000) suggests that teachers who only rely on lectures may encourage a superficial understanding of concepts and facts. As he states, lecture may "encourage a surface approach and discourage the very intellectual skills that . . . education claims to foster" (p. 61). Bligh suggests that teachers can help promote more active and "deeper" thinking by providing students with graphic organizers, by being aware of students' ability to sit attentively in class, by interjecting discussion questions into the lecture, and by teaching note-taking skills. We will describe how to engage students during lectures later in this chapter.

The lecture method presents other challenges for students and teachers. The teacher organizes the lecture as he or she believes is best, but this may not be the order that promotes understanding for every student. For example, a teacher may decide to lecture on the characters in a novel before describing the plot, but some students may want to have an overview of the storyline prior to knowing details about the characters. Even more prevalent is the teacher who "moves away from the topic" or "gets off track" from the main topic of the lecture. These occur from a student's question or simply because the teacher believes he has an interesting story to tell. While these are opportunities to make the lecture more engaging, students are often frustrated by these stories because they confuse what is important from what is tangential. Similar to this, students often have difficulty keeping track of lecture content in their notes. Even though some have identified strategies for effective note-taking (Saski et al., 1983), teachers seldom teach them to their students. Students are put in the difficult position of receiving a large amount of information without the skill of knowing how to record and remember it (Ormrod, 2006). Students with listening deficits, language difficulties, and writing disabilities are put at an even greater disadvantage (Sandock, 2000). It is a difficult task for all students to identify important lecture content and record it accurately and efficiently in their notes. A student with learning disabilities could easily write one idea in his notes and miss the next two key ideas in the process (Hughes and Suritsky, 1994). We mention these concerns not to discourage lectures, but to point out concerns with relying too heavily on this strategy.

Direct Instruction

Direct instruction is a term that is often synonymous with **"explicit teaching"**; the teacher explicitly or directly provides information or guides the students in learning step-by-step skills. Therefore, the instruction is controlled by you, and the students will look to you for guidance about what to do during the class. Direct instruction is a scripted and sequential approach for helping students learn by anticipating students' responses and questions. It allows students, often in special education programs, to master specific knowledge and skills that have been determined to be important (Engelmann and Carnine, 1991; Kame'enui et al., 1998). The learning theory of direct instruction contends that learning can be greatly accelerated if instruction is clear, removes opportunities for misinterpretations, and facilitates generalizations. As a result, students are placed in appropriate instructional groups based on their performance, and as they progress they are regrouped to stay with those similar to them. To a certain degree, direct instruction is based on behaviorism (you may want to refer to Chapter 1 to review this idea). Teachers clearly define the tasks they expect of their students; they explicitly teach concepts and skills by telling and demonstrating them to students, students respond with hand signals, choral responses, and other ways to demonstrate their understanding, and the teacher adjusts the lesson to accommodate student learning (Kame'enui et al., 1998). Siegfried Engelmann and colleagues have developed lessons for reading, writing, mathematics, social studies, and most other content areas that provide the specific scripts and learning objectives needed for a direct instruction lesson.

We mention direct instruction in a chapter about lecturing, because we can learn from its research about leading students. Rosenshine has suggested that ten general principles should be adhered to while writing an explicit or direct instruction lesson plans (Rosenshine, 1987, p. 76; Burden and Byrd, 2007, p. 168):

1. Provide students with a concise statement of goals.
2. Review prior knowledge that is necessary for the day's lesson.
3. Present new information in small chunks, and allow students the opportunity to practice frequently with the new information.
4. Clearly explain and describe new skills and information.
5. Provide opportunities for student practice with the skill or knowledge.
6. Check students' understanding by posing frequent questions.
7. Guide students during initial practice.
8. Provide feedback that includes praise and correction on their skill and/or understanding.
9. Provide independent practice through specific activities and seatwork exercises.
10. Continue practice until the skill or content is mastered.

Much of the research and ideas about direct instruction apply to lecture and several other instructional strategies. Chapter 6 on Questioning and Chapter 7 on Concept Formation both tap into some of the Rosenshine principles outlined above. Rather than providing step-by-step procedures for a direct instruction model, we chose to introduce it here, and then integrate particular principles of direct instruction into several instructional strategies to improve their effectiveness in promoting student learning.

If you would like to know more about direct instruction, and how it might assist students, you may want to examine some examples online at the National Institute for Direct Instruction (www.nifdi.org) or the Association for Direct Instruction (www.adihome.org) once you have identified specific needs of individual students in your class.

STEP-BY-STEP PROCEDURES FOR PLANNING AND IMPLEMENTING LECTURE

For the remaining sections of this chapter, we will focus on helping you consider how to plan and deliver effective lectures.

Teachers use different types of lectures to meet different purposes in the classroom. As mentioned above, lectures can be to the whole class, or to small groups of students.

Lectures might be short, as when briefly describing the expectations of a chemistry laboratory, or they may be lengthy, as when describing the lymph system in the human body. When planning to lecture, teachers are aware that they need to be prepared for being in front of their students. If you plan to lecture all period, and you teach five 1-hour periods, you need to be ready for 5 hours of talking. This has implications for your content knowledge as well as for your physical stamina and the attention span of your students. In this chapter, we examine five key steps for lecturing: (1) planning the topic outline; (2) planning the lecture; (3) student note-taking skills and preparing the audio/visuals; (4) delivering the lecture; and (5) concluding the lecture.

Step One: Planning the Topic Outline

We suggest that teachers write a topic outline for every lecture they will present. This outline allows the teacher to think about the sequence in which content should be presented, as well as the level of detail that the students need. If you are lecturing on the elements of fiction, then your topic outline might have the following key points of Freytag's dramatic arc in this order:

> characterization
> conflict and rising action
> climax
> falling action
> denouement/conclusion.

Each key point should then have definitions, minor points, and other details that will help students understand the facts and concepts. This topic outline also allows you to begin estimating how much time you want to spend talking about each point. Beginning teachers often find that a challenge of lecturing is deciding what to leave out. In the above example, you likely know examples of "conflict and rising action" from many different stories (and likely from many different genres of fiction). If you determine that you only have time to describe two conflicts, you will need to omit the many other excellent examples. That is difficult to do. You will often know more information about a topic than you will present in a lecture. The lecture should only include information that is critical for the students to know. This will help keep the lecture focused on important content.

Step Two: Planning the Lecture

After the content of the lecture has been outlined, you will create a lesson plan that has your lecture notes, opportunities for student interactions, and questions you want to ask during the lecture to assess student learning. Objectives for a lecture will usually fit two categories: content objectives and skill objectives (these were explained in detail in Chapter 3). Teachers usually highlight the key ideas of the topic outline in their notes, with additional information included to help remind them of the content. These key ideas will comprise the content objective(s) for the lesson. The skill objective of lectures will describe how students will develop their skills at synthesizing information or at note-taking. Examples of these two types of objectives for a planned lecture on the construction of the North American transcontinental railroad would be as follows:

- Students will be able to list in their notebooks two reasons why investors were willing to fund the building of the railroad (information objective).
- Students will demonstrate their ability to identify key ideas during a lecture by taking accurate notes about the building of the transcontinental railroad (skill objective).

Many teachers will write out an entire lecture (much like a speech) and then bring a script to class. These teachers either read this script to their students or refer to it when they talk about a particularly difficult topic. Scripting is a very effective strategy, because it lets you think through the content and the manner in which you will present it to your students. The process of writing the script helps you estimate the amount of time needed for the lecture, and provides you the opportunity to think through the words you will use to help make an idea clear and understandable. Of course, if you simply read your script to the class, you will not be engaging, dynamic, or flexible with the content. Opportunities to interact with the class will be further restricted if you only keep to the pre-written words. We suggest a balance by using scripts, when planning a lecture, and outlines or topical notes during the lecture. The scripts can be with your notes but not the main document you refer to. If you lose track of the topic, or need to present a very technical or difficult concept, then the script is available to read. The rest of the time, the script provides a backup for the detailed outline of the lecture topic.

Step Three: Student Note-Taking Skills and Preparing the Audio/Visuals

The third part of the lecture is to consider the audiovisual components that you will use. Students need help with taking notes and focusing on key concepts. You may want to provide copies of your topic outline to your students. This could provide them with a framework or outline on which they can add additional points and details gleaned from the lecture. If these notes are so detailed that you are merely repeating the information on the handout, then your students could be less engaged in your lecture. If you intend to write notes on the board, then we suggest planning out the key ideas that you want students to learn from the lecture to ensure that you write them accurately on the board. If your students have not had much practice taking notes, then they will need explicit directions from you. Students will record in their notes whatever you put on the board, overhead, or in computer notes, so these notes need to be planned thoughtfully and written logically. Provide students with a format for recording notes, and tell them how to record their ideas. For example, you can tell them, "This is the main idea," or, "This is a supporting point under the main idea that you just put in your notes." An outline format is most common, but teachers might also use a web format, such as Figure 5.1.

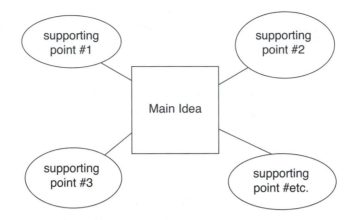

FIGURE 5.1: Sample "Outline Web" of Main Ideas

Students might also find it useful to have a blank or partially completed web to serve as an "advance organizer." Advance or graphic organizers can be used with any instructional strategy to help students record or organize new information. If students have prior knowledge about a topic, then they can add new information to it. If students have little prior knowledge, then they may not know how to organize or think about new information. Graphic organizers serve that purpose. Have you used advance organizers as a student? Have you seen teachers use them with students? What were some of the forms of graphic/advanced organizers that you have observed?

If you will be using audio or video clips, then put a comment in your lecture notes where you want to present those to the students and your purpose for using them (e.g., if you are going to play audio of a protestor who is afraid of a group of policemen, you could tell students, "Please listen to the fear in the voice of this civil rights protestor").

Step Four: Delivering the Lecture

Effective teachers use an introduction or hook to focus the students on the content and help students to engage with the content. This hook activity is important because it sets the stage for the ensuing content. These activities will vary greatly depending on your personality, the make-up of your classroom, and the content being examined. We have seen teachers use hooks such as playing a song, reading a poem, showing a video clip, or viewing a webcam. We have also watched teachers dress-up in a costume, display an old artifact or primary source document, and have a skeleton set up in front of the classroom. In addition to generating student interest, teachers may also introduce a lecture with a brief overview of the content they will examine, a statement of the learning objectives for the day, and the purpose of the day's lesson.

Keep the following things in mind, when delivering a lecture. As an instructor, you wish to minimize student distractions and maximize student learning. Clearly talk through your notes or scripts. Pace and pause to engage students' interest and allow them to note important points. Most of the hard work will have been done when preparing the lecture outline and lesson plan. The delivery is now your verbal presentation of these notes. Be sure your voice is clear, that you clearly enunciate your words, and that your mannerisms help your lecture. For example, standing motionless behind the lectern will make you appear separated or nervous. Move and incorporate hand gestures to emphasize particular points and key ideas.

In addition to presenting the information accurately and enthusiastically, the single most important element of lecturing is to be acutely aware of your students. Throughout the lecture, look to see if they are engaged and attending (this will be evident through body language, eye contact, note-taking, and other behaviors). Look to see if they are keeping up with you in their notes. When we work with teachers, we encourage them to pause and look at their students' notes to see how closely they align with the teacher's lecture notes. If students are not following, then you need to revisit the content, slow down, or remember who is having difficulty and provide more one-on-one attention after the lecture. It will be rare that all of your students will be able to learn the same amount of information from a lecture. Attention deficits, English language skills, or even the weather outside influence students' learning during a lecture—especially when you are lecturing to the whole class. You must closely monitor students and assess their learning so that you are able to follow-up with individuals who do not learn from your lecture.

This close monitoring of students also provides you with insight about student note-taking skills. It is very important to tell students that they should "include this in your notes," or "write a synopsis of what I just said in your notes," or to give other prompts to help students' note-taking skills. While students are learning academic content from your lecture, you will also need to help them learn the skills of synthesizing information, writing notes, asking questions for clarification, and other advanced thinking skills.

Effective teachers do not merely present; they help students understand what they are presenting. This is more important when students have had fewer opportunities to take notes during a lecture. Therefore, middle school students will need more time spent on these thinking skills than most high school students. As a teacher, the more time you spend on these skills, the less time you will have for lecturing on content. However, by contextualizing note-taking skills into your lecture, you will better prepare the students to learn how best to receive information from a lecture. Periodic questions, or checks of students' understanding should also be used, while you deliver the lecture (questioning is addressed more in Chapter 6). These questions should focus on specifics of your topic outline and not be generic. For example, if you just finished describing different cloud formations, a question such as "Could you explain the differences between a cumulous and stratus cloud?" is more effective and focused than "Do you have any questions about clouds?"

Step Five: Concluding the Lecture

Typically, the conclusion of a lecture will involve a review of the main points that you want your students to remember. You also should remind them of the overall purpose of the lecture. The conclusion is also an excellent place to tell students how the information from the lecture will connect with the next day's class. For example, if an earth science teacher just finished a lecture on volcanoes, he or she may end the lecture by telling students:

> This lecture provided you with a general understanding of how a volcano erupts. Look over your notes to be sure you have the following six points listed (teacher lists the six points). You should also have a few details that explain each point in more detail. Does anyone need help with these six points? The information we explored today will prepare us for tomorrow when we look at Mt. St. Helens in Washington State.

We also encourage teachers to collect students' notes at the end of class, or to have students complete "**exit cards**." Exit cards are documents that your students must have ready when they leave the class and if they query about specific content (e.g., name two characteristics of human bones) and not general questions (e.g., name two new ideas from today's lecture), then exit cards become a quick assessment of student learning. These could be lecture notes from the day, answers on a note card (e.g., "Write the titles of the five themes of geography that I described to you"), verbal responses ("As you leave today, tell me one metaphor, simile, and hyberbole), or any other concise strategy for checking students' understanding of specific content from lecture. Assessments will be addressed later in this chapter.

The following lecture/presentation planning chart provides a helpful format for planning lectures. The right column is useful for you to write your responses to the prompts in the left column. We adapted this chart from work by Wingert (2001) and from the University of Minnesota's Center for Teaching and Learning Services (http://www1.umn.edu/ohr/teachlearn/tutorials/lectures/planning.html):

BEGINNING THE LECTURE/PRESENTATION	
What would you like your students to do/know by the end of your presentation? (Short-term objective.)	
How will you share your objective/goal (including how and why it is important) with your students?	
Introduction: (Think of an overview, anecdote, question, problem/case study, question, demonstration, quotation, relevant fact/statistic)	
DELIVERING THE LECTURE/PRESENTATION	
First segment of information (10–15 minutes):	
List the main points you will present:	
List the audiovisual aids you will use (handouts, PowerPoint presentation, video, overhead projections, notes on chalkboard, etc.):	

Active processing/participation activity: (What might students do to help them think about the content? Share with a neighbor? Take a brief quiz? Participate in a question/answer session?)	
Second segment of information (10–15 minutes):	
List the main points you will present:	
List the audiovisual aids you will use (handouts, PowerPoint presentation, video, overhead projections, notes on chalkboard, etc.):	
Active processing/participation activity: (What might students do to help them think about the content? Share with a neighbor? Take a brief quiz? Participate in a question/answer session?)	
If applicable, third segment of information (10–15 minutes):	
List the main points you will present:	
List audio/visual aids you will use (handouts, PowerPoint, video, overheads, notes on board, etc.):	
Active processing/participation activity: (What might students do to help them think about the content? Share with a neighbor? Take a brief quiz? Participate in a question/answer session?)	
ENDING YOUR LECTURE/PRESENTATION	
Wrap-up: (How will you know students have learned/mastered what you intended [refer to the assessment section of this chapter]?)	

To see a teacher using a lecture teaching strategy in the classroom, visit the companion website.

LOGISTICAL CONCERNS, INCLUDING BENEFITS AND OBSTACLES

Many of the courses you have taken in college have utilized lectures. A "lecture hall" at a university is a very common structure. Rooms designed for lectures usually have rows of desks or tables that face the front, a screen for a projection unit, chalkboards or whiteboards, and a podium or table for the speaker's notes, computer, or other equipment. These rooms usually seat a large number of students. Thinking about the structure of these rooms reveals much about the lecture strategy: the teacher is the focus of attention, students do not interact much with one another, a large number of people can hear the lecture without much opportunity to interact with the teacher, and audio/visual aids help the presentation.

When you lecture to your future high school or middle school students, you will be in a classroom, not a lecture hall. You will also be talking to a smaller number of students who do not necessarily have the needed note-taking skills or discipline to concentrate during a lecture. As a result, several logistical considerations will help your lectures. The setting of the classroom is an important initial consideration. Determine if all your students can see you and can see your visual aids. Students who have auditory or visual impairments should be close enough to see and hear you.

The following eight recommendations can help make your lectures more effective. They have been adapted from assessments of effective teaching conducted by Cashin (1990, pp. 60–61):

1. *Fit the lecture to the audience*

   Be sure that the words you use, the examples with which you illustrate your ideas, and the content of the lecture will engage your students. Middle school students will need direction from you about what to focus on during the lecture, while high school students may have had more experience with lectures. With any age student, recognize that you will be more active than your students during a lecture, so you must be sensitive to their attention spans. There is not an ideal length for a lecture, but the more concise you can be, the better.

2. *Focus your topic—remember that you cannot cover everything in one lecture*

   Focus on the key ideas, skills, facts, and/or principles that your students will use after the lecture. Do not think of the lecture as an end in itself, but as a lesson that helps students gain information that they will use during other activities.

3. *Organize your points for clarity*

   The topic outline should help you decide the best order for presenting the main points of the lecture. This order should move from less-complex to more-complex ideas so that students are able to build upon their prior knowledge. Hand out notes or a graphic organizer that will help students follow along during your lecture.

4. *Select appropriate examples or illustrations*

   As mentioned above, these should help the students understand the information. Therefore, the examples and illustrations should be appropriate for your students' age, experience, and interests.

5. *Present more than one side of an issue and be sensitive to other perspectives*

   Since you are leading the class during a lecture, your students are a captive audience. By that we mean that they cannot leave (in general, students will not often question a teacher's authority, and the teacher must be aware of this power dynamic). As a result, the teacher must be aware of different opinions, experiences, and ideas that students could bring to the classroom. If an issue is controversial, or multifaceted, then you need to consider how to represent multiple perspectives during your lecture.

6. *Be aware of your audience—notice their feedback*

   As mentioned earlier, you need to be acutely aware of your students. Watch them during the lecture for nonverbal feedback that will help you know their interest level, degree of engagement, and their understanding of the topics.

7. *Repeat points when necessary*

   Students benefit from your overemphasis of key ideas and points and from your willingness to explain a complex topic multiple times.

8. *Be enthusiastic*

   You don't have to be an entertainer but you should be excited by your topic. If you lack enthusiasm for the topics, students will notice. However, if you model enthusiasm, then students will likely be more interested in the topics examined.

CLASSROOM MANAGEMENT AND MOTIVATION

During a lecture, the students' attention will be up front and on you (or on the audio/visual aid you are using). Lectures do not require students to talk, unless you ask for their insight, ideas, and questions. As a result, your expectations for them to listen must be very clear. Many beginning teachers try to lecture when their students are talking quietly, looking about the room, or simply not paying attention. When you are lecturing, you must require that the classroom is quiet, that the students are not distracting one another, and that the learning environment is conducive to listening and taking notes. This means that if several students are talking, you will request them to stop. If the sunshine is making a glare on the board, then you will close the blinds. If students do not have paper and pencil with which to take notes, then you will either provide that to them or have them get the needed materials.

Your proximity, or location, during the lecture will help with many management issues. For example, if two students are talking to each other during the lecture, then you can move next to them as you talk. Your physical presence will often make the students pay closer attention. If you cannot move next to a student, then stop the lecture and ask the students to please stop and listen (e.g., "I need you two to listen because your talking is distracting me and others who are trying to learn from the lecture"). If students continue to talk, then you may need to rearrange seating assignments. As we mentioned in Chapter 1, however, discipline problems this severe usually reveal a relationship problem and may require more long-term interactions with the student(s). The bottom line during a lecture, however, is that the classroom needs to be quiet and focused for all students to have opportunities to hear what you have to say.

Lecture is a teacher-centered activity. As such you, the teacher, will need to be sure you are ready to "lead the class." Students should clearly understand your expectations of them during the lecture. Possible expectations include:

- bringing pencil and paper to class;
- reading any assigned texts;
- listening to the teacher;
- actively taking notes;
- raising hands when questions arise.

You should also set high expectations for yourself. If you prepare your notes and are knowledgeable about your lecture topic, move the lesson along at a pace that keeps the students engaged, continually monitor your students' level of engagement (e.g., Are they actively taking notes? Gazing out the window? etc.), and show enthusiasm and excitement about the topic, then you will experience fewer management and discipline concerns.

Student motivation during lecture is a significant issue to consider. Many students welcome lectures because it is an opportunity for the teacher to tell them what they need to know for the test. These students are motivated extrinsically. Thinking about course content is limited to repeating what they heard from a lecture or from assigned readings. However, look for opportunities to communicate to the students that a lecture is not merely presenting information for a test. Inform students why you are lecturing to them so that they know the purpose of the lecture. If you are planning to lecture about the safety procedures in the science laboratory, be sure that your students know why this information is important and how it will be used in the future. Similarly, if a Spanish teacher is lecturing on Mexican holidays, the content will seem more relevant if he or she also explains why this content will help them understand Spanish language and culture that will be learned in the coming units. In each of these cases, the students see the relevancy of the lecture beyond preparation for a test.

During a lecture, the teacher is active. Students need to also recognize that they should also be actively listening, thinking, and taking notes. Hearing a lecture can be a very passive activity for students, unless you help them engage with the content. For most adolescents, however, "engaging with the content" is too abstract. Instead, the teacher can facilitate this by asking the students to engage in higher-order thinking tasks with the lecture content. For example, they can compare and contrast important information, predict outcomes to events, or write a personal reflection paper about new facts they learned during the lecture. Another approach for motivating students to remain engaged during lectures is to consider whether or not their own experiences might add to the lecture. By knowing your students' background, you are in a position to help incorporate their ideas and stories into your lecture. This could occur as you plan the lecture, or if you allow students to interject their ideas while you lecture. Either approach will provide a greater sense of ownership by the students, which often increases their motivation to learn and helps you manage the learning environment.

An old adage with teachers is to change the instructional mode every 20 minutes. We have heard some teachers tell that the length of a lecture in minutes should not exceed the age of the student. For example, middle schoolers will only be attentive for 11–15 minutes. While there is little research to support or refute this claim, most teachers have ample anecdotal evidence that students struggle to sit for an entire period. Students might engage in and learn from your lectures if you limit them to half of a class period, or intersperse other activities. Later, in Chapter 6, we will consider questioning strategies, and in Chapter 10 we will describe discussion. In the assessment section below, we explain about the **"think-pair-share"** strategy. These all may help you to engage the students during the lecture.

REALITY CHECK

When you see teachers lecturing, what are their topics?

What are students doing during the lecture? Are they taking notes or using advance organizers?

How long are the lectures? What other activities does the teacher intersperse during the lecture? Does this seem to be effective in helping the students learn? You may want to review the video of a lecture at our companion website.

APPROPRIATE ASSESSMENT TECHNIQUES TO USE WITH LECTURE

Lecture presents students with information but does not allow students many opportunities to apply the information. As we mentioned earlier in the chapter, this is a criticism of lecture. The relatively passive role of the students also has implications on how you assess student learning. Consider the following example:

A middle school art has teacher just finished a lecture on several shading techniques that artists use when drawing portraits. Her lecture was full of examples of many artists' work, detailed notes, and her own demonstrations of several techniques. Students listened at their desks, took notes, and asked periodic questions about the techniques.

When this teacher is going to assess her students' understanding of the information presented in her lecture, she must take into consideration the following ideas:

- What content did the students learn?
- How might they show an understanding of the content that is consistent with how they learned it?

These questions are useful for any teacher to consider when preparing to assess students' learning after a lecture. The general answer to the first question is that students were to have learned the content described in the "topic outline" of the lecture. In the above example, the students learned about shading techniques. The second question, however, is a bit trickier. The teacher will only be able to assess students' understanding of the topic outline by using assessments that are consistent with the lecture technique. A valid assessment technique for the art teacher would be for students to write on a piece of paper two techniques that create depth and shading to a portrait. An inappropriate assessment would be for the students to demonstrate their skill at shading. The lecture presented the facts and skill required, but it did not allow for students to use or apply the facts or skills. Assessments after a lecture, therefore, should be limited to the content presented in the lecture. The following assessments are valid and reliable techniques for determining what students learned from a lecture:

Exit Cards

These were described in the "Step-by-Step Procedure" section above. In brief, an exit card is as assessment of the key points a student learned from the lecture. These are usually short and concise assessments (1–5 minutes of writing). If you collect students' notes, then you can identify what they wrote down, but you cannot assess what they learned. Having students write what they learned will be a more accurate assessment.

Journal of Facts and Feelings

We encourage students to record a "facts and feelings" section in their notes. This can also be a separate journal that the students keep. Students record new facts and ideas that they learned during the lecture, and then describe their feelings and questions about these new facts. This allows the teacher to assess students' thinking and understanding of the information presented during a lecture. The following is an example from a facts and feelings section of a student's notes:

- Fact: I never knew that Lewis and Clark were leaders of an official Army Corp sent by Jefferson.
- Feelings: This makes the Lewis and Clark expedition seem more official, because they were on government business. I can imagine that many were excited to hear about what they found. I also wonder if this was the beginning of confrontations between the U.S. government and Native Americans.

The facts and feelings entry is also useful for having students write what they consider to be the most confusing or complicated part of a lecture. This often allows you to determine if a portion of your lecture was unclear. This is also a useful technique when students complete a reading assignment, or listen to a presentation.

Think-Pair-Share

This assessment technique is an informal strategy. The teacher provides students with a prompt or question from the lecture, then asks the students to "think about the question, pair with a partner, and share your answers." These questions should be about the content of the lecture, but they can push the students to apply the content to other situations. For example, after a mathematics teacher finished a brief lecture on Pythagoras' Theorem, she might ask her students to "think of how this theorem is used in our community." The students would then pair and share. The teacher can listen to the pairs' comments, ask students to share their comments after they share with their partner, or ask students to write what they shared on a piece of paper.

Recall of Specific Information

Students can be given a writing assignment where they must recall specific facts and details from a lecture. These could take the form of a true–false test, fill-in-the-blank quiz, or essay examinations, but they can also be written or verbal explanations of information presented during the lecture. These recalls are not necessarily memorization tasks. Students could be asked to compare and contrast information learned during the lecture with information they learned in previous class session or readings.

The key point to remember is that if the students have learned the content, they should be able to use and apply it in a variety of tasks. However, if the assessment requires skill or knowledge that they have not learned from the lecture, then the assessment is an invalid measure of what they have learned. Consider the following assessments following a lecture on literary devices:

* Finish this sentence so it uses alliteration: "The snake _____ silently through the grass."
* Why might a writer use similes?
* What is a recent story you read that uses symbolism?
* Write a short poem using metaphors and similes.

The first three examples are valid assessments, because all the information was presented in the lecture. The fourth requires writing skills that need practice and could not be addressed in a lecture—this should not be used as an assessment of what students learned. Assessments that follow a lecture determine student learning, and they provide insight into how effectively you presented the information. If all students are confused about the same information, then you should consider how you revisit that information to promote their learning.

ENHANCING STUDENT LEARNING WITH TECHNOLOGY

PowerPoint or Powerpointless?

We believe technology can be a wonderful enhancement to lecture. YouTube videos of exploding volcanoes, mento-propelled rockets, an individual stopping a tank in Tiananmen Square, or other film clips used as hooks can be excellent. Digital models or 3D imaging for atomic structures, web-based maps for current or historical events, and other imagery have been used to assist with focusing the students on lecture topics in an interesting way. With that said, the most commonly used computer technology for organizing lectures has been the presentation software PowerPoint (although others are available, see Google Docs, for example). Most university students have had, or will soon have, a course on creating good "PowerPoints." This software can be a very useful organizer of the main points of a lecture along with embedded video, maps, models, graphs, and other visuals. If however, using PowerPoint leads to an endless listing of bulleted points or even worse, full pages of text that the class reads while the teacher is talking about something else, well, what is the point? The question to ask while using software with a lecture is "what value is added?" Below is a listing of ideas to help you with creating PowerPoint presentations that add value to your lecture:

1. *Why are you talking?* Prepare your lecture first and then create the PowerPoint to aid your lecture points instead of creating the PowerPoint and then adjusting your lecture to fit the visuals you have found.
2. *Stop, Drop, and Roll.* Well, at least pause once in a while, and if you really want to express yourself and add interest, you probably could drop and roll. Just because you have plenty of great visuals does not mean you forget about public speaking skills. Pause to make a point, add emphasis, or for dramatic effect. Remember to use vocal variety (pitch, pace, volume) to avoid the monotone drone. It isn't about the flashy PowerPoint you made; it is about your message.
3. *Techno no-nos.* Don't put too much text on each slide, include too many flying objects that distract, use text color that is similar to the background, have a busy background, or use text size that is smaller than 18 pt. When teaching about effective slide design, we like to use examples. A good layout example that includes non-examples can be found at the International Association of Science and Technology Education website www.iasted.org/conferences/formatting/presentations-tips.ppt.
4. *Visualize.* Using visuals is probably the most important reason to use PowerPoint. We think that every slide could have a visual of some sort and that the best slides add visual meaning to support you, the speaker. This could be a photo, graph, chart, symbol, or some other image that informs that portion of your lecture. The best slides will be those that are of little use to someone that misses your narration. It may even be appropriate to print an outline of your notes and use slides that have very little text whatsoever. If you choose to use video, embed the footage in the slide if possible so that you are not internet-dependent.
5. *Keep it simple.* Keep it simple, keep it simple. If you spent too much time tweaking your PowerPoint, you have not spent enough time on the content of your lecture. PowerPoint glitz is passé and distracting. Use impact visuals with lots of white space that aren't flying all over the place.

In the following section, you will probably notice that some of the conversation around the benefits of using PowerPoint also apply to assisting ELLs in your class.

MAKING A LESSON MORE MEANINGFUL FOR ELLs[1]

Lecture can be an effective way to assist ELLs. Oftentimes, students who have recently immigrated feel more comfortable with the teacher-centered model. In their culture, many of our student-centered approaches may either be unheard of or counter to cultural norms. In addition, as you read in Chapter 1, most students acquiring a new language go through a period of adjustment in which they prefer to listen rather than create language. When using this strategy, consider ways you can adapt for the ELLs in the class:

- Activate prior schemata: Make connections to the students' background knowledge, or provide contextual information to help provide that background:

  - Have you ever . . . What do you remember about . . .
  - I remember when I was in high school classes and the teacher would lecture . . .
  - Look at the pictures on the wall with a partner. Write down what you think the picture is about, or a question you have about the picture.

- Provide the objective: Let them know at the start what you want them to be able to do at the end of the lecture that they couldn't do at the beginning:

  - At the end of today's lecture I want you to be able to list six ways to help students retain new information and ideas from your lecture.

- Provide a graphic organizer to help them take notes and categorize what they are hearing (examples of these are available on the companion website):

  - a partially filled in outline (the amount left to be filled in can be modified for different students within the same class—those with the strongest listening skills can have more blanks);
  - an information grid with headings—students fill in the appropriate cells;
  - a flow chart showing cause and effect to fill in;
  - Cornell note-taking technique, using frequent discussion times to identify what "key words" can go in the review column.

- Use visuals to clarify what you are talking about—it helps students who may not understand every word or follow along and make logical guesses about the vocabulary they are hearing.

  - Visuals don't have to be fancy. Learn to use a document camera effectively, write important points on the board when you say them.
  - Imagine (or actually try by videoing) listening to a recording of your lecture with the sound off. How much about the topic would the viewer be able to grasp?

- Interrupt your lecture every 10 minutes and ask a question (which you've prepared in advance) that pairs can quickly discuss for 30 seconds to 2 minutes:

- What are the three reasons for . . . that I just mentioned?
- How would you feel if you were in the situation I just mentioned?
- Explain to your partner how . . . and . . . are different.

• Be aware of your speech.

- Second language learners need to see your face and hear your words.
- Don't speak slowly or overly loudly—but *do* enunciate.
- Avoid slang or sayings, unless you "sandwich" them with more spoken language.
- Use academic language; students need to hear it and learn it. *But* be sure to "sandwich" this academic language with brief spoken language versions. For example, "We will write an autobiography, writing about you, autobiography."

We also believe that all of us are learning to speak, understand, and use English more effectively. As a result, we are all learning English. Each student in your classroom will benefit from the adaptations described above. Even though these are proven methods to assist ELLs, they are also highly effective modifications and approaches for helping students who speak English as their primary or only language, and we suggest incorporating them into your teaching.

GUIDELINES FOR DECIDING IF A LECTURE IS APPROPRIATE FOR THE CONTENT OF A LESSON

The lecture is a valuable part of a teacher's instructional repertoire, if it is not overused and if it is not used when other methods would be more effective. When lecturing to your students, you must have solid knowledge of the content, speak clearly, highlight main points and key concepts, engage students with periodic questions, and monitor student note-taking and learning. Since lecturing is a teacher-centered strategy, students can easily become passive learners when you lecture to them. The concern over this is that students will not stay engaged in the topic and their attention span will be limited. Good and Brophy (2003, p. 371) have summarized suggested criteria that we believe would provide an excellent set of guidelines for determining when to use lecture:

• When the objective is to present information that is not readily available from another source, is original, or must be integrated from different sources.
• When the material must be organized and presented in a particular way.
• When it is necessary to arouse interest in the subject.
• When it is necessary to introduce a topic before students read about it on their own or to provide instructions about a task.
• When the information needs to be summarized or synthesized, for example, following a discussion or inquiry project.
• When curriculum materials need updating or elaborating.
• When the teacher wants to present alternative point of view or to clarify issues in preparation for discussion.

- When the teachers want to provide supplementary explanations or material that students may have difficulty learning on their own.

Many students may not readily learn content that they hear during a lecture, and it is widely accepted at all levels of education that content presented during a lecture is rapidly forgotten by students (Bligh, 2000; Edwards et al., 2001). This is often called the "curve of forgetting"; Cross found that one week after a lecture, students recalled only 17% of the information (1986). This percentage is higher if students use the information after a lecture (in ways we describe earlier in the chapter). Still, this forgetfulness is a concern, and we believe that lecture is too often the default approach for teaching. When students' primary language is not the same as the language used for the lecture, and when students have learning difficulties that are exacerbated when listening to someone speak, lecture is not an appropriate strategy. However, lecture is one of many powerful instructional strategies. Use it when you have confidence that it will enhance student learning more than other instructional strategies.

A NOTE ABOUT PRESENTATIONS FROM GUEST SPEAKERS AND STORYTELLERS

Guest speakers can provide your students with excellent insights and perspectives. Imagine the information that your students might learn from speakers such as a medical doctor, attorney, therapist, artist, writer, athlete, historian, or politician. Some community organizations have a speakers' bureau that you can contact to line up a speaker for your class. If the speaker has presented to adolescents before, he or she may have a preplanned series of activities for your students. Usually, however, a speaker will come to your class and lecture or present information. Herein is the caveat for inviting guest speakers. You will take many courses in preparation for becoming a middle school or high school teacher. These course, much like this book, are designed to help you facilitate student learning, and to use class time effectively and efficiently for this purpose. A guest speaker usually does not have this experience. Since he or she will be speaking to your students, you want to be sure that he or she is able to teach and that your students will learn from the presentation. Guest speakers should help your students learn information and skills that are different from what you can provide. We suggest that teachers ask the following questions when considering whether to invite a guest speaker:

- Will he or she provide information or skills equal to or more effectively than you?
- What experience has he or she had speaking to students?
- What evidence do you have that the speaker will help your students learn?
- Do you know the specific content to be presented?
- Can you provide guiding questions or topic for the speaker?
- Does the content fit in with your curriculum scope and sequence?
- Do parents need to be notified?
- Why will your students benefit from hearing the speaker?

- What preparation should your students have prior to the speaker? For example, should students read a text or prepare questions ahead of time?

Storytelling is another type of presentation or lecture that is a powerful supplement to your instructional strategies. Stories incite the imagination and provide narratives and descriptions that help information come alive. Most of us have heard someone who is a good storyteller. They can engage listeners in a unique manner that captivates their attention. Several organizations promote storytelling, and have lists of storytellers who can come to your classroom (e.g., the website www.storyarts.org/ provides lesson plans and ideas incorporating storytelling into the classroom; www.storynet.org is the home page of the National Story Telling Network and provides resources and ideas for teachers). These are usually professional speakers, but the above questions should be asked for them as well.

MAKING IT WORK IN YOUR CONTENT AREA

Consider the subjects you will be certified to teach at the middle school or high school level. Considering Good and Brophy's (2003) guidelines for selecting lecture, determine a topic that you believe will be appropriate for a lecture. Effective lectures are a result of careful planning. Return to the "Lecture/Presentation Planning Chart" above, and consider the following:

1. Construct a topic outline for the lecture.
2. Write lesson targets:

   - targets dealing with the information students will learn;
   - targets dealing with the intellectual skill of taking notes.

3. Describe the rationale for choosing the issue:

   - What makes this a good topic for a lecture?
   - What topics will immediately precede and follow this lecture?

4. Lesson procedures:

   - Identify the key topics of your lecture, including at least two sub-points for each topic. Remember that you will probably have more than two sub-points, so you will need to choose the most important topics and sub-points.
   - Write a script for the opening of your lecture. For the next point or topic of the lecture, write detailed notes. Decide whether you are more comfortable with notes or scripts, and complete the lecture using detailed notes or scripts for the rest of the topics you identified above.
   - What graphic organizers, overheads or computer slides, or other audiovisual aids will help with your lecture?

- Write out some questions you could pose to your class to assess their understanding of your key points. These should be interspersed throughout the lecture to help your students understand your main ideas.
- Reread the section on assessing student learning from lectures and determine which ideas you might use. Consider whether you want to assess them through written work or through an oral review.

CHAPTER REVIEW

- Research support for using lectures and other interactive presentation techniques:

  - *Lecture* is an instructional strategy where the teacher presents a specified set of information to students.
  - Students who make frequent, relevant responses during a lesson learn more than students who are passive observers.

- Step-by-step procedures for selecting, planning, and using lectures:

  - planning the topic outline
  - planning the lecture
  - preparing the audio/visuals
  - delivering the lecture
  - concluding the lecture.

- Managing the classroom/learning environment during lectures and presentations.

  - Nine recommendations can help make the lecture approach more effective.

- Assessing student learning appropriately during and after lectures.

  - What content did the students learn, and how they might show their understanding of the content that is consistent with how they learned it?

- Using technology to enhance learning:

  - Technology provides great tools, such as YouTube, computer models, and even authoring and editing software.
  - PowerPoint or other presentation software benefits and caveats.

- Considerations for ELLs during lectures:

  - activate prior schemata
  - provide the objective
  - provide a graphic organizers
  - use visuals to clarify
  - interrupt your lecture to pose questions
  - be aware of your speech.

NOTE

1 This ELL section was created in association with Trish Skillman and Maria Timmons-Flores, Western Washington University.

CHAPTER 6

Questioning

CHAPTER OBJECTIVES

In this chapter, you will learn about:

- research support for using questioning;

- step-by-step procedures for selecting, planning, and using questioning;

- managing the classroom/learning environment during questioning;

- assessing student learning appropriately during questioning;

- using technology to enhance learning;

- considerations for ELLs during questioning.

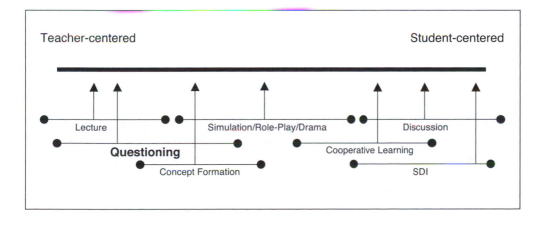

Teacher-centered   Student-centered

Lecture   Simulation/Role-Play/Drama   Discussion

Questioning   Cooperative Learning

Concept Formation   SDI

Marie Taylor stared blankly at her Biology teacher. It was the second month of class of her junior year and she just wasn't in the mood for "playing school." The teacher again asked, "How much of the earth is covered with water?" She had stayed up late last night doing the reading and thinking about the guiding questions the teacher gave to them as homework. The answer to the question was stated on the overhead right in front of them. "This is so obvious it's embarrassing," she thought. She remained quiet as, finally, one of her classmates answered the question. The teacher then asked: "How is water different from other substances, and why is it so necessary for life?" Marie perked up a bit but let several other students give responses. Her teacher then asked: "What are ways you are dependent on water, and what are some threats to our fresh water supply?" Marie had read about threats in last night's homework, and had some ideas she wanted to share. She turned to her partner and began to talk. By the time the teacher brought them back together to further prompt them toward a deeper exploration of the issue, Marie was ready. . . .

OVERVIEW

During the years of schooling, the average student has been asked over a million questions. Some researchers have found that a teacher may ask as many as three to four hundred questions in a single day (Wilen, 1991). Others have found that questioning is one of the most dominant teaching strategies used in middle and high school classrooms, second only to lecturing (Gall, 1984). Of course, many believe that both of these strategies are overused, and often misused. In this chapter, we will offer a description of questioning as an instructional strategy, propose procedures for planning and implementation, and discuss logistical concerns, classroom management, and assessment issues. Finally, we will propose guidelines to help you decide if questioning is appropriate for the content of a lesson.

DEFINING QUESTIONING

While you have heard, answered, or asked innumerable questions at school, you probably have not considered the significance of using questions for learning. Not all teacher questions used during a lesson are part of questioning. The instructional strategy of questioning, as used in this text, is a teacher-centered approach that encourages students to think more deeply. Some might call this strategy a question-and-answer session, or "questioning to learn." The teacher uses a series of questions to lead the class or the student toward the lesson's objectives. Often, questioning is either blended or confused with discussion. While questions are certainly a part of a discussion, in this text we will speak of these as different strategies with different purposes—the primary distinction between the two being that questioning is teacher-centered and discussion is student-centered. During a discussion, the teacher may choose to move to the background; during questioning, the teacher remains an integral part of the strategy. Discussion is a strategy used to give students opportunities to engage in substantive dialog, while exchanging ideas and examining a variety of perspectives. Questioning is a strategy used by a teacher to help students develop and use a variety of thinking skills. Some teachers have designed and used methods to merge the two strategies to help achieve lesson objectives (Henning, 2004). The instructional strategy of discussion is presented in detail in Chapter 10. In addition, some teacher questions are used as an assessment technique and not as part of an instructional strategy; these questions will be addressed later in this chapter.

In the same way, there is also a distinction between student questions and the questioning strategy. Student questions are usually either an essential part of **inquiry learning**, another student-centered strategy (see Chapter 11), or are used simply for clarification purposes. It is possible that some student-generated questions will help a teacher move the class toward the lesson objectives related to higher-order thinking and, in that case, may be examples of the highest form of questioning. At some point, the distinction between all these types of questions blur. Of course, the common denominator is that what we really want as teachers is improved, thoughtful, oral participation on the part of students. However, a clear understanding of what we mean by questioning as an instructional strategy is important as we move toward using it effectively.

A DESCRIPTION OF QUESTIONING AND RESEARCH FINDINGS

Purposes for Teacher Questions

As we have noted, there are many reasons teachers purposefully ask questions. Most of these questions will fall into one or more of three categories: (1) as part of instruction; (2) as part of classroom management; and (3) as part of assessment. Questions are used to help students move between what is commonly referred to as higher- and lower-order thinking, or as an attempt to encourage student participation and investment in learning. Questions can be used for classroom management purposes to create an open and inviting atmosphere, to encourage self-monitoring of behavior, or to manage the pace or direction of the class. Finally, questions can be used formatively during a lesson to check for student understanding, summatively as a test, or to help a teacher reflect upon the effectiveness of a lesson.

Myths about Teacher Questioning

As a new teacher, you may be tempted to go by your intuition, when it comes to using questions. After all, you have seen this strategy in practice several times over your years of schooling and may have developed some strong opinions based upon your observations. Our purpose in the following paragraphs is to help you glean highly effective uses of the questioning strategy, as noted by research on teachers using questions. Wilen (2001) proposes nine common myths about the questioning of students, and offers research-based principles for a pedagogically sound approach to counter the "myths."

Myth 1: Questioning Is a Natural Teaching Behavior that Does Not Require Planning

To effectively lead students beyond **recitation** of factual information, teachers should plan most questions but allow for some spontaneous questions related to student answers. Planning questions provides structure and direction, increased engagement, and increases the likelihood that thinking and understanding will occur. Challenging students to think deeply has been found to increase and enhance participation and interest (Wilen, 1990; Newmann et al., 1992).

Myth 2: The More Questions a Teacher Asks, the More Students Will Learn

Research by Good and Brophy (2000) has shown that frequent questioning *does* help students recall factual information. It does not show that frequent questioning helps students think at higher levels. The *quantity* of questions is not as relevant as the *quality* of questions in situations where students would need to analyze an issue or evaluate a response. Unless a teacher wants students to recall factual information, it is better to focus on fewer questions of a higher quality that lead to higher-order thinking.

Myth 3: There Are No Bad Questions

This myth generally applies to student questions. In an attempt to encourage students to think and clarify their understanding, teachers will often tell students that "any question is OK to ask," or "there are no bad questions." As far as teacher questions are concerned, however, there is a difference between good and bad questions. Good questions are easily understood and stimulate student thinking. These questions are usually brief, naturally phrased, adapted to students in the class, and sequenced to help students reach objectives. Bad questions are those that frustrate or intimidate students, call for guessing or responding with a simple yes or no, give little direction, or intimidate a student into agreeing with the teacher. They may be "trick" questions (e.g.,Which is correct: the yolk of an egg is white, or the yolk of an egg are white?), or questions where the answer is so obvious that students are hesitant to answer (e.g., In what "house" does the President live in Washington, D.C.?) (Groisser, 1964; Gamoron and Nystrand, 1992).

Myth 4: Higher-Level Cognitive Questions Are More Critical than Lower-Level Questions

A person might think that with the emphasis on moving students toward higher-order thinking, this might be true, but it is not so. In fact, lower-level questions can be more important at times because they can help a teacher diagnose a student's readiness to move into higher-order thinking. In addition, recalling of factual information might be the objective for a particular lesson, and thus lower-level questioning might be appropriate. Ultimately, the goal for adolescent students is to be able to solve problems and make decisions that will assist them in becoming competent citizens. Being able to answer critical and evaluative questions must be based upon lower-level thinking (Wilen, 1990; National Council for the Social Studies, 1994).

Myth 5: Higher-Level Cognitive Questions Elicit Higher-Level Answers

Several studies have uncovered this to be untrue (Mills et al., 1980; Costa and Lowery, 1989; Hunkins, 1995). It is interesting to note that it has been found that the cognitive level of student responses align only 50% of the time with the cognitive level of teacher questions. Students tend to answer at a lower level, while teachers tend to assume student answers are at the same level as their questions. Teachers do not always inform students of their own expectations for student responses or explain why they are questioning them. Teachers should inform students of the types of questions they will be asked, and why they are being asked them. Teachers who use action verbs in their questions that correspond with a particular cognitive level more clearly express their expectation for student responses. For example, it is helpful to use verbs such as *identify*, *compare*, *predict*, or *judge* in a question to lead the student to a particular cognitive level. Using these approaches will assist a teacher in establishing a stronger relationship between the cognitive level of the question and the response.

Myth 6: Teachers Should Ask Lower-Level Cognitive Questions before Progressing to Higher-Level Questions

Many see the use of Bloom's Taxonomy as hierarchical in that one level cannot be reached until the previous level has been reached. Because of this, many believe that a student should start at the bottom and work his way up, as if climbing rungs on a ladder. It may be necessary to review the basic facts and concepts before proceeding. For example, it would be difficult for students to compare the Russian Revolution with the American Revolution before they understand the basic facts of each. At times, however, starting a lesson with a higher-order question could be appropriate if there is no need for review or a teacher wants to use the question as a lesson "hook" to stimulate interest (Bloom et al., 1956; Good and Brophy, 2000).

Myth 7: Teachers Give Students Enough Time to Answer Questions

Researchers (Rowe, 1986; Newmann, 1992) have found that while this may be true for factual recall questions, it is not the case for questions that call for more complex thinking. In classrooms where teachers gave students enough time to think through their responses, it has been found that the quality of student responses increased dramatically, student participation increased, and responses were more thoughtful. We have observed that student teachers will commonly wait for as little as one second after asking a question. Rowe (1974) and Tobin (1986) found that waiting as long as three to five seconds for a response to difficult questions will have positive results. This makes sense when you consider that students need to think when answering difficult questions, and thinking takes time to do well.

Myth 8: When Questioning Students, Teachers Should Call Only on Volunteering Students

This myth probably stems from classroom experience in which a student is painfully embarrassed or intimidated. On the other hand, research findings (Wilen and White, 1991; Kelly, 1993; Wilen et al., 2000) show that students learn more when actively involved in class, that answering questions gives students an important opportunity to practice oral communication skills, and that there is a positive relationship between calling on students who do not volunteer and achievement gains. Some argue that students, as all citizens, have an obligation and responsibility to engage in public dialog and so should practice this process in the classroom. The classroom expectation should be that all students participate. However, students should be given the option of nonparticipation if questions are of a sensitive nature and they feel their privacy is threatened.

Myth 9: Teachers Encourage Students to Ask Questions

Research findings (Dillon, 1988; Hunkins, 1995; Brice and Johnson, 1999) have shown that adolescent students do not ask many questions in class and that they do not expect to ask questions in class but to answer them. This is primarily because many teachers spend over 75% of class time talking. With so much of the class time centered on teacher talk, there is little time left for student talk. One main reason students do not ask many questions is because they are not encouraged to do so by teachers. Questioning by students increases interactive involvement and student thinking and can be encouraged by teachers who model how they pursue answers to their own questions and by teachers who value student questions.

STEP-BY-STEP PROCEDURES FOR PLANNING AND IMPLEMENTING QUESTIONING

As we have seen, good questions can serve to engage, motivate, and challenge students. On the other hand, poorly designed questions can frustrate students and turn them off. Have you ever been in a class where no one responds to a teacher's question because the answer is embarrassingly obvious? We mention other common questioning errors later in this chapter. There are a variety of proposed schemas designed to help you create effective questions that help students think critically. We will focus on one that is research-based, and build upon what has been described in this text about the way students learn.

Framing Questions and Prompts

Chapter 3 noted that Bloom's Taxonomy has been widely used to help design instructional objectives. In the same way, it has been a primary means by which effective questions for learning have been constructed. You will recall that recent updates to this taxonomy addresses six cognitive levels, from lower order to higher order: remembering, understanding, applying, analyzing, evaluating, and creating. Questions designed for the lower levels, especially for remembering and understanding, will focus students on recitation (Dillon, 1988). Questions at the other levels will ask students to move increasingly into more complex and difficult thinking (Dantonio and Beisenherz, 2001). Below, we offer sample questions at each of the cognitive levels to help you consider the type of questions you might ask in your content area. Notice how any of the action verbs that reflect a particular cognitive level can easily be turned into a question or be used in "command" form to ask a question through the intonation of the teacher's voice. For example, "List the main characters in the play" can become "Can you list the main characters in the play?" or "Who are the main characters in the play?"

Remembering

Overarching question: Can students recall information?

Sample action verbs that reflect this cognitive level: *list, locate, define, describe.*

Sample questions: What is the formula for the Pythagorean Theorem? Who are the main characters in the play?

Understanding

Overarching question: Can students explain ideas?

Sample action verbs that reflect this cognitive level: *explain, describe, estimate, paraphrase.*

Sample questions: How does communism differ from socialism? How would you describe the life cycle of a cell?

Applying

Overarching question: Can students use ideas?

Sample action verbs that reflect this cognitive level: *chart, predict, compute, classify.*

Sample questions: How could you use the formula for a triangle's area in a real-life situation? How would you say "I would like to eat at the restaurant" in Spanish?

Analyzing

Overarching question: Can students see relationships?

Sample action verbs that reflect this cognitive level: *analyze, compare, contrast, solve.*

Sample questions: What are some positive and negative characteristics of Lady Macbeth? Why did the Soviets side with the Nazis and not with England?

Evaluating

Overarching question: Can students combine ideas and make judgments?

Sample action verbs that reflect this cognitive level: *arrange, compose, formulate, hypothesize.*

Sample questions: What would happen if we mixed these two chemicals? What other times and settings might you use for *Hamlet*, and why would the other time-period work?

Creating

Overarching question: Can students develop their own ideas or point of view?

Sample action verbs that reflect this cognitive level: *judge, diagnose, apprise, assess.*

Sample questions: Should Truman have ordered the dropping of the atomic bomb? Who are the five greatest composers of all time, and why?

A diagram that may be helpful is the question construction wheel designed by the St. Edwards University Center for Teaching Excellence (see Figure 6.1). Notice how the

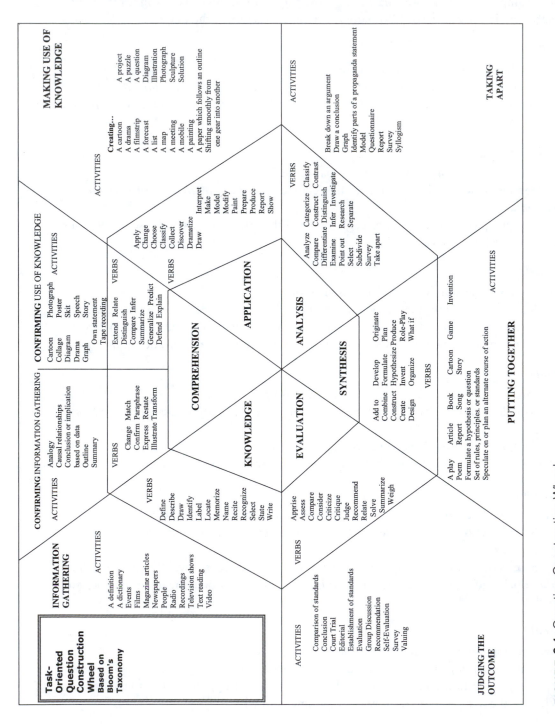

FIGURE 6.1: Question Construction Wheel

Source: "Task Oriented Question Construction Wheel Based on Bloom's Taxonomy," © 2004 St. Edward's University Center for Teaching Excellence.

wheel offers not only the verbs for question construction but also contains project suggestions for lesson enhancement. The drawback with the wheel is that it is based on Bloom's original taxonomy and not the newer thinking/update on his work. We refer to both the original and new taxonomy in Chapter 3, so you may want to go back to that section of the book to clarify the levels. We believe that the benefit of using this chart to guide your questions outweighs the drawback of it being keyed to Bloom's initial work.

While you are becoming comfortable using Bloom's Taxonomy to help guide your questioning, it might be helpful for you to become familiar with a simple technique. Many teachers use the idea of convergent and **divergent questions** to begin planning. *Convergent questions* are those that allow for only one or a few correct responses. These questions tend to be lower-order questions; for example, "What year did the Civil War begin?" "How many spark plugs are in a six-cylinder engine?" "If a circle has a radius of 3 m, then what is its circumference?" or "What are three examples of symbolism in *The Raven* by Edgar Allen Poe?" The questions focus on (literally, they converge upon) a specific response. *Divergent questions* are those that require greater deliberation and encourage broader responses. There could be a number of appropriate responses to these types of questions and typically they require higher-order thought processes; for example, "What theme did you think the author is trying to develop in this short story?" "How might this theorem be helpful for navigation?" "Should we develop genetically altered corn? Why?" or "In the musical score we just heard, what is the composer trying to communicate by choosing to feature the flute with the French horn in the second movement?" Keeping these two types of questions in mind when you begin to plan your interactions with students can be a helpful way to get started—or to think quickly on your feet during class. It could help a new teacher avoid the "deer in the headlights" look as she stands in front of the class while processing the six cognitive domains.

At this point in the chapter, we need to caution you against asking questions when you have a set answer in mind. *Recitation* is a term often used to characterize questions during a teacher-dominated classroom activity (Bellack et al., 1966; Gall and Gall, 1990; Wilen and White, 1991) that typically entails an interaction pattern between teacher and student similar to:

teacher initiated statement/question → student response → teacher feedback/evaluation

Recitations often take the form of a "verbal quiz," because the teacher evaluates student comments. We will describe the use of this type of questioning later in the chapter, but if you always expect students to answer questions to which you have a specific response in mind, then you will reduce this instructional strategy to lower-level thinking tasks.

REALITY CHECK

In a middle school or high school classroom, write some convergent questions and divergent questions that the teacher asks the students. Record student answers to these questions and consider what level of thinking students are engaging in during the class.

If you are able to teach students, make a list of questions you could ask, and predict what answers they might give to the questions. How close were your predictions to actual student responses?

Compare questions asked by teachers in different content areas. What are some questions an algebra teacher asked? How about a biology teacher or U.S. history teacher? To see a teacher using questioning in the classroom, visit the companion website.

Leading Effective Questioning Sessions

You might hear questioning sessions called *Socratic seminars*, after the Greek philosopher/teacher who made this instructional strategy famous. Even Socrates had to begin developing his questioning expertise at some point—we just don't have a record of all the mistakes and gaffes he made while learning. He interacted with his students through dialogs and responded to their questions with questions instead of answers. This process encourages divergent thinking, rather than convergent thinking. At the heart of this approach is the ability to ask meaningful questions that help students think about the content, more so than coming up with the "right answer." Students actively listen and paraphrase classmates' comments, and build on the comments with additional questions to clarify or support a comment. To help lead you more quickly into effective use of the questioning strategy, we offer the following suggestions.

Plan Your Questions Carefully

You may recall that the first myth of using questions relates to planning. Consider your lesson objectives. Do they call for recitation? Do they call for higher-order thinking? What is the purpose of the questions? Are you trying to build classroom atmosphere in this way? Thoughtfully write down as many questions as you can that will help lead students to the lesson objective. You may need to ask questions from all cognitive domains, or you may need to ask questions from only one or two. Remember, as you plan, that the purpose of this strategy is not to start a discussion but to help students share orally their thinking at higher levels or to recite factual information.

Don't Be Afraid to Depart from Your Written Questions While Staying with the Plan

If you have planned carefully, you will know where you want to go with this strategy. You will be more prepared to come up with questions spontaneously in response to students in a natural way. This can be done while staying with your overall plan as defined by your objectives.

Consider Who You Are Teaching

What time of day is it? Are the students tired? What about those who are learning English or have other special needs? Think about ways you can encourage shy students without being intimidating. What kind of relationship do you have with your class? How can you use this strategy to improve your classroom atmosphere?

Consider Classroom Management and Assessment Techniques

Every objective will call for an assessment. How will you assess students' oral communication? Every instructional strategy has its own unique issues related to classroom management. Have you thought this through? We will discuss this later in this chapter.

Close the Lesson on a Strong Note

As with any lesson, it is important not to allow any teaching session to fizzle. What can you do to close the lesson? Is there some type of interesting closing activity that uses another learning style such as pictures or music? Is there a bookend to a "hook" you may have used at the beginning? Can you debrief orally or ask a student to summarize? Evaluate how the teacher closes a questioning lesson in the video sample at our companion website.

MAKING IT WORK IN YOUR CLASSROOM

Questioning for Cognitive Variety

Review the "Framing Questions and Prompts" section in this chapter. Choose a topic for a course you will be endorsed to teach. Perhaps consider an entry level course you would likely teach during student teaching or your first year, such as world or U.S. history, algebra 1, earth science, language arts, health, etc. Write an objective for that topic that requires evaluative thinking. Create at least six questions (one from each cognitive level) that you could ask the students to help lead them from knowledge through evaluation during one lesson. Share this with a colleague and ask for feedback.

Feedback prompts might include:

- How will the questioning session you design help your students achieve the lesson objective?
- Were you able to create a question from each cognitive level? Would any need clarification? Would it affect student achievement of the objective, if you skipped one of the levels?
- How will you assess learning?
- How do you envision these questions fitting in with a lesson?

THE ROLE AND PURPOSE OF STUDENT QUESTIONS

While the questioning strategy is teacher-centered and focuses on teacher-generated questions, we cannot overlook the importance of student-generated questions. These are important for a variety of reasons, the most important being that curious students learn. In this text, we have chosen to dedicate Chapter 11 to inquiry learning that addresses the development of students' questions and the process of helping them find answers to those questions. Chapter 10 will examine the use of classroom discussion as a strategy for promoting student thinking and also uses student questions. However, a good teacher will constantly be encouraging the students' curiosity and the environment of that teacher's classroom will promote questioning. We have all noticed how younger children are full of a constant stream of questions—questions that at times seem they will never end. Sadly, for adolescents, the desire to ask questions at school has been discouraged by peer pressure or instructional practice. Teachers can help counter this by encouraging students to ask questions in class, by allowing time for written questions, or having students work with a partner to devise questions.

SOCRATIC SEMINARS

A Socratic seminar is a teaching technique that can blur the line between questioning and discussion strategies. These seminars help students develop critical thinking, while practicing listening and speaking skills. Essentially, a Socratic seminar is a dialog usually about a reading, musical score, or piece of art. The class can be highly directed at times through questions by the teacher or other students but generally the goal of the teacher is to become a participant and not speak more than students. There are several ways a seminar can be run successfully but we have included below a list of step-by-step guidelines as suggested through conversations with teachers as well as www.journeytoexcellence.org. The handout below provided to student teachers by Bruce Mansfield at Bellingham High School shows expectations for quality seminars.

Step-by-step guidelines for teachers:

1. Choose a text that is interesting to students.
2. Design possible questions.
3. Teach background information prior to the seminar.
4. Arrange seats in a circle.
5. Choose a couple of students as outside circle observers and dialog mappers (see example below).
6. Start by explaining the Socratic seminar to the students.

   a. What are the learning targets or goals?
   b. Explain that the conversation is theirs, and that your question is a starting point which they can move away from as they pose ideas and questions as long as the new ideas and questions can be discussed in terms of the text. You may need to pose follow-up questions to deepen thinking or you may ask other students to take on the role of asking clarifying questions during the seminar. Some teachers will also ask students to take other roles such as being the person who asks: "Can you tie that comment to the text" or "What evidence from the text do you have to support that comment?"
   c. Tell the students to direct their comments *to other students* and explain to them that you will not comment on what they say, since this will cause them to talk to you rather than to each other. It may help if you look down or avoid eye contact until the discussion takes off on its own.
   d. Encourage the students to think before they talk, try to comment, or add on to what others have said. Listen to others.

7. End the seminar when it feels done and you or others have no more probing questions.
8. Debrief:

   a. Get feedback from the group about your expectations for the seminar (see the description of great Socratic seminars below).
   b. Get feedback from the observers; ask them to share their maps (Figure 6.2, below, is an example of a student's map).

WHAT DOES A REALLY GREAT SOCRATIC SEMINAR LOOK LIKE?

1. *Everyone comes prepared with the assigned text, read and marked up.*
   Have I read and marked up the text? Do I have something to say?

2. *Students do most of the talking and thinking.*
   Are we doing more work than Mr. Mansfield during seminar?

3. *Students speak with each other.*
   Am I responding to what others say or just waiting for my turn to speak?

4. *The seminar stays focused on the assigned text.*
Are all my comments and questions centered on the text?

5. *Students ask questions to each other.*
Am I asking students for help when stuck? Am I asking questions that can't be looked up or answered right now?

6. *Students avoid speculating and guesses are challenged respectfully.*
Am I careful to support my ideas with evidence from the text? Am I respectfully asking students to support their comments?

7. *Students help others meet the daily goals.*
Do I know what today's goals are? Am I helping others meet today's goals?

8. *Students are writing a lot—on the text itself, the white board, on big paper, on word wall slips, and in their own notebooks.*
Am I writing with purpose to help me make meaning from the text?

9. *The debrief is honest and focused on the day's seminar goals.*
Are we meeting the seminar goals? What did you see that shows we've met the goals?

Adapted from work by Bruce Mansfield, Bellingham High School.

WHAT DOES A BAD SOCRATIC SEMINAR LOOK LIKE?

1. Only some of the students have read the text and are prepared to speak.
2. The teacher talks too much and is doing all the work and all the thinking.
3. Students are mostly looking at the teacher and talk to him.
4. The seminar gets off the topic easily—students talk about things only a few have experienced.
5. Students don't ask for help—they stay quiet and confused.
6. Lots of speculation and guessing without much evidence offered in support.
7. Students ignore the daily goals and aren't preparing to meet weekly or unit goals.
8. Students stay in their seats and won't use the classroom space to support seminar—no writing on the white board, no big paper, no word wall words, notebook writing without purpose.
9. The debrief is shallow and doesn't help improve the seminar—lots of "I agree" and "pass" responses.

Adapted from work by Bruce Mansfield, Bellingham High School.

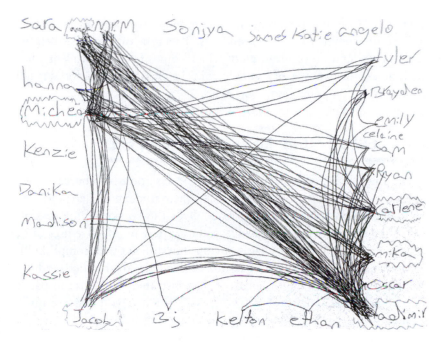

FIGURE 6.2: Example of a Student Map Created During a Socratic Seminar

ENHANCING STUDENT LEARNING WITH TECHNOLOGY

You will likely be able to locate some drill-and-practice software or websites that may be useful as part of your questioning strategy, but keep in mind that they rarely function beyond lower-order questioning. It might also be difficult to find software or websites that relate to the exact topic you are addressing with your lesson. Some teachers choose to ask more advanced students in the class to create helpful questioning games. For example, jeopardy-type games can be created in PowerPoint and used during class. You or your students can easily find directions and templates by searching the internet for jeopardy templates.

You might also consider the following activity for generating student questions. This is an example activity that could be modified for other content areas.

After reading a chapter in the book *All Quiet on the Western Front*, have students go to the computer lab. Ask students to write a question that they would like to explore further or would like to have clarified. Instead of writing a simple question, students should be encouraged to write nonstop about the question until it leads them to a conclusion or perhaps another question. Why did they think of it? Is it related to an event or character? Why is it relevant? Why is it important to them? After several minutes of writing, ask them to switch computers with a partner and continue the writing on that partner's computer. Here, the students should write an exploratory response to the other student's initial question and continue the writing until another question emerges. Continue the exchange of computers so that students read, respond to, and add to the comments of other students. This type of writing is helpful for the generation and exploration of ideas, all of which comes from the students themselves.

As with most effective uses of technology in the classroom, the focus is not on the technology itself but on your lesson objectives.

MAKING A LESSON MORE MEANINGFUL FOR ELLs

Research on English as second language (ESL) classroom discourse suggests that effective teachers of ELLs use questions to help their students understand concepts in class and to understand the texts they read. Over the course of the school year, a student's language proficiency may change. In her review of effective uses of questions in classrooms, Kim (2010) found what is obvious but difficult to accomplish: "Effective teachers reformulate and refocus their questions based upon their understanding of what ESL students know about English language demonstrated in classroom participation and use of English oral language" (p. 114). As a teacher, you can use questions to scaffold students' learning about the course content and help them better understand their own learning of the English language. Kim's research helps us understand how questions might scaffold learning by thinking of three different types of questions. "Coaching questions" are those where the teacher has the highest level of control and authority. "Collaborating questions" are when the student has the highest degree of authority. Between these two are "facilitating questions." The following examples clarify these roles (Kim, 2010, pp. 130–135):

- Coaching questions occur during activities such as before a teacher begins a new activity (e.g., Does anyone know about quick writing?), to add information (Can I add one more idea to your comment?), to assess students' knowledge or understanding (e.g., Does everyone have an idea of what a raccoon looks like? What do I mean when I say "give you credit"?), and to help students think about the focus of a class activity (What is the format of the equation? What is the outline of this story?).
- Facilitating questions serve purposes such as to invite students' input (Do you have more to add on the list?), to help students deepen their understanding (Can you think of another word that begins with "un"? Can you guess what the author wanted to tell us by using this title for the story?), to help students articulate and elaborate (What do the leaves look like? How can you find out about the names of the leaves? Can anybody say that in your own words?), and to find out students' opinions (Is anyone interested in going to the computer lab to work?).
- Collaborative questions are used to help students reflect on learning and teaching (Which piece shows your best work?), and starting conversations about course content (Did you like the special presentation on glaciers yesterday?).

It might seem obvious that while these questions help ELLs, they will also be effective for students who speak English as their primary language. If you have the opportunity to observe an ESL teacher, try to identify instances when she "coaches," "facilitates," and "collaborates" with questions, and share what you observed.

Online, a great resource for teachers is the Internet TESL Journal (ITESLJ.org). This site has excellent lesson ideas for ESL teachers and students. For example, and specific to questioning, the journal has a list of over 200 categories of "Conversation Questions for the ESL/EFL Classroom" (http://iteslj.org/questions). Many of these are for specific content area topics. We provide links to these lesson ideas for ELLs at the companion website.

LOGISTICAL CONCERNS, INCLUDING BENEFITS AND OBSTACLES

We have indicated the importance of planning when preparing an effective questioning seminar. At some point, however, it will come down to how you perform in the classroom. Having the skill to ask good questions is something that will take practice. You can quicken your development if you think through several logistical issues.

One way for you to improve your questioning technique is through attention to an element that researchers have called *wait time*. This refers to the amount of time teachers wait after asking a question (called *wait time 1*) or before responding to a student or asking another student to respond (called *wait time 2*). The concept is simple, but most new teachers struggle with it, thus stifling participation and learning. When it comes to asking questions, teachers tend to be a very impatient group. In fact, Rowe (1974) and Wilen (1991) have found that it is common for teachers to wait less than one second before speaking again to rephrase the question, answer it themselves, ask another question, or fill the quiet in some other way. Perhaps in the many years of your own schooling you can recall instances in which you were about to respond to a question when the teacher began talking.

Waiting for students to respond has been shown to have a number of positive effects. When teachers increased the wait time to just 3–5 seconds, there were positive results, according to research done by Rowe (1974) and Tobin (1986), who found that

- the length of the student response increased;
- the number of times students failed to respond decreased;
- students asked more questions;
- students were more confident;
- unsolicited responses increased;
- students with a broader range of abilities participated.

It is interesting that something as simple as being aware of and applying principles of wait time can have such impact on classroom interaction.

Improving your wait time is something that will take practice. Keeping this in mind will likely help you develop good habits from the start. Some teachers choose to count to themselves for 4–5 seconds after asking a question and before allowing themselves to speak again. Some choose to do the same before responding to a student. Others will tape-record themselves to help self-assess their technique. You will need to decide what will work for you, given all the variables of a classroom. Of course, you should understand that just waiting for a few seconds will not necessarily produce dynamic classroom interaction. In fact, there are times when a "popcorn" approach (having students pop up and respond very quickly) can be effective, such as during recitation lessons or times when exploring affective thinking. Clearly, however, when students are asked to think at a more complex level they need time to respond.

Good questioning seminars depend upon a positive environment in the classroom. You will need to create an atmosphere in the class where students want to participate and interact. If you happen to student teach in a classroom where students are not encouraged to speak (the proverbial lecture class), it will be difficult for you to have a high-quality questioning seminar or discussion. If you haven't established this questioning atmosphere in your first class session, it will likewise be difficult. It may take some time for you to establish an atmosphere conducive to verbal interaction in a lesson. You will need to share your expectations with the class, as well as let them know that it is psychologically safe for student talk. This becomes a function of classroom management that is clearly related to the questioning strategy.

CLASSROOM MANAGEMENT AND MOTIVATION

There are a number of different elements related to classroom management that have a profound impact on the effectiveness of this instructional strategy. You will recall that in this text, when we refer to *classroom management* we are not only speaking of controlling or redirecting a student's behavior but also speaking of creating and maintaining a positive climate for learning. There is no formula by which you can create this atmosphere. However, implementation of these elements will help you create an atmosphere more conducive to using questioning strategies with your students.

Responding to Student Responses

The way a teacher responds to students is very important and impacts further student participation specifically and classroom atmosphere in general. We would like to include a good flow chart for how to respond to students (if they say *this*, you should say *this*), but in reality productive responses will depend on careful listening and quick thinking. There is probably no better analysis, synthesis, and evaluation practice for a teacher. With that in mind, there are two basic types of responses to students that enhance learning.

Prompting

Students will often need to examine further their responses. Their responses may show that they misunderstand, or that they have not responded at the level of thinking that you require. Do you think that a student gives an incorrect response because she misunderstands your question? Do you think the student needs to work on her analysis? Does she want to apply a principle without careful consideration of implications? Does she evaluate a situation but not show that she has a complete understanding of the facts? Maybe you should rephrase the question, gently redirect it to another student, and ask that student to ask a clarifying question of another student, or quickly paraphrase the pool of information the student would need to respond correctly. Perhaps you need to restate their answers while allowing time for them to clarify.

Expanding

At other times students need to be asked to extend their thinking beyond the original response, or to be challenged. Do you think the student is correct and can go further? You might want to ask the student to analyze or evaluate information. For example, if a student has stated that the Nazis allied themselves with the Soviets, you might ask why they formed the alliance, or what would have happened if they had not formed such an alliance. Do you think a student offers an in-depth evaluation? It might be helpful to challenge the student by asking another student for an opposing evaluation or a differing view from outside of class. For example, "How would you respond to the writer of this article, who disagrees with your evaluation?" Remember, however, that engaging in a direct disagreement with a student in which you "win" the argument rarely enhances a lesson and can shut down others who were thinking of responding. Of course, even this will depend upon the atmosphere that has been established and to what degree the students trust you. Do you think a student's response is off-the-charts amazing? Most of the time praise should be reserved for private conversations.

The environment in your classroom that enhances a questioning session can be destroyed by comments that aren't respectful of students. Obviously, comments that intimidate or embarrass students will not encourage participation. Sometimes, a teacher does not realize how his tone or nonverbal responses to students can impact the class. A frown, smirk, roll of the eyes, or blank stare all communicate as much as a smile or an interested look. In much the same way, tone of voice can turn the same statement from an encouraging prompt to a put-down.

Participation Patterns

One reason teachers use questioning sessions is to give students an opportunity to participate orally. However, many times those who participate are the usual volunteers or those "go-to" students the teacher uses when a correct answer is needed. One way to help assess your pattern of questioning is to employ an observer grid, through which an impartial observer uses a seating chart to place a check mark by the name of each student who participates. It is interesting for a teacher to note after a lesson that most of the responses came, for example, from the right front corner or from the boys in the class. Feedback from this type of observation can help the teacher to create a more equitable and encouraging classroom.

The eighth myth of questioning claimed that only volunteering students should participate. Research implications show that, within reason, all students should be encouraged and expected to participate. For example, a teacher should expect all students to respond during a review of factual information in a reading assignment. A teacher may opt to allow a student to pass if, for instance, he is asked a question related to his political beliefs regarding a presidential candidate. Some teachers choose to do this through random calling. This could be done through the use of two decks of cards: each student is given a card from the first deck, and the teacher has another deck from which she randomly draws a card that corresponds with the card of the student who will participate. Other teachers will simply choose students at random, trying to get all students involved. Some will go around the room, having students respond one by one but allowing for a student to pass. As you consider when you will call on volunteers and when you will solicit responses, you will also be deciding whether you want your students to "raise their hands," answer without permission, or be called upon by the teacher. This logistical issue goes hand in hand with your thinking about participation.

One final consideration about student participation is related to culture. White (1990) has found that different ethnic groups communicate orally in different ways. In the classroom, as much as possible, consideration should be given to the student's cultural background when encouraging oral participation. In addition, students who speak English as a second language may have considerable difficulty participating at a high level in a questioning session. Alternative strategies should be used to reach this population, or perhaps questions could be provided in written form. Students could follow the text during class or be able to use the text with a helping partner or during an ESL-supported study hall. It may also be helpful to give additional wait time to allow such a student to comprehend the question. Students could also be given several minutes of free-writing time after some questions; this would improve responses from all students without singling out some.

Common Classroom Management Errors

As we have noted, there are many different elements to consider, while establishing or maintaining an atmosphere conducive to an effective questioning session. Below, we offer some common errors that are made in this area:

- Questions aren't clear, so students become frustrated.
- The "guess what's in my brain" game, in which the student must try to verbalize what the teacher is thinking. This becomes a "give me what I'm looking for" session.
- The teacher calls on favorites or the reliable few with answers, and does not include the whole class.
- Negative uses of questions, thus intentionally or unintentionally embarrassing or intimidating students.
- Asking more than one question at a time.
- Not giving enough time for responses.
- Poor follow-up, which stifles students' desire to respond.
- The questions are so simple that no one wants to respond because it's embarrassingly obvious.
- The teacher commonly answers his own questions, and students are thus confused about responding.

- Questions leave out a large portion of the class. The teacher fails to frame learning through the use of questions that build to higher-order questions.
- Teacher not listening well. Perhaps, she is thinking about the next question or a response the students might give or should have given.
- Negative nonverbal cues. The teacher uses cues, such as looking at papers, at the clock, raising eyebrows, rolling eyes, and so on, to show disinterest or displeasure in a response.
- Rewording an answer into an idea the teacher wants to hear.
- Teacher talks too much.

Refer to the companion website to observe what you might do differently than (or the same as) the teacher in the video.

APPROPRIATE ASSESSMENT TECHNIQUES TO USE WITH QUESTIONING

Assessing questioning can be difficult, as can assessing any oral participation strategy. The daily learning targets for the lesson will again be key in determining how to go about assessing students. You may have had a number of purposes in mind when choosing to question the students. The lesson target may be related to critical thinking skills, participation, or practicing verbal skills. A rubric similar to the "Clipboard Checklist" (p. 265) shown in Chapter 10, "Classroom Discussion and Debate," could be used to assess any of these objectives. This would be done with a checklist-style rubric that could quickly be used to rate a response. However, unlike with discussion, this strategy is teacher-centered. There likely will be little time to fill out a rubric, while fully participating in leading a questioning seminar. Instead, a teacher will commonly use the strategy to support objectives that call for a different type of assessment. Take, for example, this objective: *Student will be able to show her ability to evaluate the effects of the Vietnam War on foreign policy decisions during later presidential administrations by writing a two-page editorial according to guidelines on the provided rubric.* Here, the objective indicates that the point of the lesson is to teach students to evaluate. The teacher may have chosen to use questioning to help students practice their evaluation skills. However, the formal assessment of those skills will be completed during the written assignment. The teacher will formatively, through listening and observation, assess student ability to evaluate during the oral questioning seminar. Most assessment for questioning will be formative and eventually used to modify future lesson objectives or prepare for a summative assessment. If done well, and if you can avoid the "common errors" listed in the previous section, then questioning can become a powerful formative assessment tool. You can literally check on students' thinking as they form their understanding.

One reminder may be important here, and that is that questions are commonly used as an assessment strategy. For example, a teacher may ask questions as part of a lecture to assess student comprehension. This use of questions *specifically for assessment* is not part of a questioning seminar.

GUIDELINES FOR DECIDING IF QUESTIONING IS APPROPRIATE FOR THE CONTENT OF A LESSON

Questioning for learning is thought to be a useful strategy for the promotion of higher-order thinking skills. If you decide that your students need assistance moving from recitation of memorized fact to being able to analyze or evaluate information, this strategy can be helpful. A skilled questioning seminar leader can have a strong influence on the student thought processes. Students often need this guidance to be able to think critically. Simply *asking* a student to evaluate isn't *teaching* a student to evaluate. For example, a student might "evaluate" a character's action as "dumb" by simply depending on his own impressions or emotions. Questioning can help a student go back and look at the factual information and make judgments based on supporting evidence. This interaction between teacher and student can have long-lasting positive results.

The unique student characteristics of a class should also be considered when deciding if this strategy is to be used. If your class has a high percentage of ESL students, it would be problematic to consistently use questioning. In addition, consideration should be given to the types of learning styles that you have in your classroom. Most experienced teachers will tell you that any group of students forms a unique personality. Some seem to be more verbally oriented than others. However, within this class personality, there will be students who do not have the same learning style as others. Because this strategy is so verbally oriented, it may or may not be the right choice for habitual use. Using a variety of instructional approaches is key to being able to attend to the needs of the diverse group of learners that will be in your class.

At times, questioning is used to encourage student participation and investment in learning. Studies have shown that when students become more actively involved rather than passive recipients they learn more. This strategy is one that encourages teacher-led student participation and thus could assist a teacher with purposeful student engagement. Keep in mind, however, that these teacher-centered activities have been commonly overused with adolescents.

MAKING IT WORK IN YOUR CONTENT AREA

Questioning for Cognitive Variety

Review the "Framing Questions and Prompts" section in this chapter. Choose a topic for your content area. Write an objective for that topic that requires evaluative thinking. Create at least six questions (one from each cognitive level) that you could ask the students to help lead them from knowledge through evaluation during one lesson. Share this with a colleague from the same content area and ask for feedback.

Feedback prompts might include:

*   How will the questioning session you design help your students achieve the lesson objective?

- Were you able to create a question from each cognitive level? Would any need clarification? Would it affect student achievement of the objective if you skipped one of the levels?
- How will you assess learning?
- How do you envision these questions fitting in with a lesson?

CHAPTER REVIEW

- Research support for using questioning:

  - Questioning is a teacher-centered approach that encourages students to think more deeply.
  - Questions, high-level thinking, and student participation.
  - Questions can be used for assessment.
  - Nine myths about questions.

- Step-by-step procedures for selecting, planning, and using questioning:

  - Bloom's Taxonomy provides guidance.
  - Convergent and divergent questions.
  - Questions need to be planned ahead of time.
  - Socratic seminars are more student-centered than conventional questioning, and focus on asking meaningful questions that help students think about the content more so than coming up with the "right answer."

- Managing the classroom/learning environment during questioning:

  - responding to student responses;
  - prompting student responses;
  - expanding on student answers/comments;
  - promoting an open/safe learning environment.

- Assessing student learning appropriately during questioning:

  - the written objectives
  - rubrics
  - teacher listening and observation.

- Using technology to enhance learning:

  - Online games are useful for review activities.

- Questions help keep students focused when researching a topic on the internet.

- Considerations for ELLs during questioning:

  - Help students understand concepts in class and in the texts they read.
  - Teachers use questions to scaffold students' learning.

CHAPTER 7

Concept Formation

CHAPTER OBJECTIVES

In this chapter, you will learn about:

- research support for using concept formation;

- selecting, planning, and using concept learning activities;

- managing the classroom/learning environment during concept learning;

- assessing student learning appropriately during concept formation;

- using technology to enhance learning;

- considerations for ELLs during concept formation lessons.

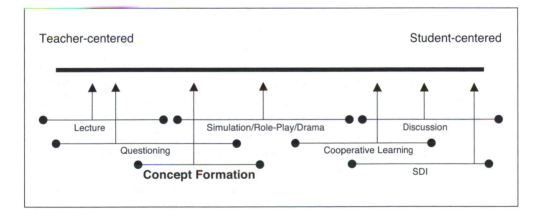

Teacher-centered   Student-centered

Lecture   Simulation/Role-Play/Drama   Discussion

Questioning   Cooperative Learning

Concept Formation   SDI

In early August, Steve signed a contract to teach five sections of creative writing at a local high school. The school district specified that the creative writing curriculum would involve a series of writing prompts, and would mainly focus on writing fiction. Other teachers mentioned that one of the elements of fiction that was difficult for students was that a story's plot needs conflict. Many conflicts are possible, but a fundamental understanding of conflict was an important building block for future writing. Steve decided that forming an initial understanding of conflict at the start of the course would be useful. During the semester, Steve returned to this concept as his students incorporated different types of conflict (e.g., character versus character, character versus nature, character versus society, character versus self). Throughout the year, his students added to their understanding of the role of conflict as part of the plot of a story, and were able to build on their initial understanding of conflict so that it became increasingly robust.

OVERVIEW

A concept is the same as an idea. We create concepts to help categorize or classify the world. As Parker (2005) explains, concepts are

> abstract categories or classes of meaning. For example, island is the word label for a geographic phenomenon consisting of land completely surrounded by water. Kauai is one specific example of such a set of conditions. There are thousands of other specific examples of the concept island . . . concept definitions, therefore, tell us only about those qualities or attributes that a group *has in common*. They do not tell us about the unique features of particular examples.
>
> (p. 191; emphasis in the original)

Many of the words we use refer to an idea, and not to specific or tangible "things." For example, *books*, *liquids*, *artifacts*, *cultures*, *rules*, *theorems*, and *characters* are all concepts. Usually, when we use a word such as *book*, people around us know what we mean: books all share specific attributes that most people agree make something a book. In your future classroom, however, you will be helping students learn concepts that they have not learned. Then, as they explore specific **examples of a concept,** they will become better able to categorize and organize this information.

The purpose of the **concept formation** strategy is to help students form a robust understanding of significant concepts in your content area. Too often we use concepts and have limited understanding of what we mean. Middle school students may be able to use the concepts of *democracy* and *freedom* in a sentence but often cannot articulate the meaning of these terms. Consider, for example, the difference between the words *bravery* and *courage*. Most people will acknowledge that they are not synonyms but will find it difficult to specify the differences. Some have referred to this as the "rattle of empty wagons" (Taba, 1967; Parker and Perez, 1987). With this metaphor, wagons are thought of as the word, or label, we use for a particular concept, and the content of the wagon is the understanding of the concept. When we use **concept labels** without fully understanding their meaning, we rattle along like an empty wagon.

Each of the instructional strategies described in this book promote student learning of facts, skills, and concepts. In this chapter, however, we examine a specific strategy that helps students form a deep and flexible understanding of a concept that the teacher determines is critical for students to understand. We believe that helping students gain conceptual understandings—literally understanding big ideas—is a critical element of any instructional strategy. Helping middle school and high school students learn concepts is important because it helps them organize information. Concept formation is an approach to learning where students examine examples of a concept and draw conclusions about those examples. In addition to learning about the concept formation strategy, we also intend for this chapter to challenge you to think about concepts that are important in your content area. As we explore this strategy, continue to consider those ideas that are important for your students to learn during the school year and consider the instructional strategies that will promote student learning of these important ideas.

A DESCRIPTION OF CONCEPT FORMATION AND RESEARCH FINDINGS

We often present the following idea to pre-service teachers: *Thinking is how people learn. Therefore, always be aware of who is doing most of the thinking/learning in your classroom.*

Imagine that a local high school or middle school teacher in your content area asked you to come in and teach for 55 minutes. This teacher gave you a concept that she wants her students to learn, and you have 3 days to prepare. Preparing for this will require several hours to determine valid assessments of student learning, preparing learning activities, and writing the lesson plan. In addition, you will also spend a significant amount of time thinking about the concept, and finding relevant examples of it. It is during those hours of thinking and exploration that you develop a robust understanding of the concept you will be teaching. If you only have 55 minutes of class time, students cannot spend the same amount of time you spent preparing. And you would not want them to. What activities can you have your students do that will help them learn the concept that you learned while preparing? Often, teachers spend time preparing a lesson and learning the content, and then use class time to simply tell students what they learned. This is what we call *concept telling*; you tell students about a concept. The problem with concept telling is that deep conceptual understanding occurs during the hours of preparation that *you* spend before you teach. By simply coming to class and telling students about a concept, they miss out on the opportunity that you had while preparing—the opportunity to think about and learn the concept.

Concept formation is a strategy that takes your students through a process whereby they work to understand a concept. Rather than you telling them, the students form their understanding of a concept. This approach taps into Vygotsky's theory of learning (1978). You may recall from Chapter 1 that Vygotsky suggested that a "zone of proximal development" exists between our current understanding of something and the next, more robust level of understanding. Usually, we need help attaining this new level. According to Vygotsy's theory, people learn when they have proper scaffolds in place to help them reach this next level of understanding. This strategy provides a step-by-step process for helping students learn a new concept.

Consider Figure 7.1 as a description of different levels of learning.

Facts, concepts, and generalizations rely on each other to help promote deeper understanding. A *fact* is something that can be verified through observing, experiencing, reading, or listening. Facts are necessary for building conceptual knowledge and generalizations. They are the building blocks of concept development. As we stated earlier, a *concept* is an idea for organizing and classifying experiences and facts into groups with common qualities. Concepts are timeless and abstract. *Conflict*, *change*, and *perspective* are three concepts. Examples of the concept *change* can be found in social studies (historical events), earth science (erosion), literature (character development), and music (tempo). *Generalizations* are descriptive statements of relationships between two or more concepts. To state that "social change often brings about conflict" is a generalization about two of the concepts stated above. You can make this statement only if you have understood the concepts of *change* and *conflict*, and if you have examined many examples and facts about social reform movements. *Generalizations*, as the word implies, are "generally true. They can also be called conclusions" (Parker, 2005, p. 201).

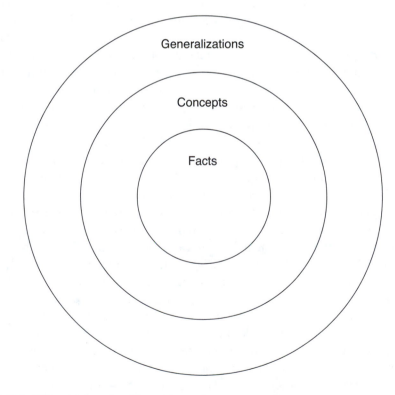

FIGURE 7.1: Different Levels of Learning

Before we proceed to the step-by-step procedures for helping your students form their understanding of concepts, we need to define five key terms:

1. *Concept*: A concept is an idea.
2. *Concept label*: Since concepts are ideas, they only exist in our minds. Words are labels that we use to talk about the ideas. A concept label is the word or phrase that people use when referring to a particular concept. Consider the concept of *cooperation*. We all have an idea of what cooperation is, but in order to talk about it we need to use the word or label.
3. **Critical attributes**: These are the traits or characteristics that every example of a particular concept will have. If we return to cooperation, we would conclude that every example of this concept involves at least two people who are working together toward a common purpose. For something to be an example of cooperation it must have these three attributes—therefore, they are critical to the concept.
4. *Examples of a concept*: Every example of a concept has all of the critical attributes. An example of cooperation might be a group of four students helping each other complete a task assigned by the teacher. Another example might be a football team successfully executing a play. Both are examples because they have all of the critical attributes.
5. **Non-examples of a concept**: Non-examples simply lack one or more of the critical attributes. If any of the critical attributes of cooperation do not exist, then it is not an example.

This quotation by Parker (1987) provides an additional example of how these terms work together:

> For instance, the idea *sentence* (or democracy, equation, mammal, or experiment) does not exist physically, but there are numerous examples of sentence, such as the one you are now reading. What makes it an example is that it has the critical characteristics all sentences must have in order to be called by the label *sentence*: it has a subject, verb, and direct object, either present or implied; it expresses a complete thought; it has a beginning, ending, and, as needed, transition signals.
>
> (p. 57)

Before we explore the planning procedures for a concept formation lesson, it is important to understand where a concept's critical attributes come from. *Epistemology* is the study of knowledge that seeks to explain how we know—literally how we obtain, use, and think about knowledge of the world around us. Concepts help us think and understand the world, so studying concepts is an epistemological venture. When you help your students learn a concept, you are helping them to think and study how they know something to be true. Concepts help us categorize the world. As a result, anyone is able to create a concept that helps him to categorize the world. Concepts are proved to be accurate ideas, when they are tested. In other words, when we have experiences that require us to make judgments using a concept, we either verify or discredit the concept. Left to our own devices, we might create concepts that appear accurate simply because our individual experiences have not allowed for many judgments using the concept. When others use our concepts, they increase the number of experiences and prove or call into question our category. Consider, for example, the concept of *democracy*. Two important attributes of this idea are that democracies require a free and fair election process. It is not all that important to know who decided this, as much as it is important to know whether these are defining attributes with which we all agree. As a society, we test the idea of democracy by making judgments about different systems of governance. If examples of this concept all include free elections and a fair election process, then these critical attributes are confirmed, and the concept is valid. On the other hand, there has been much debate over the concept of *family*. The debate is about the critical attributes of a family, and whether these attributes are accurate when we determine if different scenarios are examples of a family. We all agree that *family* is a good concept label, but many disagree on the critical attributes. There is not an overall agreement on what defines a family. In the next section, we refer to *established* and *dynamic* concepts as one approach for determining if the experiences of the greater society have verified the critical attributes. It will be helpful for you to engage in some epistemology and think about how well you know the key concepts in your content area, and how these concepts have emerged.

STEP-BY-STEP PROCEDURES FOR PLANNING AND IMPLEMENTING CONCEPT FORMATION

Concept formation is an inductive approach that will help students learn the critical attributes of a given concept. As we suggested earlier, telling students the attributes that we, the teachers, have discovered does not promote mastery learning as effectively as helping students engage in a process whereby they actually think about the concept. In brief, concept formation provides students with the opportunity to examine several examples of a given concept in light of the critical attributes, and then draw conclusions about the similarities and differences among these examples. Students' conclusions about the similarities are then generalized to be true about other examples of the concept they examined. To promote the type of thinking that will engage students, concept formation follows a sequential eight-step process.[1]

Step 1: Selecting a Concept

The first step in developing a concept formation lesson is selecting a concept that students need to know. Teachers often tell us that this first step is the most difficult part, because the teacher needs to determine the concept on which the students will focus. Think about a few powerful ideas and issues that you want your students to build on and explore in your class. It might be helpful to follow this process: first, given all the potential topics that could be mentioned during the 180 hours you will have in class with your future students (far too many topics to teach well), identify five or six topics that are critically important for your students to learn. In previous chapters of this book you thought of many topics that you might teach in your future classroom; you might return to one of those. When you are teaching, you will also have curriculum guides that provide many topics. Next, reflect on these topics and identify concepts that are an integral part of each topic. Think of concepts that you believe students must know well, and upon which other course content can be built. It is from this select list of concepts that you will select the big ideas, the important and powerful concepts for your students to explore. In a course on American government, you might select the topic *constitutional government*. With this topic, the concepts of *democracy*, *checks and balances*, and *e pluribus unum* are all significant concepts. In an earth science course, you might decide on the topic *rock cycle*. Possible concepts could include *sediment*, *erosion*, or *weathering*. Select concepts that are difficult for students to grasp, and that are ideas you can build upon in future lessons. For example, a teacher might decide that the concept of *authority* is critical for understanding U.S. history. This concept will help students compare and contrast authoritarian forms of government with forms of government that gain their authority from the people (an authoritative government). The concepts should also have critical attributes upon which your local community has some agreement. While we all could agree on the critical attributes of *symbiosis* or *improper fractions*, we would have more difficulty agreeing on the critical attributes of *love*. We refer to concepts with easily agreed upon attributes as **established concepts**, and concepts with more disagreement as *dynamic concepts*. Concepts are established to help us make sense of the world around us. As a result, previously agreed upon attributes may change as societal expectations change. Dynamic concepts are often learned best through inquiry projects, lecture, or classroom discussions (please refer to the chapters on these instructional strategies).

REALITY CHECK

What are some concepts that teachers use in your endorsement area? Talk with teachers to identify the concepts in the curriculum. Ask the teachers how they help students learn these concepts, and how they assess student learning. Look at the standards for your endorsement area to indentify key concepts. How well do you understand these ideas?

Step 2: Studying Examples and Gathering Data

Once an established concept has been selected, you will need to develop a graphic organizer of some form to help students gather and record information about several examples of the concept. This organizer can take any form but must contain two components: (1) a list of three to five examples for students to study and (2) a set of three to five focus questions that direct students' attention to the critical attributes of the concept. As such, you will need to come up with examples of the concept, identify the critical attributes of the concept, and develop questions that address each of the critical attributes. Many times teachers feel perplexed as they try to identify examples and attributes of a concept. It is hard work, because you must think in depth about the concept. We find that you can identify the most critical three to five attributes efficiently by looking up the concept label in dictionaries or web sources related to the course you will be teaching (even the oft-criticized Wikipedia [www.wikipedia.org] provides a good starting place to consider what some think to be the critical attributes of a concept), having conversations with fellow teachers or other experts on the concept, and closely examining examples of the concept. Consider the following sample of a chart that a high school social studies teacher developed for the concept *social caste*, and possible student responses to the focus questions (Table 7.1). Four critical attributes for *social caste* are (1) hierarchical; (2) tied to occupation; (3) based on ideas of purity/cleanliness; and (4) inherited and rigid. By the way, a sociologist will likely be able to come up with more attributes. The attributes you select do not have to be an exhaustive list as much as a list of the most relevant and important attributes, given how you will use this concept in the classroom. As you look at Table 7.1, you will notice the four focus questions across the top, and their relation to the critical attributes of this concept. Down the left column are three examples of the concept that the teacher located online and modified so that his students could understand the descriptions better.

TABLE 7.1: Data-Gathering

	Is this country's social organization hierarchical?	Is the social organization tied to occupation?	How does the idea of purity/impurity contribute to a separation of the social groups?	Can people move out of the social groups into which they were born?
The *burakumin* are a social group in Japan whose occupations consist of unwanted jobs. These jobs include that of executioners, disposing of dead animals, and sweeping and cleaning. Historically, the emperor was the exact opposite in Japan. The people believed that he was a deity. In between the Emperor and the Burakumin were several social groups. During the middle ages, at the height of this social system, individuals were born into their social group and could not leave it.	Yes	Yes	Burakumin perform unwanted jobs	No

continued . . .

TABLE 7.1: Data-Gathering . . . *continued*

	Is this country's social organization hierarchical?	Is the social organization tied to occupation?	How does the idea of purity/ impurity contribute to a separation of the social groups?	Can people move out of the social groups into which they were born?
In India, one social group called the *panchamas*, or untouchables, are required to perform work that is considered to be "unclean." A higher social group in India, known as the *brahmans*, performs religious duties. Members of both groups are born into these roles, and individuals cannot change their membership in a group. To maintain "purity," marriage among members of different groups is not allowed. In addition to these social groups, there are others in India. The origins of this social structure are based on religion.	Yes	Maybe	Untouchables perform work that is considered "unclean"	No
Members of the *ñeeño* social group in Senegal inherit their status from their parents. The ñeeño are characterized by their occupations, such as blacksmiths, leatherworkers, and griots (musicians and storytellers). The *geer*, members of a higher social order, traditionally has discriminated against the *ñeeño*. Historically, the idea of pollution and impurity prevented intermingling between the ñeeño and other social groups. The *ñeeño* and other social groups are fixed within their social status.	Yes	Yes	Ideas of pollution and impurity prevent intermingling between groups	No

You may have noticed that the words this teacher used in the focus questions and in the descriptive examples might be difficult for younger students or for students who do not speak English as their first language. You need to structure a concept lesson to allow all of your students to learn. A student who is less proficient in English can be partnered with a student who speaks English as a first language. For "social caste," you could add alternative words to the examples and the focus questions. For example, the first focus question reads:

Is this country's social organization hierarchical?

To assist ELLs, you might pose this question as follows:

Is this country's social organization hierarchical? In other words, in this country do some groups of people always have more (or less) power than other people?

A teacher may determine that some of the words in the examples or the focus questions are too difficult for students who speak English as their first lanquage. Again, modifying word choice to help students understand is an important consideration, when developing the lesson.

Providing students with a chart helps them study particular examples of the concept (examples that have relevance to your course content), and helps students to consider the examples in light of the critical attributes. This is undertaken as they think to answer the focus questions. These charts will not necessarily use descriptive paragraphs such as the example above. They may present students with examples of a concept by providing video clips (e.g., clips of different examples of cell division in a biology class), words or phrases (e.g., examples of racism in the media during a current-events

TABLE 7.2: Charting Concepts: Fruit

Mango
Where does this grow on a plant? What purpose does this part serve for the plant? Does this contain seed(s)?
Tomato
Where does this grow on a plant? What purpose does this part serve for the plant? Does this contain seed(s)?
Pumpkin
Where does this grow on a plant? What purpose does this part serve for the plant? Does this contain seed(s)?

unit), pictures (e.g., examples of contrast in a graphic design class), or even skits (e.g., examples of compromise). One teacher gave his students three examples of *appeasement* along with five focus questions, and then had the students spend a day in the library researching each example and answering the questions.

The focus questions can follow each example, or be placed in a chart. The above Table 7.2 (adapted from Ehrenberg, 1981, p. 37) could be useful for the simple concept of *fruit*.

Step 3: Reporting Information

During this step, the students report to a group or to the whole class what they found out from thinking about the examples and answering the focus questions. By reporting on the data they collected, students compare their findings with others. This allows students to clarify any questions they could not answer, and verify their findings with others in class. As we mentioned above, placing students in small groups to do this step allows for peer tutoring and differentiating the instruction. This is also helpful for assisting ELLs in your classroom.

Step 4: Noting Differences

At this point in the lesson, the teacher talks with the whole class about the examples they have examined, and their answers to the focus questions. During this step, the teacher helps the students focus on the differences among the examples. An effective prompt for this is, "Look at the examples, and describe how these are different from each other." This is an important cognitive step because it requires students to consider how examples of a concept can have very different attributes but still be an example. In the above example of fruits, attributes such as the color, climate in which they grow, or size would not be critical attributes. Or, consider all of the different examples of dogs, which all possess the critical attributes for a canine.

Step 5: Noting Similarities

After contrasting the examples in Step 4, you as the teacher will proceed to have students compare the examples and help them identify how the examples are similar. An effective prompt for this is, "In what ways are the examples all alike?" This question directs students' attention to the answers (data) they provided for each focus question. You should list these on the board for use in the Step 6, "Synthesizing." These similarities match the critical attributes that you came up with when preparing the focus questions. You have not told them to your students, but they have come up with them on their own as a result of thinking about the different examples. You will keep asking them to identify similarities, and the students will identify all of the critical attributes by using their own thoughts and words. Look again at the data-gathering chart we gave for "social caste"; you can imagine how the attributes are identified by sharing similarities.

Step 6: Synthesizing

In this step, the students form the concept by combining the similarities into a sentence or statement. At this point, the students write their own definition of the concept, being sure to incorporate all of the similarities, on the chalkboard. The students then share aloud their sentences, and check each other to ensure that they have mentioned each similarity; the teacher engages with the students to check their definitions. These definitions will be accurate descriptions of the concept, but they will be in the students' own words and not be given to them by the teacher. Instead, the students will have developed these through their own thinking about the examples.

Step 7: Labeling

Although the concepts are abstract, the word or label that we use when referring to a concept is tangible. The concept label *cooperation* makes a lot of sense because the label is closely related to the critical attributes (*co-* means "more than one," and *operate* means "to do something"). The concept label *fruit* makes less sense because the label does not seem closely related to the critical attributes. At this step in the lesson, students think of labels that they believe capture the essence of the critical attributes. These labels do not need to be the actual words for the concept. In fact, the teacher focuses more on the reasons why a student selected a label than the actual label. Labeling is another type of synthesis, and it ensures that the students understand the gist of the concept. An effective prompt by the teacher might be, "Think of a word or phrase that you think captures the idea of your definition and the similarities we listed on the board. In a minute I will have you share what you came up with, and why that word is a good choice." Consider for a minute the concept of *compromise*. A student may suggest that a good label is "give and take," and another may suggest the label "negotiation." Both labels are acceptable *if* the students are able to explain why they are related to the critical attributes of the concept. After several students have the opportunity to state and explain their labels, the teacher provides them with the conventional word for the concept. Just as the students did, this is also a good place to add any insight into why this word is used when referring to this concept. In other words, see if you can provide any etymology for the word. This allows students to add to their understanding of the concept by learning the word that "adults use" when referring to the concept they have just explored. One final note on labeling: students may say the conventional word when they are thinking of a label. That is great; the teacher should follow up with the same request that students explain why they think this is an appropriate label.

Step 8: Assessing with Classifying Tasks

At this point, the concept has been formed and labeled. Now the teacher assesses students' understanding by asking them to engage in a series of classifying tasks. We will highlight three tasks that become increasingly complex, and that give you increased confidence that the students have learned and can use the concept. These tasks are addressed in the next section of this chapter.

These steps might be better understood with the following diagram:

1. Teacher selects a concept that will promote students' understanding.

2. Students study examples and gather data by answering the focus questions.

3. Students report what they discovered about each example.

4. The class notes differences among the examples.

5. The class notes the similarities among the examples, and a record of these is made on the board.

6. Students synthesize the similarities into a statement.

7. Students come up with their own label for the concept and learn the conventional word or phrase.

8. Teacher leads assessment with classifying tasks.

To see a teacher using concept formation in the classroom, visit the companion website.

APPROPRIATE ASSESSMENT TECHNIQUES TO USE WITH CONCEPT FORMATION

Assessment is so closely tied to the concept formation strategy that it really is an extension of Step 8, above. To assess students' understanding, you will determine if students can note how non-examples may resemble examples, but more importantly how they differ from them (Ehrenberg, 1981). You are also checking to see if students can make the generalization that all examples of a concept must have all of its critical attributes. For instance, if they finished forming the concept *war*, they should be able to identify why the "Vietnam Conflict" was close to, but not officially, a war (i.e., they should be able to identify which attribute of "war" is missing).

The most efficient and valid assessment of your students' conceptual understanding is to engage them in the following three types of classifying tasks: (1) distinguishing examples from non-examples; (2) producing examples; and (3) correcting non-examples (Parker, 2005, p. 198). The great advantage of these three types of concept practice is that they get students thinking about the critical characteristics of the concept. We describe each type below:

Type 1: Distinguishing Examples from Non-examples

In this classifying task, you present the students with a list of examples and non-examples all at once. For the concept *fruit*, the following mixed list might be used: *avocado*, *celery*, *carrot*, and *pinecone*. The instructions are, "Study these items and decide which ones are examples of *fruit*, and which items are non-examples. Also, note the items that you cannot determine. In a minute, I will ask several of you to support your decisions." Or, you might have them write their support as part of the assignment. Whichever way you prefer, be sure to give lots of students, if not all of them, the opportunity to support their decision.

Type 2: Producing Examples

This task is different from Type 1 because you do not provide any examples or non-examples. Rather, you give students only the concept label and ask them to come up with an example of the concept. This time, the instructions are, "Now that we have studied the concept called (state the concept label), I want you to find (or make/ write/produce/construct/look for, etc.) an example of it. Remember, in order to be an example, it must have all the critical attributes we identified in our definition. After you have produced your example, be ready to support it by telling us why it is an example and not a non-example." The students' support for the concept they produced is what you use to accurately assess their conceptual understanding.

Type 3: Correcting Non-examples

Most teachers consider this the most difficult type of classifying practice, which is why it is the final classification task (the first type is considered the least difficult). Unlike in Type 1, where you give students the label and several items, and Type 2, where you only give them the label, in Type 3 you give them the label and a non-example. Now the instructions are, "Here is a non-example of the concept we call (state the concept label). Your task is to make the necessary changes in this non-example to make it into an example. Then, I'll ask several of you to support the changes you made." Cognitively, your students will be comparing the critical attributes of the concept with the critical attributes of the non-example, *and then* they will identify which attributes are missing and make the needed changes. Earlier in the chapter we commented that *courage* and *bravery* are related but different concepts. If the concept that the students learned was *courage*, then having them change an example of *bravery* to be an example of courage would be a Type-3 task. Or, if the concept was *interdependence*, then being able to correct a non-example of interdependence would require them to understand the concept well enough to identify the missing critical attributes of the example and make the needed changes.

Of course, other assessments could be used in which the students engage in tasks that require them to use their conceptual understanding. For example, students in a chemistry class could demonstrate their conceptual understanding of neutral, acidic, and base chemicals. You might ask them to test ten different chemicals, using purple cabbage water and turmeric-stained parchment, categorize the chemicals into one of the three areas, and provide a rationale. The emphasis of all these assessments is to have students work with examples of the concept, and to demonstrate their understanding of the critical attributes that are part of each example (and that are missing in non-examples).

LOGISTICAL CONCERNS, INCLUDING BENEFITS AND OBSTACLES

As we mentioned before, preparation before the lesson is extensive. First, you need to select an established concept upon which you can explore future course content, and identify the three to five critical attributes common to every example of the concept. Next, you need to compose focus questions that address each critical attribute, and locate three to five examples of the concept. We described ideas for developing the examples earlier in the chapter, but some general thoughts bear repeating here, under logistics. Often the concept and examples will determine how students will gather data. For example, if students are exploring the concept of *propaganda*, then the examples will likely be statements, phrases, and/or images, because these are usually the forms that propaganda takes. These may best be viewed online or as a handout. If the concept is *theme*, then the examples will be fully developed themes of stories that the students need time to read. The examples need to provide enough information so that the students can answer the focus questions. As a result, you need to consider your students' prior knowledge as you prepare the examples. If you are teaching the concept *civilization* to sixth graders, you should not have the term *Mesopotamia* as an example. While this is a fine example of the concept, your students will not know enough about Mesopotamia to answer the focus questions. Instead, a paragraph description of Mesopotamia that emphasizes the key characteristics of all civilizations will facilitate students' forming of the concept. Therefore, you need to allow student opportunities to find and use information about the example. At times, this can occur simply from the examples given on a data-gathering chart. At other times, this may require more in-depth examinations of the examples.

Listing the similarities (Step 5) requires patience on your part as the teacher. Remember, you have already thought about the concept, but this is the first time your students will do so. The temptation is to turn this step into a question-and-answer session in which the students feel that they are trying to guess what you want. If you are patient, the students will come up with a list of similarities that very closely resembles the list of critical attributes you identified during your preparation. If students find this step difficult, prompt them with, "Look closely at the focus questions across the top and see if any of your answers reveal how the examples are alike." You might also need to model this for the students. For example, if the concept is *photosynthesis*, then you might model for your students how to identify similarities in this manner: "When I look at my answers to the focus question about sunlight, I see that I have the same answer for all the examples. So, one way these examples are alike is that they all require sunlight. How else are they alike?" Again, since you know the similarities, you need to exercise patience and allow your students the thinking time required to form the concept. The similarities must be listed on the chalkboard for use in Step 6, Synthesizing.

The synthesis step may require more time than you originally think. During this step, students write their definition of the concept from the list of similarities. Students will originally do this independently, and revise their definitions to ensure that they incorporate all of the critical attributes. You should have many students share their definitions. As they do, encourage the class to cross-check the definition with the similarities listed on the board, noting any gaps. After a student shares, initial definitions may need revisions. Allow time for this, so that all students eventually have a definition that incorporates all of the similarities. This step allows for you to assess student progress and understanding. It is a step where comments from each student are considered together. Students who have a strong grasp of the attributes are able to explain their thinking (which helps them understand the concept even more). Students who are having difficulty understanding are able to hear from peers about the critical attributes of the concept, and compare that with their current understanding. Students who are learning English as an additional language will benefit by hearing others in class share their ideas. If they have an English-speaking partner, then this is a great time for them to pair up and discuss what the class is developing as a definition.

CLASSROOM MANAGEMENT AND MOTIVATION

Each of the eight steps in the concept formation strategy guide the students in their understanding of the critical attributes. The principal classroom-management issues involve ensuring that you are monitoring the students, guiding them through the steps, and providing ample opportunities for them to share their ideas. It is during the sharing that you can assess their learning, and that they can learn from each other's ideas. Therefore, concept formation requires the teacher to facilitate students' independent work and whole-class interactions. The independent work will occur when students gather data, write their synthesized definitions, develop labels, and engage in the classifying tasks (Steps 2, 6, 7, and 8, respectively). The whole class interactions occur when students report their findings, consider differences and similarities, share their labels, and explain their classifying decisions (Steps 3, 4, 5, 7, and 8, respectively).

When students work independently, you may want them to work individually or with a partner (*independent* work is not always the same thing as *individual* work). We suggest limiting the size of these work teams to two or three, because the steps of the lesson require students to think on their own about the examples and focus questions. The use of partners is to assist this thinking and help with understanding the critical attributes; it is a great opportunity to pair an English speaking student with an ELL, or to pair a highly capable learner with a student needing extra assistance. If students are in large groups, they may rely on others for answers and not think as deeply about the examples and attributes of the concept. During the independent work period, the students must have time to answer the focus questions and think about the topic. By watching students closely, you will be able to decide when they have had adequate time to think. We have worked with teachers who have not allowed enough time (the result is that students do not gather adequate information to accurately form the concept), and with teachers who provide too much time (the result is that the lesson loses momentum, and the students disengage). Because the data gathering precedes a classwide reporting session, you do not need to wait until all students have fully completed the data-gathering phase. However, you should be aware of who is not finished, and watch them closely so that you are able to ensure that they complete their data gathering as the class reports on its findings.

The whole-class interactions need to allow as many students as possible the chance to share their ideas. To manage this, it is often helpful to ask for volunteers and to call on students. The only time you need to be up front writing on the chalkboard or on an overhead projection is when students report similarities and when they suggest labels for the concept. The rest of the time, you can walk around the room encouraging student participation. Since students may work with partners and share their ideas with the entire class, consider how the desks might be arranged to facilitate both. The conventional rows of desks or tables facing the front will work well (students then lean across the rows to interact with a partner), but so will any seating configuration in which students are facing the front of the room: they must be able to easily see the board or screen during the synthesis step.

During the entire lesson, you will want students to listen to and critique their classmates' thinking. When students gather data, be sure you are interested in what they are finding. You will need work at this, because you have already thought about the concept and its critical attributes in preparation for the lesson. You do not want to give the impression that your students are trying to guess what you want; rather, you need to impress upon them that you want them to think about the examples and come up with their own answers to the focus questions. It is a subtle difference, but one that helps motivate students to think for themselves, and not think for the teacher. For example, if you present the students with a data-gathering chart, be careful that they do not think it is merely a worksheet that they need to mindlessly complete. Instead, promote the idea that they need to think about the examples and questions. Show enthusiasm and curiosity for their answers as they report their findings, note differences, and suggest similarities.

ENHANCING STUDENT LEARNING WITH TECHNOLOGY

We have found that having students access a variety of examples of concepts online, after they have formed an understanding of a concept, helps accentuate their understanding. In addition, locating examples beyond the walls of the classroom becomes a powerful approach to enhancing learning. Students who learned about "political revolution" can access news accounts online about current revolutions. Student who learned about "climate change" are able to see this concept by visiting webcams, first-hand accounts, or even university lectures on the topic. Students who learned about derivatives can explore actual examples for taking the derivative of a function to find the velocity of an object. The world, full of concepts, comes into the classroom to help students examine a wide range of examples, and notice missing attributes of non-examples. You might, for example, provide your students with case studies of different phenomenon (e.g., different symbiotic relationships, different cultural traits) and ask them to search for examples online and then identify the crticial attributes in the examples.

We have also found online sources useful for you, the teacher, in devloping your own understanding of a concept. Searches for examples, definitions, and critical attributes will provide you with many learning opportunities. Years ago, a teacher might have hesitated to help students learn a concept because he lacked background knowledge about the idea. Today, learning about any concept is literally at our fingertips. Our companion website contains links to help you identify critical attributes for many concepts. We have also provided links to help you and your future students locate and evaluate primary source materials/resources.

MAKING A LESSON MORE MEANINGFUL FOR ELLs

Throughout this chapter, we have interjected several ideas for assisting ELLs during the concept formation lesson. More advanced ELLs will benefit from word formation excerises. In fact, advanced level English examinations, such as the TOEFL, use word formation as a portion of their assessment. Charting concept nouns, personal nouns, adjectives, and verbs helps students see the relationship between these categories and improve fluency. Students can use the word formation chart for language development in many ways such as by creating additions to the chart or creating sentences using words from the different columns. An example chart with hundreds of words listed from A to Z can be found at http://esl.about.com/od/vocabularyadvanced/a/a_wordforms1. htm or at our companion website.

Table 7.3 is a brief example of words from this site.

In Chapter 11, we mention "word walls" in the section on helping ELLs. That strategy is also useful for helping students see, recall, and use basic concepts and strategies. Word walls are lists of words written on butcher's paper and plastered on walls around the classroom to assist with vocabualry development. Often teachers ask students to help create the lists and add to the list as appropriate. In addition, the "labeling" step of the concept formation lesson allows students to think of their own

TABLE 7.3: Charting Word Formations for Concepts

Concept noun	Personal noun	Adjective	Verb
Absenteeism	absentee	absent-minded	to be absent
accounting	accountant	accountable	account
accusation	accuser/accused	accusing	accuse
calculation	calculator	calculated	calculate
law	lawyer	lawful/lawless	enforce the law
migration	migrant	migratory	migrate
theory	theorist	theoretical	theorize
volunteering	volunteer	volunteered	volunteer

word or phrase for the concept. Concepts are often specific to subject areas (e.g., theory, culture, fiction, scarcity, and metamorphosis), and as a result, the English words we use to label a concept can be very academic and confusing. Allowing students to label the concept allows them to attach a label that makes sense from a conceptual perspective and an English language perspective.

GUIDELINES FOR DECIDING IF CONCEPT FORMATION IS APPROPRIATE FOR THE CONTENT OF A LESSON

The concept formation strategy is an effective tool for helping your students think through the critical characteristics of a concept. It should not be used to teach vocabulary words to your students, but should be used to explore a few important concepts that will provide a foundation for future learning. One teacher we know uses the concept of *tradition* when teaching a unit on Japanese culture because she believes that exploring this concept in depth will help students understand the nuance of Japan's history and culture. Another teacher begins a geometry course by engaging students in a concept formation lesson about vectors. If understanding a complex idea is important for learning additional content in your course, then consider introducing the idea with the concept formation strategy.

Earlier, we mentioned the difference between *established* concepts and *dynamic* concepts. The critical attributes of established concepts are agreed upon by most people, but this is not the case with dynamic concepts. If you cannot identify three to five critical attributes that are clearly established, then this strategy will not be effective. Consider the important concept *culture*. Would you consider it dynamic or established? Your answer will help determine the appropriateness of the concept formation strategy. Similarly, reserve the concept formation strategy for those significant and/or more complex ideas that students have difficulty understanding, or for those ideas that students often misunderstand. For example, *institutional racism* is more complex than *prejudice* and may be the better concept of the two to explore with this strategy.

Because concept formation lessons take time to develop and teach, be sure you have the time to develop the lesson fully. If the focus questions are not complete, or if they do not focus students on the critical attributes, then the students might miss an important attribute. Use this strategy after you have double checked that the critical attributes are clearly identified, the examples are descriptive and appropriate, the focus questions are clear, and you have enough class time to develop the lesson. Usually, a concept formation lesson requires 40–50 minutes. If the students engage in extra research on the examples, then the lesson could take two days.

MAKING IT WORK IN YOUR CONTENT AREA

In Step 1 of the step-by-step lesson procedures, we had you consider a process for selecting a concept you might teach in your content area. We want to build on that a bit more in this section. Our intention is for you to identify how to use the concept formation strategy to help the students learn at least one "big idea" in your content area. We will restate what we put in that section, and then build on that activity. Work through the following twelve steps on your own or with a partner.

1. Given all the potential topics that students need to learn in your future classroom, identify five or six topics that you believe are critically important for your students to learn. Next, reflect on these topics and identify ideas or concepts that are an integral part of each topic. From this select list of concepts, select one that is complex and powerful enough for your students to explore.
2. State the concept that your students will learn (actually list the concept label).
3. Ascertain the origin of this label; often the origin, or etymology, provides insight into the label's critical attributes.
4. Ascertain your rationale for asking students to build on this idea. Why is it significant in your content area? What will precede this lesson? What will follow it?
5. Ascertain the critical attributes, and list them.
6. List three or four examples, and briefly describe how students will learn about these examples—for example, will they read about the example or view a video clip?
7. List three or four non-examples for the classifying tasks.
8. Ascertain which format will be best for the data-gathering chart. Will it be a matrix? Paragraphs and questions? A webpage?
9. Develop a data-gathering graphic organizer that lists examples and focus questions.
10. Develop a list of at least two examples and two non-examples of your concept that students can explore during the first classifying task.
11. Come up with a non-example of your concept that students can change into an example during the third classifying task.

12. Write lesson objectives for a concept formation lesson that incorporates the ABCD structure (see Chapter 3). It is important to note that objectives should be written before the lesson is written. Since concept formation has the single objective of helping students learn an important concept, we are here having you write the objective after you have thought through and applied each step of the concept lesson. In future concept lessons, however, you should write the objective(s) at the beginning.

CHAPTER REVIEW

- Research support for using concept formation:

  - Students often learn information superficially.
  - The purpose of the concept formation strategy is to help students form a robust understanding of significant concepts.

- Selecting, planning, and using concept learning activities:

  - Facts, concepts, and generalizations rely on each other to help promote a deeper understanding.
  - Concept formation is an inductive approach that follows a sequential eight-step process.

- Managing the classroom/learning environment during concept learning:

  - monitor students;
  - guide them through the steps;
  - provide ample opportunity for them to share their ideas.

- Assessing student learning appropriately during concept formation relies on classifying tasks:

  - distinguish examples from non-examples;
  - produce examples;
  - correct non-examples.

- Using technology to enhance learning:

  - accessing examples of concepts from around the world;
  - using the internet to identify critical attributes of a concept.

- Considerations for ELLs during concept formation lessons:
  - partnering with an English-speaking classmate;
  - word walls of key concepts;
  - charting concept nouns.

NOTE

1 This procedure was developed by Parker (2005, 2012) and is based on the work of Taba (1967) and Ehrenberg (1981).

CHAPTER 8

Cooperative Learning

CHAPTER OBJECTIVES

In this chapter, you will learn about:

- research support for using cooperative learning in the classroom;
- step-by-step procedures for selecting, planning, and using cooperative learning strategies;
- managing the classroom/learning environment during cooperative learning;
- assessing student learning when working in cooperative groups;
- using technology to enhance learning;
- considerations for ELLs during cooperative learning activities.

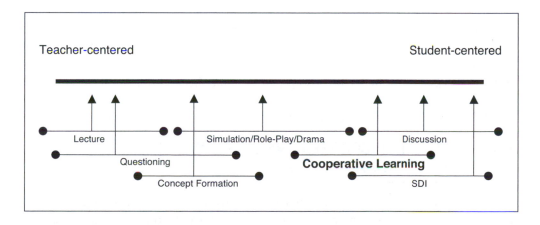

Mr. James placed the students in his seventh grade mathematics class into groups of four. He intentionally created the groups so that each group had students with a range of ability when it came to the unit they were learning (graphing and ratios), a mix of ethnic background, and a balance of gender. He gave each group a sheet of paper that described the task: graph the relationship between their height and their arm span, create a data table, and develop a poster. Each group had a meter stick for measuring, and a worksheet for recording the data. After the group found the height and arm spam for each member, they sat down together and graphed the data by placing their heights on the x-axis and their arm spans on the y-axis. Mr. James required each member to graph their own measurements, and asked each member to help others in the group complete the tasks and understand what they were accomplishing. They then made a small poster with a data table of the group members' measurements, a graph of the data table, and a summary of the relationship between height and arm span. They made the poster together, with each member being responsible for one of the poster features. The groups were free to make the posters colorful and creative, and then each signed their name and displayed them in the hallway and cafeteria for the rest of the school to see.

OVERVIEW

During lessons that use cooperative learning, students work together in groups to help each other learn content and skills. Cooperation requires students to accomplish shared goals. During cooperative learning activities, students work to complete tasks that help them learn individually and also help group members learn as well. In short, cooperative learning places students in groups to maximize their learning. In the process, students learn to use critical social skills. Cooperative learning groups typically range from three to seven students, with the ideal number being four or five. Keeping the size of the groups small encourages students to work together and to more actively participate. Cooperative learning is not group work. In this chapter, we will help you understand the difference between cooperative group learning and conventional group projects. Many of the instructional strategies mentioned in Part 2 of this book could use cooperative learning groups. Cooperative learning, therefore, is an instructional strategy that involves placing students into groups, and helping them work together to complete a given task.

A DESCRIPTION OF COOPERATIVE LEARNING AND RESEARCH FINDINGS

Educational researchers have examined cooperative learning extensively for several decades. Research studies consistently find that cooperative learning has positive effects on student achievement, because the process of interacting with others promotes learning. Students often learn more and learn more quickly when compared to students working alone or who are not working in cooperative groups (Johnson et al., 1994).

Student achievement is highest when the cooperative learning activity requires group members to work together "to earn recognition, grades, rewards, and other indicators of group success" (Slavin, 1989/1990, p. 52). Said another way, group goals and tasks requiring students to depend on each other and work together to attain group goals lead to higher levels of achievement. What causes this increase in achievement has been the focus of many years of research. Most research studies conclude that group goals and individual accountability decreases competition among students and motivates them to help each other learn and enhance their own learning. Cooperative learning has at its core the idea that students must both "pull their own weight" and work together to accomplish a task. The cooperative tasks are designed so that one person is not able to complete the group's assignment alone. By holding members individually accountable, the group is positioned so that members help each other, work interdependently (and not independently), and learn more. Students often complain about "working in groups," because they feel as though they have to do all the work, or because they have had previous experiences in groups where partners "slack off," or "do nothing." This takes place because a teacher does not have a method in place for holding all the group members accountable. Often teachers assign a group grade. This is in conflict with cooperative learning research, because group grades will not promote individual achievement the way group goals and individual accountability will. Consider the following example of one approach for holding students individually accountable: a biology teacher places students in groups of three and assigns them the task of analyzing water samples from six different streams. The teacher then specifies that each student needs to analyze two samples, and that each student needs to compose a report comparing his or her two analyses with the other group members' analyses. The group must produce a PowerPoint presentation on the "state of water in our community," and the students each receive a grade for their analysis and comparisons. The PowerPoint presentation is recorded as either satisfactory or unsatisfactory. The teacher grades in this fashion so that the students will analyze their samples and hold each other accountable for completing the analyses. The group is interdependent, but each member is assessed on their individual work. What other examples of **group investigations** can you come up with for your content area that have this mix of individual accountability and group rewards?

Findings from 164 research studies on cooperative learning specify that placing students in groups (as opposed to having students select their own groups), assigning a task where they must work together, and teaching specific social skills have a positive effect on student achievement (Johnson et al., 2000). Research in these areas reveals that when students cooperate, and the emphasis on competition and individual achievement is decreased, student learning increases. For example, placing students in heterogeneous cooperative learning groups at least one time a week has a significantly positive effect on learning (Marzano et al., 2001). Similarly, students spend more time on task, are more motivated to complete the assignments, and are more capable at transferring their learning to other contexts during cooperative group activities (Kohn, 1993; Johnson and Johnson, 1999). In contrast, when students with lower abilities are grouped together, their academic performance decreases (Kulik and Kulik, 1987; 1991), and when students are placed in groups *without* support structures that reduce competition and increase interdependence, they do not attain higher academic levels of achievement (Anderson et al., 1997).

Cooperative learning has a positive impact on social interactions among students, because students learn how to interact with one another. When you teach, you will model for your students how to work with others. One of the most consistent findings is that "when students of different racial or ethnic backgrounds work together toward a common goal, they gain in liking and respect for one another" (Slavin, 1989/1990, p. 53). Why do you think this might be true?

Cooperative learning has also been shown to increase classmates' acceptance of students who are traditionally marginalized because of low academic ability (Slavin, 1989/1990, p. 54; Cohen, 1994; Cohen and Lotan, 1997). Students are marginalized, or placed outside of the mainstream of the classroom, for reasons such as ability, ethnicity, wealth/poverty, or appearance. Elizabeth Cohen has examined how student "status" leads to different behaviors in groups thus leading to different treatment by peers. As she states,

> A status characteristic is an agreed upon social ranking where everyone feels it is better to have a high rank than a low rank. Examples of status characteristics are race, social class, sex, reading ability, and attractiveness . . . high status individuals are expected to be more competent than low status individuals across a wide range of tasks that are viewed as important. When a teacher assigns a task to a group of students, some of whom are higher and some lower on any of the status characteristics described above, these general expectations come into play . . . those who are higher status come to hold a high rank in the status order that emerges in the group interaction. Those who hold lower status come to hold a low rank on that status order.
>
> (1994, p. 33)

No one formally assigns status to students, just as no one formally assigns status to people in society at large. It is one aspect of a diverse society that perpetuates the status quo and the current power structure in the society. High-status students are expected to be better (and they come to expect it of themselves), and low-status students are not expected to make important contributions to the group (and they begin to believe they have little to offer). Members of a group often promote some members to be active (high-status students), and some members to be subordinate (low-status students). If left on their own, most student groups will reiterate the existing status of students. Even when groups are changed, a student's status often follows him or her to the next setting (Cohen and Lotan, 1997). However, cooperative learning has been found to increase the status of marginalized students. By assigning students to groups, structuring tasks to require interdependence, reducing competition, and proactively teaching students how to divide the work load, understand group goals, listen, paraphrase ideas, and encourage each other, teachers can help students overcome the barriers of status and marginalization. In addition, students increase friendships with group mates after working together in cooperative learning groups or teams, and over time students increase their abilities to listen to others, consider ideas from all members of a group, assign tasks equally, and have a greater sense of concern for the success of all members in a group. We often hear from people in a wide range of occupations (e.g., teachers, doctors, lawyers, contractors, retailers, small business owners, and community service workers) that the ability to work with others cooperatively is a critical "job skill." We add to this idea that it is also a critical skill for citizens of a democracy. The research clearly suggests that cooperative learning promotes learning of skills and content. The idea that cooperative learning promotes pro-social behavior among students is an added value of using cooperative learning strategies.

The question that arises in the midst of this research support is "What are these strategies?" Cooperative learning is much more than simply placing students in groups and assigning them a task. This simplistic approach fosters behavior where one or two capable students "take over" and complete the task. Students who are marginalized by peers and even by the larger community because of reputation, ethnicity, gender, lower ability, or other social factors are often further separated from the assignment. At its worst, group work becomes an activity in which students merely go through the motions of interacting with one another. Resentment is stirred up in the student who ends up completing the task on his or her own, and students who do not participate in class might even be pressured to contribute to a lesser degree. Groups, thus, can create resentment, reinforce stereotypes, and benefit some students to the detriment of others. The teacher must structure group work. We think that merely asking students to work in groups (even if you assigned them to the groups) can at times do more academic and social harm than good. Very specific attributes are needed to promote **positive interdependence** (which we believe is another name for cooperation). Johnson et al. (1994, p. 26) have developed the following five "essential elements" of cooperative learning that we believe will help you structure your future use of student groups:

1. positive interdependence
2. face-to-face interactions
3. group goals and individual accountability
4. interpersonal and small-group skills
5. group processing.

The following overview of these elements is intended to help you clarify the importance of each when you plan to use cooperative learning.

1. *Positive interdependence*
   When people cooperate they have positive interdependence on each other. Students must see that they need each other to accomplish a task and to learn. Many techniques are available for teachers to use in promoting this. Teachers might request that students share resources, materials, and information so that the students genuinely need each others' ideas and information. For example, in a biology class, each group member might be responsible for learning a different example of a symbiotic relationship, but the group needs to use all the examples together. Each member informs group mates about the information she gathered. The teacher could also have the group establish mutual goals about how members

might help each other learn the content or skills. A group might have the goal that each member will complete his research about a symbiotic relationship in the next two days. Or, the group might set the goal that everyone will provide a paragraph description and a photo of the symbiotic relationship. Goals could also specify the role of each member during a class presentation.

Positive interdependence can also be fostered when the teacher provides group awards. This could be in the form of praise (e.g., applause and commendations after an effective presentation to the class), extra credit points (e.g., points awarded if all members' test scores are above a certain percentile), or other incentives that the whole group receives other than a grade. Finally, interdependence is fostered by assigning roles within the group that are necessary for the group to progress. For example, students in a group might take on the following roles: (1) the *coordinator* (someone who allocates responsibilities and keeps the group on task); (2) the *checker* (someone who makes sure all members of the group are participating and understanding the content); (3) the *recorder* (someone who takes general notes for the group and organizes the final group solution); and (4) the *skeptic* (someone who keeps the group from leaping to premature conclusions) (Heller et al., 1992; Johnson and Johnson, 2004). These are simply suggested roles, and you will develop your own based on the needs of your students. These roles are assessed and monitored by the group and by the teacher. Students hold themselves accountable, and exhort or encourage each other to fully complete their role. As the teacher, you must remember that you are helping students learn content (e.g., symbiotic relationships) *and* that you are helping students learn interdependence. You must monitor student interactions with both in mind. We will discuss this in more detail in the assessment section of this chapter.

2. *Face-to-face interactions*
   Many of the cognitive and social benefits of cooperative learning occur during face-to-face group interactions and discussions. Requiring students to meet and work as a group is essential. These meetings may occur during class so you can monitor student interactions, or they may occur outside of the classroom if the group needs to complete tasks as homework. Students cannot work toward many of the interdependent elements listed above without meeting face-to-face. Likewise, these interactions require students to engage in higher-order thinking, such as summarizing, explaining, elaborating ideas, and seeking clarification. The interactions promote content and skill learning. It is also during these interactions that students cooperate in earnest with others who may be "different" from themselves. As the teacher, you need to assess the degree of cooperation that occurs. We will explore this more in the assessment section of this chapter.

   Your students will likely lack social skills that promote interdependence with others. Face-to-face interactions are a critical element for "developing harmonious interracial relations in desegregated classrooms" (Cohen, 1994, p. 17) that the research on cooperative learning suggests. At times you may need to stop a group project and work solely on interaction skills. The following experience of one student teacher serves as an example:

Jill placed students in **heterogeneous groups**, and assigned them to hypothesize about underlying causes of the Civil War. After the first day, she noticed that most of the groups were not working together. The assigned task required interdependence, but the ability and ethnic diversity of the groups seemed to hamper students' willingness to work together. Jill decided to work on the relationships of the students, and spent two days engaging in "trust building" and "team building" activities (e.g., leading a blind-folded partner around an obstacle course, identifying positive character traits of group members). She plainly told students that she placed them in groups with classmates they did not know well, and that she would be watching to see how well the groups worked together. She told them that she wanted little competition in the groups, and that each student would assess his own performance and his group members' performance in helping the group work together. After the assigned two days, she resumed the Civil War assignment, and closely monitored student interactions. At least twice a week she had students turn in the group and individual assessments of their progress. Jill used these assessments to teach specific social skills to the class. After working in the groups, every student received at least 85% of the total points possible for the project!

3. *Group goals and individual accountability*
    Cooperative learning groups will have goals such as completing a task or assignment, working to accomplish a project by cooperating, and the mutual goals listed above (in the "positive interdependence" section). In addition, each student must be held individually accountable for her own learning. Cooperative groups have not met their goals until every member of the group has learned. Group members need to work hard at their own learning, and work to support each other. You may think of creative ideas for holding students accountable, but a few common ideas include: (1) dividing a large group project into smaller tasks that are divided among the group; that way the group is responsible for the larger project, and each member is responsible and held accountable for completing one or more critical tasks; (2) quizzing or testing each member individually over material the group was learning together. This will keep students accountable to learn content and to teach it to each other; or (3) having one member answer for the entire group. This way the students will prepare together so that all members can provide answers effectively.

4. *Interpersonal and small-group skills*
    Most people do not have adequate preparation to work cooperatively in a group, and your students will be no exception. Cooperative learning is dependent on you helping your students learn effective interpersonal or social skills. These are taught in the context of the group project. Students need to learn trust, decision-making abilities, conflict management skills, and motivation techniques. For example, the ability to criticize an idea and not the person presenting the idea is difficult to learn. Learning this while working on a group project will allow students to develop this skill in an authentic setting. Similarly, confronting students who are not sharing the workload is difficult, but necessary, and a cooperative group becomes a

powerful setting for learning how to do this. Many times the interpersonal and group skills are identified because a group is struggling to work together. Rather than fearing this, you need to take full advantage of "uncooperative" group work by identifying and helping students learn the social skills that will help the groups work together more effectively. More on how to do this follows in the section on "logistical concerns."

5. *Group processing*

    You eventually want your students to learn how to work cooperatively, assign roles, hold each other accountable, and promote group mates' learning. Therefore, you must allow students the time to analyze how well their groups are working, how well classmates are learning, and how well they are using social skills. Not only does it help you and your future students determine if they are learning but it also promotes effective relationships among the group members. The structure for facilitating group processing will vary, but generally it involves students reflecting on how well they are meeting goals, identifying any obstacles or problems that might prevent them from cooperating, and developing action plans for overcoming the problems. Some teachers observe their students during group tasks and provide written feedback about how well the groups worked together, and areas that need to be improved (some teachers even have the students do these observations). We like to think of this as a debriefing period. It demonstrates to your students that you value group work, and that you are not interested in the product alone; the process is important enough to discuss and improve on so the next group project is even better.

Implicit in all of these elements is the point that the teacher helps students learn the process of working together. Students are assigned to groups, intentionally by the teacher, to maximize their learning of content and social skills. Cooperative learning usually requires that students are placed in "heterogeneous" groups. In other words, the students do not form or select their own groups, but the teacher forms the groups with mixed ability, mixed ethnicity, and mixed gender. Students will tend to choose to work with classmates who are similar to themselves in terms of culture and ability. This type of *homogeneous* grouping does not necessarily help students learn content more effectively, and it does not promote the social benefits of cooperative learning. High-ability students do not have opportunities to deepen their understanding by helping group members learn key concepts, and low-ability students do not have peers who can help them attain a deeper level of understanding (Slavin, 1993). **Homogeneous groups** have no positive effect on increasing students' understanding of culture or viewpoints different from their own (Mitchell et al., 2004); therefore, teachers need to place students in groups purposefully (as opposed to randomly). We suggest grouping the students as heterogeneously as possible. When placing students, consider the ethnicities, genders, and ability levels of your students, and try to group students in a way that cuts across these categories. Personalities of students, previous experiences working together, knowledge of the topic they are exploring, and the amount of time you are able to spend working on social skills will also impact your placement of students. We find that placing students in groups is a very difficult task, because so many variables interact. However, your thoughtful work in placing students will help promote the type of student achievement reported in the cooperative learning research and is well worth the effort. As you get to know your students better, you become more insightful at grouping them, and you begin to see how the group projects benefit your students.

The idea of cooperation is neither new nor is the goal of having students work cooperatively in groups. What we want you to think about in this chapter is the intentional grouping of students so that they are able to work effectively together to accomplish tasks. Cooperative learning is not easy to accomplish, because time and effort are needed to place students in groups, assess their progress, and determine both the social and academic needs of your students. In Chapter 3, we described three categories of learning objectives: content, skill, and social. Cooperative learning will help students learn academic content, intellectual thinking skills as they research and complete assigned tasks, and social interaction skills as they learn to work interdependently with group members.

STEP-BY-STEP PROCEDURES FOR PLANNING AND IMPLEMENTING COOPERATIVE LEARNING

To take full advantage of the content learning and the social benefits of cooperative learning, you will need to make preparations before your students begin working.

Step One: Forming Groups

You should usually plan on forming groups with three to five students. Groups of this size allow for the benefits of mixed groups, while still being small enough to promote interdependence and individual accountability. Often teachers will place students in groups randomly, or they will allow students to select their own groups. As we wrote earlier, cooperative learning research clearly suggests that the teacher places students in groups to serve a purpose. Usually, this means that each group is made up of students who are different from one another in several categories: ethnicity, ability, gender, and so on. We suggest that you think about the task you will have students complete, and place students in groups accordingly. Consider the following examples:

- A social studies teacher wants his students to create a policy recommendation to the local city government about developing a vacant lot. The space could become a park, shopping center, or community center. How might he place students in groups? He might be sure each group has a student who has some artistic skills so the group can provide a sketch of their recommended land use. He might decide that the perspective of boys and girls need to be considered, so the groups will be of mixed gender. He might also decide that groups with mixed ability will promote better learning of the issue for all the groups' members.
- A language arts teacher wants her students to write a team biography on the courage of Rosa Parks. Each team member is responsible for learning and writing about a

different event in Parks' life that demonstrates her courage. The group will turn their individually written events into chapters, and work to ensure that all the chapters flow together. The group will also develop and timeline of Parks' life, a cover page, and an introduction to the biography.[1] The teacher might decide to place the students so that each group has a member with strong research skills, and a member who needs help with research skills. She might also create groups of mixed ethnicity.

• Students in a biology class are exploring cellular reproduction. The teacher worries that the students are socially immature. She might decide to create groups that are of mixed ability, but of the same gender. The groups are comprised of all girls or all boys, but within each group the students' abilities are diverse.

The point of these examples is to consider how the content will best be learned with groups, and how placing students purposefully in groups may best promote student learning. Remember, the research on cooperative learning clearly states that mixed groups promote student learning. Research studies consistently find that high- and low-ability students learn and benefit from working in mixed-ability groups. How you mix them will depend on how well you know your students, and on the task you are assigning.

Step 2: Conducting the Cooperative Learning

Any classroom activity using cooperative learning will follow the same general sequence: An introduction to the task; an invitation or request to work interdependently on the task; a final product or performance by the group that is assessed. During the introduction, you will place students in groups and provide an overview of what you want the groups to accomplish by the end of their time working together. Following this you will assign the task(s) the groups will accomplish, help the groups get started with materials and resources, and assist them as they begin working together. The final part of the sequence involves the groups showing what they have accomplished, and while it is a group product, individual work in developing the final product should be clear.

We find it useful to consider cooperative learning activities as being "informal" or "formal" (Johnson et al., 1998). *Informal cooperative learning* involves quickly formed groups that may work together for a few minutes or a whole class period. You might have these groups focus their attention on the content they are learning, talk through a problem, or clarify student understanding (In Time, 2004). If you use informal cooperative learning, you will likely place students in groups spontaneously without a lot of planning. The task may be quickly stated ("Please look at your answer to Problem 4 with the person sitting next to you," or "I would like you to quickly form groups of three and recall two reasons in favor and two reasons against drilling for oil in wildlife preserves"). And though the task may require students to work together and cooperate, it does not necessarily possess all of the critical cooperative learning elements that researchers have identified.

An example of an informal cooperative learning strategy can be found in "Numbered Heads Together" (Kagan, 1992). With this approach, the teacher asks a question to the group. Each member of the group has a number (one through five, depending on the size of the group). The group members consult to make sure everyone knows the answer. The teacher then calls out one number and the students in each group who were assigned that number must produce the answer. This is an effective review strategy. Another example of a review strategy is "think-pair-share" (see Chapter 5). With this approach, the teacher poses a question, students pair with a classmate near them, and they share their ideas and thoughts about the question. A third example of informal cooperative learning is the use of "buzz groups." This is the equivalent of small-group brainstorming in which the teacher presents a topic or question to students in small groups, and they then talk (or "buzz") with each other about the topic. For example, if you teach a social studies or an earth science class, your students might form buzz groups to brainstorm answers to the question: "Where should we haul our community's garbage?" Students in a literature class could buzz about their predictions of what will happen next in a story they are reading. Buzz groups, such as the think-pair-share method are also useful as a preparation for whole class brainstorms or discussions. Students are more likely to talk in small groups (especially if they have worked with each other on previous projects), and after they have talked together in groups, students may feel more comfortable sharing with the larger class.

Formal cooperative learning groups work together longer—usually from one class period to several weeks. You can structure any assignment to fit within formal co-operative learning (In Time, 2004). As Johnson and his colleagues note, "Formal cooperative learning groups ensure that students are actively involved in the intellectual work of organizing material, explaining it, summarizing it, and integrating it into existing conceptual structures. They are the heart of using cooperative learning" (1998, p. 7).

Informal cooperative learning is useful for specific tasks that are completed fairly quickly. Not a lot of time is spent helping students learn "how to cooperate," but time is spent completing assigned tasks. If students lack cooperation and social skills, then informal cooperative learning may be difficult to use. Formal cooperative learning helps students learn content *and* social skills. It requires additional time to teach social skills. Teachers grade students more so during formal cooperative learning, because of the structure and time students spend together. We will address this more in the assessment section of this chapter.

To see a video of a teacher who has organized students into cooperative learning groups, visit the companion website.

THREE COMMON TYPES OF COOPERATIVE LEARNING

In this chapter, we present three common formal cooperative learning strategies for you to consider: (1) **student teams achievement divisions (STAD)**; (2) **jigsaw**; and (3) group investigations. A fourth formal strategy, **structured academic controversy**, fits more appropriately as a discussion technique. In this strategy, students interact with one another to form an opinion about a controversial issue. We describe it in detail when examining classroom discussions in Chapter 10. Obviously many forms of cooperative learning exist, and you may develop your own forms that have all of the critical elements. These four strategies are ones that many teachers and researchers consider to be the most common and effective to use. Each strategy involves the important elements listed above (teacher selected groups, positive interdependence, face-to-face interactions, group goals and individual accountability, interpersonal and small-group skills, and group processing).

Student Teams Achievement Divisions

This method (Slavin, 1983; 1988; 1995) involves competition among groups and is useful when reviewing information and preparing for a quiz/test. Competition *within* groups destroys cooperation because students become independent (and not inter-dependent), but competition *among* groups may actually draw members within a group closer. To use STAD you need to follow three essential steps. First, you must present the content to your students through lecture, reading assignments, or other instructional strategies. Second, you must place your students in mixed groups of three to five members and ask them to complete a series of worksheets and activities that review the content and help them master the information they just received. The students help team mates learn the content. Those who need help in understanding learn from those who understand the content. The students who already understand the content increase their understanding as a result of explaining or teaching it to students who needing assistance. The third step is the assessment. Each student takes quizzes on the information as individuals, and the team receives points based on the level of individual improvement over previous scores. The students are graded on their performances on the quiz, and the groups receive bonus points based on members' improvements.

STAD is appropriate for a variety of subjects that focus on material with specific "correct answers" (Newmann and Thompson, 1987). Consider the following example: A mathematics teacher wants students to review the use of trigonometry when working with right triangles. She could place students in teams, and provide a number of exercises using sine, cosine, and tangent for solving problems with right triangles. After a class session of the teams working together, the students take a quiz on using these principles. The teacher sets aside the next class session for the groups to meet and correct wrong answers and help each other clarify their conceptual understanding. This is followed by a final quiz over the material, and the group is rewarded for improved quiz scores. As you can see, STAD is a long-term cooperative activity where the students work together for several days or possibly several different times during the year. It is not an approach that can be used for a single segment during the day, because the groups need to work together with an eye toward improving every member's level of understanding and achievement.

The Jigsaw Approach

This cooperative learning method (Aronson et al., 1978) effectively uses groups to examine information that the whole group is studying. Whereas STAD focuses students on specific facts, ideas, skills, the jigsaw approach focuses students more on connections and relationships among the content. For example, each student in a five-member group is given information that comprises only one of the five parts of the information. Each student in the group is responsible for a different piece of information. Students leave this original "home" group and join other students who have been given the same information. These are referred to as "expert groups"; all students with the same piece of information get together, study it, and decide how best to teach it to their peers in the original group. When the experts are finished, the students return to their home groups (which are now composed of one expert on each of the five topics), and each teaches his or her portion of the lesson to the others in the group. Students work cooperatively in two different groups, their home group and the expert group, and are held individually accountable by the performance of their group on an assessment over all five parts. This strategy was later updated to "Jigsaw II," which includes the idea that all students are presented with all of the information first, and then they are separated into expert groups. This updated approach becomes one of clarifying and learning information that everyone has already seen at least one time.

The jigsaw approach is complicated until you have observed them in use, or tried teaching with them, so we offer a very simple example to help clarify the strategy:

A class of 30 students in a literature class is reading a novel (this is for sake of an example. Students might just as easily be in an algebra class completing word problems; in a physics class experimenting with the formula $E = mc^2$. You get the idea and can think of your own endorsement area). The teacher wants to be sure that all the students understand the first five chapters of the novel. After students read the first five chapters, he places students in home groups of five and assigns each student one of the five chapters.

Home Group A: Student 1, Student 2, Student 3, Student 4, Student 5

Home Group B: Students 1, 2, 3, 4, 5

Home Group C: 1, 2, 3, 4, 5

Home Group D: 1, 2, 3, 4, 5

Home Group E: 1, 2, 3, 4, 5

Home Group F: 1, 2, 3, 4, 5

All of the students assigned to chapter one then meet together (as do all of the students assigned chapters two, three, four, and five), and clarify the characters, setting, and plot of their chapter. Their goal is to become an expert on their assigned chapter. In the classroom, the students would be in five groups (one for each chapter) with six students in each group.

Chapter 1 Experts: 1, 1, 1, 1, 1, 1

Chapter 2 Experts: 2, 2, 2, 2, 2, 2

Chapter 3 Experts: 3, 3, 3, 3, 3, 3

Chapter 4 Experts: 4, 4, 4, 4, 4, 4

Chapter 5 Experts: 5, 5, 5, 5, 5, 5

Students then return to their home group. Since each of the five chapters is again represented, each student tells the group about the chapter on which he or she became experts, and collectively the group members receive an overview of the five chapters.

Home Group A: Student 1, Student 2, Student 3, Student 4, Student 5

Home Group B: Students 1, 2, 3, 4, 5

Home Group C: 1, 2, 3, 4, 5

Home Group D: 1, 2, 3, 4, 5

Home Group E: 1, 2, 3, 4, 5

Home Group F: 1, 2, 3, 4, 5

Group Investigation

This method (Sharan and Sharan, 1989/1990) provides students with a significant amount of choice and control. Groups are mixed, but they are additionally formed to match students who share an interest about the same topic. For example, if the teacher wants students to examine stem cell research, some students may be interested in cloning, others in controversies surrounding cloning research, and others in stem cell potential. The group members help plan how they will research the topic and how they will present it, and divide the work among themselves. The teacher facilitates this task based on the needs of the group. Each member then carries out his or her part of the investigation, and the group summarizes the work and presents their findings to the class (Sharan and Sharan, 1989/1990, p. 17). This strategy requires the teacher to act as a resource person, while providing direction and clarification as needed. The teacher's task is to create a stimulating work environment. Six specific stages comprise group investigation. To contextualize these stages, think through how each might help students in groups of four who are asked to work on a science fair project explaining how boats float (adapted from Blosser, 1992; Sharan and Sharan, 1989/1990, pp. 17–20):

- The teacher identifies the general topic and students identify subtopics.
- Students work together to plan how they will carry out the investigation of their subtopic or set of questions, and they equally assign tasks.
- Students investigate the topic, and work to complete their tasks.
- In their groups, students analyze and evaluate the information they have collected and plan how to present this information to the rest of the class.
- Each group presents a summary of the results of its investigation so that all students gain a broad perspective of the general topic. The students teach the class about their topic.
- The teacher solicits feedback from the class about the presentations, and feedback from the group members about the topic, the process, and the presentation. The teacher also assesses each student's part of the investigation.

REALITY CHECK

Observe a classroom in your endorsement area when students are working in groups. Why are they working in groups? Did the students select their own group members? What type of cooperation is taking place? Are the students assigned particular roles? What social skills do the students need to work well together? Share your answers with others from your same endorsement area and with others who will be endorsed to teach a different subject. Also, compare your observations with the cooperative learning video on the companion website for the book.

CLASSROOM MANAGEMENT AND MOTIVATION

When students work in cooperative learning groups, the classroom needs to be managed in a unique manner. In Chapter 1, we mentioned that a characteristic of effective teachers is that they do not sit down while teaching. Instead, they monitor the classroom by interacting with students and assisting them (Doda et al., 1987). During cooperative learning activities, you will need to actively monitor each group's progress to ensure that they are progressing according to your plan, that they understand the task and have appropriately divided the workload among themselves, that their questions are answered, and that you provide them with guidance for working together to complete their task.

When you monitor the groups, you are assessing both their group progress and each member's individual progress. Every member of a group should be able to explain both the group task and his individual part in accomplishing that task. When monitoring groups, a good question to ask students is "How are you helping your group right now?" If they are cooperating, all students should be able to tell you their own progress and the group's progress. If a student is not working very hard, then you will refer him to his role as part of the group and request him to work on completing that task. For example, if a group is in the computer laboratory to locate different types of volcanic activity around the world, students may each be examining a different region for "hot spots." Each student should be able to tell you his or her progress in locating volcanoes, as well as how this fits into the group task. If you come across a student who is off task, you can easily determine what this student should be doing, and ask him or her a question such as: "What does your group expect you to be doing right now?" In this way, the student will need to answer to the group norms and expectations.

As we mentioned earlier in this chapter, placing students into groups does not guarantee cooperation. Even purposefully placing students into groups to create a mix of ability levels, ethnicities, skills, and gender does not necessarily result in interdependence and cooperation. As the teacher, you will need to establish group norms and expectations. Using cooperative learning requires that you are willing to teach cooperative skills to your students. These skills may not be part of your content area, but they are critical if your students are to work interdependently. The first task is to help students recognize the need for a particular social skill. We have seen this need emerge when groups cannot get along, fail to complete a task, or come and complain to the teacher about a group mate. A less frustrating approach for students is for the teacher to communicate to the class before problems arise why different skills are important. You may use skits, video clips, examples from real-life experiences, or other strategies to help students recognize the importance of cooperation. As the teacher, you need to help students understand particular cooperative or social skills. One effective approach for this is to model the skill as the teacher and incorporate the use of a "T-Chart," or a "looks-like/sounds-like chart." These charts help students identify behavioral expectations for specific cooperation skills. They are called "T-Charts" because they have two columns and are shaped like the letter "T." Consider the example in Table 8.1 (adapted from Johnson et al., 1994, p. 72).

The whole class, or each group, completes the T-Chart. When they complete the first column, they consider what they would see when watching a group of peers working together in a group. For the second column, they come up with comments that they might hear (note that these exact phrases are not what is important, rather it is the idea behind each comment). We suggest posting these in the classroom as an additional form of accountability. This could be a type of rubric that students adhere

TABLE 8.1: T-Chart for "Working Together in a Group"

Looks like	Sounds like
Eye contact	"Good idea"
Facing group mates	"Have you thought about this?"
Interested/engaged in the talk	"What is your idea?"
Listening	"That is interesting"
One person speaking	"I don't agree, because . . ."

to during group projects. We have seen teachers develop T-Charts for cooperative skills, such as "Criticizing Ideas and Not People," "Encouraging Group Members to Pull Their Own Weight," "Disagreeing with Someone's Idea," and "Coming to a Group Consensus." As we mentioned earlier, these often arise during the class interactions. For example, when groups are struggling to divide the work load evenly, it may be a good time for you to help them develop a T-Chart for that skill. It is an effective tool for accountability because the students develop it, and because the expectations are clearly delineated. Other social skills that require you to model to your students and help them learn to use include setting goals, brainstorming with others, encouraging all members of the group to participate, dividing the workload equally, and solving problems together.

One of the key management tasks during group projects is to be aware of the progress each group is making. Just as students will finish at different times when they are working individually, groups will complete their tasks at different times. If it is important that all groups finish at approximately the same time, then you may need to modify the task so slower groups are able to finish on time, or add enhancements to the task so faster groups are able to continue learning, while the other groups finish. Consider this example from a literature class: You want your students to think about the themes of seven Native American legends. You decide to place your twenty-eight students into seven groups of four, and assign each group one of seven different legends. You plan to use the jigsaw approach, and ask the expert groups to take 15 minutes to identify the main characters in the legend, the plot, and possible themes. One group is struggling to complete these three tasks in the time you allotted, and two groups are close to finishing 5 minutes after starting. If you approach the "slower group," you may find they are not on task, not understanding the task, or some other reason for not moving along efficiently. Check with them shortly after they begin working on this assignment (recall that in Chapter 1 we referred to the work of Jones who suggested that teachers visit all groups quickly at the start of an assignment to ensure that all students understand the task given to them). An additional clarification of the task may be all they need to complete the work on time. However, you may identify other reasons for their delay, and you may need to modify the task. You might ask them to not worry about the characters, and focus only on the plot and the theme. This modification might be just enough for the group to finish with the others. As for the "fast group," often groups finish quickly because they do not complete the task completely. A group that has answered too superficially needs to recognize where they could have gone into more depth, and asked to finish the original task more completely. If the group has completed your task adequately, then you have the opportunity to challenge them to explore new ideas or content. This group might consider how foreshadowing is used, or how their legend compares to myths they have read. These enhancements should be thought of ahead of time, and they should not be construed by students as "busy work." You should reward students for their efficiency, not "punish" hard work by assigning irrelevant "extra work."

When we talk with teachers, they often share a paradox of using student groups: students do not know how to work in groups, but they can only learn how by working in groups! As a result, you will find that each successive group project may work more effectively than the previous ones. Many teachers have groups of students complete classroom tasks as a way to help them learn cooperative skills. For example, a group of four students may be assigned the task of designing a bulletin board for an upcoming unit; another group might serve as a teacher's steering committee that gives advice about upcoming projects or field trips. A third group might help the teacher update the class website. These duties are then rotated monthly so all the groups are able to work on the different projects. The idea here is to provide opportunities for students to practice working interdependently, plan together, set group goals, and develop mutual trust. When the students are asked to work on a more academic task, they have the chance to develop an initial cooperative skill set from the classroom tasks.

LOGISTICAL CONCERNS, INCLUDING BENEFITS AND OBSTACLES

Because cooperative learning requires students to work interdependently, you must set up the room in a manner that is conducive to group work. Desks and chairs should be positioned so that students can meet in their groups and interact face-to-face. The groups need to be far enough apart so that students are not distracted by other groups. If the physical space of your classroom is small, then be sure students talk in soft voices. As the groups start working together to accomplish tasks, individual students may need to leave your classroom for the computer laboratory, art room, library, etc. Be sure you know school policies about allowing students out of the room. Similarly, think about the role of homework for projects that require several days of work. If you allow class time for the work, then you are able to closely monitor the groups and students do not need to coordinate their busy schedules. The drawback of this is that you must use class time. We find that a combination of class time and homework is effective. At the start of the task, provide time in class until the groups have identified how they will work interdependently. After that, you can offer short 10- to 15-minute "class meetings" for the groups to check progress and/or exhort one another. By providing class time for meetings, students can complete tasks on their own and then bring their ideas and answers to the group during the next class meeting.

One of the largest concerns of cooperative learning has to do with group assignments. We examined this earlier in the chapter, but it is worthwhile to restate that students benefit from working in groups that are purposefully formed by the teacher and are not self-selected. Often students have had negative experiences working in groups (and so have their parents), so it is important to provide a rationale for using cooperative teams for students or parents. We find that handing out a list of the group members, and telling each group where to meet and what their task should be is a great help in helping groups get started working together. For example, if a group of students are meeting to explore American child labor practices in the early 1900s, you might hand out a sheet of paper that has each group numbered and that lists the names of each group member. You might say, "On this sheet of paper I listed the group in which you will each be working. You will notice that each group has a number from one to seven. I would like all members of group one meet at the table by the door, all members of group two meet by my desk, etc. Move to these locations very quickly, so we do not waste time. When you have arrived, the first order of business is for each member to tell the group at least one idea about child labor in America during the early 1900s that you learned from your reading last night, and all of you should record these ideas in your notes." This type of script will get the groups into place quickly and help them get started. You could also prepare a handout with a series of procedures that you want the students to follow, and a timeline for the completion of each task. Rather than waiting for your direction, the worksheet provides structure for the groups' work.

If you plan to assign specific roles to students in the group (as we described in a previous section), you need to have the roles clearly described prior to the activity. You also need to think about how successful each student will be in an assigned role, and whether you are adequately serving traditionally marginalized students.

We described the jigsaw approach earlier, but here we revisit one logistical problem specific to this approach. Remember that during a jigsaw, students are in two groups: an expert group where they learn with others about specific information and a home group where they share their newly formed expertise. If you are able to form groups that have the same number of students, then jigsaws work smoothly. When one or two groups have a different number of students than the others, then logistic problems can arise. For example, a class with thirty students can be divided into five expert groups of six students each. When each of the six "experts" rejoin to make their home group, there will be six groups with five members in each group. Consider how you will move students from expert to home groups if you have 29 students. Thinking through this scenario will prepare you ahead of time for using the jigsaw approach.

APPROPRIATE ASSESSMENT TECHNIQUES TO USE WITH COOPERATIVE LEARNING

Teachers need to assess the content learning that is taking place and they need to assess the social interactions and relationships of the students in the group. Many times teachers will need to intervene with a group to help re-establish expectations for interactions during group work, to assist in the division of the workload and tasks, and to facilitate students in understanding the content. The T-Charts described in the section on classroom management can be used as a rubric for expected student behavior, and students can be held individually accountable for how closely they meet the expectations described in the chart. You could even assign a grade on how well the students met the criteria stated on particular T-Charts.

Self assessment and group assessments are effective tools for determining how effectively the groups worked together, and for having students reflect on their contributions to the group goals. Box 8.1 is an example of how a rubric can assist students to reflect on the process of working in groups:

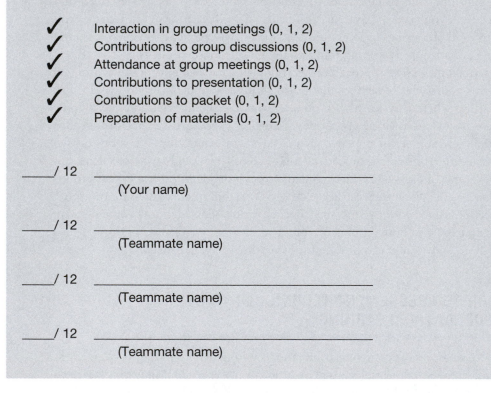

Box 8.1

GROUP AND SELF EVALUATION

Please award each member of your project/presentation group a score reflecting their effort in the group work. Score each of the six categories on a scale of 0 to 2, and enter the total score in the space next to each name. A 2 means you/they were excellent; 1 means you/they were adequate; 0 means you/they did not meet expectations. Under each name/score, please provide a succinct explanation for the score that you gave. Write these in clear phrases/sentences/statements.

✓   Interaction in group meetings (0, 1, 2)
✓   Contributions to group discussions (0, 1, 2)
✓   Attendance at group meetings (0, 1, 2)
✓   Contributions to presentation (0, 1, 2)
✓   Contributions to packet (0, 1, 2)
✓   Preparation of materials (0, 1, 2)

_____ / 12   _____
           (Your name)

_____ / 12   _____
           (Teammate name)

_____ / 12   _____
           (Teammate name)

_____ / 12   _____
           (Teammate name)

In addition to a self assessment tool, you can also provide the groups with a document that outlines all of the components of the group task. For example, the following is a tool that could be used if students are working in cooperative groups to produce a group biography (Box 8.2). Each member writes his or her own chapter, and the group works interdependently to complete several additional components of the biography (this example is adapted from Parker, 2005):

Box 8.2

GROUP BIOGRAPHY PLANNING SHEET

Please complete this with your team members and hand in *before* the end of class today. You will be assessed on how well you complete the task(s) you have signed up to complete for the group.

Group Members: _____

_____

Critical Events/Chapters and Illustrations:

Title of Chapter One: _____ by: _____

Title of Chapter Two: _____ by: _____

Title of Chapter Three: _____ by: _____

Title of Chapter Four: _____ by: _____

Name(s) of who will complete this task:

Foreword   _____

Introduction   _____

Map   _____

Timeline   _____

Bibliography   _____

"About the Authors" page   _____

Cover Page   _____

Formatting   _____

This document is helpful at the beginning of the task, because students can use it to identify all of the tasks that need to be completed. This follows the idea of making expectations clear to students at the start of a project that we described in Chapter 3 (Wiggins, 1990). This document is also useful as an assessment tool, because you will be able to connect different aspects of the task to particular students. The group needs to promote excellent achievement from all of the members, but sometimes not all students perform up to this expectation. A form that identifies each student's task allows you to hold students accountable.

You will also develop rubrics for grading the overall quality of student work. Again, the group does not receive a grade, but each student does. You will assess students on their contribution to the group goals, and on their individual contribution to the end task/product. When you have determined a project for your students, you may want to refer to Chapter 3 and reread the section on designing valid assessment tools and developing rubrics.

ENHANCING STUDENT LEARNING WITH TECHNOLOGY

Computer technology can be used in many ways to enhance and support cooperative learning. Most often this will depend upon the group's task. For example, a group that wants to gather census data can be directed to appropriate websites or a group attempting to interpret a song can download the music and lyrics. While information gathering is a common use of technology by cooperative groups, an increasingly common method is using that information and an online application to create a collaboratively written article. One example of this type of writing is given by Jon Orech of Downers Grove High School:

> . . . this is an assignment I have recently given to students. While studying *Lord of the Flies*, students are placed in small groups (no more than four students) and read the book through a particular "lens" which guides their study and discussion. As they read, they research sources that analyze and support their particular lens. Since they are the ones becoming "experts" in their lens or theme, it becomes their responsibility to share their findings with classmates. To do so, they create a collaborative article analyzing the specifics on the theme complete with links to authoritative sources. The final step is to create two "foundation questions" (Inquiry Research) related to the theme and make them available. As a final class assessment, students read the analysis of themes done by classmates (total of four) and answer the foundation questions using the novel as well as their peers as sources to support their answer.
>
> (Orech, 2009)

This article could be created for the public on a website or for private viewing on a shared document. A wiki, a collaboratively created website, is a way that many teachers support these publicly viewed articles. One free site we find useful is www.wikispaces.com. If you prefer a more private format, it is not difficult to set up shared documents for specific viewers using http://docs.google.com.

As with any use of technology in your classroom, you should consider what value you are adding. In the above example, how is the technology being used to support proven pedagogy for cooperative learning? What could be done to help facilitate this? Oftentimes inquiry learning is used together with collaborative learning. To see other ideas for enhancing these strategies with technology, refer to Chapter 11, "Student Directed Investigations," and visit the companion website for this book.

MAKING A LESSON MORE MEANINGFUL FOR ELLs

In many cultures of the recently immigrated, cooperation is valued far more highly than individualism. For these students, cooperative learning may have added benefits. In addition, the informal cooperative learning ideas presented in this chapter, such as think-pair-share, or buzz groups may be especially helpful for ELLs as they learn to negotiate the nuances of English in smaller focused groups before trying their ideas with a large group. The following are some specific ideas that may help ELL students become more successful.

- *Grouping*. It is often more successful when you plan who will work with whom prior to class.

    - Partner students for different purposes.

        - Often pairing students who share a first language provides an opportunity to build background and conceptual knowledge or clarify class content in the L1, and "catch up" before being asked to produce in English.
        - Working in mixed language and proficiency groupings provide opportunities to practice and use English language to talk about academic topics.

- *Circulate*. It helps to get down at eye level with your students.

    - Student discussion time is not time to catch up on your organization work. This is when a lot of your most productive teaching happens.
    - ELLs, along with other students, will ask you questions much more frequently in the context of a small group.

- Take enough time to stop in the small group so that you really hear the discussion. You might not get to all the groups, but you can make a note of it and come to them next time.
- Provide the words and language patterns to carry out those roles. All students need to practice academic vocabulary and academic language patterns orally.

    - Consider providing a list of "formal" language either for the discussion or the report back, or both.

        - On a poster in room, or in student folder, for discussion language:

            - I see what you mean, but I think . . .
            - You've got a point, but I've found that . . .

    – Could you explain that some more?
    – I believe _____ because _____
    – Can you give me an example of that?
    – I agree with you because _____
    – I can see where you are coming from, but have you ever thought about _____?

- You can make a paragraph with blanks, or provide sentence stems, to help guide students during the report back. This makes it easier for the ELL to do the report back if the entire group fills it in together. It also exposes students to the academic language they are asked to understand when they read.

    – We agreed on _____, but we disagreed on _____
    – Some of the group expressed the idea that _____
    – Although _____ thought _____, others believed that _____
    – Despite some disagreement, we now all agree that _____

- Provide participation roles and cooperative guidelines. This step is essential to ensure that group members all participate and have a reason for ensuring that their group mates understand.

  – Provide an outcome project for the group that has included a way to report everyone's ideas.
  – For some activities, assign or have students self-assign "roles":

    - reporter and recorder: demand high language proficiency;
    - participation officer: makes sure everyone is heard and that no one dominates—language is not an issue here;
    - artist, chart maker (copies onto poster board from the recorder's draft), actor, timer, and so on. See cooperative learning techniques, for more ideas. Language is not as much of an issue with these roles.

  – Ask for written notes or a poster that has every student write in a different color—makes it easier to see if people are taking over.
  – Instead of assigning group roles in a discussion, use the technique of assigning students report back numbers prior to discussion.

    - Out of a cup, pull numbers written on tongue depressors. The group member with that number needs to be ready to answer the question.
    - Even if an ELL is called, classmates can coach the answer, as long as the ELL repeats it back. A group can always ask for "more group discussion time" so that they can coach someone who hasn't been able to answer—takes the pressure off—but remember to come back to them.
    - Give a round of applause or points to the ELL and the group for being supportive.

GUIDELINES FOR DECIDING IF COOPERATIVE LEARNING IS APPROPRIATE FOR THE CONTENT OF A LESSON

We believe that cooperative learning can be used to teach in most content areas. However, it is important for you to consider the following five factors when determining its usefulness for your classroom.

Time: Cooperative learning is a time-demanding instructional strategy. It takes time for students to think about content together, to work together, and to teach or practice using the social skills that are necessary for working together. Cooperative learning promotes content learning and social skill development. If you have enough time to work with students in both of these areas, then cooperative learning will be effective.

Group formation: Do you have enough information about your students to place them in mixed groups that will promote learning? You may want to wait a week or more into the school year before using cooperative learning so you are able to get to know your students. You also need to consider if the cooperative learning be formal or informal. Informal cooperative learning groups are formed with convenience in mind to allow for quick assignments (e.g., four students are grouped because they are sitting near each other, or a group is formed because the teacher has them number off by fours).

Social skill development: As we mentioned under "time," cooperative learning is based on you placing students into groups. Often groups have conflicts until they learn to cooperate with one another. This will require you to motivate and facilitate the students to work together as a group. Consider if you are willing and able to help the students respect differences, interact with peers who are from different cultures, religions, ethnicities, or socioeconomic groups.

Clear task expectations: If you have a clearly stated task for students to perform, consider why working in groups will benefit the students more than working independently. How will a group project enhance student learning of this content? How will it enhance student satisfaction with their learning experience? Formal cooperative learning strategies serve specific purposes. STAD is best used when you want students to learn specific answers to questions. It is an effective review task. Jigsaws allow you to efficiently examine a complex topic by dividing the information among the group and having the group members teach each other. Group investigations, unlike STAD, allow groups freedom in completing their tasks. It is an effective approach for inquiry and student-led research projects.

Assessment: Can you separate the task so that the students are able to be held individually accountable? Could you create a rubric that clearly states the group goal or task (e.g., to make a presentation on the formation of the National Park System) and that assesses students individual work in the group (e.g., each student is assessed on his or her contribution to the research and presentation on the National Park System).

MAKING IT WORK IN YOUR CONTENT AREA

Select a topic that you believe students will be able to learn about while working in groups. From the list of three "formal cooperative learning" approaches (STAD, jigsaw, and group investigations), select the one that will be effective for helping students learn the content. If you are working with a group of students, consider how you might divide them into groups of four or five. Since you must know your students before you are able to effectively place them in groups, you may not be able to consider the formation of the groups at this time. That will come when you begin teaching. Next, consider the following:

1. List the topic students will work on together. Develop a clear question or statement such as "How does the Columbian Exchange still impact us today?" or "Determine the defining attributes of the following geometric figures."
2. Write lesson objectives:

- Social objectives dealing with what students are to learn about working together.
- Academic objectives dealing with the knowledge base to be explored.

3. Forming groups:

- Describe the rationale for choosing the cooperative learning strategy and for placing students in mixed groups.
- In addition to ability, gender, and ethnicity, what are other attributes to consider when placing students in groups for this project?
- What makes this a good issue to explore in groups?
- How does it fit with the curriculum?

4. Lesson procedures for conducting cooperative group work:

- Student preparation and helping the groups work:
  What needs to take place before the groups work together? Will students learn new material during the group project, or will they work with material already introduced? What social skills do you think need to be learned before the project begins? How will you teach those skills to the students (e.g., with a T-Chart? role-play?). Also, write down what you will do while the groups work. How will you monitor their progress? What will you do with groups that finish early? What might you do with groups that are moving at a slower pace?
- If you are using STAD, how will you present the material to your students? What handouts or supplements will the groups need when working together to review and learn the information? Have you designed the quiz or quizzes that you will need at the end of the group work? How much time will the groups need to learn the content?

- If you are using jigsaw, what preparation will the students need before the group work? How will you divide the task so that the students can become experts on one part of the material? What information will they use to build their expertise (e.g., handouts, internet, books, etc.), and how will you facilitate their learning? How much time should you allow for the expert groups to work?
- If you are using a group investigation, how will you present the general idea of the project so that the students are interested in the topic? Have you posed the task as a clear statement that the students can understand? How can you facilitate the students as they divide the work load among the group members? How will they learn the information? Do you need to reserve a computer laboratory, library, telephone for interviews, and the like? How will the groups present their information?

5. Assessment:
   Reread the section on assessing cooperative learning, and determine how you might assess student learning. Consider how to assess their "social skills" and/or their understanding of the content.

CHAPTER REVIEW

- Research support for using cooperative learning in the classroom:

  - Emphasis on competition and individual achievement decreases as student learning increases.
  - Students of different racial or ethnic backgrounds gain in being liked and respected.
  - Classmates' acceptance of students who are traditionally marginalized because of low academic ability is increased.
  - Five "essential elements" of all cooperative learning activities.

- Step-by-step procedures for selecting, planning, and using cooperative learning strategies:

  - Informal cooperative learning
  - Formal cooperative learning:

    - student teams-achievement divisions (STAD)
    - jigsaw
    - group investigation.

- Managing the classroom/learning environment during cooperative learning:

  - Assess both group progress and each member's individual progress.
  - Establish and assess group norms and expectations.
  - Teach cooperative skills to your students.

- Assessing student learning when working in cooperative groups:

  - Assess content learning and social interactions.
  - Self-assessment and group assessments.

- Using technology to enhance learning:

  - Computer technology can enhance and support learning.
  - Use information and an online application to create a collaboratively written article.

- Considerations for ELLs during cooperative learning activities:

  - grouping
  - circulate
  - practice academic vocabulary and academic language patterns.

NOTE

1 This idea is adapted from the work of Zarnowski (2003).

CHAPTER 9

Simulations, Role-Play, and Dramatization

CHAPTER OBJECTIVES

In this chapter, you will learn about:

- definitions and support for using theatric strategies;

- step-by-step procedures for selecting, planning, and using simulations, role-plays, and dramatizations;

- managing the classroom/learning environment during simulations, role-plays, and dramatizations;

- assessing student learning appropriately during theatric strategies;

- using technology to enhance learning;

- considerations for ELLs during simulations, role-plays, and dramatizations

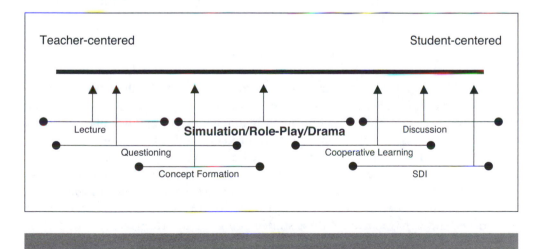

Pierre Cauchon, Bishop of Beauvais, waited anxiously for the jury to return with the verdict. He had been overseeing the trial of Joan of Arc for two days and was sure the verdict would be rendered soon. He wondered if the riveting testimony given by Nicolas Loiseieur would convince the jury that she was guilty of heresy or if they would be convinced by those that testified in her defense. As the jury filed in, the murmur in the courtroom dissolved into silence. "Have you reached a verdict?" Bishop Cauchon asked the jury foreman.

"We have Sir. We find Joan of Arc to be . . ."

About a week prior to "the verdict," Mr. Johnson had assigned each student in his world history class a role in the trial of Joan of Arc. A student jury was to decide if she was freed or burned at the stake. He explained that this was part of the culminating project for their unit on medieval Europe. Some students were assigned key roles because they had shown they were up to the challenge and responsible for the preparation. Others were selected for major roles randomly. Several were selected for the jury because they had a history of poor attendance and the role-play could continue if they were absent. He found detailed role responsibilities in a curriculum guide but decided to include an essay at the end of role-play to better assess student learning. Now, as he looked at his classroom filled with students dressed in thrift-store medieval wear, he knew that they had had fun, and he knew that they had been engaged and participating as they prepared the trial and learned their roles. At the end of the trial, he would have a focused debriefing session with the class about the trial, the roles, and what they learned. He would have to wait for their essays on Joan of Arc to finally have enough assessment information to determine if the role-play was effective.

OVERVIEW

Using a simulation, role-play, or **dramatization** can be a fantastic experience. Students have fun and are engaged in learning. Teachers see a learning environment develop, just as they had hoped. Using an instructional strategy that involves a high degree of student interaction, participation, and autonomy can be challenging to manage. At the same time, however, students will have a high degree of engagement when their emotions and opinions combine. If you ask practicing teachers about using these strategies, you will probably find mixed responses. Teachers report that some of the risks associated with this strategy include: students who see it as "dumb" and refuse to participate; students who feel uncomfortable performing anything seriously and will play the clown to be disruptive; classes that become out of control; and students who fully participate and have fun but are uncertain if they learned anything. Of course, the rewards of enthusiastic, energetic, and effective teaching and learning are possible as well. It is also possible that this might just be *the* unique way to interest some of your students. As in many worthwhile endeavors, there is a high degree of risk. We think the risk of trying is worth it, and so have included these strategies for you to investigate.

In this chapter, we introduce three theatric strategies: *simulation*, *role-play*, and *dramatization*. These instructional strategies involve some aspect of the stage—a scene change, a particular role, or the use of scripted material. We will offer a description of these theatric strategies, propose procedures for planning and implementation, and discuss logistical concerns, classroom management, and assessment issues. Finally, we will propose guidelines to help you decide if these strategies are appropriate for the content of a lesson.

DEFINING THEATRIC STRATEGIES

If you have attended a play recently, you will have noted the set designs, the performed roles by the actors, and the oral interpretation of scripts. These three aspects of stage communication are key to understanding and utilizing instructional theatric strategies. Fortunately for most of us, we don't need to become professional Shakespearian actors to be able to use these strategies in the classroom. Simulations, role-play, and dramatization that effectively create sets, establish roles, and utilize scripting can be important elements of learning in your classroom. Many times it may not be important to precisely determine if an activity is a simulation, role-play, or dramatization; there certainly can be overlap among these methods. However, an understanding of how these strategies are similar and different may help you choose one that best fits your objectives. A simple way to distinguish among the three is to remember that *simulation* focuses students on a change in their environment (this could be thought of as the set design), *role-play* focuses on the actor's role, and *dramatization* focuses on scripted dialog.

Simulations allow students to experience simulated phenomena and then debrief about their reactions. They are more concerned with students reacting to the environment in which they find themselves than taking on a particular role or personality. Much like the creation of a set to establish a scene in a play, a simulation establishes an alternative environment within the classroom that reflects another scene of life. Part of the classroom may be turned into a spacecraft or a covered wagon, for example. This environment may be reflective of something they could encounter in the real world (the stock market) or it may not (a colony on another planet). Students are asked to engage and interact with the alternative environment or with others situated within that environment. As you will see, this physical set change in itself does not necessarily make an activity a simulation.

A simulation will ask students to take on a functioning part within the alternative environment (a president, a farmer, an engineer, a waiter) and will give the student enough information (news reports, documents, maps, expert advice) about a specific issue or problem to be able to make appropriate decisions or interact with others. A simulation will not ask a student to change her personality but will ask her to deal with the responsibilities of her job or task within the situation or environment in which she finds herself. A person might become the president of a country but will not be asked to take on the values or attitudes of another person (to role-play that person). She may be responsible for a particular part but will always keep her own personality. For example, a student may be asked to take the part of school board member deciding a controversial curricular issue but will not be asked to play the personality of a particular member of the local school board.

In role-play, students learn about and act as someone (or something) different from themselves. This involves taking on the personality of a person in order to empathize, understand, or explore feelings, attitudes, conflicts, or values. Others may ask students to assume the characteristics of some type of matter (e.g., an atom) in order to learn about its structure or relationship with outside influences (e.g., heat). Role-play is more concerned with acting a part or imitation than it is with exploring an environment or situation. Role-play, as opposed to simulation, is usually brief and performed in front of an audience of classmates. Typically, the information provided to students would be related to the role to be played rather than the situation in which students find themselves. Simple examples of role-play would include having students act like atoms under extreme temperature changes, asking students to play various European leaders (such as Neville Chamberlain) during the Sudetenland crisis prior to World War II, or having students explore attitudes or values by choosing roles related to an instance of interpersonal conflict.

At times, teachers will combine simulations and role-play so that students experience a phenomenon as they are acting in a particular role or so that roles played by some students will impact the environment of the other students. For example, during a civil rights lesson related to the Harper Lee novel *To Kill a Mockingbird*, several members of the class might be asked to play the role of the "enforcer" so that only boys can sharpen their pencils during class time. Another common example is that of a middle school classroom turned into a medieval feudal system: students are assigned roles (queen, jester, peasant, knight) in the feudal hierarchy. "Oregon Trail" is a popular role-play/simulation where students take on the role of pioneer and engage in a computerized environment as they "move west."

Dramatization takes students one step closer to the stage. During this strategy, students act in a given role, during a scene, and often with a script. Using this technique can involve professionally written scripts or those written by the students themselves. Dramatization can be as simple as having volunteers do an oral interpretation of a text selection from a magazine, as involved as a culminating research project that scripts an historical event, as innovative as a pantomime, or as elaborate as a full-class play including props, costumes, and purchased scripts. Usually, this technique is used to help students empathize with a particular viewpoint or better understand an event, but it can also be effectively used to help improve student communication skills.

A DESCRIPTION OF THEATRIC STRATEGIES AND RESEARCH FINDINGS

Classroom teachers choose to use these strategies for several reasons, but primarily because they require a high degree of student participation in a somewhat atypical activity. For many, this could lead to increased motivation and engagement. Simulation can be a particularly stimulating strategy, since it requires complex thinking that involves difficult moral choices based upon values and beliefs (Greenblat, 1987; Bransford et al., 2000). These dramatic strategies can help create an environment to examine a variety of perspectives and develop empathy for those from different cultures

(Fisher and Vander Laan, 2002). Teachers at times want to have their students become more physically involved in a lesson, and these strategies certainly discourage passivity. Many see the somewhat unusual nature of these activities as helpful in creating an environment to practice communication skills. Partly because of this, these strategies are particularly popular with students speaking English as a second language (ESL) and in world languages classrooms. While there are many possible reasons for using these strategies, the research literature suggests that the strengths of theatric strategies are important to student learning.

One of the strengths of these strategies is student engagement. While many find these strategies *fun*, the real goal is to get well beyond mere enjoyment. An activity that is "just for fun" is not a learning activity; it may be important for establishing a positive environment, but something more is needed to make it a learning activity. Most educators would agree that an important aspect of learning is engagement. An engaging strategy would be part of a lesson that is thought-provoking, interesting, and energizing. In feedback from teacher workshops conducted by Wiggins and McTighe (2005, p. 195) it was found that learners are engaged when work

- is hands-on;
- involves mysteries or problems;
- provides variety;
- offers opportunity to adapt, modify, or somehow personalize the challenge;
- balances cooperation and competition, self and others;
- is built on real-world or meaningful challenge;
- uses provocative interactive approaches, such as case studies, mock trials, and other types of simulated challenges; and
- involves real audiences or other forms of "authentic" accountability for the results.

It is easily noted that theatric strategies encourage most, if not all, of these components in one way or another. Different strategies will have unique strengths for developing an engaging lesson.

Role-play and simulation, especially, are highly interactive strategies that usually require authentic intellectual work—that is, work that requires application of knowledge and skills that go beyond a routine use of facts and procedures. This type of work moves a student from learning about an ecosystem or watershed, for example, toward learning to apply information to protect the environment while considering the concerns of other interest groups. This involves students using their own ideas to make decisions and solve problems. Researchers have found that interactivity and authentic intellectual work have a positive impact on student achievement. One study examined the link between different forms of instruction and learning. This study of elementary and middle school students and teachers in Chicago showed that interactive teaching methods were factors in increased learning in reading and math (Smith et al., 2001). Another study of middle school students examined the relationship between the type of assignment given in class and the quality of student work and achievement on standardized tests. Assignments were rated according to how "authentically" the students were asked to perform work. These researchers concluded that students from a variety of socioeconomic backgrounds benefit from assignments calling for more authentic intellectual work as shown by both classroom assessments and standardized tests (Newmann et al., 2001). Several recently published reports on the use of theatric strategies by classroom teachers suggest that students benefit from the unique way in which they focus on analysis in a contextualized learning environment (Steinbrink, 2004; Leonard et al., 2005).

Theatric strategies in general, but especially dramatization, make use of physical activity during the lesson. As you have seen in Chapter 1, Gardner (1999) has developed a theory of multiple intelligences. This theory suggests that society tends to value those with linguistic or logical abilities while overlooking those with other skills. To the degree that school is a reflection of society at large, this would imply that students with acting, musical, dancing, or other artistic skills are being overlooked in the classroom. Theatric strategies are particularly strong in the areas of bodily kinesthetic, musical, interpersonal, and intrapersonal intelligences. The use of strategies that utilize these intelligences would be beneficial to a diverse group of learners—which, of course, includes those from all classes. When Gardner refers to *intelligences*, he is thinking of aptitude, not learning styles (Gardner, 2003). However, even if a learning style or preference isn't an intelligence, it could still be important to consider for the variety of students in your classroom. Learning preferences may very well include one of the theatric strategies.

Another benefit often associated with theatric strategies is improved communication skills and confidence building. These strategies not only offer an opportunity for practice but also, as Jones suggests, the "power of a simulation arises from the reality of the communication skills" (1995, p. 7). Learning about communication can also be achieved through drama. Scenes with scripts have a communication component that is very different from communication in a simulation or role-play. As we have noted, many times teachers use dramatization in connection with learning about, empathizing with, or understanding a person or event; for example, dramatizing a court hearing, reading during a reader's theater, or exploring a different culture that uses a non-English language. At other times, the lesson objectives deal primarily with communication or preparing students to communicate their learning (e.g., recite a dramatized script about how to use pi to determine the length of a traffic roundabout that has recently replaced a traditional intersection). In these instances, teachers have found dramatization to be useful (Heathcote, 1992; Farris and Parke, 1993; Johnson, 1998).

REALITY CHECK

Simulations take many forms. We often categorize simulations as being "historical," "process," or "symbolic." Consider the following:

Three "Types" of Simulations

*   *Historical simulations*: Re-enacting historical events, such as striking grape workers, Boston Massacre trial, colonization, or westward movement.

- *Process simulations*: Simulating meetings or procedures, such as the legislative process, the stock market, elections, a budget process, Model United Nations, mock trials.
- *Symbolic simulations*: Enactments of cultures or other events where students are unaware of what is being represented until the debriefing stage of the simulation. For example, Bafa Bafa, "brown eyes/blue eyes," or others that address complex issues such as apartheid, culture clashes, war, conflicts, or slavery.

We situated most of these examples within social studies to highlight their differences. Ask teachers to share examples of simulations that they have used/seen in their classroom. Answer this question for each of these three types: "What would be an engaging and effective simulation in my class that will help them learn?" Be prepared to share ideas for simulations with those in endorsement areas other than yours.

USING TONE TO COMMUNICATE

If you emphasize the italicized word in the sentences below it will change the meaning of the entire sentence each time. Can you hear all four different meanings?

I like that answer.
I *like* that answer.
I like *that* answer.
I like that *answer*.

Next, try changing the following two sentences from pointed commands into questions or encouraging statements using tone.

Combine those two points of view.
Criticize that argument.

Now, try changing the meaning of the sentence "Someone add to Michael's answer." Start by making the sentence a put-down and change it to an encouraging question just by changing the tone and not the words.[1]

Extension: Most teachers don't have a background in theater and may be a bit apprehensive to try or may not be aware of exercises that can help in this area. Three areas vital to effective communication are the use of visuals, vocals, and verbals. Oftentimes, there are several people in class who have some theater background and can be used as "experts." Through personal class experience or by looking through resource materials, brainstorm theater exercises might be helpful for your future class in developing communication skills. To see a teacher using theatric strategies in the classroom, visit the companion website.

STEP-BY-STEP PROCEDURES FOR PLANNING AND IMPLEMENTATION OF SIMULATION, ROLE-PLAY, AND DRAMATIZATION

Theatric strategies vary widely in terms of purposes for the classroom. As we have indicated, a simulation would most likely serve a different purpose from that of a drama or role-play. We have discussed the distinct characteristics of these strategies to help you understand which might fit your purposes. In this section, we discuss ways to effectively implement each of these strategies so that you can learn from the experiences of others who have been successful. Remember, using these strategies can be risky, because you are allowing the students freedom to express their ideas and thoughts; of course, that is exactly why they are compelling and engaging for students. Some teachers have been frightened off because they have had less-than-successful experiences. However, there is no reason to think you will not become one of the many who successfully use and enjoy these strategies regularly. Teaching adolescents isn't hard— it just isn't easy.

Simulation

The way the facilitator talks about the simulation can lead participants to have expectations and behaviors that do not reflect the simulated environment. One simulation expert suggests "appropriate" and "inappropriate" terminology for use during a simulation. You'll note that in general, Jones is promoting language that helps communicate that the event is not play or game time, but instead an opportunity to participate as oneself (not play a role) in a unique situation that requires thoughtfulness and problem solving. The suggested language helps others understand that someone views the simulation as a way to interact with others in the way they would in the "real world." A participant wouldn't try to "win" unless the simulation environment caused her to think that it was important in some way. She wouldn't act like another person unless the simulated environment required it. For example, if the simulation asks groups of students to give advice to the U.S. president and the Soviet premier during the Cuban Missile Crisis, they would not be told that they were going to play a game where they will role-play political advisors. Nor would they be told that the team that gives the best advice will win.

While use of a specific word may not sabotage your simulation, the words do reflect underlying attitudes about what you are trying to accomplish and can be important. Table 9.1 is a list of terms (adapted from Jones, 1995, p. 14) for your consideration.

When implementing a simulation, it is important for you, the future teacher, to recognize that your role has changed. No longer are you the know-it-all behind the desk with all the correct answers. During a simulation, the teacher will likely have four facilitating roles (Joyce et al., 2000):

1. *Explainer*: At the outset the class will need to know how to participate in the simulation. Students need to know the general goals, context, and environmental

TABLE 9.1: Appropriate Terms for Simulations

Appropriate Terms	Inappropriate Terms
simulation, activity, event	game, drama, role-play, exercise
participant	player, actor, puzzler, trainee, student
facilitator, organizer	teacher, trainer, instructor
behavior, function, profession	playing, acting, staging
role (functional)	role (acting a part)
real-world responsible behavior	winning (losing) the game
real-world responsible ethics	point scoring, just for fun
professional conduct	performing the game or exercise

particulars that make up the simulation. Students won't need to know everything about the experience, as much will occur that cannot be predicted. There will be plenty of questions to answer, however.

2. *Referee*: During the simulation, someone will need to help negotiate disputes or make decisions about the simulation that involve the group. This should already be built into the simulation but nonetheless such intervention may be necessary. This should be done in as limited and nonintrusive way as possible.

3. *Coach*: According to Joyce et al. (2000), the teacher should be prepared to intercede as coach to assist participants when necessary. This supportive component would assist the learning during the simulation. However, Jones (1995) argues that a teacher should not intrude into the simulation as coach. There would be no "coach" at a business meeting, or at a United Nations meeting, or at most real-world events. Coaching would disrupt the student "ownership" of the simulation and be counterproductive. We pass this information on to you along with the reminder that a simulation is an *untaught event*, and adolescents may need some prompting.

4. *Discussion leader*: At the completion of the simulation, it is important to have a debriefing time. The teacher will need to be prepared to facilitate this discussion.

Most simulations come with clear instructions and step-by-step procedures. There are at least four common phases that each simulation should go through (Joyce et al., 2000). The first phase is *orientation*, during which the teacher presents the simulation overview and explains the learning objectives for the simulation. The second phase involves *organizing* the simulation; in this phase the teacher establishes the simulated environment by explaining rules, assigning roles, and explaining the type of decisions that may need to be made. Some teachers will hold an abbreviated practice session if they feel some students may not completely understand. During the third phase, the simulation is *operational* and there may be opportunities for feedback or time for metacognitive reflection. The final phase, *debriefing*, is one that is sometimes overlooked but is essential for effective simulation; during this phase, students are given the opportunity to summarize and analyze events and offer insights while comparing their perceptions with those of other students. Students are also asked to discuss how the simulation compared to the real world. Finally, students are brought back to the learning objectives to discuss how the simulation helped them learn. This would also be a good time to discuss ways the simulation could be improved for future classes.

KEY CONCEPTS FOR SIMULATION PROCEDURE

Allow for and expect mistakes or errors of fact by students. These can be recorded and dealt with during the debriefing if they are not addressed by others within the simulation. Also keep in mind the following:

- A simulation is an untaught event.
- The teacher should let the simulation run its course even if it is heading in an unintended direction. Again, this can be dealt with at the debriefing.
- Resist the temptation to become involved or to intercede. Sometimes, of course, it is necessary to intercede, but try to stay out of things.
- A debriefing time at the end is vital.
- A metacognitive time is helpful during or after a simulation.
- Simulation is not a game and not about winning or losing. It is possible that winning or losing might be a natural part of the simulated environment (i.e., the stock market or an election), but winning should not be a fixation of students during the simulation.
- A simulation strategy involves the reproduction of a simulated environment not a reproduction of characters as in a role-play.

Role-Play

As we have noted, role-play takes us one step closer to theater. Because this strategy isn't quite as free-flowing as a simulation, it probably isn't as complicated. It does, however, have its own set of issues and should be considered carefully. Shaftel and Shaftel (1967) suggest nine phases for conducting role-play for learning about personal and social dimensions of education. For example, this model would be good if you wanted students to explore their feelings or attitudes about an interpersonal conflict at school. These phases can also be of benefit for teachers choosing to use role-play for other types of objectives but may need to be modified.

1. *Warming up:* A problem is identified or introduced and questions posed to the class that help focus students on key issues.
2. *Selecting participants:* The roles are analyzed and volunteers are selected.
3. *Setting the stage:* The participants show that they understand their roles and ask questions.
4. *Preparing the observers:* The peer observers and the teacher decide what to observe and assign focused tasks.
5. *Enacting:* Role-play is executed.
6. *Discussion and evaluation:* The class or small group reviews the action of the role-play, discusses major focus areas with observers, and develops modification ideas for next phase.

7. *Reenactment:* Participants play modified roles or extend role-play to suggested alterations.
8. *Discussion and evaluation:* Repeat Phase 6.
9. *Sharing and generalizing the experience:* The class or small group relates the role-play exercise to the real world and explores principles of behavior.

Dramatization

Unless you plan to be a theater teacher, you will be less concerned about the quality of the acting and more about what students are learning about your subject. When planning for dramatization, we suggest you consider the following guidelines.

Targets

The reason you are asking students to perform should be very clear to you and stated in your targets. Why are you using this strategy?

Class Environment

Creating an environment in class that supports and enhances this strategy is key. This is discussed further in the "classroom management issues" section of this chapter.

Time

It is usually best to think of this strategy in terms of skits rather than plays. Your curricular schedule will probably limit your time, but you will also need to consider the attention and interest level of the students you have in class.

Props

Use limited props as needed, but don't become overwhelmed by this detail, as students can easily use imaginative props. Keep an eye out at garage sales for odd-looking props and have students bring props from home. Simple props, such as a hat or umbrella, can add a lot and may be all that is needed.

Scripts

You can find scripts on the internet, from creatively like-minded teachers, or from published sources; or you can use scripts written by you or your students. Also, remember that oral interpretation, a form of dramatization, makes use of any text such as scenes from novels, magazine or newspaper articles, diaries, or movie scripts.

Casting

It is probably best to ask for volunteers for the various available roles. Assign key parts to those who are motivated and interested and not necessarily to those who are the best actors. More limited roles can go to those who are less interested or less willing. It is usually not in the interest of all involved to require a student to participate in dramatization, but keep in mind that many adolescents will need encouragement to try.

Rehearsal

Make it as serious or as light-hearted as you think is warranted for the script and the particular students involved. Be sure that if it is a group project, all the students are interpreting the script and the expectations for the assignment in the same way. Hurt feelings occur when several in a group see this presentation as meaningful and personal and one person wants to make a joke out of it.

Performance

Be sure to give the audience the expectations for the dramatization. Is it a spoof? Is it about a serious personal issue? The classroom audience should know your behavioral expectations in advance based upon your expectations for the dramatization.

Debriefing

Consider taking some time following the drama for a large group debriefing. It may help to have a guided, written, individual reflection time prior to the debriefing time.

REALITY CHECK

Examining a Theatric Idea

Decide if the following medieval fair—adapted from an idea created by middle school core (English/social studies) teachers at Fairhaven Middle School in Bellingham, Washington—is a simulation, a role-play exercise, a dramatization, or a combination of these; explain why. What ideas do you like? What might improve this idea or add your unique twist to the idea? (How would you select the king? How much time would you give students to prepare and participate? Can you describe any other contest ideas?) Talk with teachers about their use of role-plays, simulations, and dramatizations. Can you think of an idea similar to this one for your content area or for high school?

The Medieval Fair

Kingdoms

Each seventh grade teacher will have her two core classes choose:

- a name for their kingdom;
- a symbol for their kingdom;
- royalty for their kingdom: a queen, a king (royalty must also meet qualifications for knighthood).

Knighthood

Knighthood will be open to both girls and boys. Requirements for knighthood are:

- all assignments for a three-week period in core classes must be turned in;
- a 3.0 grade point average;
- demonstration of knightly conduct: respect, courtesy, and promptness.

Heraldry

Each kingdom will have its own symbol for its own coat of arms. Each kingdom will be responsible for making a banner displaying their coat of arms. In addition, each knight and each student will have his own coat of arms, which must include the symbol of the kingdom.

Activities

1. *Jousting Contest (Outside)*
   One must qualify as a knight to participate in the jousting contest.
   Equipment for jousting:

   Steeds: big wheels
   Swords: rubber bats
   Armor: football helmets, shields
   Target: egg
   Shield: to be provided by participants, made of cardboard only! It should be 18" × 24" and decorated with the knight's own coat of arms.

   Jousters will make two passes on big wheels; then may engage in open combat until one breaks the egg of the opponent. Jousting contest will be an elimination contest until we are down to three people. At this time, the kings and queens may challenge one of the knights to a jousing contest until there is but one unvanquished foe.

2. *Magic Acts*
3. *Juggling: Exhibition*
4. *Riddles and Court Jesters: Exhibition*
5. *Music*: Gregorian Chants, instrumental, vocal (a cappella)
6. *Plays: Romeo and Juliet; Pyramus and Thisbe*
7. *Poetry*
   Selections to be read by students. Medieval poetry; selections include:

   Shakespearean sonnets
   Beowulf
   Chaucer's *Canterbury Tales*
   The Song of Roland
   Tales of 1001 Arabian Nights

8. *Chess/Checkers/Backgammon Tournaments*
   To be held in the kingdoms at the teacher's discretion.
9. *Excalibur*
   Costumes: knight, lady, jester/Minstrel, monk, nun, beggar, wizard (Merlin), squire

Also consider non-European costumes of the period: Japanese feudal period costumes (daimyo, samurai) or Arabian.

- The Excalibur event: Split the log and gain royalty. To qualify for a chance to swing the axe and split the log, the royal adzman will require five push-ups. Each qualifying contestant will have just one chance.

Learning Stations

Each classroom has learning stations that relate to at least one of the following topics:

castles	the Crusades
siege weapons	guilds
catapult competitions	torture
the Church	merchants
cathedrals	chivalry
monasteries	Gregorian and Julian
stained glass	calendars
village life	medieval names
manor life	education
city life	science
knights	entertainment
feudalism	medieval holidays
music	falconry
the Plague	heraldry
dress and food	architecture
the Islamic world	monk day
the Byzantine world	the medieval banquet.

LOGISTICAL CONCERNS, INCLUDING BENEFITS AND OBSTACLES

Probably the biggest logistical concern about using these strategies is the ability to acquire appropriate and interesting ideas. However, planning ahead of time, ensuring that resources are available and ready, thinking through how you will place students into groups, and facilitating the step-by-step process that the students will follow can be daunting and will be unique for each strategy. For example, if a biology teacher wants to simulate the formation of protein chains, she will need to think through how to divide the class into groups, how to assign groups the roles of particular atoms, when to allow the groups time to research the behavior of their atom, and how to allow the groups/atoms to interact. This will be a very different type of planning than a literature teacher will need to think about when helping the students choose a character and scene from a Shakespeare play, analyze their chosen character, and then act out the scene for the class. The step-by-step procedures for the theatric strategies provide a process for thinking through logistics.

ENHANCING STUDENT LEARNING WITH TECHNOLOGY

Below, we offer resources for ideas related to simulation, role-play, and dramatization that have been used by classroom teachers. There are many websites that contain helpful ideas, and we provide annotated descriptions and links to a variety of these on the companion website for this book. Several online sources are "link sites," where you are able to search by the name of the theatric strategy and find hundreds of ideas. You could search online for other educational production companies that provide high quality simulations, role-play exercises, and dramatizations; some are free and some charge. A few sample free sites follow:

Free Online Resources

Teaching English as a Second Language
http://iteslj.org/links/TESL/Lessons/Role_Plays/

Reluctant Writers
www.readwritethink.org/lessons/lesson_view.asp?id=217

Free Databases that Can Be Searched by Theatric Strategy

www.learnnc.org/lessons
www.lessonplanspage.com
www.eduref.org/Virtual/Lessons
http://teachers.net/

We found that thousands of educational simulations exist online. The quality and reliability of these vary greatly. For example, Tech Trekers is a private site that provides links to online simulations for most content areas. You may want to visit it (www.techtrekers.com/sim.htm) to see what is listed for your endorsement area. The companion website for this book has additional links to online simulations, including subject-specific simulations and/or role-plays. These are meant to serve as initial ideas for what is possible. For example, the following site has a variety of applications that simulate math and physics concepts such as sound waves and electrostatic fields: www.falstad.com/mathphysics.html.

MAKING A LESSON MORE MEANINGFUL FOR ELLs

ESL teachers will tell you that role-play and dramatization are especially good fits for ELLs. These strategies are natural ways to encourage listening, speaking, and reading

English in fun and interesting ways, while giving ample opoortunity for support. Of course, each individual will need careful consideration prior to the presentation. This might include an evaluation of levels of English proficiency before assigning roles or tasks in a simulation or role-play exercise. Students having special needs with reading English may need additional time in advance to look through scripts or other directions that are not usually given to other students. This is especially important if it avoids awkward or embarrassing situations for these students in front of the class. For example, after evaluating individual needs, time may need to be provided for small groups to practice reading their parts or the teacher may need to take special time to work with several students to prepare. Some teachers choose to give scripts (or rewritten simplified versions) to their ELLs several weeks in advance and instead of minimizing their role, encourage them to take on roles that stretch their comfort zones without setting them up for failure.

It is important for all students to have a chance to debrief after using one of the theatric strategies. This is probably even more critical for ELLs. One way this can be done effectively is by using the debrief strategy, *Numbered Heads Together*. Students are given review sheets with debriefing questions and put into groups. Group members are given time to reflect on the theatric activity, discuss the questions, and come to a consensus. The teacher will call a number and a student with the corresponding number from each group will stand and give a response for their group. The teacher will facilitate discussion and correct reponses as necessary. Students will continue to use listening, speaking, reading, and writing skills with group support until the conclusion of the debriefing.

CLASSROOM MANAGEMENT AND MOTIVATION

The environment of your classroom is key to using theatric strategies successfully. You do not need to be a drama coach; you do not need to be able to recite the major themes of any of Shakespeare's plays; you do need to have an environment established in your classroom that encourages creativity, active learning, student responsibility, and experimentation. In this section, we will discuss this type of environment in connection with simulation, role-play, and dramatization.

One of the reasons to use these strategies is to promote a lesson-design philosophy that encourages intrinsic rather than extrinsic motivation. Theatric strategies have natural attributes that encourage student-generated enthusiasm and interest. A classroom in which students have been passive and consistently motivated by external factors will have a difficult time in instantaneously transforming itself for a simulation. Warning: student interns may be set up for failure if trying these strategies in this type of a classroom environment. In classes where students are used to passive learning, it is a good idea to bring students along with smaller activities. For example, before using a full role-play try a series of theater games such as that suggested in the "Using Tone to Communicate" section, above. Take the time to thoughtfully build the commonplace of *milieu* as described in Chapter 4.

A classroom in which these strategies will thrive will be one where a climate of trust and support has been established. This is important, as students are taking a risk and may be made to feel uncomfortable. A classroom climate that is energized, fun, and supports risk takers is necessary. Students need an environment where they know it is okay to make mistakes and learn from them. Theatric strategies will thrive in an environment where creativity has been encouraged and supported—where it would not be seen as unusual or strange to play a quick theater game or do some other unusual activity as a lesson "hook." This would be an environment in which students' original work is proudly displayed or presented at parent nights.

Theatric strategies are active strategies. Sometimes, students get a bit feisty and noisy. Other teachers may wonder what is going on in your room, and if you are able to "control" your students. You will need to come to peace with that. As with test pilots flying at supersonic speeds, you will at times "push the envelope." This will require you to have acquired skill in efficiently dealing with off-track behaviors and helping students understand what behaviors are acceptable during a simulation but not in other classroom settings. You will need to clearly and consistently let students know behavioral expectations during a theatric strategy. They will probably need to be reminded what you want them to accomplish and what type of behavior is appropriate and inappropriate. New teachers sometimes have difficulty with this consistency and send mixed messages. This causes an increase in inappropriate behavior and the "tiger-by-the-tail" syndrome.

Clearly stated expectations are important to maintaining a positive environment. During an early phase of each of these strategies, students should be told the purpose of using the strategy as well as expectations during certain events. For example, hurt feelings or misunderstandings will occur if some students are operating in a simulation mode (not playing another personality) and other students are operating in role-play mode (pretending they are someone else and acting with another's values or beliefs). During dramatization, some students will want to be comedians, while others will want to be dramatic. These differences will need to be resolved early to avoid conflict and withdrawal.

When using theatric strategies, it will be important for you to consider effective ways to form and work with groups. In Chapter 8, "Cooperative Learning," we discussed strategies for holding individuals within a group accountable as well as considerations for group formation. We will now turn your attention to techniques to be used while assessing these strategies. A scoring guide can also include criteria from the area of classroom management. You should consider including credit for this process learning, as described in the next section.

APPROPRIATE ASSESSMENT TECHNIQUES TO USE WITH SIMULATION, ROLE-PLAY, AND DRAMATIZATION

Assessing theatric strategies presents its own set of unique issues, but we can also draw from general assessment ideas that are common to other instructional strategies. If you have well-thought-out objectives in mind, it will help with assessment focus, just as it does with other strategies. For example, if the purpose of using a dramatization is to help students learn to *empathize* with different perspectives during a conflict, the assessment should focus on whether students learned to empathize. Can they share the thoughts, feelings, or emotions of several different people after the dramatization? Can they say, "Oh, this is why that was such a terribly difficult decision?" Sometimes, however, when using unique teaching strategies, the process of learning, rather than the intended learning, is evaluated. In other words, should how well a person acts during a dramatization be included in a rubric if acting skill is not the intended learning? It would depend upon where the objectives are guiding the lesson.

This is not to say that these processes of learning (performance, participation, responsibility) can't be included in an assessment in some minor way, but that they should not be a focus of the assessment unless they are part of the lesson objectives. The process could be assessed to the degree that you are assessing participation or responsible behavior in the class as a whole. Most classroom teachers aren't as concerned with how a student performs during simulation, role-play, or dramatization. It is likely that knowledge or skills associated with the course content are the focus of the lesson objective. Because of this it would follow that a well-thought-out assessment design would probably include a clear assessment related to process objectives (performance, participation, responsibility) as well as another means of collecting assessment data related to the lesson objectives. For example, a U.S. history teacher has an objective that states: *After participating in a simulation students will be able to evaluate three perspectives on the dropping of the Bomb at the close of World War II according to the rubric provided.* To assess the *process*, the teacher designs a simple score sheet that is to be completed first by the students and then completed by the teacher. He does this to hold the students accountable for their individual work within the groups and because the course syllabus states that participation is expected. Box 9.1 is an example.

Box 9.1   Simulation Score Sheet

Student Name: _____

1 = Poor
2 = Average
3 = Good
4 = Excellent

Performance __/4
Performed duties of assigned team role

Participation __/4
Communicated with others to enhance the simulation

Responsibility __/4
Work was completed and presented on schedule

Total_____/12

TABLE 9.2: Persuasive Paper Rubric

Criteria	1	2	3	4
Position and perspectives	Position and perspectives unclear	Position stated, poorly maintained, missing viewpoints	Position clearly stated and maintained, missing other viewpoints	Position clearly stated and maintained while showing understanding of two other perspectives
Supporting evidence	Unrelated or unreliable evidence	Limited or questionable sources	Clearly related and reliable but limited	Clearly supportive and sufficient evidence
The six traits of writing[2]	Need for revision outweighs strengths	Strengths and need for revision about equal	Strengths outweigh weaknesses; minor revisions	Shows control and skill

To assess the *lesson objective*, the teacher requires a persuasive paper, accompanied by the above rubric (Table 9.2).

As we have shown, theatric strategies are a way that teachers can reach students who may be hard to reach. It would follow that the assessment techniques used with these strategies would be unique and address what students are learning from multiple perspectives. Often, teachers will look at products from the experience to help assess student learning. For example, at one high school, as part of a simulation, students made tools that Native Americans were using at a given time period. The rubric used by the teacher required students to show an understanding of techniques (drying a deer skin), needs (making a fish hook), and materials of the period (bone or rock), appropriate artistic symbols (what anthropologists have discovered), as well as a certain amount of creativity (making a basket). Another teacher had students choose the type of product from the simulation they would like to create to show their learning as guided by a rubric. This can be a good opportunity for student involvement in choosing how they would like to show what they are learning.

GUIDELINES FOR DECIDING IF THEATRIC STRATEGIES ARE APPROPRIATE

As we have noted, there are a number of reasons that theatric strategies are thought to be useful. They are thought to be interesting and motivating strategies that require a high degree of student participation in a way that is uncommon. Simulations, in particular, can be intellectually stimulating, as they require complex thinking that involves difficult moral choices based upon values and beliefs.

These strategies can help create an environment for examining a variety of perspectives while encouraging active, physical involvement. Many teachers see these as helpful in creating an environment conducive to practicing communication skills. As with all instructional strategies, the theatric strategy a teacher chooses should reflect the purpose of the lesson—the objectives—because one strategy will be better suited to certain purposes than another. For example, in general, while simulation may require a high degree of analysis or evaluative skills, dramatization may not. As you look at your objectives, see if any of the above strengths of theatric strategies align with what you are trying to accomplish. As you revisit the understanding by design model (Wiggins and McTighe, 2005) in Chapter 3 you will recall that the model calls for this type of "backward design."

Simulations, role-play, and dramatization are some of the most effective strategies available for ESL and world language teachers. Based upon the *total physical response* premise that students learn best when they become physically involved in learning a new language, theatric strategies provide an ideal way to accomplish this. They encourage thinking and creativity as they enable students to develop and practice a new language in a fun way. However, many ESL students come from backgrounds where they are used to direct instruction. They may be uncomfortable trying these strategies at first because of their background and their perceived English language deficiencies.

Sensitive issues can cause unique difficulties for theatric strategies. Many teachers will avoid a student performance about a sensitive issue for fear that some students will react in immature and insensitive ways. For example, middle school students with the "giggles" may embarrass themselves and others by unthinkingly and innocently laughing at friends during a performance about the Holocaust. It would be wise to consider the maturity level of your class before using these strategies with sensitive issues. For example, it would probably be better to use dramatization rather than simulation with a group of immature students if the subject was civil rights—or to choose a different strategy altogether.

MAKING IT WORK IN YOUR CONTENT AREA

With a partner, create an outline for a theatric strategy lesson for your future classroom. If possible, work on a lesson that is related to a unit you are developing. The lesson might be symbolic, or an attempt to recreate/simulate an actual event or occurrence. You need to be prepared to do this by fully thinking through the process yourself. (Note: you could do this activity by gathering a specific simulation, role-play, or dramatization exercise from resources available to you, or this can be done in a more general way without a specific simulation/role-play/dramatization in hand.) The following items should be included in your lesson plan:

1. Lesson objectives
2. Simulation preparation

Your preparation: Based on the objectives listed above, consider what needs to be done before the simulation/role-play/dramatization exercise. Consider the roles of students and teacher, the procedures that will be followed, the rules of the activity, background information that you will need, handouts, and "stuff" that will be used during the activity. Some of this is material preparation, some is thinking through the logistics.

Student preparation: Within what unit of study will this fit? What background do the students need? How will they learn/gain this background information? What will precede this lesson? What will follow? How will students learn their roles, context of the activity, procedures?

3. Initiation and direction

   Describe how you will begin the lesson. Set up the activity for the students, direct them to the proper spots, initiate the day/activity so that the students know what is necessary for this to be a successful simulation/role-play/dramatization.

4. Describing the scenario

   How will you explain to the students the scenario in which they will be operating? You have already told them what they will be doing (simulation/role-play/dramatization), but now you tell them about the specifics.

5. Assigning roles

   Briefly describe how students will be assigned to different roles. Consider doing these assignments "on purpose" rather than randomly, and having the purpose be to enhance student learning in some way (e.g., mixing students by gender, or across ability levels, etc.). How will the students know the part(s) to which they are assigned?

6. Enactment

   Describe what should happen during the simulation/role-play/dramatization. What will the students be doing? What will *your* duties be to ensure that it goes as planned?

7. Debriefing

   Describe how you plan to examine what happened, examine emotions, draw parallels, and connect the simulation/role-play/dramatization to the content/curriculum and, of course, to life outside of the classroom. Script a good portion of this—at least script the questions you could ask after the activity ends.

Watch the teacher using a theatric strategy in the classroom and determine how these steps were addressed by visiting the companion website.

CHAPTER REVIEW

- Definitions and support for using theatric strategies:

  - Strengths of the theatric strategies include student engagement, interactivity, complex thinking, and motivation to learn.
  - Simulations allow students to experience a replicated environment.
  - Role-play helps students learn about, and act as, someone else.
  - Dramatization gives students an opportunity to act in a given role, during a scene, and often with a script.

- Step-by-step procedures for selecting, planning, and using simulations and role-plays:

  - warming up
  - selecting participants
  - setting the stage
  - preparing the observers
  - enacting
  - discussion and evaluation
  - reenactment
  - discussion and evaluation
  - sharing and generalizing the experience.

- When planning for dramatization, consider the following guidelines:

      objectives
      class environment
      time
      props
      scripts
      casting
      rehearsal
      performance
      debriefing.

- Managing the classroom/learning environment during simulations, role-plays, and dramatizations:

  - a classroom climate of trust and support;
  - theatric strategies are active strategies;
  - clearly state expectations.

- Assessing student learning appropriately during theatric strategies:

    - well-thought-out objectives will focus assessments;
    - performance, participation, and responsibility can be assessed;
    - rubrics.

- Using technology to enhance learning.

    - Many websites that contain helpful ideas.

- Considerations for ELLs during simulations, role-plays, and dramatizations:

    - These strategies are natural ways to encourage listening, speaking, and reading English.
    - Students having special needs with reading English.
    - The debrief strategy *Numbered Heads Together*.

NOTES

1 This exercise is modified from an activity described in Tanner (1972).
2 Six trait writing is an assessment approach focusing on elements of writing. These six traits include word choice, organization, sentence fluency, content, voice, and fluency.

CHAPTER **10**

Discussion and Debate

CHAPTER OBJECTIVES

In this chapter, you will learn about:

- research support for using classroom discussions and debate;
- step-by-step procedures for selecting, planning, and using classroom discussions;
- managing the classroom/learning environment during discussions;
- assessing student learning appropriately during classroom discussions;
- using technology to enhance learning;
- considerations for ELLs during classroom discussions.

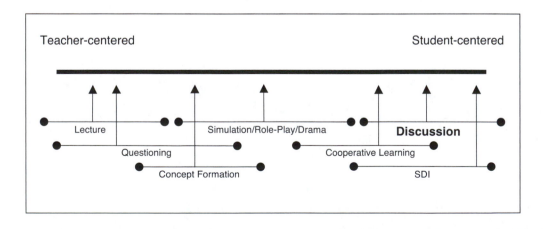

An upside down black umbrella, littered with playing cards, sat encircled by empty chairs in the middle of Chris Allen's high school chemistry classroom. She sat at her desk looking at the scene, wondering if the discussion had worked and, if it did, to what degree? She had hoped that providing each student with three cards to toss into the umbrella when they spoke would encourage the "talkers" to limit themselves and the others to participate. As she reflected on her plans, she thought it seemed to work but it seemed a bit contrived. Some of those who were starting to get excited about the topic ran out of cards and ended up mumbling to those sitting next to them. Other students weren't enthusiastic but made minimal comments so they could toss one of their cards into the umbrella. It wasn't a bad idea, she thought, but how could the idea be improved?

As Chris reflected upon the discussion she began to quickly think through Schwab's four commonplaces—the class environment, the students' familiarity with the topic and motivation, her own preparation, prompting, and leadership, as well as the topic she had chosen. It seemed to her that this discussion could be improved if she simply had more confidence in her students. They were mature enough overall to handle the responsibility of the discussion. Maybe she didn't need to be so controlling and so involved. Chris realized that she really wasn't focusing on their discussion *skills* in this lesson but instead wanted them to discuss the topic to better learn the content. What would happen if she tried to simplify the discussion by breaking the class into small groups of five or six and gave them the discussion prompt? She could walk around the room listening or giving additional prompts if asked or needed. What if she asked for an exit slip listing the major points of three different perspectives on the topic?

OVERVIEW

During discussions, students and teacher interact with one another by listening, thinking, and sharing. As the participants discuss a topic, they think about different points of view and new information. Although discussion is a useful instructional strategy to help students learn in any content area, its dependence on social interactions and participation also encourages students to "learn how to talk" with others. This is a powerful skill for citizens in a democracy, where one of the many roles is a willingness and ability to interact with others on matters of common concern (Gross and Zeleny, 1958; Engle and Ochoa, 1988; Parker, 1996; Hess, 2000). Contradicting this positive view of discussion, however, are research findings that suggest that it is rarely used in America's classrooms. As we mentioned in the chapter on questioning (Chapter 6), recitation persists in classrooms, despite its frequent criticisms (Hoetker and Ahlbrand, 1969; Stodolsky et al., 1981; Goodlad, 1984; Cazden, 1988), and despite the fact that teachers claim to use discussion frequently. As an example, researchers have observed that a teacher talked for 87.8% of the class period during the portion of the lesson he claimed that he used discussion (Swift and Gooding, 1983). Before exploring discussion further, it is important to briefly review the difference between classroom discussion and recitation. Recitation and discussion are two methods of instruction with different characteristics. *Recitation* is characterized (Bellack et al., 1966; Gall and Gall, 1990; Wilen and White, 1991) as a teacher-dominated classroom activity; a "procedure in which students repeat orally or explain material learned by individual study or previously presented by the teacher and in response to questions raised by the teacher" (p. 478). In contrast to this, Wilen and White (1991) define *discussion* as a "structured conversation in which participants work cooperatively to present, examine, compare, and understand often diverse views about an academic topic or issue" (p. 492).

A DESCRIPTION OF THE STRATEGY AND RESEARCH FINDINGS

Classroom discussion serves several educational purposes because it is a unique form of classroom talk. Discussion requires students and teacher to talk back and forth at a highly cognitive and affective level. Dillon (1994) has examined classroom discussion and notes that what students and teachers talk about is "an issue, some topic that is in question for them. Their talk consists of advancing and examining different proposals over the issue" (p. 7).

In a summary of literature about the use of discussion in instruction, Gall (1985) has reported that discussion is an effective way to promote higher-level thinking, develop student attitudes, and advance student capability for moral reasoning. In short, discussion provides opportunities for student thoughtfulness about a chosen topic or issue. Attempts to suggest the necessary and sufficient conditions for discussion have been made (Bridges, 1979, 1987; Haroutunian-Gordon, 1991; Miller, 1992), as have characteristics of different types of discussions (Roby, 1988; Alvermann et al., 1990; Gall and Gall, 1990; Larson, 1997), and the influence of teacher questions on classroom discussion (Roby, 1988; Dillon, 1994; Hunkins, 1995). These attempts characterize discussion as a structured activity in which the process of discussing encourages the students to pool ideas and information and illuminate alternative perspectives. Students develop skills and abilities in civil discourse, criticism, and argument. These skills are extremely important for two reasons. First, democratic life requires citizens to interact using civil, critical discourse to make policies about important public issues (Barber, 1989; Parker, 1996). The classroom holds the potential for students of different race, gender, and social status the ability to learn how to engage one another in discussions about issues of common concern (Dewey, 1916/1985). Second, discussion requires students to learn the content so that they can talk about it.

Teachers who do use discussion, however, use it as a label for many types of teacher–student interactions (Dillon, 1984; Roby, 1988; Larson, 1997; Hess, 2000; Larson, 2000, 2003). Regardless of the type of discussion, certain attributes must be apparent if a discussion is to promote student learning. Bridges has examined the use of classroom discussion (1979, 1987), and established a list of conditions that are necessary if people are to learn from a discussion. Bridges (1987 p. 34) has theorized that there are three defining guidelines or conditions for discussion. Each is presented below with a parenthetical rephrasing to help clarify his points:

- Discussion involves a general disposition on behalf of members of the group to listen, to consider, and to be responsive to what others are saying. (You cannot have a discussion if the members of the group are unwilling or unable to listen.)

- Discussion involves members of the group contributing from their different perspectives, opinions, or understanding. (You cannot have a discussion if everybody is saying the same thing or nobody is saying anything.)
- Discussion is guided by the central purpose of developing the group's knowledge, understanding and/or judgment on the matter under discussion. (It is different from group talk, from negotiation of power, from debate aimed at winning votes or defeating one's adversary, from group therapy—none of which have this central purpose.)

According to Bridges, discussion must be a rule-governed, structured activity so that it encourages collaborative and exploratory development of hypotheses, the pooling of ideas and information, and the illumination of alternative perspectives. It also develops students' skills in criticism and argument. Thought of in this manner, the three necessary and sufficient conditions for discussion provide a disposition, a set of general rules, and a structure to classroom discussion. Bridges suggests that discussions contribute to discussants' understanding of topics by expanding each discussant's information on a topic with information from other discussants; fostering different perspectives on a topic; providing opportunities for discussants to present alternative ideas about a topic; providing opportunities for other discussants to criticize, accept, or refute these alternative ideas; and encouraging mutual modifications among discussants' opinions to produce a group decision or consensus. Group interaction is the important component for each of these as it shapes and directs the exploration of a topic.

REALITY CHECK

Before we begin to look at the procedures and different forms of classroom discussion, it will be helpful to see how teachers lead discussions with their students. What types of interactions with students and teacher do you see when discussion is being used? Are discussions similar or different than a "questioning session"? How?

If you can observe a discussion in your endorsement area, keep track of who is talking. With a seating chart, put a check by a students name to record both who is talking, and how often a student talks. By looking at these patterns, what might you infer about participation during this discussion?

How does the teacher assess students during discussions? Talk with the teacher afterward about assessment of discussions. In addition, watch a video of a teacher using classroom discussion on the companion website for this book.

STEP-BY-STEP PROCEDURES FOR PLANNING AND IMPLEMENTING DISCUSSION AND DEBATE

Teachers use different forms of discussion to serve different purposes in the classroom (Larson, 2000). Whole-class discussions will serve a different learning objective than will small-group discussions. Classroom discussions will vary according to the purpose of the discussion, use of questions, and the issue being discussed. This chapter examines six effective types of discussion. While each serves different purposes, each is appropriate for examining current, controversial, and/or perennial issues. Teachers report that simply planning to have a whole-class discussion with students often is too vague an aspiration. Very few students actually talk, and valuable class time is often wasted with irrelevant comments and student behavior problems. The six types of discussion described below are "tried and true" ways to promote student involvement in classroom discussions. They will be effective in both middle school and high school classrooms. They provide specific structure for engaging students in small-group and whole-class discussions. The six types are:

1. **taking a stand**
2. the **issues/values continuum**
3. the **future's wheel discussion**
4. the **fishbowl discussion**
5. the structured academic controversy (SAC)
6. the **electronic threaded discussion**.

While debate has completely different learning objectives than discussion, it is also examined at the end of this chapter. It is important for you to know how to use this strategy as well. By identifying seven different strategies for helping students talk with each other about course content (six types of discussion and debate) you can better ensure that the strategy is aligned with your learning objectives.

Taking a Stand

This type of discussion is useful with large classes (Oliver and Newmann, 1972; Larson, 1997). It is best used when teachers want students to consider opposing viewpoints around a controversial issue. The primary focus is to clearly and systematically discuss public policy issues in the classroom by aiming conversations "at *persuasion, problem solving* and *clarification* when discussants take a stand on public issues" (Oliver and Newmann, 1972, p. 6; emphasis in the original). Students consider the pros and cons of an issue, devise solutions to problems, and determine a specific policy or action to implement. During policy discussions, the teacher continues to pose questions that encourage students to follow a rational process, consider multiple points of view, and decide on a course of action that the class advocates as a group. Discussants have to think on two levels. First, they must choose a position about an issue and think of reasons to defend it; second, they must reflect on the discussion process itself (the process of verbally interacting with classmates). A *taking a stand* discussion has five steps:

Present an Overview of the Issue, and the Opposing Sides

Begin the discussion by presenting an overview of the issue. For example, provide a handout describing the predominant reasons for the controversy, without detailing specifics of the controversy. Phrase the issue as a question requiring a choice or a decision for action so that the students form an opinion on the issue by responding to the question. Following this, present two opposing sides of the issue in a *point/counterpoint* format. After the overview, point, and counterpoint, Encourage the students to ask questions and clarify their understanding.

Divide the Class in Half, Assigning Each Half One of the Two Sides of the Issue

Divide the class in half randomly. One half moves to one side of the classroom and assumes the *point* side, while the other half moves to the opposite side and considers the *counterpoint*. Be quick to acknowledge to the students that they were assigned these perspectives. Later, they will have the opportunity to stand on the side they truly support. Once in their groups students pair with someone standing near them, and share in their own words the most compelling points on their side of the issue. This puts each student in a position to talk face to face with someone about the one side of the issue. Select students from each side to tell the class these compelling points. By doing so, the issue is described in students' words, and students' understanding can be informally assessed.

Encourage Students to "Go with Their Own Beliefs"

With the two sides of the issue restated in their own words, ask students to take a stand based on their own belief about the issue, and move to one of three locations in the room: one side supports the *point*, one the *counterpoint*, and a location in the middle represents the *undecided*. Once the class is divided, have each student consider why he moved, and explain the reasoning behind his move to someone standing in the same location. These three locations are to represent students' current thinking only. Encourage them to move freely among these locations, based on the ensuing discussion. Occasionally, one side of the room may be left empty—no students have moved to that position. If this happens, you may ask students why they did not move there, or you, yourself, may need to represent that side of the issue. Your preparation needs to be such that you know how to articulate the main views of the point and counterpoint positions.

Encourage Student Interactions and Descriptions

To begin the large-group discussion, ask three or four students on the *point* side of the room to explain their strongest arguments for deciding to stand on that side. After *each* explanation, ask the students on the opposite side of the room (the *counterpoint* side) to respond *only to the comments* they heard from their classmates. The interactions proceed in this manner until both the point and counterpoint sides have presented what they believe are the most significant arguments for their side of the issue. The teacher's role during this initial voicing of opinions is to keep the responses focused on specific lines of reasoning and commentary. When no additional information or ideas are contributed to the discussion, each group gathers in a circle and begins to develop an answer to the question, "What is a solution to this issue/problem?" Students must consider the pros and cons they have heard on *both sides* of the issue, and determine an appropriate policy decision. With three policy options/solutions roughed out (one each from the point, the counterpoint, and the undecided), come back together as a large class and explore together, through discussion, these options. Ask the students to try to combine the three so that the class can reach a consensus. Often, students will request more information about the issue, and you should allow time for research at home, in the library, and/or on the internet.

Dialogical Reasoning on Paper

Since the purpose of this activity is to encourage students to deliberate about public issues, focus them away from winning an argument or defending a particular side of an issue. Instead, you want the students to consider competing positions as well as their own and be able to represent the arguments each might make. After the class discussion about an acceptable policy, ask students to write a four-paragraph essay. The paragraphs address the following topics, respectively (Parker et al., 1991):

> Paragraph 1: Introduce the issue by providing an overview of the main points and major areas of controversy.
> Paragraph 2: Describe the primary arguments presented by the "point" side.
> Paragraph 3: Describe the primary arguments presented by the "counterpoint" side.
> Paragraph 4: Conclude the paper by suggesting a policy that might meet the interests of the two sides.

The Issues/Values Continuum

This technique allows the teacher and students to assess the diversity of opinions in the classroom, while requiring students to think about their own positions on issues. This strategy also allows students to describe perspectives to their peers and explore their own opinions and ideas. You can use this strategy with historical issues by placing students in a specific time period or use it to let them reflect on current or controversial issues. These can be in-depth discussions if the students are able to research and prepare before the class meeting; there will be brief discussions if students rely only on knowledge they bring to the class without any chance to prepare. This type of discussion has four steps:

Making the Continuum

Draw a line from one side of the chalkboard to the other. The end points of the line represent extreme points of view. Label the end points to represent dichotomous positions of the issue. Common points on the continuum are, "strongly agree," "agree," "disagree," and "strongly disagree."

Moving on the Continuum

Select an issue that is related to your course content. Pose a solution to a problem to the class. These might be current events, such as *Gun control laws need to be stricter*; or *Casinos should be allowed on American Indian reservations*. These issues can also examine specific opinions about course topics, such as *Hemingway has a clear theme in* The Old Man and the Sea, or *Farmers should be encouraged to grow genetically altered vegetables.* Students indicate their positions by moving to the point on the line that reflects their view.

Explain Placement

Allow students from each end and the middle to explain their views; allow students to change their placement if they hear persuasive arguments.

Follow-Up Activity

For an ongoing exploration of an issue, you might tape a paper continuum to a wall. Have students write their names on pieces of paper and tape them onto the continuum. As they gain new knowledge or insights they—literally—change their positions by moving their name along the continuum. At the end of your exploration of the issue, debrief with students about when and why they may have changed their opinions.

The Future's Wheel Discussion

This technique focuses classroom discussions in a way that leads to decision making. Students think through the implications of potential outcomes on any issue, and begin to think about the future, and the implications of decisions on future decisions, actions, and policies. This activity can be completed in small- or large-group discussion settings and is comprised of the following five steps:

Describe the Issue

Draw a circle on the chalkboard with a clearly articulated problem or issue in the middle of the circle. Have students think about this problem and come up with possible solutions.

Brainstorm

As students brainstorm possible solutions, place their ideas on the board in circles surrounding the main issue/problem and attach them with arrows (like the spokes from the center of a wheel). The more ideas the students can generate, the better. Figure 10.1 provides a graphic for these brainstorm sessions.

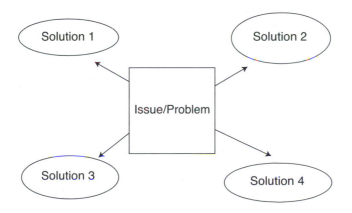

FIGURE 10.1: Future's Wheel Brainstorm Web

Look to the Future

Extend the wheel one step further and examine possible results of each solution and write them on the board. For example, if we decided to solve the problem with Solution 3, then what consequences would result? This can be done as a whole class, or in small groups. These "second generation" outcomes are attached with arrows as well. These steps can be repeated to the third, fourth, and even fifth generations.

Analysis

Students analyze the "future's wheel" to determine *desirable* outcomes—those can be marked with a *D*. Students also identify what they think will be the most *probable* outcomes with a *P*. Have students consider:

> Which outcomes are probable and desirable?
> Which outcomes are probable but not desirable?
> What can be done to make these less probable or more desirable?
> Which consequences are desirable but not probable?
> What could be done to make these more probable?

Consequences

Students consider how consequences imply relationships between factors they might not always think about, such as technological, economic, political, sociological, or psychological factors.

Extension

Have students make a decision or choose a solution to the initial problem and write about why they chose their solution, considering all the implications of their choice.

The Fishbowl Discussion

This technique is used to help students develop effective group skills of participation and observation (Mail, 1968; Gorman, 1969; Hoover, 1976; Priles, 1993). While fishbowl discussions follow a wide variety of formats, they all are used so that discussants learn about the topic of discussion *and* develop the requisite skills and attitudes needed to listen and talk during a discussion. It is a technique that helps teachers navigate between using discussion as a method of instruction and having discussion ability be a curriculum outcome. Fishbowl discussions place one small group of discussants within a larger circle of observers. The smaller group is "in the fishbowl," and as they discuss they are observed and critiqued by classmates outside of the "bowl." A fishbowl discussion has six basic steps:

Grouping the Students

The class is divided into three equal groups. Members of Group 1 and Group 2 are paired. Group 1 sits in a close circle. Group 2 sits in a circle outside of Group 1. Members of Group 2 position themselves to see the face of their counterparts in Group 1. Members of Group 3 form the outer circle and sit outside of the second group in no particular order.

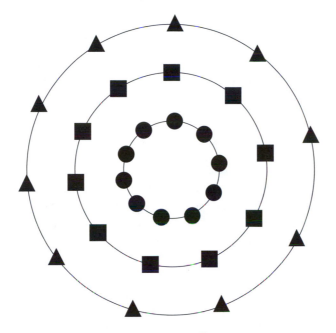

FIGURE 10.2: Diagram of a Fishbowl Discussion Seating Arrangement

Engaging in a Discussion

Select an issue related to the curriculum that has some degree of controversy. It does not need to be highly controversial, just an issue that will promote some differences of opinion. The students in the inner circle (Group 1) begin to discuss the controversy. To promote participation by all of the students in Group 1, the teacher may limit the speaking of students until all have shared. For example, the teacher may allow each student to share one time until all others in the group have spoken, unless the student asks a question of another student. If a student wants to speak a second time but others in the group have not spoken for the first time, she can only speak to ask a question of someone who has not talked. In that way, all students are limited in their sharing, but all students also serve to encourage each other to share during the discussion. Let the discussion run for 15 minutes, unless the talk drops off before that.

Observations

During the fishbowl discussion, members of Group 2 observe their partners and take notes on how they interacted with others. The goal of Group 2 is to create an accurate recollection of the participation in the discussion. While members of Group 2 observe their partners in Group 1, members of Group 3 observe and take notes on the interaction patterns of Group 1. They do not critique individuals, but observe the whole process to identify how the discussion flows, who the leaders are, what behaviors were observed, and how cooperative/cohesive the group appeared to be.

Debriefing

After the 15-minute discussion, student pairs in Groups 1 and 2 meet. The pairs talk about the discussion, and critique the role of the Group 1 member in the discussion. Ideas and suggestions are made that might improve the interactions and enhance the discussion. Members in Group 3 meet with the teacher and talk about the process they observed. They address the notes that Group 3 took during the observation. At this point, the teacher may want to share with the large class some observations about the process.

Reassembling

The groups reassemble and continue to discuss the original issue. Each class member assumes his original role, and discussion lasts for 10 minutes. At the end, students are asked to write their responses to the discussion, what they learned about the issue being discussed, and what they learned about discussion.

Switching Roles

At the next class session, Group 1 moves to observe the whole discussion, Group 2 moves into the fishbowl, and members in Group 3 observe an assigned partner in Group 2 (i.e., all the groups rotate through the roles. The first four steps are now repeated.

Now, switch again; the roles are rotated a final time, and the first four steps are repeated once again.

The Structured Academic Controversy

Using academic conflicts for instructional purposes is a powerful approach to discussing controversial issues in the classroom. The SAC allows for an organized approach that enhances cognitive and affective learning. This strategy is often considered to be a type of cooperative learning (Chapter 8 examines cooperative learning in more depth), because students work together to understand a controversial issue. It also requires students to discuss the issue and provides excellent structure for small-group discussions (Johnson and Johnson, 1988). The purpose for using this approach is similar to the *taking a stand* discussion, with the difference being that the interactions take place in small groups and not with the entire class. The "structure" in an SAC holds all students to a high level of accountability. Students are required to talk in their groups and to examine different sides of a controversial issue. The format for organizing controversies consists of four steps:

Choosing the Discussion Topic

The choice of the topic depends on the interests of the instructor or students and the purposes of the course. Two well-documented positions need to be prepared, and the topic needs to be age-appropriate, so select a topic that has information available.

Preparing Instructional Materials

The following materials are needed for each position:

- a clear overview of the controversy;
- a definition of the position to be advocated with a summary of the key arguments supporting the position;
- resource materials that provide evidence and support for the arguments.

Guiding the Controversy

To guide the controversy, the teacher gives students specific instructions in five phases:

Learning the Positions

Students plan with a partner how to advocate the position effectively. They read the materials supporting their position, and plan a persuasive presentation. They attempt to master the information supporting their assigned position and present it in a way that will ensure the opposing pair will comprehend and learn the information.

Presenting Positions

As a pair, students present their position forcefully and persuasively to the opposing pair. Each pair listens to the other and attempts to learn the opposing position. Students take notes and clarify anything that is unclear.

Discussing the Issue

Students argue forcefully and persuasively for their position, presenting as many facts as they can to support their point of view. Students listen critically to the opposing pair's position, asking them for the facts that support their viewpoint. Each pair presents counterarguments.

Reversing Perspectives

Working as a pair, students present the opposing pair's position. The goal is to be as sincere and forceful about this position as possible. This is also a food formative assessment of how well the pairs listened to each other during the previous steps. Any new insights and facts should be added to this presentation. Students elaborate on this perspective by relating it to other information they learned previously.

Reaching a Decision

At this phase, the students "leave their allegiance" to a particular point of view, and together the two pairs summarize and synthesize the best arguments for both points of view. They then attempt to reach a consensus on a position that is supported by the facts. Follow a format, perhaps, similar to that of the fifth step of the *taking a stand* discussion.

Debriefing

Debrief as a class about the decisions, the process, and the dynamics of SAC. Ask such questions as:

Did you understand all sides of the issue?
What are the strongest points of your decision?
What are the weak points of your decision?

Describe the benefits and difficulties of building a consensus.
What insights do you now have about committees work?
What insights do you now have about public policy making?
What are questions or issues for future discussion?

The Electronic Threaded Discussion

During **electronic threaded discussions**, students "talk" with one another electronically and asynchronously through computer. Discussions are typically referred to as "forums," and comments made by students are called "posts." Thus, when students engage in the threaded discussion, they enter a discussion forum and either post a new response to the initial question (known as beginning a new thread) or respond to a classmate's message (known as adding to an existing thread). Merryfield's (2000) description of what such a forum looks like is helpful:

> The "threads" develop as an outline of message headings and grow longer and more complex as people post messages on new topics or respond to messages already posted. Threads can be . . . only one message or quite long with 10–15 messages.
>
> (p. 507)

By clicking on the thread, the full message is opened for the reader. Figure 10.3 is an example of what students see on the computer.

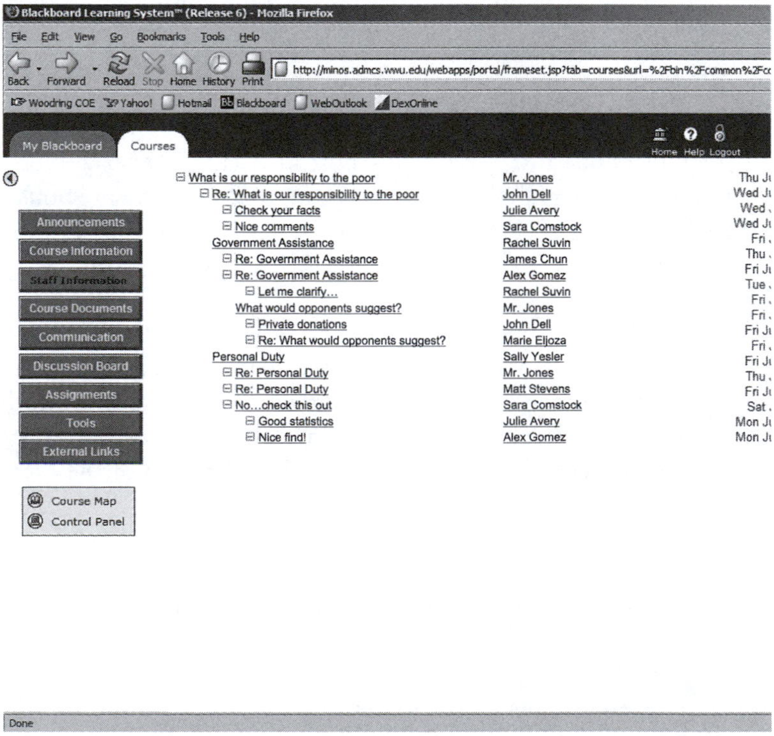

FIGURE 10.3: Screen Shot of Threaded Discussion

A threaded discussions forum is useful for students in interacting about public and controversial issues. Students' responses demonstrate that threaded discussions allow for solid academic interactions with others. Not all quiet students will add to discussion boards, but those students who are quiet thinkers may benefit from sharing their ideas with classmates if they perceive an electronic format to be more conducive for them to "talk." Threaded discussion does not replace classroom discussion. The face-to-face talking that occurs in the latter provides students with a powerful opportunity to interact about an issue and practice using the social skills needed by participatory citizens in a democracy. However, the threaded discussion supplements classroom discussion in the same way that a follow-up writing assignment supplements a face-to-face discussion (Larson, 2003). In addition, the teacher is able to formatively assess students' understanding of the topic under discussion. Complete, accurate records of what was "said" during the discussion are posted at the forum. While it takes a considerable amount of time for students and teachers to read these, it is a very accurate approach for determining who is participating and to assess the quality of the interactions. Threaded discussions follow three steps:

Posting the Initial Thread

Once the site for threaded discussion is established, a topic is posted on the electronic discussion board, and the students are asked to respond.[1] An example of a posted question might be, "Most communities have people who are poor and/or homeless. What responsibility to the poor or homeless do the 'not poor' or 'not homeless' have? Does local/state/national government have a responsibility to aid the poor/homeless? Why?"

Student and Teacher Responses

This is where the discussion takes place. Students respond at least twice: once to the initial question and once to another classmate's comment. You may decide to reply to your students' postings, or you may decide to let them interact with each other. The time that is needed for these discussions is significant, because students must read classmates' comments, select the appropriate comment(s) to respond to, and compose a written response. More details about this third step are addressed in the "Logistical Concerns" section below. While the other discussion techniques involve skill in listening and speaking, threaded discussions do not. Instead, they require skill in reading and writing.

Optional Debriefing

Students may respond to the following prompt: "What do you think about your participation in the threaded discussions?"

The Structured Debate

By strictly timing a debate and establishing a sequence for who speaks when, you can ensure wide participation in classroom debates. These debates can be planned for thirty students or fewer, depending on the availability of teacher assistants/parents who will help with the supervision of the process. This strategy works best with issues that have two dominant sides (e.g., a point and a counterpoint). Debate is more competitive than the six discussion approaches, because it has the strongest emphasis on a "winner" of the debate. Learning about the issue occurs as your students research and prepare for their side of the issue, and prepare responses to arguments from the opposing side. The structure of a debate promotes learning about an issue, and thinking logically, but does not provide students with experience of "everyday conversations" about public issues.

Selecting an Issue and Assigning Groups

Choose an issue with clearly opposing views. Place students into groups of six to eight. These groups need to be divided in half. In other words, each group of six will be two groups of three; each group of eight will be two groups of four. These two groups will represent the opposing sides of the debate. You can assign students to these groups randomly or have students choose the side that reflects their own opinion—the goal is to end up with two groups of equal size. Depending on the number of students in your class, you may have three or four groups of students ready to debate an issue. A class of thirty-two will have four groups of eight. If this is the case, you might have them all debate the same issue, or each group could investigate a different issue.

Preparation and Background

Preparation is important: provide students with readings (or access to readings and have them do a pre-debate inquiry) that will help them establish the main arguments for each side of the issue.

Establishing the Rules for Debate

Observe the following rules:

> Flip a coin to see which side starts.
> Allow a three-minute opening statement from each side.
> Allow each side to present supporting one- or two-minute speeches.
> Each student on each side must speak before anyone can speak a second time.
> No one can talk but the recognized speaker.

Regrouping

After everyone on each side has had a chance to speak, give each side five minutes to regroup and discuss their arguments. Continue the debate, this time cutting speaking time to 30 seconds. You can continue to alternate sides, but recognize students at random.

Switching Positions (Optional)

After an additional 8–10 minutes of debate, make the groups switch and argue the other side of the issue. This is similar to the "Reversing Perspectives" step in a *SAC*.

Variation Possibilities

Allow some students to start out undecided and join sides as they decide; have groups list the main points they have made when they regroup; have a panel of student judges who record the most persuasive arguments for each side.

LOGISTICAL CONCERNS, INCLUDING BENEFITS AND OBSTACLES

If you have ever been part of a classroom discussion in a lecture hall, you know the importance of room size and layout. It is difficult to talk with classmates when seated in rows facing the front of the room (and looking at the back of the head of the person in front of you). The layout of the classroom is important. Moving student desks or tables into groups of four or six or seating students in a semicircle are easy ways to encourage more face-to-face interactions. Some of the discussion approaches described above specify student location. For example, the *taking a stand* and *issues/values continuum* discussions have students stand up and move about the room. Chairs and desks might be pushed to the side of the room. Fishbowl discussions require students to sit in a series of concentric circles. Many teachers design seating charts in the shape of a square or semicircle so they do not have to rearrange the classroom whenever they want to plan a discussion. If you engage all your students in a whole-class discussion, be sure to monitor all your students' levels of engagement.

Good discussions depend on knowledgeable discussants. You will need to allow your students some time to gather information prior to a classroom discussion. This is often called *prior knowledge*—knowledge that students have before an activity begins. Not only will student participation increase when they know about the topic, but opportunities to expand on their prior knowledge will occur during the interactions with classmates. Before you lead a discussion, you need to determine your students' prior knowledge. If the topic is new to them, then you will plan for a discussion after students learn pertinent information. If you determine that students' prior knowledge is adequate, then the discussion will allow for deeper understandings. For these reasons, classroom discussions are excellent activities immediately following a research project, class reading, or homework. The discussion allows students to talk about what they have learned and in the process think about the information anew. They are also useful when examining current events or controversial issues about which students have some prior understanding.

Sometimes discussions will give students the false impression that issues are dichotomous—that only two points of view revolve around a topic. For example, dichotomizing the issue of cloning results in two points: (1) scientists should clone or (2) scientists should not clone. Obviously, cloning is a more complex issue, and it oversimplifies the topic to think of it this way. Consider the *taking a stand* discussion approach. It begins by dichotomizing an issue into two sides, point and counterpoint. However, at the end, the students are asked to develop a policy statement about the issue, and multiple points of view are incorporated. In other words, structuring the discussion as a point/counterpoint initially oversimplifies the issue, but ends by promoting students to think outside these two positions.

How you present the issue to your students is also a very important part of a discussion. Consider this issue: a city's drinking water supply is a nearby lake. This lake is also a recreation center for fishing, waterskiing, and other water sports. In addition, the lake is ringed with houses. The drinking water supply is becoming increasingly polluted. Depending on your content area, you may ask a number of questions. A biology teacher might explore water quality, pollutants, and/or bacteria in lakes from recreational use. A mathematics teacher might encourage students to calculate the flow of water, or whether the amount of water in the lake will effectively dilute the contaminants. A social studies teacher might consider the history of the city's water supply, and historical uses of the lake, or she could have students develop a policy recommendation for the city council about future use of the lake. Finally, an English teacher might have students write an editorial letter to the city paper, where they argue in favor of a particular use of the lake. In each of these cases, the teacher must be careful about posing the question so that a maximum of thinking and talking is encouraged. A poorly formed question will dichotomize the issue. For example, posing the question as "Should this city outlaw the use of outboard motors on the lake?" limits answers to *yes* or *no*. A better question is, "What might the city do about its drinking water problem?" Posed this way, the problem has a wide range of possible solutions, including but not limited to outlawing outboard motors. The point of these examples is that the issues and questions provided to the students need to be carefully designed ahead of time so that maximum thinking is encouraged through the discussions.

CLASSROOM MANAGEMENT AND MOTIVATION

Discussion strategies depend on students talking. From the above examples of discussion, you may notice that students may speak to the whole class, to a small group, or even to a single partner. During whole-class discussions, you can easily step in and control the interactions; you can correct errors, challenge student comments, instruct students to respect classmates, and even help them understand that the goal of discussion is not to win but to understand the topic better. However, many students are able to "slip through the cracks" and not participate. They can rely on the more verbal students to carry the conversations. This is problematic for a couple of reasons. First, students who do not engage in a class activity are unable to meet the learning objectives. If a student is able to avoid talking during the whole class discussion, he may not be learning from the talk. Second, students may feel inhibited from talking to the whole class because of their gender, race, or status in the classroom. As Parker states, the second problem, "discussion may appear open and democratic while masking domination" (2001, p. 111). Moving students into groups encourages more participation and usually is more engaging for a larger number of students. However, groups limit the control you have over the discussions; instead of monitoring one discussion, you will need to oversee several. Discussions, therefore, require management strategies for whole-class discussions and small-group discussions. Both will be examined in this section. However, a set of guidelines for student behavior is helpful to ensure that the behavior is conducive to learning. For example, the following ideas could be presented through an overhead projector or classroom poster:

EXPECTED BEHAVIORS

Discussants are to ask themselves:

- Am I listening to what other people are saying or did I miss an important point?
- Am I clearly making claims and supporting claims with facts?
- Am I critiquing ideas and not individuals (keeping a high respect for human dignity)?
- Are we developing together a shared understanding of the problem or issue?[2]

Whole-Class Discussions

As mentioned above, during whole-class discussions you have control over the interactions, but participation by all the students is often limited. For example, if your class has thirty students, and you have one hour for a discussion, each student will be able to talk for two minutes. In all likelihood only about ten students will talk, and the others will listen to them. The think-pair-share strategy (see Chapter 5) is a simple yet powerful approach for promoting student engagement and helping move a discussion along. You pose a question and ask the students to *think* about a possible solution, *pair* with a partner (or somebody sitting next to them), and *share* their thoughts about the question. By following this with a whole-class discussion of the same question, students may feel more at ease "going public" with the thoughts they have just given to their partner. Thought of in terms of writing, think-pair-share is their rough draft, and the whole-class discussion is their second draft. Some students may have difficulty pairing with someone near them. It is a good idea to place them with partners (e.g., by simply saying, "You two will be a pair," or "You three will talk together"). This is also helpful to ensure that no one is left out, and that the groupings are not too large. During whole-class discussions it is imperative that all your students are listening to the person talking. Equally important, however, is for you to ensure that one student is not dominating the conversation. In other words, you want to make certain that all students are listening, and that no one is talking too much. This is a difficult task. Many teachers have students raise their hand so that they can call on students and help spread out participation. Others teachers do not want to play this gatekeeper role and want students to direct their comments to each other and not the teacher. Teachers often move to the back or to one side of the room as a way to encourage more student-to-student interaction. You still must monitor student comments to be sure that they are representing their ideas clearly and factually.

Small-Group Discussions

Cohen, a sociologist who studies student interactions, has suggested that the size of a group impacts participation. Groups larger than seven encourage many students to not participate. If students are in a group with seven or fewer classmates, greater participation by all students occurs (Cohen, 1994). Most of the discussion approaches mentioned above require having students in smaller groups. As with the think-pair-share activity during the whole-class discussions, students often need help forming these groups. Again, the most straightforward approach is to group students who are near each other. If you know of students who do not work well together, then you will want to form the groups to maximize the learning. Students can form their own groups, but you need to monitor closely that all students are included. Most of the research on group work suggests that the teacher should place students in groups for a purpose. You may want to mix the groups so that they are heterogeneous in regard to areas such as experience, communication skills, gender, ethnicity, or other categories that will enhance student learning. You may even want to group students in homogeneous groups. For example, middle school students often benefit by talking about controversial issues in same-sex groups. Once they are in the small groups, monitor the students to be sure that they understand the task, know of any time limits, and are engaged in the project. The key at this point is to move continually among your students as they interact. Do not engage in lengthy conversations with your students; rather, encourage them to talk with their partners/group mates about the topics. If you talk in depth with students, they will not develop their own understanding of the topics, and you will not be able to observe all of your students. Your primary tasks during large groups discussions are to be sure that the students understand the question you have asked them to discuss (e.g., "What are the strongest points on your side of the issue?"), that they are discussing this with their partners, and that these discussions are not taking up too much class time. By reminding them to focus on the question and topic, you can help keep them engaged.

APPROPRIATE ASSESSMENT TECHNIQUES TO USE WITH DISCUSSION AND DEBATE

Assessing classroom discussions create unique challenges. Once you decide the purpose for a discussion, assessment becomes much easier. Consider these two purposes:

> Discussion is used as an instructional strategy, where the purpose is to have students engage in verbal interactions so that they learn the content.
> Skill in discussing becomes the desired outcome of this strategy.

If you solely have the first purpose, then you may not want to assess students' participation during verbal interactions. A report, presentation, and/or written response will allow you to adequately assess learning (e.g., the *dialogical reasoning on paper* step of the *taking a stand* discussion). However, if you solely have the second purpose, then you assess much more of the process during the discussions. For example, during a fishbowl discussion, students are assessed on their skill in explaining their ideas and thoughts rather than merely recounting memorized facts and details.

Formative assessments of discussions help students listen and respond to each other appropriately. By teaching students how to discuss, the benefits for using discussion in the classroom can be extended to all areas of students' lives. Most teachers believe that discussion skills need to be taught, that students left to their own will not engage in fruitful discussions. Certain notions—such as supporting opinions with facts and criticizing an idea rather than the person suggesting the idea—require skill. As such, they need to be learned by the students and assessed by the teacher. Once these are learned, however, the very process of discussing a topic may facilitate abstract learning processes (Bridges, 1979, 1987). Usually, you will assess both your students' engagement in the discussion and how well they learned the content. Table 10.1 is one type of rubric that will help you assess both.

Use this checklist on a clipboard to keep track of students on a daily basis. You can assess students' discussion skills on a three-point "scale": (1) consistent; (2) emerging; (3) not seen/not observed. Five to eight students can be targeted for observation each day, taking care to vary the days each student is observed. After several weeks, several

TABLE 10.1: Clipboard Checklist for Classroom Discussions

Date of Observation: Activity: C = Consistent E = Emerging N = Not seen/Not observed Student Name	CLASSROOM OBSERVATION	Describes issue clearly	Elaborates with relevant examples	Asks thoughtful questions re: issue	Restates arguments/then counters	Gives relevant support	Notes gaps in logic	INDIVIDUAL WRITTEN WORK	Summarizes others' ideas	Develops on thesis	Gives arguments to support thesis	Examples strengthen argument	Organizes main points to build argument	Strong closing

clipboard checklists can be combined to complete individual rating scales for each student. This allows for more accurate generalizations about students. This rubric has two sections. The first section, labeled "Classroom Observation," assesses students during the discussions. The second section, labeled "Individual Written Work" assesses student learning through a presentation, written paper, or some activity after the discussion ends.

Allowing the students to self-assess their participation allows you to compare your perceptions with theirs. Figure 10.4 is a rating scale that might be given to students to complete, and then completed by you.

This rubric requires that you and your students decide the gradations between a score of 0 and 6. In other words, you decide before the discussion what scores of 1, 3, or 6 might be. Often this is a helpful rubric when using a fishbowl discussion, a threaded discussion, or a debate.

Both of these rubrics are appropriate for formative and summative assessments. Formative assessments are very important in helping students learn the skills needed to engage in discussion. Formative assessments of student understanding also occurs during the think-pair-share segments of discussions and also as the students talk about

---

Student Name:_____   Period:_____

You will see a one number on each line. The numbers represent how you rated in each of the 3 discussion. Your score is on the right of each category and the total score is at the bottom of the page.

No mention   **Integrated into your discussion**
(0 pt)   **(6 pts)**

⟵————————————————————⟶

Building on other student ideas   _____/6

⟵————————————————————⟶

Using information from the text   _____/6

⟵————————————————————⟶

Using information from the handout/readings   _____/6

⟵————————————————————⟶

Integrating new ideas/outside information   _____/6

Total _____/24

FIGURE 10.4: Discussion Rating Scale

the compelling points of the issue. You assess their comments for accuracy. A threaded discussion has the comments in text for review. You and your students can refer to the postings to assess their contributions and/or complete a rubric.

You will have students who are disinclined to talk. A student who is shy may not feel comfortable speaking and will require opportunities to talk in smaller groups. Gender has been shown to influence speaking in classrooms. Some studies suggest that girls may talk less frequently than boys, especially if the conversations are perceived as combative. Culture is also an influence on student talk. Some cultures promote talking out loud, while others view excessive talking as disrespectful. In any of these cases, it is imperative that you are aware of your objectives and your students' needs. You can work with your students (and talk with their families) to help negotiate how they might engage in meaningful classroom discussions.

ENHANCING STUDENT LEARNING WITH TECHNOLOGY

Computer technology can support a discussion. To help students prepare, teachers will often lead them to websites or organize their own digital-guided inquiry. These might be as simple as hyperlinked questions in a Word document that lead students to rich online information. Aside from helping students prepare for face-to-face discussions, technology can also be used to hold the discussion itself. This leads to a unique take on our spiraling themes of logistics, classroom management, and assessment.

Logistics: In the above text, we mention online threaded discussions. These discussions can be created using a variety of applications. You may be familiar with BlackBoard, a commonly used e-learning application found in universities. Unfortunately, this software is probably too expensive for your future district's budget. We have found that two good options are the free web applications Moodle or Google Groups. These are applications we are most familiar with, but there are other good open source options such as eFront, Dokeos, Claroline, Ilias Learning Management, Sakai Project, or Olat.

Classroom Management: Electronic threaded discussions posit a management issue slightly different than the other discussion strategies. Often students read the initial question(s) put forth by the teacher, and respond to that prompt with a lengthy statement. Reading and responding to classmates' postings seemed to occur less frequently as the discussion continued. Somehow the energy that is present at the beginning of the discussion needs to be perpetuated. Clearly, as students post more messages, the reading task becomes more burdensome. Changing the discussion topic, or attempting to post "refocus questions" periodically helps reduce the backlog of unread messages.

As with face-to-face discussion, students need instruction about "how to" discuss electronically. Identifying a structure that allows the teacher's voice to be "heard" is important. While classroom discussions typically take one or two hours, threaded discussions can last an entire semester because the internet allows the interactions to transcend the time and place restrictions of meeting in a classroom. When the students are together in a computer lab, momentum is not a concern. When students post during their own time, it is. Experienced teachers who use threaded discussions put limits on how long students can post to a given forum. For example, you may limit the threaded discussions to three days. Since students interact over a short period of time, they know their comments will be read, and responses will be posted quickly. Students' interest in visiting the discussion forum is heightened when they know "new comments" will be posted frequently. Of course, some students will need to be reminded that all classroom expectations for respectful face-to-face conversations also apply online even though the medium is different. For example, face-to-face we don't yell at each other and online WE DON'T FLAME!

Assessment: As you review the checklist and rubric in this chapter, you will notice that most of the criteria will also apply here. A threaded discussion has the comments in the text for review. You and your students can refer to the postings to assess their contributions and/or complete a rubric. You may notice that some of your more reserved students begin to come out of their shell as they have a medium to communicate that suits them. For all students, you should consider criteria in your rubric that explains your expectations for number and length of posts.

MAKING A LESSON MORE MEANINGFUL FOR ELLs[3]

Providing discussion time in class between native and ELLs is an outstanding aid to language and content learning. Age-peers are likely to speak in a way that is more comprehensible for the ELL, and the ELL may feel more comfortable with a partner or peers in a small group, because it is less "public" than the whole class instruction. Pair discussion, small-group discussion and large-group discussion can be successfully used, but they need to be sequenced and well-planned to provide the scaffolding ELLs need to actively participate.

- Build background:

  - Before jumping into "discussion," provide a reminder of what we have been talking about.
  - Provide a model of what a good discussion might sound like.
  - Introduce (or review) important content vocabulary and concepts and provide visual reminders for students to refer to as they discuss.

- Provide the objective of the discussion:

  - Let them know at the start what you want them to be able to do or produce at the end of the discussion.

- Choose the discussion size strategically:

  - Do pair discussion or small-group discussion *before* a teacher–whole-class discussion if you want to increase participation.
  - Frequency of student speaking activity can be increased dramatically.

- Brief pair discussion allows student to put ideas into English words before having to participate in a small group.
- Large-group discussion is best to close up a class discussion time.

- Structure the debriefing.

  - Be especially clear during the debriefing about what was accomplished. Consider writing the outcomes of the discussion on the board or in some visual format.

- Discussion styles vary significantly from culture to culture:

  - American whole-class discussion often seems more like brainstorming, or ping-pong, with the frequency of response often more valued than the depth or reflectivity of the thought. Discussion might be seen as a learning experience in which everyone, prepared or not, can participate. The speed demanded by this kind of discussion is challenging for those who may be searching for words in a second language.
  - Some students may come from cultures in which challenging the intelligence of someone's ideas is not seen as a challenge to the individual's intelligence. This can come off as rude and shocking in the American classroom.
  - Some students may come from cultures in which the concept of debating and disagreeing strongly is not acceptable. Some come from cultures where speaking out is viewed as arrogant or challenging the teacher's knowledge. These students may become very quiet in discussions, and seem uncomfortable. Often they excel, however, in discussion where compromise and cooperation is expected and encouraged.
  - Some students may come from cultures that place a high value on reflection before speaking. Turn taking, with everyone having the opportunity to speak without being interrupted, is comfortable.

- Provide the words and language patterns to carry out those roles. All students need to practice academic vocabulary and academic language patterns orally.

  - Consider providing a list of "formal" language either for the discussion or the report back, or both.

    1. On poster in room, or in student folder, for discussion language:

       i. I see what you mean, but I think . . .
       ii. You've got a point, but I've found that . . .
       iii. Could you explain that some more?
       iv. I believe _____ because _____
       v. Can you give me an example of that?
       vi. I agree with you because _____
       vii. I can see where you are coming from, but have you ever thought about _____?

    2. You can make a paragraph with blanks, or provide sentence stems, to help guide students during the report back. This makes it easier for the ELL to do

the report back if the entire group fills it in together. It also exposes students to the academic language they are asked to understand when they read.

   i.   We agreed on _____ , but we disagreed on _____
   ii.   Some of the group expressed the idea that _____
   iii.   Although _____ thought _____ , others believed that _____
   iv.   Despite some disagreement, we now all agree that _____

- Provide a graphic organizer to help them take notes and categorize what they are hearing (many samples available online):

    - an information grid with headings—students fill in the appropriate cells;
    - a Venn diagram for noting agreement and disagreement while people are talking;
    - demonstrate this on the overhead or document camera.

GUIDELINES FOR DECIDING IF A STRATEGY IS APPROPRIATE FOR THE CONTENT OF A LESSON

Each discussion strategy listed herein serves specific purposes. Those purposes were identified as part of the discussion for each strategy. This section, however, suggests general guidelines for determining the appropriateness of using discussion in helping students learn. While the majority of all classroom talk is synonymous with recitation-style approaches, significant social and cognitive changes have been reported to occur in students when classroom talk shifts more toward adult "conversations" (Cazden, 1988). Cazden explains this move away from recitation and toward discussion as

> [o]ne important shift is from recitation to something closer to a "real discussion" . . . talk in which ideas are explored rather than answers to teacher's test questions are provided and evaluated; in which teachers talk less . . . and students talk correspondingly more; in which students themselves decide when to speak . . .; and in which students address each other directly.
>
> (p. 55)

Discussion is thought to be a useful teaching technique for developing higher-order thinking skills that enable students to interpret, analyze, and manipulate information. Students explain their ideas and thoughts rather than merely recount, or recite, memorized facts and details. During discussion, learners are not passive recipients of information that is transmitted from a teacher but are active participants. Their active involvement with each other and the course content helps them construct a deeper and more flexible understanding of the topic (Tharp and Gallimore, 1988; Johnston, et al., 1994).

When students interact during discussions and debates, they need to have a deep and flexible understanding of the content, and they need to have skill in discussion itself. The following questions should help you consider whether or not classroom discussion will be an appropriate activity to plan for your students.

Will the Discussion Help Students Learn about the Issue/Topic?

For discussions to educate students, they should be serious interactions through which students "support their ideas with evidence, where their opinions are subject to challenge by their peers as well as the teacher, and where the teacher's ideas are equally open to criticism" (Engle and Ochoa, 1988, p. 47). The purpose of probing questions and discrepant viewpoints is to encourage interactions and to encourage the students to respond with the most powerful evidence available to them.

Can Students Discuss Issues?

Teachers think of discussion as a skill that requires practice sessions. As such, they often pre-teach discussion skills to their students in an attempt to front-load behaviors, attitudes, and interactions that they consider critical for classroom discussions. They set time aside to prepare students for discussions; some begin this preparation the first day of school. Teachers tell students about courtesy, respect, and manners for talking—and possibly disagreeing—with classmates. They tell students to view the class as a community to encourage more interaction. This is something that does not happen without effort on the part of the teacher and willingness on the part of the students. Teachers make efforts to earn students' trust, and students are held accountable to respect their classmates. One teacher we know reported this as a training process: "I train them from the beginning to become a learning community . . . there is an atmosphere of trust."

What Types of Interactions do You Want during the Discussion?

Parker (2001) theorizes that discussions can have the "look and feel" of a seminar or of a deliberation. The purpose of a seminar is to improve the understanding about a topic, book, and/or idea. He suggests that seminars start with a question such as "What does (the topic of the discussion) mean?", and proceed in a way that is conducive to improving everyone's understanding. Deliberations start with a question such as "What should we do?" As such, deliberations intend not only to improve the discussant's understanding but also to reach a decision about a shared problem (Parker, 2001, p. 114). Consensus building and compromise are more prevalent in deliberations. With any discussion, however, the emphasis needs to be taken off "winning an argument." Classroom discussions need to value the learning that comes from the process of interacting.

MAKING IT WORK IN YOUR CONTENT AREA

Consider the courses you will be certified to teach at the middle school or high school level. Select a topic that you believe will engage students in a discussion. Productive discussions are a result of careful planning. Consider the following:

1. Identify the topic students will discuss.
2. Write out lesson targets:

   a. targets dealing with what students are to learn about discussion;
   b. targets dealing with the knowledge base to be explored.

3. Describe the rationale for choosing the issue.

   a. What makes this a good issue to discuss?
   b. How does it fit with the curriculum?

4. Decide what type of discussion will best help students learn the issues.
5. Lesson procedures: Explain why you chose the type of discussion technique you did and how it will help students learn. Consider the following:

   a. Student preparation:

      i. How will you prepare students to engage in a discussion on this topic?
      ii. What experiences, readings, and information will they need ahead of time?

6. Discussion questions:
   Write out actual questions you would pose to your class:

   a. opening questions (to help students recall information and establish facts);
   b. interpretive questions (to help students draw relationships and compare/contrast information);
   c. opinion questions (to encourage your students to draw their own conclusions and articulate them).

7. Assessment:
   Reread the section on assessing classroom discussion, and determine how you might assess student learning. Consider whether you want to assess their "discussion skill" and/or their understanding of the discussion topic.

CHAPTER REVIEW

- Research support for using classroom discussions and debate:

  - Teachers value classroom discussions, but struggle using it frequently.
  - Discussion helps students learn content deeply and helps develop key interaction skills needed for citizens in a democracy.

- Step-by-step procedures for selecting, planning, and using classroom discussions:

  - identification of six discussion types:

    - taking a stand
    - the issues/values continuum
    - the future's wheel
    - the fishbowl discussion
    - SAC
    - the electronic threaded discussion;

  - **structured debate** serves a different purpose.

- Managing the classroom/learning environment during discussions:

  - logistics and establishing a conducive classroom tone;
  - clarify goals of the discussion;
  - develop a set of guidelines.

- Assessing student learning appropriately during classroom discussions:

  - assess student participation and content learning;
  - rubrics.

- Using technology to enhance learning:

  - researching discussion topics;
  - online discussions.

- Considerations for ELLs during classroom discussions:

  - Pair discussions, small-group discussions, and large-group discussions can be successfully used, but they need to be sequenced and well-planned in order to provide the scaffolding.

NOTES

1 Information about setting up an electronic discussion can be found in the technology section of this chapter, and on the companion website.
2 These guidelines are developed from work done by Barber (1989); Larson (1997); and Parker (1996).
3 This section was created in association with Trish Skillman and Maria Timmons-Flores at Western Washington University.

CHAPTER 11

Student-Directed Investigation

CHAPTER OBJECTIVES

In this chapter, you will learn about:

- research support for using student-directed investigations (SDIs);

- step-by-step procedures for selecting, planning, and using SDIs;

- managing the classroom/learning environment during SDIs;

- assessing student learning appropriately during SDIs;

- using technology to enhance learning;

- considerations for ELLs during SDIs.

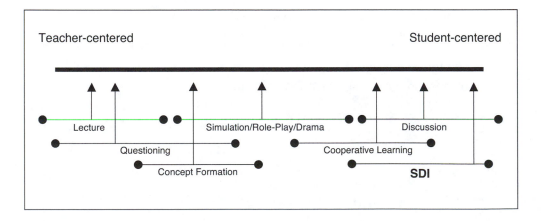

If an outsider walked into Lil Rios' world language classroom conducting a SDI, it might appear somewhat chaotic. Some of her students, sitting in the back corner of this rural high school Spanish class, would be taking notes while viewing a documentary about the stories of recent immigrants. Other students would be asking for permission to go to the library computer laboratory to analyze data and research statistics on ELLs and state test scores. One student might be giving a fellow classmate a survey. Another student would be composing interview questions that will query community members about their traditional customs.

At first glance the class looks hectic, but it is actually a highly planned student-centered strategy allowing for differentiation during an inquiry lesson. Ms. Rios had been considering how she could get her students connected with the local Spanish-speaking community. She hoped that by creating an inquiry project her students could generate questions that interested them and then pursue them in a variety of ways with her and community partners' support. She planned for these questions to move students out into the community. Since they were working in teams, some of the higher-level Spanish speakers could assist those that were not as fluent. She gave them the topic — "Learning about recent immigration from Spanish speaking countries." So far, teams have come up with these questions:

- What interesting stories can we find of recent immigrants trying to earn a living?
- What was the town they came from like?
- How difficult is it for a recent immigrant to learn English and go to school?
- What are jobs like for the recently immigrated?
- Do all immigrants work in the fields? Has anyone gone to college?

The students were working hard at refining their data-gathering ideas so they could get interviews and not just information from text as required in their guidelines. Ms. Rios was looking forward to inviting some local community members into her class so that they could hear the results during student presentations.

OVERVIEW

Students in Ms. Rios' class are similar to their adolescent peers elsewhere in that they want learning to be engaging. According to Tomlinson (2003), there are three trends that strike at the core of effective teaching and learning in today's schools:

- Classrooms are more diverse than at any time in our past and this trend will continue.
- Due to this trend in diverse classrooms, teachers are looking to teach in more flexible, personalized ways.
- There is an escalating demand that students acquire high-level knowledge and skills.

Increasingly, teachers are using the term *differentiated instruction* when they design plans that address these trends. One of the ways to meet the educational needs of all the students in the classroom is to focus on curriculum that both *promotes understanding* and *engages* students. SDI is an important component of a classroom that accomplishes this. After considering this approach, you will be able to better evaluate the curriculum you develop using the criteria for high-quality curriculum in the "Making It Work" section at the end of this chapter.

DEFINING SDI

You may have heard the old proverb, "Tell me and I forget, show me and I remember, involve me and I understand." The strategies that you have been exploring through this text have varying degrees of student involvement. No teaching approach has greater potential for student involvement and engagement than SDI. This approach includes several varieties of investigation that share certain critical attributes. Different types of SDI would include inquiry learning, discovery learning, **problem-based learning**, project-based learning, experiential learning, and service learning. SDI offers an opportunity to learn through experience in an environment that:

- involves the "real world" and offers meaningful, personally interesting challenges;
- requires active learning;
- provides opportunities to solve problems, answer questions, or address real needs;
- allows for student ownership, responsibility, and choices;
- offers students an opportunity to perform as experts or professionals.

Precise definitions of the various types of investigation are difficult and somewhat nebulous. However, when you hear these terms used at a school, you can assume that they include the characteristics referred to above for learning directly related to the course curriculum in addition to the following variations:

Problem-based learning has two types:

1. *Inquiry learning*: A focus on asking and investigating personally relevant questions. The conclusion is not as important as learning the thinking process. These questions might be controversial or have conclusions that are difficult to ascertain.
2. *Discovery learning*: Those who use this type of learning will focus on discovering the solution to a particular problem through a process respected by professionals in the field. Specific solutions or conclusions are as important as learning the thinking process and will deal with settled rather than controversial issues.

Project-based learning: A focus on the process used to develop a product or other creation. This may or may not be problem-based.
Experiential learning: A focus on learning through an experience usually not associated with a traditional classroom environment.
Service learning: A focus on learning through an experience of service to the community usually outside of the classroom or school.

A DESCRIPTION OF SDI AND RESEARCH FINDINGS

As you may have noted, SDI is grounded in constructivist learning theory. With this in mind, now is a good time to quickly review the basics of two predominant approaches to learning as described in Chapter 1—*behaviorism* and *constructivism*. Much of the experimental data that serves as the basis for the behaviorist view was first generated by Skinner (1968). This view suggests that knowledge is universal, objective, and independent of the student. The behaviorist teaching approach is primarily focused on direct instruction because knowledge is transmitted to the student and received through the senses. The primary role of the teacher would be to break information and skills into meaningful packages, build them back together through a series of presentations or activities and, when finished, test to see if students have learned. Behaviorist classrooms tend to focus on teaching skill sequences, stress individualized rather than group work, and emphasize methods such as lecture, teacher-directed questioning, skill worksheets, teacher-led activities, and objective tests.

Constructivist theory has a different view of knowledge and therefore holds a different view of approaches to learning. While proponents of this theory hold a variety of opinions about knowledge and learning, they would agree with the underlying belief that knowledge is constructed by people through their personal prism of experiences. Constructivists believe that what a person knows is not a function of detached observation but created through interaction with the world and that knowledge and reality are subjective (Fosnot, 1989). Those holding this view give attention to the social context in which learning occurs. Learning environments similar to those in the "real world" are best suited to enhance learning. Constructivists support learning that focuses on the use of authentic tasks—that is, the every day practices of a particular group such as scientists, historians, or filmmakers. These tasks would be similar to on-the-job experiences or apprenticeships (Cognition and Technology Group at Vanderbilt, 1990; Collins et al., 1994). Proponents of this view would have classrooms focus on problem solving, independent investigation, the pursuit of personal interests, and the utilization of higher-order thinking skills.

A brief overview makes these two perspectives appear to be mutually exclusive and to some they are just that. In practice, however, perspectives fall on a wide continuum somewhere between two poles (Duffy and Jonassen, 1992; Scheurman, 1998). For example, some teachers may not agree with the idea that reality is created by the individual but are still proponents of student-centered approaches to learning. However, through this discussion, you can see how what you believe about the way students learn has a profound impact on the instructional choices you make in the classroom. This can be reviewed further by revisiting Chapter 1.

Many teachers of adolescents have noticed that the naturally inquisitive nature of children seems to slowly fade. Sadly, our traditional system of education has not always encouraged the pursuit of independent inquiry. Instead, too often, students use almost all of their time in a required pursuit of the test answers. The facts, of course, are important, but so also are the understanding and the use of information. Research in cognition, authentic learning, and student engagement support claims that SDI is a beneficial strategy for developing these attributes (Brown et al. 1989; Brooks and

Brooks, 1993; Scheurman and Newmann, 1998). Others have described environmental approaches associated with this strategy such as independent inquiry and self-regulation to be advantageous approaches for developing understanding and application of knowledge (Wisker and Brown, 1996; Boekaerts, 1997). According to a summary of research on learning conducted by Bransford et al. (2000) there are three implications for classroom teachers that are components of SDI. First, students should be placed in settings that prepare them for flexible adaptation to new problems and settings; second, students should organize information into the main ideas that structure a discipline—its most important theories or concepts and their interrelationships; third, students show understanding when they know how and when to put knowledge to use.

STEP-BY-STEP PROCEDURES FOR PLANNING AND IMPLEMENTATION

The various types of SDI will serve different purposes, and because of this, one type may be a better match for a learning objective than another. We have found these strategies to be equally effective at both the high-school and middle-school levels even though students' maturity levels vary drastically. Teachers will consider other variables such as time constraints, community resources and contacts, transportation, and the course schedule, when determining which type of investigation to pursue. The following common types of SDI share the commonalities that we describe in the preceding sections of this text and are very similar in many ways. However, they are unique in emphasis and require different considerations in planning because they are different procedurally.

Problem-Based Learning

Problem-based learning was originally designed for medical school programs when concerns were raised that students knew the medical information but lacked critical reasoning skills to use the information wisely. Some see this approach as a type of (or synonymous with) inquiry learning, as the two are very closely related. There are three primary features of problem-based learning: "initiating learning with a problem; exclusive use of ill-structured problems; and using the instructor as a metacognitive coach" (Gallagher et al., 1995, p. 137). In other words, from the outset, the students are presented with a complex problem that has many variables and likely has several solutions. Students will be supported by a teacher to help them as needed but will not be given a process to follow. Many times students who are confronted with problems to solve do so only as an extension to a teacher-directed lesson; it is viewed as an activity to reinforce what the teacher has presented. Granted, this would be an effective way to extend a teacher-centered lesson; however, often the students do not know why they are learning the material. At the same time, they *do* learn to assume that in the real world all the information needed will be at hand in order for them to proceed. Problem-based learning confronts students with an ill-structured problem at the onset, allowing for problem-solving through information resources and scaffolding.

Ill-structured problems are an important aspect because they are, well, *messy*. This mirrors the problems that people face regularly in life outside of school. During this approach, students are encouraged to consider problems that need plentiful exploration and careful consideration that can lead students along several different paths or alternate solution routes. These are problems that may have more than one correct answer or unclear solutions, and often require the use of key course concepts that can be readily transferred to other problems.

Many times teachers will substitute actual problems that face students with interesting generated problems that reflect the real world. One chemistry classroom used the following problem for a lesson on the effects of industrial pollution:

> Richard, who is 15 years old, lives near an oil refinery. His family, which includes three children, one only a month old, has been living there for three years. His mother has noticed that since they moved to that house, her silver teaspoons became tarnished quickly (West, 1992).

The class then began with the problem (silver teaspoons becoming tarnished) and began looking for the solution. Of course, the teacher encouraged them to begin thinking about a solution that involves chemistry. In another class, a middle school math teacher wanted to get students thinking beyond routine application of formulas and avoid the confusion surrounding area and perimeter. After using some pre-problem warm-ups to garner interest, the teacher introduced a problem related to pizza pricing. Students were given a menu with prices for various individual slices from different sized pizzas (9 inch, 12 inch, and 15 inch). The students used various techniques (string, making grids, etc.) to determine circumference, radius, and area of each pizza. The students were then asked to explain why one of these measurements was most closely related to price and to determine which pizza they considered to have the best value. To follow this, students were asked to extend their learning by investigating the relationship between diameter and circumference by measuring other objects in the classroom and making tables and graphs to share their findings. Finally, students had the more challenging task of using the same techniques to compare radius and the area of circles (Harris et al., 2001).

One procedure, of many, for the implementation of problem-based learning would be to include the following steps. These steps can be easily modified depending upon the requirements of the discipline or if the problem is to be worked on by the class, small groups, or individuals. For ELLs, these steps can be modified by having them work with an English-speaking partner or intentionally placing students in heterogeneous groups that incorporate a range of ability levels.

- The teacher frames the learning objectives, essential questions, and desired results.
- The teacher discusses objectives and assessment methods with students.
- Begin by identifying a problem that relates to a significant course concept. This could be student- or teacher-generated.
- Brainstorm what students know, what students need to know, and the process they can use to find out unknowns.
- Students collect and test data.
- Students manage and analyze the data.

- Students generate a plan or solution and test it.
- Students reassess their plan or solution and retest.
- Students present or publish their findings.
- The teacher facilitates debriefing to summarize learning and assess process.
- The teacher assesses student learning and teacher (self-)facilitation, and evaluates overall process.

Inquiry Learning

Another common approach that encourages students to think like professionals in the field (i.e., to think scientifically, like a literary critic, or to "do geography") is inquiry learning. Again, this approach is similar to problem-based learning in many ways, but we separate the two here to help illuminate the different emphases and forms of implementation. With inquiry learning, the emphasis is on the pursuit of questions, making hypotheses, investigating, forming theories, and the possibility of taking action based upon evaluative judgments.

There are three basic types of inquiry that teachers use depending upon their objectives and other limiting factors. First is *structured inquiry*, in which students are given a research question or direction, a method, and materials, but not expected outcomes. Another type is *guided inquiry*. Here, students are given a research direction and materials but need to determine the research method themselves. A third is *open inquiry*, in which students determine the research question, methods, and necessary resources.

You will be ready to begin the written phase of planning after determining what type of inquiry is most appropriate for your classroom. Some teachers have found that inquiry-oriented lessons are improved if there is a clear focus and direction for students. Students are not productive learners if they are unclear about what they are trying to accomplish or become frustrated by a lack of direction. Box 11.1, adapted from the work of Exline (2004), is helpful with the development of an inquiry plan that gives focus and direction. It is useful for planning in any content area but may need to be modified depending upon the short-range (one hour?) or long-range (one month?) nature of your lesson idea. Some would use this template to help organize their thoughts prior to completing a more formal lesson plan as shown in Chapter 4.

Inquiry lessons will loosely follow a process of inquiry similar to that shown in Figure 11.1 below.

In general, the inquiry process begins with the questioning stage and proceeds to other stages as shown. Opportunities for metacognition and feedback occur throughout the process. While this simple visual may be of use as an overview of the process of inquiry, it is also misleading in that rarely is a high-quality inquiry lesson so neatly packaged. Many think of inquiry as more of a web. For example, after interpreting the information, the students may need to form another hypothesis and reinvestigate or ask a different question. Teachers using inquiry techniques would need to have an understanding of the basic process before they could confidently modify plans as circumstances in a fluid classroom would demand. The following suggestions for this process would need to be modified depending upon these circumstances as well as the type of inquiry (structured, guided, or open) that the teacher has chosen.

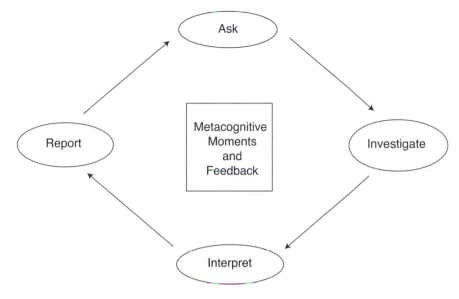

FIGURE 11.1: Stages of the Inquiry Process

| Box 11.1 | **Planning Template for Inquiry Learning Lesson** |

Learning Objectives and Expected Outcome

What is the skills development focus (e.g., research, observation, synthesis skills)?

Habits of Mind/Ground Rules Being Emphasized

What are the rules of the discipline being studied that you wish to reinforce (e.g., aspects of the scientific method; literary ideas and ideals)?

Conceptual Theme Most Important to This Lesson

What are the themes that connect the lesson to previous lessons and the important ideas in the framework of the discipline (e.g., the way the discipline explores change, the way it makes connections between one idea and another, or the way theories or ideas can be applied to different levels of analysis)?

Specific Content

What is the content that your students need to know by the end of the lesson?

Sources and Resources Needed/Available

What sources and resources are needed (e.g., libraries, professional journals, local colleges/universities, the internet, experts, materials)?

Potential Roadblocks to Learning

What problems do you see that may hinder student learning? What plan do you have to deal with these roadblocks?

Inquiry Attributes Already Possessed by Learners

What are the skill levels of the learners?
What nurtured habits of mind do the learners possess?
What are the levels of conceptual understanding of the learners?
What are the levels of content understanding of the learners?
How will you plan for enhancement and appropriate scaffolding?

Questions and Types of Questions to be Raised and Explored

What are the main questions that you hope learners will explore, bearing in mind the various types of questions (inference, questions about hypotheses, etc.)?

Ongoing Assessment

How will you formatively assess student progress throughout the lesson?

Appropriate Sources and Resources to Effectively Monitor Progress

How will you summatively assess student learning?

Professional Preparation

What do you, as a teacher, need to find out before starting this lesson?

Plans to Help Advanced Learners Become Facilitators for Learners Needing Additional Help

In what ways can advanced students work with others as the project progresses?

Stage 1: Asking

Most students will need assistance posing an appropriate question that is both interesting and challenging. Encourage students to consider what really interests them about a topic. Is the question under consideration one that can be answered with little effort or is it challenging and worthwhile? How will pursuing the question give them deeper insight into the overall lesson theme or objective? Students should be encouraged to avoid questions with simple answers, or yes/no questions, unless they need to do in-depth exploration to come to a decision. For example, *Should the Makah be allowed to hunt whales?* could be a poor question choice if students are not asked to provide in-depth supporting information from various perspectives. Care should also be given to guide students away from questions that are too broad—for example, the question, *What should be done about overpopulation?* After speaking with the students about their interest, this could be refocused to read, *What impact does the Mexican economy have on migration patterns?* Students could be asked to form conclusions or take a position after they have answered the question.

Once an appropriate question has been determined, a *need-to-know* chart can be used to help focus students. On a large visual, the teacher would write headings for three columns:

What do we know?
What do we need to know?
How do we find out?

If the class is pursuing one question together, this could be a large-group brainstorming session; if students are pursuing questions in small groups, this could be done with teacher facilitation. This step is as important as any of the others since, commonly, students who have poor inquiry experiences can trace it back to the question formulation stage.

At this early stage, students should be encouraged to formulate an investigation plan in which they meet with the teacher to determine direction and form a work schedule.

To help your understanding of this important first stage, brainstorm potential questions or problems that you might ask students in your future classroom. Have a partner look at your questions and provide you with feedback on whether these questions will help engage students. If you have access to a middle school or high school classroom, then see what questions students are interested in exploring in your content area.

Stage 2: Investigating

Each discipline will have established techniques for investigating a question. For example, obviously using the scientific method is vital in a biology class, while a history class would have its own methods. For example, the scientific method most commonly used would include the following steps:

1. Form the question.
2. Make observations.
3. Form a hypothesis.
4. Do the experiment.
5. Draw a conclusion.

Historical methods would include techniques by which historians examine primary sources and other evidence to research and write about history. Guidelines for historical inquiry would require consideration of internal and external criticisms prior to forming hypotheses through a process of historical reasoning. Investigating social issues would involve a perspective gathering component. The steps involved may be similar to the scientific method but this discipline, like all others, has its own investigative methods.

One source of information common to all fields is text-based resources. The teachers will need to be prepared to give suggestions and guidance for the selection of appropriate resources. This is especially true of the use of internet resources, as evaluating online information can be confusing and difficult for students. How does a middle school or high school student know if information is reliable? Students should be made aware that consideration of authorship, publisher, currency, perspectives, coverage, and accuracy can help determine the reliability of a source. Many students will be familiar with the online resource Wikipedia; it may be a good starting point for research and be helpful in determining related topics or other guidance to find other resources. However, students should be taught the importance of finding multiple resources and that because there is usually no author to cite in Wikipedia, it should be seen only as a starting point.

The use of face-to-face or online experts is also a good way to make resource information available. During this investigative stage, students could use the teacher for mini-lessons for small groups on an "as needed" basis. In addition, during this stage, there may be opportunities to have student experts or community experts available as resources. This stage is an excellent place in the lesson to provide extra help to ELLs and to any student who may be struggling. One of the distinct advantages of SDI is that differentiating instruction and learning is doable because the teacher is facilitating learning. As a result, you will be able to react to students' individual needs.

Stage 3: Interpreting

Students are encouraged to analyze information they have collected and draw conclusions. To do this they will need to reflect on *what* information is relevant to the question under consideration and *how* it can help them answer it satisfactorily. Both middle school and high school students will need assistance with the thinking skills needed to draw logical conclusions from the information they have collected. Some computer software—spreadsheets to create graphs, for example—can be helpful to teach students to analyze and interpret information. This example would be especially helpful for those learners with a more visual orientation.

Students can record their interpretation notes along with investigative notes in an inquiry journal. A journal like this could be used as an assessment tool by the teacher as well as a way for the student to track their learning. After the interpretation of results is completed, students can record their conclusions and begin preparing for a report of their findings.

Stage 4: Reporting

Give students an opportunity to present their findings to an audience. This audience (small group of classmates, the School Board, PTA) should be a group interested in the topic. For example, one middle school classroom used sophisticated computer software on loan from a university to investigate a question posed by the local city council: *Should we—and if so,* where *should we—place a city park for our fast-growing town?* The students took several months to investigate information and analyze data until they were prepared to make a recommendation. Their teacher, to her credit, saw this as a wonderful opportunity to have community leaders involved as part of the presentation audience. Naturally, this is neither always possible nor advisable. Some inquiry projects are small, in-class affairs where informal reports are appropriate. It is important to provide a forum for students to present findings and field questions. This could be an audience of peers, the teacher, or the larger community.

A presentation with a written document is a natural and oft-used form of report for an inquiry-based lesson. However, it is not unusual to find classrooms that take a form of social action as a result of their inquiry. This might involve writing letters to the influential, making video reports that are sent to television stations, creating websites or blogs, or other ways the class desires to draw attention to their findings.

Stage 5: Metacognitive Moments

This stage should be thought of as an integrated part of the process. Create times throughout the inquiry that allow for student self-reflection, assessment, and adjustment. For example, take a few minutes along the way to hold a questioning seminar to explore what they are concluding up to that point or what remains to be resolved. Use think-pair-share activities, exit cards ("On a card, write two specific things you learned today"), or one-minute papers ("Write for one minute about a prediction you can make based upon your experiment today"). Students could also use their inquiry journals to record questions about the process or for future pursuit and other reflective internal "talk" that may be helpful. We have also found Stage 5 to be an excellent time for making sure ELLs understand the process and are meeting learning targets. For example, by having an ELL and an English-speaking student think-pair-share, you can provide an opportunity to ensure both students understand.

Watch the video of a teacher leading students in these 5 steps of an investigation at the companion website for this book. See if you can identify each of the steps, or if some are combined.

LOGISTICAL CONCERNS, INCLUDING BENEFITS AND OBSTACLES

The attitudes of stakeholders can make the implementation of SDI challenging for some. Many educators, parents, and community members use their own experiences of school to judge what is appropriate for adolescents to learn and how they should learn it. This is commonly referred to as the impact of the *historic curriculum.* An inquiry-oriented approach may be at odds with a district that valued the memorization of content and recitation above the practical use of content through inquiry. Many of the statewide standardized tests attempt to assess student ability to think critically by having them show their thought process. However, critics argue that standardized testing is a poor format for assessing these important thinking skills. In either case, the perception of many is that inquiry-oriented approaches take time away from preparing students for "the test" and are seen by some as "fluff." Teachers using SDI should be prepared to share their rationale for its use.

Time constraints are viewed by many as the single greatest obstacle to the implementation of this strategy. These constraints involve both the lack of time for the teacher to implement a lesson of this sort and the lack of time in the curricular schedule. Teachers are pressed for time on all sides. Some have found that using collaborative techniques are helpful in the planning and implementation of lessons. Sharing ideas, plans, and resources with a small group of like-minded teachers can be tremendously helpful.

There will be many time pressures as you schedule lessons for your course calendar. This will create tension between "covering" the material and using additional portions of the schedule to go deeper. Many assume that because of the pressure of state testing, there is no choice but to attempt to cover material in survey-course fashion. However, according to one extensive study that examined middle schools over a three-year period, this may not be the case. The authors concluded that "assignments calling for more authentic intellectual work actually improve student scores on conventional tests" (Newmann et al., 2001, p. 29). You will need to be realistic about how you balance "coverage" and "authentic intellectual work," but the question really isn't *Should you do it?* but *How can you* best *do it?*

You should be aware that some challenges will involve student factors. Saye and Brush (1999) identify three of these challenges as students' lack of engagement; students' failure to consider a variety of competing perspectives; and, students' lack of content knowledge or the thinking skills necessary to apply the knowledge they possess. We have stressed the importance of teacher involvement in the process of engagement and perspective gathering. It is also important to prepare students through pre-inquiry activities. These can be thought of as practicing skills in order to get your class ready for true inquiry. By learning these skills independently, students are helped to overcome some of the challenges associated with this type of learning. Students who do not speak English as their primary language will need extra assistance. However, we find that SDIs allow you to come alongside students who need their instruction differentiated. As the focus shifts from a teacher-centered lesson to student-centered activities, you are available for students as they engage in their own (or small group) investigations. This benefits not only ELLs, especially, but also all of the students in your classroom. Two examples provided by Wilke and Straits (2005) include giving students an article with an important section (e.g., the conclusion) missing and ask them to draw conclusions from the information remaining, or posing an ethical question and asking students to discuss opinions, solutions, and opposing perspectives.

Students can be confronted with simple (but not immediately obvious) curiosities that arouse interest but also give opportunity for learning thinking skills. For example, one high school teacher wanted her students to learn about creating a hypothesis. At the beginning of class, she stood a lit candle in a pan of water and placed a jar over the top. The students noticed that as the candle flickered lower and lower the water was pulled up inside the jar. When the flame went out, the water inside the jar was raised partway up the candle. The students were given 5–10 minutes during several class periods to create and test hypotheses using a variety of candles and jars available as resources. After several days the students, who worked in teams, were asked to share their hypotheses with the large group. The teacher was using this pre-inquiry technique to teach students about the process of scientific inquiry that she would use in other labs throughout the term.

CLASSROOM MANAGEMENT AND MOTIVATION

From a distance SDI looks as if students do everything and it runs on its own. This is far from the case. For every successful SDI, you will find masterful work by a behind-the-scenes teacher. So, in the case of Lil Rios' classroom described at the beginning of the chapter, what may appear to be "chaos" is actually a well-thought-out, planned system of learning.

A great deal of attention will need to be given to the classroom learning environment. You will need to create and nurture a "community of learners." This is a common concept for classrooms involved with student-centered approaches to learning. The development of a learning community is at the heart of this approach to learning (McGrath, 2003). According to Brown (1997) there are five critical pieces that work together to create a community of learners:

1. *Active, purposeful learning.* The design of a SDI will give opportunity for active purposeful learning.
2. *A learning setting that pays attention to multiple zones of proximal development.* Brown bases this component on the work of Vygotsky, who promoted the idea that through collaborative work on important topics learners will accomplish what they would not have been able to do alone. For specifics about collaborative learning, see Chapter 8.
3. *The legitimization of differences.* Students should be encouraged to develop their individual areas of expertise for the good of the community of learners.
4. *A community of discourse.* A community is developed in which learners value methods for civil and worthwhile discussion.
5. *A community of practice.* Members of the learning community (which includes the teacher) value and respect each other and take responsibility for each other's learning through collaboration.

These five components of a healthy learning community could be explained to the class and perhaps acknowledged on paper and signed by students and the teacher as a way to show commitment to the principles.

You will notice that the roles for the teachers and students in a community of learners is somewhat unique. Teachers are thought of as colearners, coaches, facilitators, and sometime experts. Realistically, teachers can immerse themselves in the community only to a degree due to their responsibilities with evaluation and facilitation. These responsibilities naturally will affect student–teacher relationships even in the most dynamic of learning communities. Student roles will include assuming responsibility for learning, making process decisions, taking the initiative to determine direction, self-initiating, and participation as expert or coach at times.

One of the challenges for facilitating a successful SDI is to give students the responsibility for their learning while helping them stay on a pathway to success. It is important for a teacher to help monitor self-directed work time by helping students consider their work schedule and set deadlines. It would be a mistake to assume that most students could, without assistance, create a work plan and stick to it. Here are a couple of suggestions that may be helpful:

Create a Work Plan Together

Sit down with each student (or group) and help them create their schedule. Your role is not to give them a schedule but to help them understand what needs to done and when it needs to be completed—to help them learn to take responsibility on their own.

Monitor the Students' Schedule

After a schedule is created, a series of deadlines is helpful. These deadlines can be created by the students themselves or provided by the teacher. This again could be thought of as taking the responsibility of learning back from the students; however, this is a way to help students assume responsibility with the support needed for them to be successful. This series of deadlines could be part of a scoring guide or a part of a procedure with which students receive feedback (e.g., "You will need to turn in your first reflection for our service learning project on Tuesday so that I can give you feedback before our next site visit"). Some use "research accountability receipts," citation forms, or similar forms to keep track of what students accomplish with their time at the library or at home in order to assist them with their schedule. Part of the learning beyond the content is related to making and keeping a schedule to accomplish a task on time. Students will probably need your help.

APPROPRIATE ASSESSMENT TECHNIQUES TO USE WITH THESE STRATEGIES

Assessment can be difficult during SDI, because the purpose of the strategy deals with thinking skills practice and the use of content. This focus requires techniques that are different from those associated with traditional testing for knowledge acquisition. Performance assessment, or authentic assessment, is a natural fit for this type of strategy because they ask students to demonstrate their thinking. This form of assessment is detailed in Chapter 3.

There is a logical process to follow as you plan for assessment. As we discuss the assessment process, we are assuming that you will have aligned your goals and objectives and thus have identified desired outcomes for the lesson. We assume these objectives will have guided you into deciding that a SDI is an appropriate strategy to use in helping students learn. The objectives will also help you create a scoring guide that reflects your thinking on the valued outcomes. In other words, the criteria you select for your scoring guide should be aligned with the objectives you have selected for the lesson. There are many valuable lessons your students will learn during their investigation; however, they need to know what in particular you will be assessing at the end of the day. A good way to do this is by sharing the scoring guide with the students "up front."

In a performance assessment, the scoring guide is often a rubric or a checklist. This gives the teacher the opportunity to reduce (although not eliminate) the subjective aspects of this type of assessment. However, using SDI allows ample opportunity to use a variety of assessment techniques to collect multiple perspectives of student learning.

The Checklist

A checklist is similar to an analytic rubric, but without the descriptors and with more criteria—it typically is a list of criteria that can be checked off as the teacher sees evidence of students' meeting expectations. Box 11.2, below, offers an example.

The Conference

By talking with the teacher in the conference, the student explains what was learned and provides evidence. The teacher has an opportunity to ask questions or probe for understanding.

The Portfolio

A portfolio is a collection of samples of student work and reflective notes from the student and others that show progress.

The Rubric

The rubric is a matrix that provides criteria and descriptors for rating students at various levels. *Holistic* rubrics provide criteria that look at the overall quality of the task, while *analytic* rubrics breakdown the most important aspects of the task.

Table 11.1, below, is an example of an analytic rubric and Box 11.3, below, is an example of an holistic rubric.

The Student Journal

The student journal contains notes kept by the student that can be shown to the teacher or referred to by the student during a conference. The notes are from free writing exercises about learning, or responses to prompts by the teacher intended to help the student think about her learning.

Teacher Notes

Teacher notes are an "on-the-fly" record of notes the teacher makes as observations are made. For example, on an index card a teacher might record, "Observed Amelia leading the group through excellent analysis comments during . . ."

Box 11.2   Checklist for Oral Presentations

Student Name:_____ Date: _____

Reviewer Name: _____

Project:_____

Category	Responsibilities
Content	☐ The information I gave was interesting or important to others.
	☐ I was well informed about my topic.
	☐ I used vocabulary that the audience could understand or defined unfamiliar terms.
	☐ I used an effective and appropriate attention-getting device.
	☐ Logical appeals included reliable, factual information.
	☐ I used emotional or persuasive appeals where appropriate.
	☐ I added supportive detail to the main point(s).
Delivery	☐ I maintained eye contact most of the time.
	☐ I spoke to the entire audience, not just one or two people.
	☐ My pronunciation was clear and easy to understand.
	☐ My rate of speech was not too fast or too slow.
	☐ My voice could be heard easily by the entire audience.
	☐ My voice varied in pitch; it was not monotone.
	☐ I did not use filler words (e.g., "um," "uh," "ah," "mmm," "like," etc.)
	☐ My body language was not too tense or too relaxed.
	☐ I didn't fidget, rock back and forth, or pace.
	☐ I used notes sparingly; I did not read from them.
Organization	☐ I organized ideas in a meaningful way.
	☐ The information and arguments/details were easy to follow.
	☐ I stayed focused and did not stray off topic.
	☐ The introduction included a clear statement of the main point(s).
	☐ I included necessary background information about the topic.
	☐ The body of the presentation contained support for, or details about, the main point(s).
	☐ The audience could distinguish the introduction, body, and conclusion.
Presentation Aids	☐ Presentation aids were used during the speech.
	☐ Presentation aids were relevant to the speech.
	☐ Presentation aids improved the presentation or reinforced main points.
Resources	☐ I used resources that addressed the topic thoroughly.
	☐ I used credible print resources.
	☐ I used credible electronic resources.
	☐ I cited my sources using the required format.
	☐ A bibliography was available.

Box 11.3	Holistic Rubric for Fiction Writing

5—The plot, setting, and characters are developed fully and organized well. The who, what, where, when, and why are explained using interesting language and sufficient detail.

4—Most parts of the story mentioned in the score of 5 above are developed and organized well. A couple of aspects may need to be more fully or more interestingly developed.

3—Some aspects of the story are developed and organized well, but not as much detail or organization is expressed as in a score of 4.

2—A few parts of the story are developed somewhat. Organization and language usage need improvement.

1—Parts of the story are addressed without attention to detail or organization.

TABLE 11.1 Analytic Rubric for Making a Brochure

CATEGORY	4	3	2	1
Writing and Organization	Each section in the brochure has a clear beginning, middle, and end.	Almost all sections of the brochure have a clear beginning, middle and end.	Most sections of the brochure have a clear beginning, middle and end.	Less than half of the sections of the brochure have a clear beginning, middle and end.
Content and Accuracy	All facts in the brochure are accurate.	99–90% of the facts in the brochure are accurate.	89–80% of the facts in the brochure are accurate.	Fewer than 80% of the facts in the brochure are accurate.
Spelling and Proofreading	No spelling errors remain after one person other than the typist has read and corrected the brochure.	No more than one spelling error remains after one person other than the typist has read and corrected the brochure.	No more than three spelling errors remain after one person other than the typist has read and corrected the brochure.	Several spelling errors in the brochure.
Attractiveness and Organization	The brochure has exceptionally attractive formatting and well-organized information.	The brochure has attractive formatting and well-organized information.	The brochure has well-organized information.	The brochure's formatting and organization of material are confusing to the reader.

ENHANCING STUDENT LEARNING WITH TECHNOLOGY

A popular and long-standing format for online inquiry-oriented lessons is called a *webquest*. The best webquests are not just scavenger hunts but adhere to principles of inquiry we have discussed in this chapter. Information about the creation of webquests along with many teacher- and student-created examples can be found at the San Diego State University Webquest Homepage (webquest.org). Webquests have six key elements:

Introduction: provides background information;
Task: includes either a question or task;
Resources: provide links to helpful resources to give direction;
Process: provides step-by-step guidance for completion;
Evaluation: outlines expectations through a scoring guide;
Conclusion: a summary of learning goals.

After looking through examples in your discipline at the webquest homepage, you might want to choose one example and decide what type of inquiry (structured, guided, open) is proposed and discuss why you would or would not use it in your class. You could also use the QuestGarden portion of the website created or modify a webquest for your future class using the principles of Student-Directed Instruction set forth in this chapter.

Technology can be used to join or create collaborative support systems that will help save time. In addition, many websites have lessons and other ideas available so that teachers can save time by modifying investigative ideas rather than trying to create from scratch (see, e.g., www.sciencenetlinks.com or http://smithsonianeducation.org, as well as the companion website for this book).

When students engage in investigations, they need to gather and evaluate information. Obviously, this information can come from around the world. As a result, an important skill for students is the ability to evaluate online information. As the teacher, you can play an important role in helping your students become critical consumers of ideas, data, opinions, and other sources of information that will confront them when online. Below are some criteria for evaluating online information that the pre-service teachers with whom we work find useful. We have additional references on the text's companion website that will be useful for using the internet as part of student investigations.

Criteria for Evaluating Online Information[1]

Authorship

- Is the author identifiable? Never use a source whose author you cannot identify. If the author is not clearly listed within the site, use the following techniques to locate the author's name:

  - link back to the site's home page;
  - ask the web development team or sponsoring organization to identify the author.

- Is the author a professional in the field?
- If the author's name is unfamiliar, is the site linked to an established authority on the subject?
- Has this author been referred to favorably by respected professionals in the field or by a respectable website? Does the document contain links to these professionals or to the respected websites? Are there also links from these sources that go back to the site you're assessing?
- Does the author include his or her e-mail address or a postal address so that you can contact the author directly from the site?
- Does the website belong to an individual, or is it part of a site maintained by an organization, academic institution, or other group? Does it list the author's position within this group?

Publishing Body/Publisher

- Is the type of material appropriate for the assignment? Professional sources from a website include professional home pages or online professional journals. Non-professional sources include personal home pages or online general audience magazines.
- Are you able to contact the webmaster or sponsoring organization from within the site?

Currency

- Does the site include information on when it was created or how often the site is updated?

Perspectives

- Can you identify the goals of the site?
- Are these goals clearly stated?
- Does the focus of the text relate to the graphics in the site?
- Is the perspective appropriate for your paper?
- Are all sides of the issue fairly presented?

Coverage

- Is there an in-depth understanding of the related issues that shows the author's familiarity with the subject?
- Does the site acknowledge other sources within the text itself? Are there also links to these sources if they exist online?
- Is the bibliography complete and thorough?
- Are the appropriate theories, schools of thought, or techniques used in the discussion of the material standard in the field?
- If the material is based on a new theory, is coverage of the new approach detailed? Does the site cover the advantages and disadvantages of the method compared to other current methods in the field?

Accuracy or Verifiability

- Is the material comparable to related sources? The home page of an authority in the field will provide a good base of sources to use as a comparison.
- Is the methodology given so that the author's work can be replicated or evaluated?
- Do many mechanical errors (e.g., grammatical errors, typos, etc.) appear in the text? Errors suggest that the author might be careless in presenting information.
- Did you discover the site through a search engine? If so, how does the search engine you used look for information and, if relevant, rate the sites it retrieves?

Below we provide only a few sites to practice using these criteria. Our selection of sites is offered as a starting point. Ideally, you will talk with a teacher in your endorsement area about websites that they use for students to gather online information. View each site while you consider the criteria for evaluating online information listed below. You should use the questions below each criteria heading as a guide to consider the major points, as these sub-questions are general aids to thinking critically about the site and may or may not be appropriate for each site listed.

The Cuban Missile Crisis
    www.gwu.edu/~nsarchiv/nsa/cuba_mis_cri/

Commemoration Of The Holocaust
    www.ihr.org/other/tehrantimesdec05.html

Mankato, Minnesota
    http://city-mankato.us

MAKING A LESSON MORE MEANINGFUL FOR ELLs

Word Walls

Word walls are lists of words written on butcher paper and plastered on walls around the classroom to assist with vocabulary development. Often teachers ask students to help create the lists and add to the list as appropriate. During a SDI, a teacher might listen to students talking in their groups with an ear toward words that may be confusing or at some point may take some class time to ask about words "for the wall." Some teachers leave these words for all students to know at the end of a unit (and work on definitions collaboratively), others write definitions on the wall, and still others draw pictures or write in native languages. At the end of the investigation, the teacher can place the words on 3 × 5 cards or in a three-ring notebook and color code for the unit. This way the students can associate the color (or sometimes pictures are used) with the word and place it in context which helps with recall. For example, the word *engineer* might be one word written on the wall during an inquiry project dealing with naturally occurring *tessellations*. This could be placed in the red notebook and when referenced by the teacher the student may recall the inquiry project and the associated word. Of course, this type of coding would be most helpful if the teacher keeps a notebook for each unit. Teachers would assist students if they refer to the word wall and notebooks consistently and model using it.

Web 2.0 ideas for ELLs

SDI is an ideal strategy to incorporate ideas from the latest in internet technology called Web 2.0, or that many refer to as the ReadWrite web. This new generation internet is more interactive and has allowed for those with limited technology skills to publish their own blogs, podcasts, photographs, videos, wikis, and much more. It is easy to see that publishing in these ways will involve communication practice that will enable students to utilize developing English skills. Digital storytelling, a method for communicating through video, is one way this technology can be used to encourage ELLs within the SDI framework. For example, using concepts found in this chapter, students create digital stories on energy conservation by interviewing families in their neighborhoods. This process involves several pre-production techniques, such as scripting and storyboarding. You can find many ideas by searching the internet for digital storytelling or you can probably think of several ideas for your own content area. To assist you, we provide an initial set of ideas and links at our companion site for this book.

GUIDELINES FOR DECIDING IF SDI IS APPROPRIATE FOR THE CONTENT OF A LESSON

Weighing the advantages and disadvantages of SDI will be important as you determine if this is an appropriate strategy. Some of the advantages are that it is often motivating the students as they pursue topics that interest them. It can be stimulating to perhaps explore outside of the traditional classroom, especially in a venue that allows you to serve another person or the community. This approach encourages autonomy and initiative, while giving students an opportunity to think deeply about issues. Some of these advantages may be similar to what you have in mind about your objectives.

You should also consider some of the unique challenges in SDI when deciding if you should use it. It can take considerably more time to complete than other approaches. Remember, you will need to balance a need to "cover" material with an opportunity to learn through exploration and experience. You will need to have the appropriate resources, such as community experts, informational media (can you get access to the computer lab or go to the library?), and materials necessary for student to be successful. You should determine if you feel comfortable acting as a facilitator, often being pulled in many directions at one time. How is your energy level? This is not a study hall approach. Are you prepared to engage with students in an environment that at times can look like controlled chaos?

MAKING IT WORK IN YOUR CONTENT AREA

SDIs for Differentiated Learning

Tomlinson (2003) offers criteria for what she calls a *high-quality curriculum*. This is a curriculum that promotes learning for all students by being engaging and promoting understanding. Obviously, no teacher would be able to achieve all of these in one lesson or probably in one unit. However, these indicators will help you evaluate your instructional direction. After you have created a unit of instruction that includes SDI, assess your unit using the following checklist. Indicating a check, plus, or minus for each criterion may be helpful before you write self-evaluative comments about your work.

Engagement:

- is fresh and surprising to the students;
- seems "real" and purposeful to the students;
- connects with the students' lives;
- allows choice;
- requires active learning;
- is pleasurable—or at least satisfying—for the students;
- is focused on products that matter to the students;
- yaps personal interest;
- allows students to make a contribution to something greater than themselves;
- challenges students and provides support for success.

Promotes understanding:

- is clearly focused on the essential knowledge, understanding, and skills a professional in the field would value;
- is coherent (organized, unified, sensible) to students;
- attends to student misconceptions;
- deals with profound ideas that endure across years of learning;
- enables students to use what they learn in important ways;
- requires cognition and metacognition;
- causes students to grapple with significant problems;
- causes students to raise useful questions;
- necessitates that students generate (versus reproduce) knowledge.

You can also observe the online video of a teacher using SDI and assess how many of the items listed on the above checklist are addressed. You might want to discuss your findings with others to clarify any points of interest or even disagreements. The video is located at the companion website for this book.

CHAPTER REVIEW

- Research support for using SDIs:

    - promotes learning through experience in an environment that involves the "real world" and offers engaging challenges;
    - requires active learning;
    - provides opportunities to address real needs;
    - allows for student ownership, responsibility, and choices.

- Step-by-step procedures for selecting, planning, and using SDIs:

    - Different types of SDI include inquiry learning, discovery learning, problem-based learning, project-based learning, experiential learning, and service learning.

- Managing the classroom/learning environment during SDIs:

    - A great deal of attention will need to be given to the classroom learning environment and to creating and nurturing a "community of learners."

- Assessing student learning appropriately during SDI:

    - Assess content learning and skill development.
    - Align goals and targets with assessments.

- Using technology to enhance learning:

    - Gather online data.
    - Students need to be able to become critical consumers of ideas.

- Considerations for ELLs during SDIs:

    - word walls;
    - Web 2.0 allows for opportunities for interactions and networking.

NOTE

1 © 1997–2005, The Write Place. Reproduction of these criteria granted for educational purposes.

Appendices

Glossary

504 plan: A program of instructional services to assist a student with a physical or emotional disability, an impairment that restricts one or more major life activities (e.g., caring for one's self, performing manual tasks, walking, seeing, hearing, speaking, breathing, working, and learning), or who is recovering from a chemical dependency.

Action research: Purposeful ways a teacher identifies a phenomenon in the classroom, determines an approach for gaining insight into this phenomenon, and assesses if the approach was effective.

Affective domain: Learning that is tied to feelings or emotions. Learning in this domain does not require students to develop particular feelings or emotions, but it helps students use their emotions and feelings to learn.

Analysis: Breaking down whole entities into their component parts to identify relationships, make comparisons and contrasts, and look for patterns. Level four on Bloom's Taxonomy.

Anticipatory set: Some refer to this metaphorically as the "hook" by which a teacher catches students' attention, or the manner by which a teacher helps students anticipate what will be happening for the day. This could be a question, a poster, music, or even a short activity.

Application: Students practical use of skills, concepts, and information in new situations. Level three on Bloom's Taxonomy.

Assessment: A plan that allows teachers and students to monitor their progress toward meeting specified goals and objectives.

Authentic assessment: Assessments that resemble tasks that might occur outside of the school as well as in the classroom. Both the material and the assessment tasks look as natural as possible. Authentic assessment values the thinking behind the work, or the process, as much as the finished product.

Authentic task: An activity where students need to use the information and skills learned in school to complete a complex task that is realistic and might occur outside of school.

Backward design: Wiggins and McTighe (2000) describe backward design as follows: "One starts with the end—the desired results—and then derives the curriculum from the evidence of learning called for by the standard (learning objective) and the teaching needed to equip students to perform" (p. 8).

Behaviorism: A long-established approach for thinking about learning, where learning occurs when the overt behavior changes.

BICS: An abbreviation for "basic interpersonal communicative skills." This is best thought of as conversational language.

Bilingual: An ability to speak two languages.

Bilingual education: An approach to instruction that includes the continued development of the student's native language, the learning of a second language, and the use of both languages to teach academic content.

Biliteracy: The ability to read and write in two languages.

Biological development: Considers the influence of the body's physical changes on the adolescent. This applies to learning and teaching because physical changes impact adolescent body size and shape, nutritional needs, mood swings, and the many other changes that are occurring in the body.

Bloom's Taxonomy: This is a hierarchy of thinking proposed by Benjamin Bloom. At the lowest level, thinking is comprised of simple knowledge. As one moves along the taxonomy, thinking becomes more complex as it moves to comprehension, application, analysis, synthesis, and finally evaluation. Bloom's Taxonomy has been revised, and the newer thinking includes the following six levels (lowest to highest): Remembering, understanding, applying, analyzing, evaluating, and creating.

Bodily kinesthetic intelligence: One of Howard Gardner's multiple intelligences. This involves the potential of using one's whole body or parts of the body to solve problems. It is the ability to coordinate bodily movements.

CALP: An abbreviation for "cognitive academic language proficiency," or the ability to communicate beyond conversation and engage in academic learning through the language.

Canter's Assertive Discipline Model: Provides a set of clear-cut expectations for the classroom. Students can expect teachers to provide a safe learning environment, and teachers can expect students to pay attention and not disrupt the class.

Classroom management: Proactive approaches for helping students learn. It includes all of the aspects of the classroom that will promote student learning.

Cognitive domain: The thinking skills and academic content to be learned in the classroom.

Common Core State Standards: An initiative that intends to provide a consistent, clear understanding of what students are expected to learn across the country. It is a state-developed plan to have a common set of agreed upon standards across the United States. At this time standards are developing for English/language arts and mathematics.

Comprehension: Demonstrating understanding by being able to explain ideas.

Concept: An idea.

Concept formation: An instructional strategy that uses an inductive approach for helping students learn the critical attributes of a given concept. Students look at examples of a concept, then generalize their conclusions to incorporate all examples of this concept.

Concept label: The word or phrase that a group of people have agreed to use when referring to a concept.

Concept telling: The critical attributes of a concept are told to students, and students do not have opportunities to think deeply about the concept. Often concepts are reduced to vocabulary words.

Constructivism: An approach based on the idea that learners construct, or build, meaning and understanding as they learn. It usually implies hands-on activities where students spend a good amount of time processing the information so that they understand it in depth.

Content: Facts, concepts, skills, and attitudes that students learn in a class. While teachers will "teach content," it is more important for teachers to know what content the students are learning.

Convergent questions: Questions that allow for only one or a few correct responses. These questions tend to be lower-order questions on Bloom's Taxonomy.

Cooperative learning: Students work in groups to help them learn content. The five "essential elements" of cooperative learning are: (1) positive interdependence; (2) face-to-face interactions; (3) group goals and individual accountability; (4) interpersonal and small-group skills; and (5) group processing.

Criterion-referencing: Assessment against fixed criteria. Potentially everyone can pass a criterion-referenced assessment—or everyone can fail.

Critical attributes: The traits or characteristics that every example of a particular concept will have.

CSS approach: An alternative approach for considering the domains of learning where the teacher writes objectives that focus on Content, Skills, and Social interactions (CSS).

Curriculum: The expected learning outcomes of the classroom, the content students will learn, and the lesson plans that provide detailed descriptions for each class period. The curriculum has five parts: (1) the formal curriculum; (2) the delivered curriculum; (3) the learned curriculum; (4) the hidden curriculum; and (5) the null curriculum.

Delivered curriculum: Also known as the taught curriculum, and can be thought of as the instructional processes or methods used to communicate the formal curriculum.

Diagnostic assessment: Assessment techniques that usually occur prior to instruction and attempt to determine students' strengths, weaknesses, knowledge, and skills. Identifying these helps teachers differentiate the curriculum to meet each student's unique needs.

Direct instruction: A label for a prescribed approach to teaching. Often direct instruction is a scripted and sequential approach for helping students learn, though it can also be used more generally to describe teacher-led instruction.

Discipline: A reaction to student misbehavior that refers to how the teacher effectively controls the students so that their behaviors maintain a positive learning environment in the classroom.

Discussion: An instructional strategy that engages students in a conversation with one another about a specific topic. Discussion takes many forms in the classroom, and serves many purposes. Generally, discussion helps students understand a topic or issue more clearly, and it helps students learn how to communicate effectively.

Divergent questions: Questions that require deliberation and encourage broad responses. A number of appropriate responses are possible to this type of question and they typically require higher-order thought processes.

Dramatization: Students act in a given role, during a scene, and often with a script. Usually, this technique is used to help students empathize with a particular viewpoint or better understand an event, but it can also be effectively used to help improve students' communication skills.

Dreikurs/Albert model: A classroom management model that is based on the idea that classrooms need to be democratic. This has implications for classroom rules, classroom management, and the instructional strategies used by the teacher.

Dynamic concepts: Concepts that do not have an easily agreed-upon set of critical attributes.

Electronic threaded discussions: A type of discussion where students "talk" with one another electronically and asynchronously through a computer. Discussions are typically referred to as "forums," and comments made by students are called "posts."

ELL: An abbreviation for "English language learners"—students who are not proficient in English.

Epistemology: The study of knowledge that seeks to explain how we know—literally how we obtain, use, and think about knowledge of the world around us.

ESL: An abbreviation for "English as a second language." A program or system of instruction designed to teach English to those who speak other languages. This system typically will use academic content and is usually thought of as a component of bilingual education.

ESOL: An abbreviation for "English speakers of other languages." Some prefer this to ESL because it recognizes that English could be the third or fourth language of the student and that this should be acknowledged. For example, a student from Mexico may speak Mixteco (a Native language) as their first language and Spanish as their second language.

Essential questions: Questions about the big ideas or fundamental concepts that teachers want students to think about and learn during the span of a unit. By posing questions, the students and the teacher are able to focus their attention on content that will help answer the questions. Essential questions, thus, provide a focus for the unit.

Established concepts: Concepts that have a widely agreed upon set of critical attributes.

Evaluation: The highest level of the original Bloom's Taxonomy (and Level 5 or Level 6 on the revised Bloom's Taxonomy). Activities and questions encourage students to take their own points of view or to express their ideas on issues. At the evaluation level, divergent thinking is encouraged and differences of opinion are to be expected. Evaluation is also a term associated with measuring student achievement. See "Assessment."

Examples of a concept: An example contains all of the critical attributes of a concept.

Exit card: A formative assessment technique where students briefly write a response to a teacher's request on a card or slip of paper and hand this in at the end of the period/day. The teacher uses the students' responses to help determine if they understood a key point in the lesson.

Explicit teaching: A synonym of "direct instruction." Both terms imply that the teacher explicitly/directly provides information or step-by-step skills.

Extrinsic motivation: People are motivated to do something by outside, or external, factors that they believe will provide desirable results.

Fact: A phenomenon that can be verified through observing, experiencing, reading, or listening. Facts are necessary for building conceptual knowledge and generalizations.

Fishbowl discussion: A discussion technique where participants learn about the topic of discussion *and* receive explicit direction for developing the requisite skills and attitudes needed to listen and talk during a discussion.

Flow: A theory of intrinsic motivation suggesting that we have a sense of calm and increased engagement in a task when we perceive that our ability matches the requirements for completing a challenging task. Developed by Mihaly Csikszentmihalyi.

Formal cooperative learning: Student groups "are actively involved in the intellectual work of organizing material, explaining it, summarizing it, and integrating it into existing conceptual structures" (Johnson et al., 1998, p. 7).

Formal curriculum: Consists of all that educators purposefully intend to teach students. This is also referred to by some as the intended, planned, explicit, or official curriculum. This is the part of the curriculum that most think of first and it includes syllabi, unit plans, lesson plans in national and state standards or textbooks.

Formative assessment: Assessment that occurs continually during each school day so that the teacher is able to monitor student learning. Formative assessment provides information on how students are "forming" their understanding.

Future's wheel discussion: A discussion technique that focuses classroom discussions in a way that leads to decision-making. Students think through the implications of potential outcomes on any issue, and begin to think about the future, and the implications of decisions on future decisions, actions, and policies.

Generalization: A descriptive statement of a relationship between two or more concepts.

Ginott's model: A classroom management model built around the key term of congruent communication, or communication that is about situations rather than student character or personality.

Glasser's model: A classroom management model predicated on the idea that the teacher expects all students to produce quality work.

Goal: A broad general statement that allows a teacher to focus the content, skills, and dispositions that students need to learn. Goals are usually written for the entire course as well as for segmented sections of the course called units of instruction.

Group investigation: A six-step cooperative learning strategy that provides students with a significant amount of choice and control. Groups are mixed, but they are additionally formed to match students who share an interest about the same topic.

Group members help plan how they will research a topic, how they will present it, and how they will divide the work among themselves.

Guided inquiry: One of the three types of inquiry learning. Here, students are given a research direction and materials, but they need to determine the research method themselves.

Heterogeneous groups: Student groups with some combination of mixed ability, mixed ethnicity, and mixed gender. Placing students in heterogeneous groups is a requirement of cooperative learning.

Hidden curriculum: The knowledge, skills, and attitudes students learn at school that are not part of the formal curriculum. It is often not explicitly taught, but "picked up" or informally learned in the process of being at school.

Homogeneous groups: Groups that are comprised of students who are more similar than different.

Ill-structured: An authentic assessment that requires students to demonstrate learning by determining the structure and organization of their solution to a problem or task.

Imaginary audience: Elkind's theory that accounts for the teenager's extreme self-consciousness, because they feel that they are always on stage and that everyone around them is aware of their every action. Even if this audience is imagined.

Immersion: A term associated with teaching students with English as a second language. Technically, Immersion is a bilingual program developed in Canada where 90% of the early elementary-aged student's day is in the minority language (the non-mainstream language). Many times, however, this term is used in schools to refer to placing a student in a mainstream classroom (not necessarily as part of a well thought-out program).

Individualized Education Program (IEP): An individualized program that specifies educational supports and services that will help a child with a disability receive appropriate instruction. An IEP may specify instructional strategies, strategies for managing behavior, motivational techniques, and other insights about how best to help the student learn.

Informal cooperative learning: Students work in groups that are formed quickly and/or spontaneously for between a few minutes and an entire class period.

Inquiry learning: Problem-based learning that is initiated with a problem, uses student investigation and/or research, and has the teacher serve as a facilitator to the student or student group.

Interdisciplinary unit plan: Unit plans that integrate topics from more than one course around a common theme or idea.

Interpersonal intelligence: One of eight intelligences from Howard Gardner's Multiple Intelligence Theory (1983). Interpersonal intelligence is the capacity to understand the intentions, motivations, and desires of other people. With this intelligence, a person works effectively with others.

Intrapersonal intelligence: One of eight intelligences from Howard Gardner's Multiple Intelligence Theory (1983). Intrapersonal intelligence is the capacity to understand one's own feelings and emotions. With this intelligence, a person has an useful understanding of himself or herself and is able to use this information to regulate his/her life.

Intrinsic motivation: People are motivated to engage in an activity because of the satisfaction derived from the activity itself.

Issues/values continuum: A discussion technique that allows the teacher and the students to assess the diversity of opinions in the classroom, while requiring students to think about their own positions on issues.

Jigsaw: A cooperative learning strategy where students are in two groups: An expert group where they learn about specific information with others, and a home group where they share their newly formed expertise. Students work interdependently in both groups.

Jones' model: A classroom management model emphasizing the importance of a teacher's nonverbal communication, such as body language, expressions, gestures, proximity. This model also suggests that teachers provide incentives for students that are genuine, and that teachers should provide efficient and limited help to students.

Knowledge: This is the first and most basic of Bloom's Taxonomy. It addresses recall of information and whether students remember what they have read, were told, or saw. Knowledge is also referred to as synonymous with key facts and skills. In this use, student learning is referred to in terms of knowledge, skills, and dispositions.

Kounin's model: A classroom management model that emphasizes the importance of teachers engaging students in the classroom lessons. He suggested that misbehavior rarely occurs when students are actively learning.

Learned curriculum: A representation of all that a student learns in school. Some refer to this as the "realized" curriculum, and it comes into play when assessing the students and the curriculum itself.

Learning: A "relatively permanent change, due to experience, either in behavior or in mental representations or associations" (Ormrod, 2006, p. 184).

Learning objective: Attainable statements that help teachers, students, and others involved in education answer three basic questions related to teaching and student learning: What content do students need to learn? How will student learning be assessed? What activities will students engage in to promote learning?

Lecture: An instructional strategy where the teacher presents a specified set of information to students. These presentations take a variety of forms.

LEP: An abbreviation for "limited English proficient." Some prefer not to use this term because it is focused on what a student cannot do.

Lesson plan: A document used by a teacher that provides the structure, instructional strategies, and plan of action for each day.

Linguistic/verbal intelligence: One of eight intelligences from Howard Gardner's Multiple Intelligence Theory (1983). Linguistic/verbal intelligence involves abilities with spoken and written language, the ability to learn languages, and the capacity to use language to accomplish certain goals.

Logical-mathematic intelligence: One of eight intelligences from Howard Gardner's Multiple Intelligence Theory (1983). Logical-mathematic intelligence consists of the capacity to think logically, carry out mathematical operations, and investigate issues with a systematic/scientific approach. This intelligence includes the ability to detect patterns, reason deductively, and think logically.

Long-term targets: Learning objectives that are met during a longer unit, semester, or even an entire course. These tend to be more general than short-term objectives and more specific than goals.

Metacognition: Thinking about one's own thinking. Teachers use metacognitive strategies to assist students with this process.

Momentum: A characteristic of a well-designed lesson that shows smoothness, good transitions, and pacing during a lesson.

Multicultural education: "A field of study and an emerging discipline whose major aim is to create equal educational opportunities for students from diverse racial, ethnic, social-class, and cultural groups. One of its important goals is to help all students to acquire the knowledge, attitudes, and skills needed to function effectively in a pluralistic democratic society and to interact, negotiate, and communicate with peoples from diverse groups in order to create a civic and moral community that works for the common good" (Banks and Banks, 1995, pp. xi–xii).

Multiple intelligences: Howard Gardner's theory suggesting that there are eight different intelligences and that these account for a broader conception of what we think about human potential.

Musical intelligence: One of eight intelligences from Howard Gardner's Multiple Intelligence Theory (1983). Musical intelligence involves skill in the performance, composition, and appreciation of musical patterns.

Naturalist intelligence: One of eight intelligences from Howard Gardner's Multiple Intelligence Theory (1983). Naturalist intelligence involves abilities for sensing patterns in and making connections to elements in nature.

Non-examples of a concept: Non-examples are lacking one or more critical attributes of a concept.

Norm-referencing: Assessing students based upon how their scores rank in comparison with other students. This could be at the class, district, state, or national level.

Null curriculum: The content that students do not learn.

Open inquiry: A type of inquiry learning in which students determine the research question, methods, and necessary resources.

Overlapping: Kounin's term for multitasking. Having the ability to attend to two or three tasks at the same time.

Peer coaching model: A type of reflective teaching through peer teacher observations. A critical friend model.

Performance assessment: The process of assessing student learning while they are performing an authentic task.

Personal fable: Elkind's theory that teenage egocentrism stems from their thinking that they are special and unique from other people. This gives them not only courage but also a false sense of invulnerability.

Planning: The process of organizing the curriculum into long- and short-term plans.

Positive interdependence: A synonym of cooperation, this is an essential element of any cooperative learning strategy.

Prior knowledge: Knowledge about a topic that students have before a lesson.

Problem-based learning: A type of student-directed investigation that focuses on the process of solving a problem.

Progress monitoring: Formative assessment.

Psychological/cognitive development: Ideas about mental development that help teachers understand how the age of the student impacts psychological responses and cognitive ability.

Psychomotor domain: Learning with or about the coordinated use of the body's muscular system.

Questioning: A teacher-centered strategy used to encourage deeper thinking through the use of a series of questions. This is sometimes referred to as a Socratic seminar.

Recitation: A teaching activity where students "repeat orally or explain material learned by individual study or previously presented by the teacher and in response to questions raised by the teacher" (Good, 1983, p. 478).

Reflection: A process of thinking that focuses on learning from experiences. Typically used by students to consider their learning or by teachers to improve the quality of their teaching.

Reflection-for-action: Focusing reflective thinking on improving future actions.

Reflection-in-action: The process of monitoring students work and progress during the class meeting.

Reflection-on-action: Thinking critically about a lesson and on one's actions after the lesson is completed.

Relational teaching: A way of thinking about teaching that places a high value on the relationship the teacher has with the whole class as well as with each student.

Reliability: The degree of confidence that an assessment tool will produce the same results over time.

Ripple effect: A phrase used by Kounin to refer to a phenomenon where the teacher's words or actions are directed at one student but affect the behavior of other students.

Role-play: A theatric strategy that allows a student to assume another role including a change in values and attitudes. This may or may not involve a change in environment but would probably not involve the use of a script.

Rubric: A type of scoring guide typically used for a student project or performance. This chart is used to help teachers evaluate students' work and for students to understand expectations.

Satiation: Kounin's term for when students are done thinking about a topic and the teacher needs to change his or her approach.

Schwab's four commonplaces: Four interrelated aspects of the classroom that affect teaching and learning. These include the teacher, the students, the subject matter that is to be learned, and the milieu.

Scope: The breadth of content and skills students will be expected to learn.

Self-efficacy: Our self expectation or belief about what we can accomplish as a result of our efforts.

Self-referencing: An assessment by the student against himself or herself or more particularly against previous best performances. This is used to help gauge improvement.

Sequence: The order in which students will be expected to learn content and skills.

Short-term targets: Objectives that are met during an activity or after a few class sessions.

Simulation: A theatric strategy that allows for a "scene change" while students maintain their own sense of self (their own values and attitudes).

Sociological/cultural development: An individual's development of ideas related to their self-concept. Usually associated with an adolescent's thoughts about who they are while considering the many aspects of human identity.

Socratic seminar: A teacher-directed questioning session that encourages students to think deeply about issues.

Spatial intelligence: One of the eight intelligences from Howard Gardner's Multiple Intelligence Theory (1983). Spatial intelligence involves the potential to recognize and use the patterns of wide space and more confined areas.

Structured academic controversy: A type of cooperative learning strategy that uses small group discussions to explore controversial issues.

Structured debate: A teaching strategy that is competitive and helps encourage wide participation in the classroom. It serves a different purpose than classroom discussions. It is used when there are two dominant positions on an issue.

Structured inquiry: A type of inquiry lesson in which students are given a research question or direction, a method, materials, but not expected outcomes.

Student accountability: Kounin uses this phrase to refer to teacher's efforts to keep students alert and involved in the lessons. This may involve calling on students to answer questions or other requests that require students to be attentive.

Student-directed investigation (SDI): A learning strategy in which students are encouraged to pursue personal interests or questions that would include inquiry learning, discovery learning, problem-based learning, project-based learning, experiential learning, and service learning.

Student teams achievement divisions (STAD): A formal cooperative learning strategy that involves cooperation within groups and competition among groups to help them review information.

Summative assessment: The attempt to summarize student learning usually at the end of a unit, term, or course.

Synthesis: The level of Bloom's Taxonomy that deals with combining ideas.

Take a stand discussion: A form of discussion used when teachers want students to consider opposing viewpoints around a controversial issue.

T-Chart: Charts that have two columns and are shaped like the letter "T." These charts can help students identify behavioral expectations for specific cooperation skills.

TESOL: An abbreviation for "teaching English to speakers of other languages."

Think-pair-share: A discussion or cooperative learning activity in which students are asked to think about a topic, tell a partner about their reflections, and share ideas with the entire class.

Unit plan: A teacher's plan for students to learn a selected topic or portion of their intended curriculum. This usually is a plan for several weeks of the course.

Usability: The degree to which an assessment tool is difficult or easy to administer.

Valence and challenge arousal: Kounin's terms for how teachers might make activities more enjoyable/challenging.

Validity: The degree to which an assessment is an accurate and appropriate measurement of student learning.

Wait time: The time a teacher waits for a student response or before a teacher responds to a student.

Webquest: An inquiry-oriented online project developed by San Diego State University (webquest.org).

Withitness: The ability of a teacher to show awareness of student behavior throughout the classroom even while working with other students or in another part of the room.

Zone of proximal development: Vygotsky theorized that this "zone" exists between our current level of understanding and deeper understanding.

APPENDIX **B**

Summary Chart of the Instructional Strategies

When using:	Your purpose is to:	Benefits	Obstacles	Management/logistic issues	Valid assessments	Differentiating instruction/ELLs	Technology enhancements
Lectures	Present a specific amount of information quickly and efficiently Transfer your passion and enthusiasm about a topic to your students	Enables you to present important content that students may not be able to learn on their own Provides students with content that is particularly important or difficult to learn directly through books, the internet, or other project-based activities Highlights keys points that best meet your students' interests and needs	Students are often passive observers during lectures and may not recall all the information from your lecture Attention span of the students Boredom Students may not understand the content in the manner you have organized it	Focus on the key ideas, skills, facts, and/or principles that your students will use after the lecture Handout notes or a graphic organizer that will help students follow along with your lecture Move the lesson along at a pace that keeps the students engaged, continually monitor your students' level of engagement (e.g., are they actively taking notes? Gazing out the window? etc.), and show enthusiasm and excitement about the topic	Exit cards Facts/feelings journal Think-Pair-Share Recall of specific information during Q/A or quizzes/tests	If an issue is controversial, or multi-faceted, represent multiple perspectives during your lecture When students' primary language is not the same as the language used for the lecture, and when students have learning difficulties related to listening skills, lecture may not be appropriate. It also becomes critical to teach note-taking skills, speak clearly, and build from graphic organizers	PowerPoint or other presentation software Dynamic visual aids (such as live cameras, video clips, and primary source documents accessed from the internet)

When using:	Your purpose is to:	Benefits	Obstacles	Management/logistic issues	Valid assessments	Differentiating instruction/ELLs	Technology enhancements
Questions	Quickly and efficiently lead students to think about content Prod students into thinking more deeply or considering other points of view Formatively assess or use for classroom management	Provides guidance for students to think more critically Does not take as much time as some other strategies	Teacher-centered strategy that may be overused Including all the students rather than a favored few	Consider appropriate wait time Planning question prompts will help assure student practice of higher-order thinking Quality seminars require a positive and safe learning environment	Questioning can be a formative assessment strategy Exit slips Journaling	The questions should be adjusted for the needs of individual students "Coaching Questions," "Facilitating Questions," and "Collaborative Questions" are all suggested for assisting ELLs in participating The internet TESL Journal (ITESLJ.org) is a great resource for teachers	Student questions can be encouraged through computer laboratory activities Hypertext documents can be used to help students obtain information from websites that help answer questions or encourage consideration of another point of view
Concept Formation	To help students form a robust understanding of significant concepts in your content area	Provides a structure for students to think through the critical attributes of a concept	Preparation by the teacher is extensive This works best for examples that possess critical	Concept formation requires teachers to facilitate students' independent work and	Three classifying tasks: Type 1 (distinguishing examples from non-examples)	The structure of the concept formation lesson allows for students to work independently. During this time, you are	The internet may allow students to explore examples of concepts in depth. You are not limited to completing a

Rather than you telling students about a concept, they form their own understanding Students follow a step-by-step process for examining several examples of a given concept in light of the critical attributes, and then draw conclusions about the similarities and differences among these examples	attributes that are "established" and not "dynamic"	whole-class interactions. Independent work occurs when students gather data, write their synthesized definitions, develop labels, and engage in the classifying tasks. Whole-class interactions occur when students report their findings, consider differences and similarities, share their labels, and explain their classifying decisions Encourage students to think of answers to focus questions and not merely try to guess. Emphasize thinking	Type 2 (producing examples) Type 3 (correcting non-examples) Quizzes	able to work with students one-on-one or in small groups Partnering an ELL with a proficient English speaker will provide language assistance/scaffolds during the lesson Word walls More advanced ELLs will benefit from word formation exercises	worksheet, but can have students go online to access photos, essays, streaming video, etc.

When using:	Your purpose is to:	Benefits	Obstacles	Management/logistic issues	Valid assessments	Differentiating instruction/ELLs	Technology enhancements
Cooperative Learning	Learn new information and broaden current levels of understanding Develop social interaction skills Work interdependently with classmates	Academic achievement increases for low- and high-ability students Students learn how to set group goals and structure interdependent tasks Increases in classmates' acceptance of others	Requires significant amount of class time to allow for group processing May reinforce stereotypes and status of students if the teacher is not carefully monitoring interactions	Actively monitor each group's progress to assess both their progress collectively and individually Reposition desks and chair to allow for face-to-face group interactions Establish group norms and expectations to keep students on task and to help students hold each other accountable. Consider using a "T-Chart" for social skill development Be aware of the progress each group is making	Self assessment Peer assessment Components of the task need to allow for individual accountability T-Charts allow for assessment of social skills STAD has assessment built into its design Rubrics for final projects and/or performances Quizzes	Differentiation is the key component of cooperative learning. Students work together to help differentiate learning uniquely for each member. The teacher needs to be sure the group has established goals for interdependent work and ensure that interactions encourage all members to participate, contribute, and succeed Provide the words and language patterns to carry out those roles	Research using digital technologies allows for in-depth explorations Student/group presentations can be dynamic, interactive, and use multimedia Projects may be posted to a class website Software that encourages collaborative writing (e.g., Google Docs)

Role-Plays, Simulations, Drama	Can be motivating	Can be intimidating or make some students feel uncomfortable	Consider ways to help move students from passive to active learning	Well-designed rubrics that include both process and lesson objective expectations	All students need to practice academic vocabulary and academic language patterns orally	Simulation software is available (e.g., Tom Snyder Productions)
Help students move into the affective and psychomotor domains						
Provide variety	Can involve students that may not otherwise participate	Can take a large amount of class time	Establish a climate that is energized, fun, and supports risk-taking		Consider providing a list of "formal" language either for the discussion or the report back, or both	
Have students consider the intricacies and difficulties of real-world problems	Can be provocative and uniquely interesting	May not be appropriate for sensitive issue	Be certain students are aware of appropriate behaviors and		Consider roles appropriate for individual learners	
Help students understand a	Encourages creativity	Teacher comfort level			Physical involvement enhances learning a second language	
					The nature of the strategy allows a teacher to work individually with	

When using:	Your purpose is to:	Benefits	Obstacles	Management/ logistic issues	Valid assessments	Differentiating instruction/ELLs	Technology enhancements
	new perspective Help students develop communication skills			expectations during unusual classroom activities Consider effective group formation activities		students or in small groups Provide scripts (or rewritten simplified versions) in advance and instead of minimizing their role encourage them to take on roles that stretch their comfort zones without setting them up for failure	
Discussions	To learn new information by interacting with the teacher and each other about class content Think critically (and use other higher-order thinking skills) about a topic To develop the democratic	Explore an issue in depth Develop interaction and social skills Develop insight into multiple perspectives around an issue	Requires a significant amount of class time (both for the discussion and for the preparation) Depends on students being in control of the interactions	Establish classroom expectations Provide adequate time for student preparation Help students learn "how to discuss" as well as learn about the topic of discussion	Dialogical essay Exit cards Rubrics for determining students' understanding of content and for their discussion skills	Help students understand nonverbal communication Require students to critique ideas and not people Assign roles to discussants Allow students who are shy, not comfortable	Threaded discussions using the internet Research with digital technologies help students gain insight into multiple points of view. This includes email and visiting websites for information

citizenship skill of interacting civilly about controversial issues	Recognize that most issues are multifaceted and have more than a "point" and a "counter point"	speaking, or non-English speakers opportunities to write about what they learned during a discussion
		Small groups may be better than whole class because they promote more talk (the smallest being a group of two during a think-pair-share activity)
		Discussion styles vary significantly from culture to culture
		Provide the words and language patterns to carry out those roles. All students need to practice academic vocabulary and academic language patterns orally
		Posting opinions and policy recommenda-tions to a class website or to an approved blog

When using:	Your purpose is to:	Benefits	Obstacles	Management/ logistic issues	Valid assessments	Differentiating instruction/ELLs	Technology enhancements
						Provide a graphic organizer to help them take notes and categorize what they are hearing (many samples available online)	
Student-directed investigations	Confront students with real-world problems and challenges Provide an opportunity for active learning	Provide students with choice and allow them to explore issues of personal relevance Independent learning while pursuing a personal interest Gives students an opportunity to perform as experts or professionals Can give students an opportunity to take action or volunteer and help meet a need	Takes a large amount of time Classroom can be somewhat chaotic as students move in different directions	Development of a community of learners Create a work plan together Monitor students' schedule	Checklists Conferencing Portfolios Rubrics Journaling Teacher notes	Students encouraged to pursue personal interests ELLs work with English-proficient partners to think-pair-share their ideas. This is appropriate for several stages of the inquiry process Word walls of key terms/ideas will help provide key academic language	Spreadsheets Databases Presentation software Internet resources

References

1 THE CLASSROOM LEARNING COMMUNITY

AECT (1994). *Instructional Technology: The Definition and Domains of the Field*. Bloomington, IN: AECT.

Albert, L. (1989). *A Teacher's Guide to Cooperative Discipline: How to Manage Your Classroom and Promote Self-Esteem*. Circle Pines, MN: American Guidance Service.

Bandura, A. (1994). Self-efficacy. In V. S. Ramachaudran (Ed.), *Encyclopedia of Human Behavior* (Vol. 4, pp. 71–81). New York: Academic Press. (Reprinted in H. Friedman (Ed.), *Encyclopedia of Mental Health*. San Diego, CA: Academic Press, 1998.)

Banks, J. A. & Banks, C. M. (Eds.) (1995). *Handbook of Research on Multicultural Education*. New York: Macmillan.

Beamon, G. W. (2001). *Teaching with Adolescent Learning in Mind*. Glenview, IL: Skylight Professional Development.

Bransford, J. D., Brown, A. L. & Cocking, R. R. (Eds.) (2000). *How People Learn: Brain, Mind, and Experience and School*. Washington, DC: National Academy Press.

Brophy, J. (2004). *Motivating Students to Learn*. Boston, MA: McGraw Hill.

Campbell, P. B. & Steinbrueck, K. (1996). *Striving for Gender Equity: National Programs to Increase Student Engagement with Math and Science*. Washington, DC: American Association for the Advancement of Science.

Canter, L. (1976). *Assetive Discipline: A Take Charge Approach for Today's Educator*. Santa Monica, CA: Canter and Associates.

Canter, L. & Canter, M. (1992). *Assertive Discipline: Positive Behaviour Management for Today's Classroom*. Santa Monica, CA: Canter and Associates.

CEO Forum on Education and Technology (2001, June). The CEO Forum school technology and readiness report: Key building blocks for student achievement in the 21st century. Retrieved February 21, 2002, from www.ceoforum.org/downloads/report4.pdf.

Charles, C. M. (1996). *Building Classroom Discipline* (5th ed.). New York: Longman.

Csikszentmihalyi, M. (1990). *Flow: The Psychology of Optimal Experience*. New York: Harper & Row.

Csikszentmihalyi, M. (1997). *Finding Flow: The Psychology of Engagement with Everyday Life*. New York: Basic Books.

Culatta, R. & Tompkins, J. (1999). *Fundamentals of Special Education: What Every Teacher Needs to Know*. Upper Saddle River, NJ: Prentice-Hall.

Cummins, J. (1979). Cognitive/academic language proficiency, linguistic interdependence, the optimum age question and some other matters. *Working Papers on Bilingualism*, *19*, 121–129.

Dacey, J., Kenny, M., & Margolis, D. (2004). *Adolescent Development* (3rd ed.). Mason, OH: Thomson Publishing. Doda, N., George, P. & McEwin, K. (1987). Ten current truths about effective schools. *Middle School Journal*, *18*(3), 3–5.

Dreikurs, R. & Cassel, P. (1972). *Discipline Without Tears*. New York: Hawthorn Books.

Elkind, D. (1998). *All Grown Up and No Place to Go: Teenagers in Crisis*. Reading, MA: Addison–Wesley Publishing Company.

Erikson, E. H. (1959). *Identity and the Life Cycle*. New York: International Universities Press.

Erikson, E. H. (1968). *Identity*. New York: Norton.

Freire, P. (1978). *Pedagogy of the oppressed*. New York: Continuum.

Gardner, H. (1983/2003). *Frames of mind. The Theory of Multiple Intelligences*. New York: BasicBooks.

Gardner, H. (1999). *Intelligence Reframed*. New York, N: Basic Books

Gardner, H. (2003). "20 years of multiple intelligences: Reflections and a blueprint for the future." Keynote address made to the general membership of the American Educational Research Association, April, 2003, Chicago, IL, USA.

Ginott, M. (1971). *Teacher and Child*. New York: Macmillan.

Glasser, W. (1992). *The Quality School: Managing Students without Coercion* (2nd ed.). New York: Harper & Row.

Gorski, P. (2005). Savage unrealities: Uncovering classism in Ruby Payne's framework. Retrieved April 4, 2006, from www.edchange.org/publications/Savage_Unrealities.pdf.

Gurian, M. & Stevens, K. (2004). Closing achievement gaps with boys and girls in mind. *Educational Leadership*, 62(3), 21–26.

Hall, T., Strangman, N., & Meyer, A. (2003). *Differentiated Instruction and Implications for UDL Implementation*. Wakefield, MA: National Center on Accessing the General Curriculum. Retrieved June 27, 2012, from http://aim.cast.org/learn/historyarchive/backgroundpapers/differentiated_instruction.

Jones, F. H. (1987). *Positive Classroom Instruction*. New York: McGraw Hill.

Kounin, J. (1977). *Discipline and Group Management in Classrooms*. New York: Holt, Rinehart, & Winston.

Ladson-Billings, G. (1995). But that's just good teaching! The case for culturally relevant pedagogy. *Theory into Practice*, 34(3), 159–165.

Lepper, M. R. & Hoddell, M. (1989). Intrinsic motivation in the classroom. In C. Ames & R. Ames (Eds.), *Research on Motivation in Education: Vol. 3. Goals and Cognitions* (pp. 73–105). San Diego, CA: Academic Press.

Litzinger, M. E. & Osif, B. (1992). Accommodating diverse learning styles: Designing instruction for electronic information sources. In L. Sharito (Ed.), *What Is Good Library Instruction Now?* (pp. 72–82). Ann Arbor, MI: Pierian Press.

Lortie, D. (1975). *Schoolteacher: A Sociological Study*. Chicago, IL: University of Chicago Press.

McCormick, T. M. (1994). *Creating the Nonsexist Classroom: A Multicultural Approach*. New York: Teachers College Press.

National Commission on Teaching and America's Future (NCTAF) (2004). *Fifty Years After Brown v. Board of Education: A Two-Tiered Education System*. Washington, DC: Author.

Nieto, S. (1996). *Affirming Diversity: The Sociopolitical Context of Multicultural Education* (2nd ed.). White Plains: Longman.

Oppenheimer, T. (1997). The computer delusion. *Atlantic Monthly*, 280(1), 45–48, 50–56, 61–62.

Ormrod, J. E. (2006). *Educational Psychology: Developing Learners* (5th ed.). Upper Saddle River, NJ: Merrill.

Ormrod, J. E. (2012). Essentials of Educational Psychology: Big Ideas to Guide Effective Teaching (3rd ed.) Boston, MA: Pearson.

Owston, R. D. (1997). The World Wide Web: A technology to enhance teaching and learning. *Educational Researcher*, 26(2), 27–33.

Padron, Y. N., Waxman, H. C. & Rivera, H. H. (2002). *Educating Hispanic Students: Effective Instructional Practices* (Practitioner Brief #5). Available: www.cal.org/crede/Pubs/PracBrief5.htm.

Piaget J. (1970). Piaget's theory. In P. H. Mussen (Ed.), *Carmichael's Manual of Psychology*. New York: Wiley.

Pintrich, P. R. & Schunk, D. H. (2002). *Motivation in Education: Theory, Research, and Applications* (2nd ed.). Upper Saddle River, NJ: Prentice-Hall.

Pipher, M. (1994). *Reviving Ophelia: Saving the Selves of Adolescent Girls*. New York: Ballantine Books.

Postman, N. (1995). *The End of Education: Redefining the Value of School*. Westminster, MD: Random House.

Prensky, M. (2001). Digital natives, digital immigrants. *In on the Horizon*, 9 (5). Lincoln: NCB University Press.

Ryan, R. M. & Deci, E. L. (2000). Self-determination theory and the facilitation of intrinsic motivation, social development and well-being. *American Psychologist*, 55, 68–78.

Sadker, M., & Sadker, D. (1982). *Sex Equity Handbook for Schools*. New York: Longman.

Sadker, M. & Sadker, D. (1994). *Failing at Fairness: How America's Schools Shortchange Girls*. New York: Charles Scribner's Sons.

Sadker, D. & Zittleman, K. R. (2012). *Teachers, Schools, and Society: A Brief Introduction to Education* (3rd ed.). New York: McGraw Hill.

Skinner, B. F. (1953). *Science and Human Behavior*. New York: Macmillan.

Thomas, W. P. & Collier, V. P. (1997). *School Effectiveness for Language Minority Students*. Washington DC: National Clearinghouse for Bilingual Education.

Thorne, P. (1994). *Gender Play: Girls and Boys in School*. Piscataway, NJ: Rutgers University Press.

Tomlinson, C. A. (1999). Mapping a route toward differentiated instruction. *Educational Leadership*, 57, 12–16.

Tomlinson, C. A. (2001). *How to Differentiate Instruction in Mixed-Ability Classrooms* (2nd ed.). Upper Saddle River, NJ: Prentice Hall.

Vygotsky, L. S. (1978). *Mind in Society: The Development of Higher Psychological Processes*. Cambridge, MA: MIT Press.

Wolpow, R., Johnson, M. M., Hertel, R., & Kincaid, S. O. (2011). *The Heart of Learning: Compassion, Resiliency, and Academic Success*, Retrieved June 2012 from: www.k12.wa.us/ CompassionateSchools/Resources.aspx.

Zwiers, J. (2008). *Building Academic Language: Essential Practices for Content Classrooms*. San Francisco, CA: Jossey-Bass.

2 CONSTRUCTING CLASSROOM CURRICULUM

Apple, M. (1986). *Teachers and Texts*. New York: Routledge and Kegan Paul.

Banks, J. A. (2003). *Teaching Strategies for Ethnic Studies* (7th ed.). Boston, MA: Allyn & Bacon.

Boyer, E. L. (1983). *High school*. New York: Harper & Row.

Carr, P. (2008). Educators and education for democracy: Moving beyond "thin" democracy. *Interamerican Journal of Education for Democracy*, 1(2), 147–165. Document available at: www.ried-ijed.org.

Cornbleth, C. (1991). *Curriculum in Context*. London: Falmer Press.

Cornbleth, C. (2002). Curriculum politics, policy, practice: Comparative questions, contextualized cases. In M. Rosenmund, A. Fries & W. Heller (Eds.), *Comparing Curriculum-Making Processes* (pp. 95–106). Bern: Peter Lang.

Cuban, L. (1996). Curriculum stability and change. In P. W. Jackson (Ed.), *Handbook of Research on Curriculum* (pp. 216–247). New York: Macmillan.

Dewey, J. (1916). *Democracy and Education*. New York: Macmillan.

Dewey, J. (1938/1965). *Experience and Education*. New York: Collier Books.

Eisner, E. W. (1985). *The Educational Imagination: On the Design and Evaluation of School Programs* (2nd ed.). New York: Macmillan.

Eisner, E. W. (1992). Curriculum ideologues. In P. W. Jackson (Ed.), *Handbook of Research on Curriculum* (pp. 302–326). New York: Macmillan.

Freire, P. (1970). *The Pedagogy of the Oppressed*. New York: Herder and Herder.

Garcia, J., Spalding, E. & Powell, R. R. (2001). *Contexts of Teaching: Methods for Middle and High School Instruction*. Upper Saddle River, NJ: Merrill/Prentice Hall.

Gay, G. (1988). Designing relevant curricula for diverse learners. *Education and Urban Society*, 29940, 327–340.

Hirsch, E. D. (1987). *Cultural Literacy*. Boston, MA: Houghton Mifflin.

Jackson, P. (1968). *Life in Classrooms*. New York: Holt, Rinehart & Winston.

Kliebard, H. (1987). *The Struggle for the American Curriculum 1893–1958*. London: Routledge and Kegan Paul.

National Commission on Excellence in Education (1983). *A Nation at Risk: The Imperative for Educational Reform*. Washington, DC: U.S. Government Printing Office.

National Council for the Social Studies (NCSS) (2006). Creating effective citizens. Retrieved April 2, 2012, from www.socialstudies.org/ positions/effectivecitizens/.

Ornstein, A. & Hunkins, F. P. (2004). *Curriculum: Foundations, principles, and Issues* (4th ed.). Boston, MA: Allyn & Bacon.

Ravitch, D. (1985). *The Schools We Deserve: Reflections on the Education Crisis in Our Lives*. New York: Basic Books.

Reed, A. J. & Bergemann, V. E. (1992). *In the Classroom: An Introduction to Education*. Guilford, CT: Dushkin Publishing Group.

Shubert, W. H. (1986). *Curriculum: Perspective, Paradigm and Possibility*. New York: Macmillan.

Sizer, T. R. (1984). *Horace's Compromise: The Dilemma of the American High School*. Boston, MA: Houghton Mifflin.

Thornton, S. J. (2005). *Teaching Social Studies that Matters: Curriculum for Active Learning*. New York: Teachers College Press.

Tyler, R. W. (1949). *Basic Principles of Curriculum and Instruction*. Chicago, IL: University of Chicago Press.

United States Department of Education (1991). *America 2000: An Education Strategy*. Washington DC: United States Department of Education.

3 PREPARING LEARNING TARGETS AND ASSESSING STUDENT LEARNING

Armstrong, D. G. & Savage, T. V. (1994). *Secondary Education*. New York: Macmillan.

Authentic Education (2011). Authentic education. Retrieved October 18, 2011, from www.authenticeducation.org/ubd/ubd.lasso.

Biehler, R. F. (1971). *Psychology Applied to Teaching*. Boston, MA: Houghton Mifflin.

Black, P. & Wiliam, D. (1998a). Assessment and classroom learning. *Assessment in Education*, 5(1), 7–74.

Black, P. & Wiliam, D. (1998b). Inside the black box: Raising standards through classroom assessment. *Phi Delta Kappan*, 80(2), 139–148.

Black, P. J. & Wiliam, D. (2009). Developing the theory of formative assessment. *Educational Assessment, Evaluation and Accountability*, 21(1), 5–31.

Bloom, B. S. (Ed.) (1956). *Taxonomy of Educational Targets: Handbook I, Cognitive Domain*. New York: David McKay.

Bloom, B. S., Mesia, B. M. & Krathwohl, D. R. (1964). *Taxonomy of Educational Targets* (two vols: *The Affective Domain* and *The Cognitive Domain*). New York: David McKay.

Boston, C. (2002). The concept of formative assessment. *Practical Assessment, Research & Evaluation*, 8(9). Retrieved November 9, 2004, from http://PAREonline.net/getvn.asp?v=8&n=9.

Congress of the United States; Office of Technology Assessment (February, 1992). *Testing in American Schools: Asking the Right Questions*. Washington, DC: U.S. Government Printing Office.

Dave, R. H. (1970). Psychomotor levels. In R. J. Armstrong (Ed.) *Developing and Writing Behavioral Objectives*. Tucson, AZ: Educational Innovators Press.

Hammond, G. (2004). Testing and evaluation. Accessed from http://xnet.rrc.mb.ca/glenh/outline.htm; March, 2006.

Hiebert, E. H., Valencia, S. W. & Afflerbach, P. P. (1994). Understand authentic reading assessment: Definitions and perspectives. In S. W. Valencia, E. H. Hiebert & P. P. Afflerbach (Eds.), *Authentic Reading Assessment: Practices and Possibilities* (pp. 6–21). Newark, DE: International Reading Association.

Kellough, R. D. & Kellough, N. G. (1999). *Secondary School Teaching: A Guide to Methods And Resources; Planning For Competence*. Upper Saddle River, NJ: Prentice Hall.

Krathwohl, D. R., Bloom, B. S. & Masia B. B. (1964). *Taxonomy of Educational Targets, Book 2: Affective Domain*. New York: Longman.

McMillan, J. H. (2004). *Classroom Assessment: Principles and Practice for Effective Instruction* (3rd ed.). Upper Saddle River, NJ: Allyn and Bacon.

Mathematical Sciences Education Board and National Research Council (MSEB) (1993). *Measuring UP: Prototypes for Mathematics Assessment*. Washington, DC: National Academy Press.

NCTM (2000). *Principles and Standards for School Mathematics*. Retrieved December 2, 2004, from http://standards.nctm.org/document/chapter2/assess.htm.

Slavin, R. E. (1999). Comprehensive Approaches to Cooperative Learning. *Theory into Practice*, 38(2), 74–79.

Stevens, F., Lawrenz, F. & Sharp, L. (1996). *User-Friendly Handbook for Project Evaluation: Science, Mathematics, Engineering, and Technology Education*. Arlington, VA: National Science Foundation.

Wiggins, G. (1990). The case for authentic assessment. *Practical Assessment, Research & Evaluation*, 2(2). Retrieved December 6, 2004, from http://PAREonline.net/getvn.asp?v=2&n=2.

Wiggins, G. (1993). Assessment: Authenticity, context, and validity. *Phi Delta Kappan*, 75(3), 200–214.

Wiggins, G. (1998). *Educative Assessment: Designing Assessments to Inform and Improve Student Performance*. San Francisco, CA: Jossey-Bass.

Wiggins, G. & McTighe, J. (2000). *Understanding by Design*. Alexandra, VA: ASCD.

4 LONG- AND SHORT-RANGE PLANNING

Erickson, H. L. (2002). *Concept-based Curriculum and Instruction: Teaching Beyond the Facts*. Thousand Oaks, CA: Corwin Press.

Harwood, A. M., Collins, L. & Sudzina, M. (2001). An examination of student teacher failure: Implications for teacher education programs. In J. Rainer & E. Guyton (Eds.) *Teacher Education Yearbook* (pp. 45–60). Dubuque, IA: Association of Teacher Educators/Kendall Hunt Publishing.

Killion, J. & Todnem, G. (1991). A process for personal theory-building. *Educational Leadership*, 48(6), 14–16.

Schwab, J. J. (1973). The practical 3: Translation into curriculum. *School Review*, 81, 501–522.

Tomlinson, C. A. (2004). *How to Differentiate Instruction in Mixed Ability Classrooms* (2nd ed.). Upper Saddle River, NJ: Prentice Hall.

Virginia Department of Education (2002). *Algebra I Standards of Learning Sample Scope and Sequence*. Richmond, VA: Virginia Department of Education.

Washington State Office of the Superintendent of Public Instruction (2003). *Social Studies Frameworks: Grades 9–12*. Olympia, WA: Washington State Office of the Superintendent of Public Instruction.

Wiggins, G. & McTighe, J. (2005). *Understanding by Design* (2nd ed.). Alexandria, VA: Association for Supervision and Curriculum Development.

5 LECTURE/INTERACTIVE PRESENTATION

Barbetta, P. M. & Scaruppa, C. L. (1995). Looking for a way to improve your behavior analysis lectures? Try guided notes. *The Behavior Analyst*, 18, 155–160.

Bligh, D. A. (2000). *What's the Use of Lectures?* San Francisco, CA: Jossey-Bass.

Brophy, J. & Good, T. (1986). Teacher behavior and student achievement. In M. Wittrock (Ed.), *Handbook of Research on Teaching* (pp. 340–370). New York: Macmillan.

Burden, P. R. & Byrd, D. M. (2007). *Methods for Effective Teaching* (4th ed.). Boston, MA: Allyn & Bacon.

Cashin, W. E. (1990). Assessing teaching effectiveness. In P. A. Seldin (Ed.), *How Administrators can Improve Teaching* (pp. 89–103). San Francisco, CA: Jossey-Bass.

Cross, K. P. (1986). A proposal to improve teaching or what taking teaching seriously should mean. *AAHE Bulletin 39*, 10–11.

Edwards, H., Smith, B. & Webb, G. (Eds.) (2001). *Lecturing: Case Studies, Experience and Practice*. London: Kogan Page.

Engelmann, S. & Carnine, D. (1991). *Theory of Instruction: Principles and Applications* (Rev. ed.). Eugene, OR: ADI Press.

Fisher, C. W. & Berliner, D. C. (Eds.) (1985). *Perspectives on Instructional Time*. New York: Longman.

Good, T. L. & Brophy, J. E. (2003). *Looking in Classrooms* (9th ed.). Boston, MA: Allyn & Bacon.

Heward, W. L. (2005). Fast facts for faculty—Guided notes: Improving the effectiveness of your lectures. Retrieved November 24, 2005, from The Ohio State University Partnership Grant Improving the Quality of Education for Students with Disabilities website: http://telr.osu.edu/dpg/fastfact/notes.html.

Hughes, C. A. & Suritsky, S. K. (1994). Note-taking skills of university students with and without learning disabilities. *Journal of Learning Disabilities*, 27, 20–24.

Kame'enui, E. J., Carnine, D. W. & Dixon R. C. (1998). Effective teaching strategies that accommodate diverse learners. In E. J. Kame'enui & D. W. Carnine (Eds.), *Effective Teaching Strategies that Accommodate Diverse Learners* (pp. 1–17). Columbus, OH: Merrill.

Ormrod, J. E. (2006). *Educational Psychology: Developing Learners* (5th ed.). Upper Saddle River, NJ: Merrill.

Rosenshine, B. (1987). Explicit teaching. In D. Berliner & B. Rosenshine (Eds.), *Talks to Teachers* (pp. 75–92). New York: Random House.

Sandock, B. (2000). Enhancing learning of students with LD without compromising standards: Tips for teaching. Retrieved initially April 17, 2006. Accessed May, 2012, from www.ldonline.org/ld_indepth/postsecondary/facultytips.html.

Saski, J., Swicegood, P. & Carter, J. (1983). Notetaking formats for learning disabled adolescents. *Learning Disability Quarterly*, 6, 265–272.

Wingert, D. (2001). "Basic Presentation Skills", Teaching Enrichment Series, University of Minnesota, Minneapolis, Minnesota. Retrieved April 19, 2006, from http://www1.umn.edu/ohr/teachlearn/tutorials/lectures/planning.html.

6 QUESTIONING

Bellack, A. A., Kliebard, H. M., Hyman, R. T., & Smith, E. L., Jr. (1966). *The Language of the Classroom*. New York: Teachers College Press.

Bloom, B., Englehart, M., Furst, E., Will, W. & Krathwohl, D. (1956). *Taxonomy of Educational Objectives, Handbook 1: Cognitive Domain*. New York: David McKay.

Brice, L. & Johnson, L. (1999). Discourse as a critical pedagogical form in social studies teaching and learning. Paper presented at the annual meeting of the National Council of Social Studies. Orlando, FL, USA.

Costa, A. & Lowery, L. (1989). *Techniques for Teaching and Thinking*. Pacific Grove, CA: Midwest Publishers.

Dantonio, M. & Beisenherz, P. (2001). *Learning to Question, Questioning to Learn*. Boston, MA: Allyn & Bacon.

Dillon, J. T. (1988). *Questioning and Teaching: A Manual of Practice*. New York: Teachers College Press.

Gall, M. (1984). Synthesis of research on teacher's questioning. *Educational Leadership, 42*, 40–47.

Gall, M. D. & Gall, J. P. (1990). Outcomes of the discussion method. In W. W. Wilen (Ed.), *Teaching and Learning through Discussion: The Theory, Research and Practice of the Discussion Method* (pp. 25–44). Springfield, IL: Charles C. Thomas.

Gamoron, A. & Nystrand, M. (1992). Taking students seriously. In F. Newmann (Ed.), *Student Engagement and Achievement in American Secondary Schools* (pp. 40–61). New York: Teachers College Press.

Good, T. L. & Brophy, J. E. (2000). *Looking in Classrooms* (8th ed.). New York: Longman.

Grossier, P. (1964). *How to Use the Fine Art of Questioning*. Englewood Cliffs, NJ: Prentice-Hall.

Henning, J. (2004). The "bow tie": A conceptual tool for opening up classroom discourse. *Curriculum and Teaching Dialogue, 6, 59–67*.

Hunkins, F. P. (1995). *Teaching Thinking through Effective Questioning* (2nd ed.). Norwood, MA: Norwood, MA.: Christopher-Gordon.

Kelly, T. (1993). Calling on non volunteers in the classroom: Democratic imperative or misguided invasion. Paper presented at the annual meeting of the American Educational Research Association. Atlanta, GA, USA.

Kim, Y. (2010). Scaffolding through questions in upper elementary ELL learning. *Literacy Teaching and Learning, 15*(1 & 2), 109–136.

Mills, S., Rice, C., Berliner, D. & Rousseau, E. (1980). The correspondence between teacher questions and student answers in classroom discourse. *Journal of Experimental Education, 48*, 194–204.

National Council for the Social Studies (1994). *Curriculum Standards for Social Studies*. Washington, DC: NCSS.

Newmann, F. (1992). Higher order thinking and prospects for classroom thoughtfulness. In F. Newmann (Ed.), *Student Engagement and Achievement in American Secondary Schools* (pp. 62–91). New York: Teachers College Press.

Newmann, F., Wehlage, G. & Lamborn, S. (1992). The significance and sources of student engagement. In F. Newmann (Ed.), *Student Engagement and Achievement in American Secondary Schools* (pp. 11–39). New York: Teachers College Press.

Rowe, M. (1974). Wait time and rewards as instructional variables, their influence in language, logic, and fate control: Part one—wait time. *Journal of Research in Science Teaching, 11*(2), 81–94.

Rowe, M. (1986). Wait time: Slowing down may be a way of speeding up! *Journal of Teacher Education, 37*, 43–50.

Tobin, K. (1986). Effects of teacher wait time on discourse characteristics in mathematics and language arts classes. *American Educational Research Journal, 23*(2), 191–201.

Wilen, W. W. (1990). *Teaching and Learning through Discussion*. Springfield, IL: Charles C. Thomas.

Wilen, W. W. (1991). *Questioning Skills for Teachers* (3rd ed.). Washington, DC: National Education Association.

Wilen, W. W. (2001). Exploring myths about teacher questioning in the social studies classroom. *The Social Studies, 92*, 26–35.

Wilen, W., Ishler, M., Hutchinson, J. & Kinds-vatter, R. (2000). *Dynamics of Effective Teaching* (4th ed.). New York: Longman.

Wilen, W. & White, J. (1991). Interaction and discourse in social studies classrooms. In J. P. Shaver (Ed.), *Handbook of Research in Social Studies Teaching and Learning* (pp. 147–157). New York: Macmillan.

White, J. J. (1990). Involving different social and cultural groups in discussion. In W. W. Wilen (Ed.), *Teaching and Learning through Discussion* (pp. 147–157). Springfield, IL: Charles C. Thomas.

7 CONCEPT FORMATION

Ehrenberg, S. D. (1981). Concept learning: How to make it happen in the classroom, *Educational Leadership*, 39(1), 36–43.

Parker, W. C. (1987). Teaching thinking: The pervasive approach. *Journal of Teacher Education*, 38(3), 50–56.

Parker, W. C. (2005). *Social Studies in Elementary Education (12th ed.)*. New York: Prentice Hall.

Parker, W. C. (2012). *Social Studies in Elementary Education* (14th ed.). Boston, MA: Allyn & Bacon.

Parker, W C. & Perez, S. (1987). Beyond the rattle of empty wagons. *Social Education*, 52(3), 164–166.

Taba, H. (1967). *Teacher's Handbook*. Palo Alto, CA: Addison-Wesley Publishing Company.

Vygotsky, L. S. (1978). *Mind in Society: The Development of Higher Psychological Processes*. Cambridge, MA: MIT Press.

8 COOPERATIVE LEARNING

Anderson, J. R., Simon, H. A., & Reder, L. M. (1997, non-published). Applications and misapplications of cognitive psychology to mathematics education.

Aronson, E., Blaney, N., Stephen, C., Sikes, J. & Snapp, M. (1978). *The Jigsaw Classroom*. Beverly Hills, CA: Sage Publications.

Blosser, P. E. (1992). Using cooperative learning in science education. *ERIC Bulletin*, SE 053 432, Retrieved February 3, 2006 from the Educational REALMS (Resources for Engaging Active Learners in Mathematics and Science) website: www.stemworks.org/Bulletins/SEB92-1.html.

Cohen, E. G. (1994). *Designing Groupwork: Strategies for the Heterogeneous Classroom*. New York: Teachers College Press.

Cohen, E. & Lotan R. (1997). *Working for Equity in Heterogeneous Classrooms: Sociological Theory in Practice*. New York: Teachers College Press.

Doda, N., George, P. & McEwin, K. (1987). Ten current truths about effective schools. *Middle School Journal*, 18(3), 3–5.

Heller, P., Keith, R. & Anderson, S. (1992). Teaching problem solving through cooperative grouping. Part 1: Group versus individual problem solving. *American Journal of Physics*, 60(7), 627–636.

In Time (2004). *Chapter One: Cooperative Learning Overview*. Retrieved February 8, 2006, from Integrating New Technology Into Methods of Education web site: www.intime.uni.edu/coop_learning/ch1/types.htm.

Johnson, D. W. & Johnson, R. T. (1999). *Learning Together and Alone: Cooperative, Competitive, and Individualistic Learning*. Boston, MA: Allyn & Bacon.

Johnson, D. W. & Johnson, R. T. (2004). *Assessing Students in Groups: Promoting Group Responsibility and Individual Accountability*. Thousand Oaks, CA: Corwin Press.

Johnson, D. W., Johnson, R. T. & Holubec, E. J. (1994). The Nuts and Bolts of Cooperative Learning. Edina, MN: Interaction Book Company.

Johnson, D. W., Johnson, R. & Holubec, E. (1998). *Cooperation in the Classroom*. Boston, MA: Allyn and Bacon.

Johnson, D. W., Johnson, R. T. & Stanne, M. B. (2000, May). *Cooperative Learning Methods: A Meta-Analysis*, [online]. Retrieved April 6, 2006, from The Cooperative Learning Center at The University of Minnesota web site: http://clcrc.com/pages/cl=methods.html.

Kagan, S. (1992). *Cooperative Learning*. San Juan Capistrano, CA: Resources for Teachers.

Kohn, A. (1993). *Punished by Rewards: The Trouble with Gold Stars, Incentive Plans, A's, Praise, and Other Bribes*. Boston, MA: Houghton Mifflin.

Kulik, J. A. & Kulik, C. L. C. (1987). Effects of ability grouping on student achievement. *Equity and Excellence*, 23, 22–30.

Kulik, J. A. & Kulik, C. L. C. (1991). Research on ability grouping: Historical and contemporary perspectives. Storrs: University of

Connecticut, National Research Center on the Gifted and Talented (ERIC Document Reproduction Service No. ED 350 777).

Marzano, R. J., Pickering, D. J. & Pollock, J. E. (2001). *Classroom Instruction that Works: Research-based Strategies for Increasing Student Achievement*. Alexandria, VA: Association for Supervision and Curriculum Development.

Mitchell, S. N., Rosemary, R., Bramwell, F. G., Solnosky, A. & Lilly, F. (2004). Friendship and choosing groupmates: Preferences for teacher-selected vs. student-selected groupings in high school science classes. *Journal of Instructional Psychology*, Retrieved April 8, 2006, from www.findarticles.com/p/articles/mi_m0FCG/is_1_31/ai_n6073185.

Newmann, F. M. & Thompson, J. A. (1987, September). Effects of cooperative learning on achievement in secondary schools: A summary of research (ERIC Document Reproduction Service No. ED 288 853).

Orech, J. F. (2009). Turbo-charged Wikis: Technology embraces cooperative learning. Retrieved May 21, 2011, from the Academic Commons website: www.academiccommons.org/commons/essay/turbo-charged-wikis-technology-embraces-cooperative-learning.

Parker, W. C. (2005). *Social Studies in Elementary Education* (12th ed.). Upper Saddle River, NJ: Merrill/Prentice Hall.

Sharan, Y. & Sharan, S. (1989, December–1990, January). Group investigation expands cooperative learning. *Educational Leadership*, 47(4), 17–19.

Slavin, R. E. (1983). *Cooperative Learning*. New York: Longman.

Slavin, R. E. (1988, June). *Student Team Learning: An Overview and Practical Guide*. Washington, DC: National Education Association.

Slavin, R. E. (1989, December–1990, January). Research on cooperative learning: Consensus and controversy. *Educational Leadership*, 47(4), 52–54.

Slavin, R. (1993). Ability grouping in the middle grades: Achievement effects and alternatives. *The Elementary School Journal*, 93, 535–552.

Slavin, R. E. (1995). A model of effective instruction. *The Educational Forum*, 59, 166–176.

Wiggins, G. (1990). The case for authentic assessment. *Practical Assessment, Research & Evaluation*, 2(2). Retrieved December 6, 2004, from http://PAREonline.net/getvn.asp?v=2&n=2.

Zarnowski, M. (2003). *History Makers: A Questioning Approach to Reading and Writing Biographies*. Portsmouth, NH: Heinemann.

9 SIMULATION, ROLE-PLAY, AND DRAMATIZATION

Bransford, J. D., Brown, A. L. & Cocking, R. R. (Eds.) (2000). *How People Learn: Brain, Mind, Experience and School*. Washington, DC: National Academy Press.

Farris, P. J. & Parke, J. (1993). To be or not to be: What students think about drama. *Clearinghouse*, 66(4), 231–234.

Fisher, J. & Vander Laan, S. (2002). Improving approaches to multicultural education: Teaching empathy through role-playing. *Multicultural Education*, 9, 25–27.

Gardner, H. (1999). *Intelligence Reframed. Multiple intelligences for the 21st Century*. New York: Basic Books.

Gardner, H. (2003). 20 years of multiple intelligences: Reflections and a blueprint for the future. Keynote address made to the general membership of the American Educational Research Association, April 2003, Chicago, IL.

Greenblat, C. S. (1987). *Designing Games and Simulations*. Beverly Hills, CA: Sage.

Heathcote, D. (1992). Excellence in teaching: what it takes to do things well. *Teaching Theatre*, 4(1), 3–6.

Johnson, A. P. (1998). How to use creative dramatics in the classroom. *Childhood Education*, 75(1), 2–82.

Jones, K. (1995). *Simulations: A Handbook for Teachers and Trainers* (3rd ed.). New Jersey, NY: Nichols Publishing Company.

Joyce, B., Weil, M. & Calhoun, E. (2000). *Models of Teaching* (6th ed.) Boston, MA: Allyn & Bacon.

Leonard, J., Davis, J. E., & Sidler, J. L. (2005). Cultural relevance and computer assisted instruction. *Journal of Research on Technology in Education*, 37(3), 263–285.

Newmann, F., Bryk, A. & Nagaoka, J. (2001). *Authentic Intellectual Work and Standardized Tests: Conflicts or Coexistence?* Chicago: Consortium on Chicago School Research. Available online at: www.consortium-chicago.org/publications/p0001.html (retrieved March 2011).

Shaftel, F. & Shaftel, G. (1967). *Role Playing of Social Values*. Englewood Cliffs, NJ: Prentice-Hall.

Smith, J., Lee, V. & Newmann, F. (2001). *Instruction and Achievement in Chicago Elementary Schools*. Chicago, IL: Consortium on Chicago School Research. Available online at: www.consortium-chicago.org/publications/p0001.html.

Steinbrink, J. E. (2004). Intervention: Simulating the war on global terrorism. *Journal of Geography*, *103*(6), 239–247.

Tanner, F. (1972). *Basic Drama Projects*. Pocatello, ID: Clark Publishing Co.

Wiggins, G. & McTighe, J. (2005). *Understanding by Design* (2nd ed.). Alexandria, VA: ASCD.

10 DISCUSSION AND DEBATE

Alvermann, D. E., O'Brien, D. G. & Dillon, D. R. (1990). What teachers do when they say they are having discussions of content area reading assignments: A qualitative analysis. *Reading Research Quarterly*, *25*(4), 296–322.

Barber, B. (1989). Public talk and civic action: Education for participation in a strong democracy. *Social Education*, *53*(6), 355–356, 370.

Bellack, A. A., Kliebard, H. M., Hyman, R. T. & Smith, E. L., Jr. (1966). *The Language of the Classroom*. New York: Teachers College Press.

Bridges, D. (1979). *Education, Democracy and Discussion*. Windsor, England: NFER.

Bridges, D. (1987). Discussion and questioning. *Questioning Exchange*, *1*, 34–37.

Cazden, C. (1988). *Classroom Discourse*. Portsmouth, NH: Heinemann.

Cohen, E. G. (1994). *Designing Groupwork: Strategies for Heterogeneous Classrooms*. New York: Teachers College Press.

Dewey, J. (1976/1985). Democracy and education. In J. A. Boylston (Ed.), *Democracy and Education: The Middle Works of John Dewey, 1899–1924* (Vol. 9). Carbondale, IL: Southern University Press.

Dillon, J. T. (1984). Research on questioning and discussion. *Educational Leadership*, *41*(3), 51–56.

Dillon, J. T. (1994). *Using Discussion in the Classroom*. Philadelphia, PA: Open University Press.

Engle, S. & Ochoa, A. (1988). *Education for Democratic Citizenship: Decision Making in the Social Studies*. New York: Teachers College Press.

Gall, M. D. (1985). Discussion methods of teaching. In T. Husen & T. N. Postlethwaite (Eds.), *International Encyclopedia of Education* (Vol. 3, pp. 1423–1427). Oxford: Pergamon Press.

Gall, M. D. & Gall, J. P. (1990). Outcomes of the discussion method. In W. W. Wilen (Ed.), *Teaching and Learning through Discussion: The Theory, Research and Practice of the Discussion Method* (pp. 25–44). Springfield, IL: Charles C. Thomas.

Goodlad, J. I. (1984). *A Place Called School*. New York: McGraw Hill.

Gorman, A. H. (1969). *Teachers and Learners: The Interactive Process*. Boston, MA: Allyn & Bacon.

Gross, R. E. & Zeleny, L. D. (1958). *Educating Citizens for Democracy: Curriculum and Instruction in Secondary Social Studies*. New York: Oxford University Press.

Haroutunian-Gordon, S. (1991). *Turning the Soul: Teaching through Conversation in the High School*. Chicago, IL: The University of Chicago Press.

Hess, D. (2000). Developing strong voters through democratic deliberation. *Social Education*, *64*(5), 193–196.

Hoetker, J. & Ahlbrand, W. P., Jr. (1969). The persistence of recitation. *American Educational Research Journal*, *6*, 145–167.

Hoover, K. H. (1976). *The Professional Teacher's Handbook: A Guide for Improving Instruction in Today's Middle and Secondary Schools* (2nd ed.). Boston, MA: Allyn & Bacon.

Hunkins, F. P. (1995). *Teaching Thinking through Effective Questioning* (2nd ed.). Boston, MA: Christopher-Gorden.

Johnston, J., Anderman, L., Milne, L. & Harris, D. (1994). *Improving Civic Discourse in the Classroom: Taking the Measure of Channel One* (Research Report 4). Ann Arbor, MI: Institute for Social Research, University of Michigan.

Johnson, D. W. & Johnson, R. T. (1988). Critical thinking through structured controversy. *Educational Leadership*, *45*(8), 58–64.

Larson, B. E. (1997). Social studies teachers' conceptions of discussion: A grounded theory study. *Theory and Research in Social Education*, *25*(2), 113–136.

Larson, B. E. (2000). Thinking about classroom discussion as a method of instruction and a curriculum outcome. *Teaching and Teacher Education, 16*(2000), 661–677.

Larson, B. E. (2003). Comparing face-to-face discussion and electronic discussion: A case study from high school social studies. *Theory and Research in Social Education, 31*(3), 348–366.

Mail, D. J. (1968). The fishbowl: Design for discussion. *Today's Education, 57,* 27–29.

Merryfield, M. M. (2000). How can electronic technologies promote equity and cultural diversity? Using threaded discussion in graduate courses in social studies and global education. *Theory and Research in Social Education, 28*(4), 502–526.

Miller, S. (1992). Creating change: Towards a dialogic pedagogy. (Report Series 2.18). Albany, NY: National Research Center on Literature Teaching and Learning. (ERIC Document Reproduction Service No. ED 349 582).

Oliver, D. W., Newmann, F. M. (1972). *Taking a Stand: A Guide to Clear Discussion of Public Issues* (rev. ed.). Middletown, CT: Xerox Corporation/American Education Publications.

Parker, W. C. (1996). Curriculum for democracy. In R. Soder (Ed.), *Democracy, Education and Schooling* (pp. 182–210). San Francisco, CA: Jossey-Bass.

Parker, W. C. (2001). Classroom discussion: Models for leading seminars and deliberations. *Social Education, 65*(2), 111–115.

Parker, W. C., McDaniel, J. E. & Valencia, S. W. (1991). Helping students think about public issues: Instruction versus prompting, *Social Education, 55*(1), 41–44.

Priles, M. A. (1993). The fishbowl discussion: A strategy for large honors classes. *English Journal, 82*(6), 49–50.

Roby, T. W. (1988). Models of discussion. In J. T. Dillon (Ed.), *Questioning and Discussion: A Multidisciplinary Study* (pp. 163–191). Norwood, NJ: Ablex.

Schwab, J. J. (1954). Eros and education: A discussion of one aspect of discussion. *Journal of General Education, 8,* 54–71.

Stodolsky, S., Ferguson, T. & Wimpelberg, K. (1981). The recitation persists, but what does it look like? *Journal of Curriculum Studies, 13*(2), 121–130.

Swift, J. N. & Gooding, C. T. (1983). Interaction of wait time feedback and questioning instruction on middle school science teaching. *Journal of Research in Science Teaching, 20*(8), 721–730.

Tharp, R. G. & Gallimore, R. (1988). *Rousing Minds to Life: Teaching, Learning, and Schooling in Social Context.* Cambridge, MA: Cambridge University Press.

Wilen, W. W. & White, J. J. (1991). Interaction and discourse in social studies classrooms. In J. P. Shaver (Ed.), *Handbook of Research on Social Studies Teaching and Learning* (pp. 483–495). New York: Macmillan.

11 STUDENT-DIRECTED INVESTIGATION

Boekaerts, M. (1997). Self-regulated learning: a new concept embraced by researchers, policy makers, educators, teachers, and students. *Learning and Instruction, 7,* 161–186.

Bransford, J. D., Brown, A. L. & Cocking, R. R. (Eds.) (2000). *How People Learn: Brain, Mind, Experience and School.* Washington, DC: National Academy Press.

Brooks, J. G. & Brooks, M. B. (1993). *The Case for Constructivist Classrooms.* Alexandria, VA: Association for Supervision and Curriculum Development.

Brown, A. L. (1997). Transforming schools into communities of thinking and learning about serious matters. *American Psychologist, 54*(4), 399–413.

Brown, J. S., Collins, A. & Duguid, P. (1989). Situated cognition and the culture of learning. *Educational Researcher, 18*(1), 32–42.

Cognition and Technology Group at Vanderbilt (1990). Anchored instruction and its relationship to situated cognition. *Educational Researcher, 19*(5), 2–10.

Collins, A., Brown, J. S. & Newman, S. E. (1994). Cognitive apprenticeship. In L. B. Resnick (Ed.), *Knowing, Learning, and Instruction* (pp. 453–494). Hillsdale, NJ: Erlbaum Associates.

Duffy, T. & Jonassen, D. (Eds.) (1992). *Constructivism and the Technology of Instruction: A Conversation.* Hillsdale, NJ: Erlbaum Associates.

Exline, J. (2004). Retrieved February 1, 2006, from Concept to Classroom Website: www.thirteen.org/edonline/concept2class/inquiry/.

Fosnot, C. T. (1989). *Inquiring Teachers, Enquiring Learners.* New York: Teachers College Press.

Gallagher, S., Sher, B., Stepien, W. & Workman, D. (1995). Implementing problem-based learning in science classrooms. *School Science and Mathematics, 95*(3), 136–146.

Harris, K., Marcus, R., McLaren, K. & Fey, J. (2001). Curriculum materials supporting problem-based teaching. *School Science and Mathematics, 101*(6), 310–318.

McGrath, D. (2003). Developing a community of learners: What will it look like and how will it work? *Learning & Leading with Technology, 30*(7), 42–45.

Newmann, F., Bryk, A. & Nagaoka, J. (2001). *Authentic Intellectual Work and Standardized Tests: Conflicts or Coexistence?* Chicago, IL: Consortium on Chicago School Research. Available online at: www.consortium-chicago. org/publications/p0001.html.

Saye, J. W. & Brush, T. (1999). Student engagement with social issues in a multimedia-supported learning environment. *Theory and Research in Social Education, 27*(4), 472–504. Retrieved January 16, 2006, from ERIC database.

Scheurman, G. (1998) From behaviorist to constructivist teaching. *Social Education, 62*, 6–9.

Scheurman, G. & Newmann, F. M. (1998). Authentic intellectual work in social studies: putting performance before pedagogy. *Social Education, 4*(3), 150–153.

Skinner, B. F. (1968). *The Technology of Teaching*. New York: Appelton.

Tomlinson, C. (2003). *Fulfilling the Promise of Differentiated Classrooms: Strategies and Tools for Responsive Teaching*. Alexandria, VA: Association for Supervision and Curriculum Development.

West, S. A. (1992). Problem-based learning— A viable addition for secondary school science. *School Science Review, 73*(265), 47–55.

Wilke, R. & Straits, W. (2005). Practical advice for teaching inquiry-based science process skills in the biological sciences. *The American Biology Teacher, 67*(9), 534–540.

Wisker, G. & Brown, S. (Eds.) (1996). *Enabling Student Learning*. London: Kogan Page/Staff and Educational Development Association.

Index